Why Do You Need This New Edition?

If you're wondering why you should buy this new edition of *Designing Visual Language* here are five good reasons!

1 **Upgraded coverage of electronic communications** invites you to explore and practice the design strategies you'll need to excel in these visual media. Added examples and textual references emphasize the importance of mastering your ability to communicate visually and present documents electronically in a world where many presentations may never leave the computer screen or projector.

2 **New color insert** featuring sample charts, graphs, diagrams, photographs, and Web pages has been added to reflect the widespread use of color in visual communication today. The color-rich pages provide added direction and clarity as you begin to create your own spectrum of visual documents.

3 **Fully revamped end of chapter exercises** feature new, more creative questions that ask you to generate your own communications. The balance of analytical and creative activities encourages you to strive for a more functional and well-rounded understanding of visual communications.

4 To keep you up-to-date on the new developments in research, theory, and practice, the authors have incorporated **updated references to new and exciting works in the fields of professional and visual communication.**

5 **Streamlined coverage** in each of the nine chapters allows for quicker, more efficient reading without sacrificing clarity.

PEARSON

Designing Visual Language

Designing
Visual Language

Strategies for Professional Communicators

Charles Kostelnick

Iowa State University

David D. Roberts

Iowa State University

Longman

Boston   Columbus   Indianapolis   New York   San Francisco   Upper Saddle River
Amsterdam   Cape Town   Dubai   London   Madrid   Milan   Munich   Paris   Montreal   Toronto
Delhi   Mexico City   São Paulo   Sydney   Hong Kong   Seoul   Singapore   Taipei   Tokyo

Executive Editor: Suzanne Phelps Chambers
Editorial Assistant: Erica Schweitzer
Senior Supplements Editor: Donna Campion
Associate Marketing Manager: Bonnie Gill
Production Manager: Eric Jorgensen
Project Coordination, Text Design, and Electronic Page Makeup: Electronic Publishing Services Inc., NYC
Senior Cover Design Manager: Nancy Danahy
Visual Researcher: Rona Tuccillo
Senior Manufacturing Buyer: Alfred C. Dorsey
Printer and Binder: RR Donnelley & Sons Company / Crawfordsville
Cover Printer: RR Donnelley & Sons Company / Crawfordsville

For permission to use copyrighted material, grateful acknowledgment is made to the copyright holders on pp. 389–390, which are hereby made part of this copyright page

Library of Congress Cataloging-in-Publication Data

Kostelnick, Charles.
     Designing visual language : strategies for professional communicators / Charles Kostelnick,
     David D. Roberts.—2nd ed.
          p. cm.
     Includes bibliographical references and index.
     ISBN-13: 978-0-205-61640-4 (pbk.)
     ISBN-10: 0-205-61640-2 (pbk.)
     1.Graphic design (Typography) 2. Business writing. I. Roberts, David D. (David Donovan),
1945- II. Title.

Z246.K77 2011
686.2'2—dc22   2009042158

1 2 3 4 5 6 7 8 9 10—DOC—12 11 10 09

Longman
is an imprint of

www.pearsonhighered.com

ISBN-13: 978-0-205-61640-4
ISBN-10:   0-205-61640-2

To my parents, Julius and Marcella Kostelnick
CK

To my son, R.D.
DDR

Contents

2   Perception and Design   46

8

Pictures   293

Foreword

by the Series Editor

The Allyn and Bacon Series in Technical Communication is designed to meet the continuing education needs of professional technical communicators, both those who desire to upgrade or update their own communication abilities as well as those who train or supervise writers, editors, and artists within their organizations. This series also serves the growing number of students enrolled in undergraduate and graduate programs in technical communication. Such programs offer a wide variety of courses beyond the introductory technical writing course—advanced courses for which fully satisfactory and appropriately focused textbooks have often been impossible to locate.

The chief characteristic of the books in this series is their consistent effort to integrate theory and practice. The books offer both research-based and experience-based instruction, not only describing what to do and how to do it but explaining why. The instructors who teach advanced courses and the students who enroll in these courses are looking for more than rigid rules and ad hoc guidelines. They want books that demonstrate theoretical sophistication and a solid foundation in the research of the field as well as pragmatic advice and perceptive applications. Instructors and students will also find these books filled with activities and assignments adaptable to the classroom and to the self-guided learning processes of professional technical communicators.

To operate effectively in the field of technical communication, today's technical communicators require extensive training in the creation, analysis, and design of information for both domestic and international audiences, for both paper and electronic environments. The books in the Allyn and Bacon Series address those subjects that are most frequently taught at the undergraduate and graduate levels as a direct response to both the educational needs of students and the practical demands of business and industry. Additional books will be developed for the series in order to satisfy or anticipate changes in writing technologies, academic curricula, and the profession of technical communication.

SAM DRAGGA
Texas Tech University

$\textbf{P}$reface

You inhabit a world teeming with information, most of it visible on paper, screen, or other surfaces. Text, pictures, charts, brochures, bus schedules, Web sites, interactive displays—the range of visible information we see every day can be broad and bewildering.

Despite the immense variety, however, all of these visible forms have two things in common: Someone had to design them, and they depend entirely on us, their audiences, to give them meaning. Like other kinds of communication, to be effective, visual design must satisfy the needs of an audience—and that simple fact drives this entire book.

As a professional communicator, you'll likely design information for a wide array of audiences—co-workers, clients, investors, volunteers, large groups and small. You're already familiar with the idea that when you write or speak, the key to your success is adapting your message to the audience. In this book we'll help you apply this principle to visual design. To achieve this goal, we'll outline a systematic approach that extends to communication design many of the rhetorical principles you've already assimilated in writing or other communication courses.

Why We Created This Book

This book responds to a variety of needs, both academic and nonacademic, in the field of professional communication. Over the past two decades, rapid advances in digital technology have made design an essential part of the professional communicator's domain. Routinely, workplace communicators at every level are responsible not just for composing their communications but for designing them as well.

This book addresses the academic needs of aspiring professional communicators as well as the needs of those already in the workplace. In trying to respond to those needs, however, we chose not to write a how-to book with formulas, templates, and lockstep rules—prescriptions that might succeed in some situations but likely misfire in others. Instead, we wanted to help students and professional communicators build a sturdier, more reliable, and more comprehensive framework for thinking about and practicing design. Our approach recognizes that design is a complex creative process that blends a variety of skills—both rational and intuitive, that this process often involves extensive revision, and that, above all else, its success depends on how well it responds to a given rhetorical situation.

Readers We Had in Mind as We Created This Book

We intended *Designing Visual Language* for a variety of readers, all of whom share the desire to design reader-oriented communications. While this audience includes a wide range of individuals across North America, Europe, and around the globe, as we developed the book we envisioned three specific groups of readers.

First, we envisioned students who are taking advanced courses in professional communication—for example, document design, technical editing, multimedia design, communication production processes, or writing software documentation. For these readers, the book will extend to visual design the writing and rhetorical principles they've applied in previous courses.

Second, we envisioned in our audience professional communicators, including technical writers, corporate communication experts, editors, and freelance writers and desktop publishers. Like academic readers, professional communicators will benefit from the rhetorical orientation of the book, which is essentially pragmatic in nature and will get results.

Finally, our book is also intended for professional communication teachers who want a compatible text for courses with a significant design component, such as business or technical communication, manuals and instructional materials, Web design, or multimodal rhetoric. By translating concepts and strategies from rhetoric, composition, and other written communication courses, this book will enable teachers of the written word to adapt their approach to visual design without having to reinvent their teaching methods.

What You'll Gain from Using This Book

Simply put, our goal is to help you adapt visual language to specific audiences, purposes, and contexts in much the same way you do when you write—in other words, to help you respond flexibly to design problems. Toward that end, we hope this book will enable you to do the following:

- Learn a basic vocabulary of design, from typography to page layout to illustrations to whole communications, and how to shape that vocabulary rhetorically. Equally important, we want you to be able to extend the rhetorical framework outlined in this book to a wider design vocabulary than we have the space or expertise to cover.

- Select conventional strategies for using this vocabulary, based on your readers' understanding of these conventions. We'll show you how to use visual conventions selectively, how they can save you time, and how they vary across organizations, disciplines, and cultures.

- Integrate into your work design strategies based on perception, research, and reader feedback. We'll outline basic principles of visual perception and show you how these principles apply to communication design. We'll also show how research can help you make informed design decisions and how feedback from your audience can help you to improve your communications.

- Understand that design, like writing, is a process that entails invention, revision, and editing. You're already familiar with the concept that effective writing often requires extensive revision. We'll translate that concept to visual design by showing you the power of revision in creating effective, reader-oriented designs.

How We Structured This Book

To meet these objectives, we organized *Designing Visual Language* into four parts, beginning with an introduction of concepts and strategies in the first part and illustrating and implementing those concepts and strategies in the remaining three parts.

Part One, Integrated Communication (Chapters 1, 2, and 3), introduces you to visual design in rhetorical terms, many of which will already be familiar to you as a writer, and to the symbiotic relationship between the visual and the verbal. Part One also introduces key perceptual principles, a system for describing visual language, and tools for analyzing communications, both those you create and those you receive.

Part Two, Text Design (Chapter 4, 5, and 6), explores a variety of text levels and a range of rhetorical strategies you can use to design at these levels. These levels include linear components (letters, words, lines of text), fields (pages, panels, screens), and nonlinear components (tables, flow charts, decision trees).

Part Three, Extra-Level Design (Chapters 7 and 8), examines several design elements that are primarily nontextual in nature and outlines strategies you can use to adapt these elements to the rhetorical situation. These design forms include data displays (charts, graphs, maps), and pictures (illustrations, photos).

Part Four, Document Design (Chapter 9), explores design elements that encompass the entire communication and strategies for shaping these elements to enhance usability. We'll show how this large-scale level of design can make or break a communication and why it's essential to plan for it early in the design process.

Although the four parts form a sequence, moving from theory to text design to graphics to the global design of the whole communication, we realize that some of you may not actually use the book in that sequence. However, if you decide to explore chapters out of sequence, we strongly suggest that you first examine the principles and concepts in Part One so you can get the full value out of the six design chapters.

The Examples We Use in This Book

As you begin exploring this book, you'll realize that we invented most of the examples and rhetorical situations ourselves. We did that for several reasons. First, we wanted to show you examples you could relate to, rather than highly polished examples created by professional graphic designers. Most of the designs you'll see in this book are within your design capabilities, and in all likelihood you'll do even better with some practice.

Second, we wanted to explore in some depth rhetorical situations and their implications for designing visual language. We also wanted to illustrate a variety of design projects that professional communicators are likely to engage in. Creating our own examples, some of which we narrate in detail, gave us the flexibility to do both.

Finally, we created many of our own examples because you already have access to a wide array of communications—from home, school, or work—items such as instructional manuals, reports, fact sheets, brochures, Web sites, junk mail, and the like. In the exercises and assignments at the end of each chapter, we'll invite you to dissect, analyze, and evaluate such communications. In this way, we hope you'll extend the design concepts and strategies covered in each chapter to communications for which *you* were the audience.

What We Changed for the Second Edition of This Book

In the nearly 12 years since the first edition of *Designing Visual Language,* some significant changes have occurred in the field of professional communication, and in addition to this we have received lots of helpful feedback from teachers and students who have used our book. Below is a brief look at the changes you will find.

First, we reduced the overall length of the book to keep the cost of the textbook down for your students. The most noticeable aspect of the length reduction is the elimination of the chapter on icons, logos and symbols, along with some tightening up of the remaining chapters.

Second, we have upgraded our coverage of electronic communications, especially Web sites and PowerPoint presentations. The rhetorical design strategies at the heart of this book apply just as well to screens (both computer and projector) as to paper, but we are aware that designs are affected by the medium in which they operate. You will find more examples and more textual references to professional communications that rarely—or never—exist as "documents."

Third, we have revamped the exercises at the end of every chapter, with our major goal being to increase the proportion of creative—as opposed to analytical— activities. Both are important to learning, of course, but users of our book have consistently voiced their desire to see fewer exercises that ask them to *analyze* communications and more exercises that ask them to *create* communications.

Fourth, we selectively updated the references to include new scholarship in the field of visual communication and visual rhetoric. Although we could hardly add everything that deserved to be included, we tried to alert our readers to some important new developments in the field, with the hope that those references would provide pathways to additional scholarship.

Finally, we have arranged to include a modest assortment of full-color figures. When we wrote our book, color monitors were the exception rather than the rule, and while color printing had been around for a long time, the cost of colorization was still a limitation in many professional venues, especially small businesses and nonprofit organizations. We hope that the full-color inserts will be helpful as well as interesting.

Acknowledgments

We would like to thank our families for their continuing support over the many months it took us to shape this book. Their patience as we faced many deadlines was what we dearly needed to complete this project and far more than we had a right to expect.

We thank the English Department at Iowa State University for providing the computer and printing resources that we needed to create this book. We would also like to thank our many colleagues in the English Department for their continual encouragement. In particular, we sincerely thank Andy Swan and Don Payne for their generous technical support throughout this project and thank Martin Teply for technical support on the second edition. We made far more demands on their time than we should have, but they never once made us feel that we were demanding. We are grateful to the students at Iowa State University in our visual communication classes who used drafts of this book while it was under development. Their needs as future professional communicators served as the impetus for the project, and we received valuable feedback and considerable encouragement from them throughout the process.

As we developed the first edition of this book, we received clear, insightful, and detailed feedback from the following reviewers: Deborah C. Andrews, University of Delaware; Dixie Elise Hickman, Georgia State University; William E. Rivers, University of South Carolina; and Rebecca Worley, University of Delaware. Their comments encouraged us at critical stages of this project and opened up productive avenues for revision. We're sincerely grateful for both. We also greatly appreciate the helpful feedback and guidance we received for the second edition from the following reviewers: Carol Barnum, Southern Polytechnic State University; Eva Brumberger, Virginia Tech; Christopher Eisenhart, UMass Dartmouth; Nancy MacKenzie, Minnesota State University, Mankato; and Tamara Powell, Louisiana Tech University.

We wish to express our appreciation to the staff at Pearson/Longman for their ongoing support as we developed the second edition of this book. We wish to thank Suzanne Phelps Chambers, Executive Editor for Pearson/Longman, and her editorial assistant Erica Schweitzer, who worked painstakingly to prepare the manuscript for production and who made our work enjoyable and efficient. We also wish to thank Donna DeBenedictis, Managing Editor, and Eric Jorgensen at Pearson/Longman for their help with production, and we thank David Mahaffey from Electronic Publishing Services, who guided us skillfully and patiently through the final production process.

We thank the organizations listed on the credits page for granting us the right to use their materials in this book.

Finally, we wish to thank Sam Dragga, series editor, for his invitation to do this project (an eternity ago, it now seems), and for his encouragement and guidance along the way.

CHARLES KOSTELNICK
DAVID D. ROBERTS

A Note on the Figures That Appear in This Book

Most of the figures in this book were created on Macintosh computers using Canvas (versions 3.5, 5.0, and 10.0), a product of ACD Systems International, Inc. (and formerly of Deneba Software, Miami, Florida) as well as Adobe Illustrator (version CS3). Several other figures in the book were created using Microsoft Word and Microsoft Excel. Typefaces were done primarily with Adobe Type Basics, a product of Adobe Type Systems Incorporated; some photos were done in Adobe Photoshop.

Most of the figures in this book were created, revised, and edited by Charlie Kostelnick, with Dave Roberts providing conceptual and editorial advice. The authors chose not to seek professional graphic design assistance, for two reasons. First, the authors wanted the illustrations to be simple, accessible, and directly applicable to the points they wished to make. Second, they wanted to demonstrate that the principles and strategies underpinning this book depend on rhetoric rather than on the allied field of graphic design.

Designing Visual Language

Rhetorical Background

Introduction to Visual Rhetoric

In the dozens of communications you engage in every day, you exercise your faculty of vision, gathering and recording information, sorting it, analyzing it, and synthesizing it. You perform these tasks in order to make sense of the world and help others do the same, and you do so through a miraculous, complex, and powerful instrument—your eye.

Sometimes your faculty of vision performs its work almost entirely alone—for example, if you're taking a photograph of your friends or using pictorial instructions to assemble a bike. Most of the time, however, in the communication tasks you perform at school or work, vision often combines with speaking, listening, writing, and reading.

- If you attend a presentation, you may listen to the speaker and also read the handouts or the slides on a screen and jot down notes for future reference.
- If you write a short report for your boss, you'll see your document take shape on your computer screen, print a draft of it, and perhaps discuss it with a colleague to get feedback.
- If you receive an inquiry by e-mail, you'll probably scan it quickly, gather information by phone or on the Web, then type out your e-mail response.

Amid all the speaking, listening, reading, and writing that we do, we can easily take vision for granted. Seeing comes so naturally to most of us that we often overlook its importance—and its power.

This book is about applying visual language as a communication tool in a variety of forms—from paragraphs and columns of text to tables, pictures, charts, and icons. We'll focus primarily on paper documents, though you'll find that the principles you learn in this book can readily apply to other forms of professional communication such as computer screens, including Web sites.

We'll explore not only a variety of visual forms but also a variety of everyday situations you may encounter in your career, whether you're designing communications as an employee in the workplace, as a consultant, or as a volunteer—and whether you're designing for managers, clients, senior citizens, or children. Throughout this book we'll explore how you can adapt your design to a variety of situations and audiences.

At this point you might be saying to yourself, "Hold on a minute! I'm not a designer or an artist, and I certainly can't draw!" You're not alone, so don't feel intimidated. Like writing, design is something you learn, a skill and an art that you acquire gradually. Of course there's an aesthetic component to design—a page can be transformed into an elegant composition—and there's no denying that visual language is an extraordinarily creative medium. But that doesn't make it mysterious and totally subjective. In fact, practical design is fairly rational—in the sense that each step of the way you can understand *why* you're making design decisions.

The good news is that you've already learned quite a bit about the *why* of effective design, though you may not realize it. Because we want to help you build on that knowledge, we'll begin with some principles you're probably already familiar with and translate them into the language of design.

It Depends: The Importance of the Rhetorical Situation

You've probably taken a writing course or two, or perhaps you've done some writing on the job or for an organization you're active in. Given that experience, when someone asks you how you create a document, you probably begin by thinking something like:

"Well, it depends. . . ."

Depends on what? Well, it depends on who your readers are. If you're writing to a friend, you might write your document one way, but if you're writing to a professor or a co-worker you might write it another way altogether. What else does it depend on? Well, it depends on what you're trying to accomplish—persuade your readers to sponsor your softball team, help your readers prepare a gourmet meal, whatever. Anything else? Well, it depends on the context in which your readers will use your document—at a meeting with the big bosses, sitting by a computer, or talking on the phone.

The act of creating any workplace communication, then, is driven by the writer's understanding of three basic elements:

- *Audience*—those who are going to use your communication: who they are, what they know about the subject, their previous experience with communications like the one you're designing, even their cultural background.
- *Purpose*—what you want your communication to accomplish: persuade your readers to think or act a certain way, enable them to perform a task, help them understand something, change their attitude, and so on.
- *Context*—the physical and temporal circumstances in which readers will use your communication: at their office desks, in a manufacturing plant, during the slow summer months, or in the middle of a company crisis.

These three elements—audience, purpose, and context—make up the *rhetorical situation*. As a writer, you may consciously employ heuristics to define these elements, or you may approach them more intuitively. When the communication is simple or routine—say, responding to e-mail—you may start writing with hardly a moment's hesitation. When the communication is more complex—say, a proposal—you may have to expend significant time and effort coming to grips with audience, purpose, and context. In either case, the rhetorical situation drives the decisions you make during the entire communication process.

You know these things about the rhetorical nature of written, and oral, communication. By now they may even be second nature to you. We'll help you to continue thinking along those rhetorical lines as you progress through this book by learning to translate concepts you use in written and oral communication to visual design. To begin, then, when others ask how you solve any sort of visual communication problem or ask you whether a visual design they're developing is likely to be effective, you'll start by thinking, "Well, it depends. . . ."

In each communication you design, you'll try to shape its visual language so that it fits the rhetorical situation—audience, purpose, and context.[1] The diagram in Figure 1.1 shows these variables.

Just as in writing, you'll continue defining the rhetorical situation throughout the design process. To illustrate how the rhetorical situation drives the communication process and applies specifically to visual design, let's examine the following scenario and its accompanying documents.

A Scenario for Applying Visual Rhetoric

Fred Noonan works as a part-time staff member of the Mapleton Community Center. Located in the old train depot on Front Street, the community center is a

FIGURE 1.1   The rhetorical situation

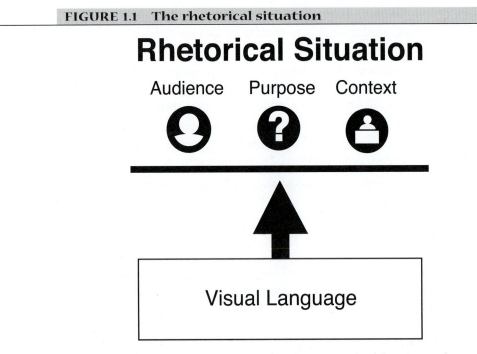

nonprofit facility that offers recreational, informational, and various other support services to people in the greater Mapleton area. The center has two full-time and five part-time staff members.

After lurching along for many years on a precarious budget—cobbled together by fund-raising efforts and a small grant from the Community Chest—the Mapleton Community Center staff was recently surprised to receive a letter from Edna Jamison, indicating her intent to give the community center five million dollars. Mrs. Jamison, one of the founders of the center, has decided that her considerable estate will do more good if she dispenses some of its resources now rather than after she passes on.

Edna Jamison's gift comes with one major stipulation: The Mapleton Community Center Board, after consulting with all members of the center, has 30 days to develop a detailed plan for spending the money. As a result, Mrs. Jamison's remarkable offer has caused a flurry of activity at the community center.

In response to this amazing turn of circumstances, the community center board held an emergency meeting at which they discussed how to fulfill the terms of the Jamison grant. The board developed two basic options for spending the money, one featuring a renovation and expansion of the current facilities in the old train depot, and the other calling for a new building to be erected on a small parcel of land a few blocks away. The board, however, remains open to other possibilities.

As a result of the board's decision, Fred Noonan finds himself charged with notifying all members of the Mapleton Community Center—people who have used the center, donated goods or money, or served as volunteers—about a special meeting to discuss the options for using the Jamison money. Specifically, the board has asked Fred to explain objectively both options—renovation or a new building—and to provide some data on membership, daily use, and expenditures to help guide the discussion.

Figures 1.2 through 1.5 show Fred's communication, an 11" × 17" foldout printed on 24-pound birch paper. (Figures 1.2–1.5 are reduced to about 70 percent of their actual size; see Figure 1.6 for a photo of the whole document.) Fred's document will be mailed to all members; copies will also be available at the door before the meeting.

How Fred's Document Responds Visually to the Rhetorical Situation

Because the rhetorical situation for any professional communication can be complex, accounting for everything that Fred has to consider as he creates his document would be impossible. But a synopsis of the rhetorical situation would look something like this:

- *Audience.* Fred's main readers will be Mapleton Community Center members, contributors, and volunteers—mostly parents and senior citizens. Because they support the center, Fred's readers will have a strong interest in choosing the right option. Younger members are also part of the audience even though they may not be decision makers.

- *Purpose.* The primary purpose of Fred's informational package is to help readers become part of the decision-making process—by presenting relevant information as clearly and objectively as possible. Although his main purpose is to enable rather than to persuade, Fred must also convince his audience to participate in the process.

- *Context.* Most readers will receive a hard copy of Fred's communication in the mail, and a PDF version will be posted on the center's Web site. After reviewing the document, readers will then bring it to the meeting so they can contribute to the discussion. Some people may see Fred's communication for the first time at the meeting.

The visual language that Fred uses in his information package responds to this rhetorical situation in a variety of ways, some of which we'll classify as global and large scale, others as specific and local.

FIGURE 1.2   Fred's Mapleton letter

Mapleton Community Center
324 Main Street, Mapleton, Indiana 41600-1234   (434) 522-3333

April 23, 2009

Dear Friend of the Community Center:

We have some wonderful news! Through the generosity of Edna Jamison, a distinguished member of the Center's founding board, we have been ffered a $5 million grant!

To the many of you who know and love Mrs. Jamison, the nature of this gesture will be no surprise. The magnitude of her thoughtfulness, however, has overwhelmed all of us, and we know you will echo our profound thanks.

Mrs. Jamison's benevolence brings with it some important work for us to do, and therefore the purpose of this letter is to ask that you attend a meeting, to be held at

Mapleton Community Center
Monday, May 11
7:00 p.m.

According to the terms of Mrs. Jamison's grant, the Mapleton Community Center must submit within 30 days a comprehensive plan showing how we intend to use the money. More importantly, the grant stipulates that whatever plan we put forth must have the support of the Community Center's organization, including not only the Board of Directors and the staff, but also the membership as a whole.

The goals for the May 11 meeting are to:

♦ reach general consensus about use of the Jamison grant funds

♦ create a committee to help the Board write a detailed plan

♦ schedule a second (and final) meeting for ratification of the plan

To facilitate discussion, on the following pages we've outlined two general plans for improving and expanding the Center with funds from Mrs. Jamison's gift. We look forward to hearing your responses to these two plans as well as any alternative ideas you have for using these funds. On the back page of this document we've also included some information about the operation, membership, and use of the Center.

We hope to see you on May 11.

Sincerely,

Fred Noonan
Program Assistant

FIGURE 1.3   Mapleton option 1 page

Option 1. Renovate the Old Depot

The existing depot, one of Mapleton's landmark buildings from the late nineteenth century, would be completely gutted and renovated. All of the depot's interior walls would be stripped bare and some would be removed. All of the heating and cooling systems would also be replaced. The renovation and remodeling would include:

♦ A new roof, all new energy-efficient windows, a new heating/cooling system, and refinishing of the exterior brick.

♦ Completely remodeled interior spaces, including the card/game, craft, exercise, meeting, and reading rooms.

♦ A new indoor water spa, with a capacity of ten.

♦ Additional office space for the staff and volunteers.

Total usable space. The renovation would result in 12,000 square feet of usable space, an increase of 4,000 square feet.

Cost. Approximately $2,700,000.

Schedule. Work would be done in stages so the Center could remain open during construction. Completion would take approximately 12 months.

Other use of funds. The remaining funds would be placed in a trust, interest on which would go toward meeting operating expenses as well as purchasing furniture, equipment, and books.

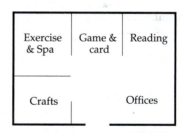

Tentative Floor Plan

Key Benefits of Option One

♦ Maintains the Center's current location in a historically significant building.

♦ Provides a stream of money that will significantly reduce annual operating expenses.

♦ Increases the usable space in the existing location from 8,000 to 12,000 square feet.

♦ Adds some new facilities such as the indoor water spa.

FIGURE 1.4   Mapleton option 2 page

Option 2. Relocate on a New Site

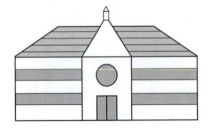

The relocation would include a three-acre site in town with total usable space of 30,000 square feet. The new building would be built in the same historical style of the depot, blending in with Mapleton's historic district. The new building would have two floors and a basement and would include:

- ◆ A card/game, craft, exercise, meeting, and reading room. Each of these rooms would be approximately twice as large as the existing rooms.
- ◆ An auditorium for concerts, plays, and other special events. The auditorium would seat approximately 400.
- ◆ An indoor shuffleboard arena in the basement.
- ◆ An outdoor wading pool, a fountain, and a walking garden.

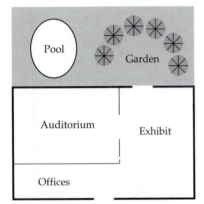

Tentative First Floor Plan

Total usable space. The new building would have 30,000 square feet of usable space, an increase of 22,000 square feet.

Cost. Approximately $3,500,000.

Schedule. The major work would take about nine months, and the Center could begin moving in shortly thereafter.

Other use of funds. All of the remaining funds would go toward furnishing and equipping the new building. No trust funds would meet operating expenses.

Key Benefits of Option Two

- ◆ Significantly increases the space available to the Center.
- ◆ Adds a 400-seat auditorium for performances, events, and meetings.
- ◆ Adds outdoor activity spaces with a wading pool and a walking garden.
- ◆ New building would need little maintenance and virtually no annual repairs.

FIGURE 1.5   Mapleton data sheet

Data about Mapleton Community Center

Expenses. Below is a breakdown of expenditures in several key areas over the past six years.

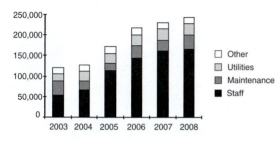

Memberships. Below is a breakdown of increases in memberships, both individual and family.

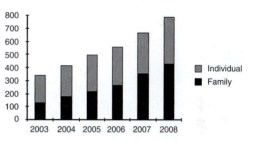

Daily Use. Below are data about the daily use of spaces in the Center during selected months.

Rooms	January		April		July		October		Ave. Monthly	
	2007	2008	2007	2008	2007	2008	2007	2008	2007	2008
Card/Game	67	138	54	145	21	47	62	174	51	126
Crafts	110	178	90	123	27	58	123	195	88	139
Exercise	233	321	114	173	84	121	211	391	161	252
Meeting	37	59	22	72	11	32	41	98	28	65
Reading	53	77	49	65	13	38	54	83	42	66

Large-Scale Responses to Audience, Purpose, and Context

On the large scale, the 11" × 17" four-panel format responds to the needs of readers who will prefer to have all the information together in a single package as they discuss issues during the meeting. The heavier paper also increases the usability of the document as it's folded, unfolded, refolded, and stuck into coat pockets and purses.

Another large-scale design element, which responds to both purpose and context, is the arrangement of the document's major elements. First, the cover letter provides necessary background as well as information about the logistics of the meeting and its goals. The interior of the document includes the options pages (placed side-by-side for easy comparison) describing and discussing the two

FIGURE 1.6   Perspective view of the Mapleton information package

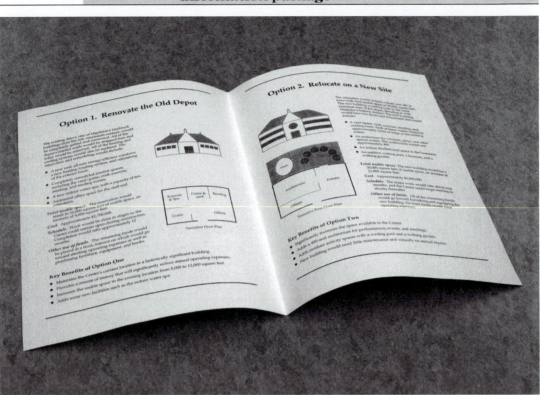

alternatives—the renovation and the new building. Finally, the back page displays some key data about the center in recent years.

Additional responses to the rhetorical situation can be seen in the document's overall appearance. The brochure-like format gives readers something more professional looking than four pages merely stapled together, something out of the ordinary—a cause for celebration. The visual demeanor responds to purpose by giving the message a level of dignity, which reflects positively on the donor, Edna Jamison, and shows the center's appreciation for her generosity.

Local-Level Responses to Audience, Purpose, and Context

The cover letter's typography responds to audience needs because it is a very readable choice for young and old members alike. The letter responds to the context by listing the time, date, and place of the meeting in large, bold type that's centered on the page. The bulleted list that outlines the goals of the meeting helps the document achieve its purpose of involving members in the decision-making process. The single-page letter also responds to context because its conciseness accommodates the four-page design.

The parallel layout of the renovate and build-new options pages helps fulfill the purpose of the document by presenting these two plans objectively. Each option description contains the same number of bullets in its lists, and each also uses the same headers and visual markers to emphasize parallel pieces of information. The parallel arrangement responds to context by placing the drawings of the buildings and the floor plans in the center of the two-page spread, enabling readers to compare them side-by-side. The narrow text columns on the options pages make these pages inviting and readable.

The last page also responds to audience needs by displaying the data in two bar charts and a table that enable readers to compare information quickly and accurately. In this way, the displays fulfill the purpose of the document by encouraging informed discussion about expenses, membership, and building use. The labels on the charts, the nearby legends, and the use of lines and gray shading in the table clarify the data by enabling readers to locate specific values more easily.

Summing Up Fred's Design Decisions

Most, if not all, of the design decisions Fred makes, then, are driven by the rhetorical situation—audience, purpose, and context. And as Fred tailors his design to the rhetorical situation, he's thinking about many of the same things he thinks about when he writes: Will readers understand how I'm arranging the information? Am I adequately emphasizing key points? Are the design elements clear to my readers? Am I getting the most mileage out of my design? What kind of tone does my design project? Will readers find my design credible, building their trust in me, the center's staff, and the information itself?

Many of these questions may sound familiar to you because you probably ask yourself the same things as you write. These are precisely the same kinds of questions that you'll start asking yourself as you *design* documents, both print and electronic. So let's talk about some of the communication terms you already know and how they apply to design. We'll call these terms *cognates* because they cross over from writing to design, as we'll show in the next section.

Visual/Verbal Cognates

Even in the short Mapleton Community Center document, the range of visual responses to the rhetorical situation may seem quite large and complex if you consider all of the design elements Fred includes in the document. Still, in terms of their rhetorical impact, many of these design elements can be categorized according to the following six strategies:

- Arrangement
- Emphasis

- Clarity
- Conciseness

- Tone
- Ethos

In the list above, we placed the six cognates in pairs because of their natural affinities. *Arrangement* and *emphasis* strategies pertain primarily to the visual structure and organization of the document. *Clarity* and *conciseness* strategies pertain primarily to functional matters of style, of making the design readable and efficient. *Tone* and *ethos* strategies relate primarily to readers' subjective responses to the visual language, its voice and credibility. In this section, we'll define each of these terms and translate them into the visual language of document design. Along the way, we'll use examples from Fred Noonan's document to demonstrate each strategy. Beyond this initial explanation, you'll have plenty of time to familiarize yourself with these strategies throughout the book: Parts Two, Three, and Four will cover them in more depth.

As in written communication, these six visual strategies, or cognates, interrelate and overlap. Just as it's not always possible to pinpoint whether an aspect of a communication—say, the technicality of its language—adds to the clarity of the writing or to its conciseness, neither can you always say that a certain design choice—say, the placement of headings or drawings on a page—is entirely a matter of arrangement rather than ethos, of clarity rather than emphasis. Chances are that many design choices, from the most large-scale to the most local and specific, fall into several categories.

Arrangement

Arrangement means order, the organization of visual elements so that readers can see their structure—how they cohere in groups, how they differ from one another, how they create layers and hierarchies. In Figure 1.7a, the placement of the numbers on the left margin creates visual cohesion among items in the sequence. In Figure 1.7b, the numbering and indentation create hierarchical relationships among the items.

In some electronic communications, such as Web pages, the arrangement is *dynamic.* That is, when the viewer looks at an individual screen, the information might be sequential (paragraphs of text) or hierarchical (text with levels of headings).

FIGURE 1.7   Arrangement through numbering

```
1.                          1.0
                              1.1
2.                            1.2
3.
                            2.0
4.                            2.1
                              2.2
5.


        a                        b
```

However, the arrangement of the screens across an entire Web site is relatively random, depending on what links the reader activates.

Visual arrangement also involves spatial orientation within a field, as in left and right, up and down. For example, in the Mapleton Community Center package, Fred places the drawings of the buildings and the floor plans in the center of the two-page layout. Alternative placements could have been both outside, both to the right, or both to the left (Figure 1.8). But Fred chooses to center the drawings because that arrangement best enables readers to compare them—a direct response, as we've seen, to the rhetorical situation.

FIGURE 1.8   Spatial alternatives for the options pages

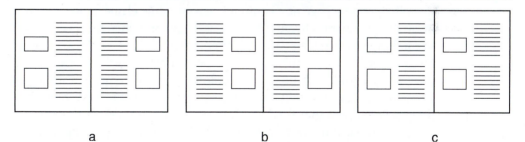

```
        a                        b                        c
```

Arrangement also governs the organization of the text itself. In that same two-page options layout, recall the way Fred places the column headings (e.g., "Total usable space") on the margin, then indents the text. Doing so makes the headings more visible, again helping readers compare options as well as maintaining objectivity through visual parallelism.

On Fred's data sheet, an arrangement strategy appears in the divided bar graphs—they're vertical rather than horizontal. The configuration of data in the table—months and years at the top, categories on the left—is also an arrangement strategy that gives readers easy access as well as fits the available space on the page (Figure 1.9).

FIGURE 1.9   Arrangement strategies for the data sheet

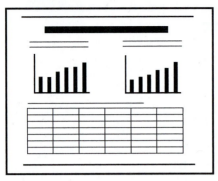

Beyond pictures, text, and data displays, arrangement also regulates page orientation, as we've seen in Fred's decision to put the data sheet in landscape format, even though the document's other pages were in portrait format. That decision also is rhetorically driven—it gives him more flexibility in presenting the data on a single page and in making that data accessible to his readers.

Emphasis

In any communication, even a single paragraph, the rhetorical situation demands that some parts are more important than others and should therefore receive more attention. This prominence or intensity of expression is what we mean by *emphasis*.

Whether on a page or a computer screen, some elements in a visual field will invariably stand out—because the type is bigger or bolder, the image is darker, and so on. Emphasis strategies are about *controlling* what stands out. For example, in Fred's cover letter he emphasizes the time and place for the meeting by centering this text, increasing its type size, and boldfacing it. This emphasis strategy is driven by the rhetorical situation: Above all else, readers need the facts about the meeting time and place, and they need to locate that information easily if they return to the letter to retrieve those facts (see Figure 1.10). Similarly, Fred emphasizes the goals of the meeting by accenting these items with bullets as well as indenting them and adding space around them, all of which give them greater visual presence on the page. On the options pages, Fred emphasizes the drawings by arranging them in the center of the two-page spread and by placing plenty of space around them. Emphasis on the data page results primarily from Fred's decision to use graphs instead of tables for some of the data and to use shading within the bars.

Emphasis at a higher level can be seen in the headers used at the top of every page in Fred's document, including the MCC letterhead on the cover letter. The headers serve as markers in the arrangement scheme, of course, but their large size is an emphasis strategy driven by the rhetorical situation: Fred's readers need a quick map that highlights the document's basic features as well as draws readers in.

FIGURE 1.10   **Emphasis strategies for the letter**

Emphasis occurs on screen as well as in print. Examples of emphasis strategies on screen include buttons, words, or other items that flash or blink; white/gray contrast to indicate operative ruler choices; or the placement of pull-down menus at the top of the screen.

Clarity

Clarity strategies help the receiver to decode the message, to understand it quickly and completely, and, when necessary, to react without ambivalence. Within the verbal domain, clarity issues occur at every level—from word to phrase, from sentence to paragraph, from section to whole communication. In the visual domain, clarity strategies span the whole gamut of visual language, everything from typefaces to charts to illustrations.

For example, in Fred Noonan's document, a concern for clarity motivates his choice of 11-point Palatino with two points of leading—a very legible typographical choice for young and old readers alike (see Figure 1.11).

FIGURE 1.11   **Fred's legible text**

According to the terms of Mrs. Jamison's grant, the Mapleton Community Center must submit within 30 days a comprehensive plan showing how we intend to use the money. More importantly, the grant stipulates that whatever plan we put forth must have the support of the Community Center's organization, including not only the Board of Directors and the staff but also the membership as a whole.

Compare the clarity of Fred's text with the same text in Avant Garde with no leading, seen in Figure 1.12.

FIGURE 1.12   A less legible version of Fred's text

According to the terms of Mrs. Jamison's grant, the Mapleton Community Center must submit within 30 days a comprehensive plan showing how we intend to use the money. More importantly, the grant stipulates that whatever plan we put forth must have the support of the Community Center's organization, including not only the Board of Directors and the staff but also the membership as a whole.

Does the text look dense and jumbled? If it does, the Avant Garde creates a clarity problem, and Fred's choice of Palatino was a wise one. Similarly, Fred's use of narrow text columns on the options pages facilitates reading, and thus clarity. Printing the document on birch-colored paper also enhances clarity because it contrasts sharply with the text. Printing the document on a dark blue paper, however, would have seriously reduced clarity.

Visual clarity also plays an important role in other elements of Fred's information package. For example, Fred achieves clarity in the table by shading two of the rows, enabling readers to follow the horizontal flow of information. The multiple shades in the divided bar charts enable readers to compare data at a glance. In the drawings on the options pages, details showing the roofs and windows and the general layout of the buildings enhance the clarity of these drawings without making them too technical.

Many of these same clarity strategies apply to e-mail, Web pages, and other electronic media. However, because designers working in a screen medium sometimes have little or no control over the equipment with which readers access these communications, even the best intended clarity strategies may evaporate into cyberspace. For example, if the user of a Web site has a small laptop screen with poor resolution, the text may not be nearly as legible as it would be if the reader had a large desktop monitor with high resolution.

Conciseness

Conciseness refers to the visual bulk and intricacy of the design—for example, the number of headings and lists, lines and boxes, colors and gray scales; the detail of the drawings and data displays; the variations in the size, ornateness, and spacing of the text. While associated with economy, visual conciseness doesn't mean designing every visual element as minimally as possible. To do so might result in an underdesigned communication that lacks visual energy. Rather, conciseness means generating designs that are *appropriately* succinct within a particular situation. You can test visual conciseness by asking yourself: Does a given design element do some rhetorical work? If it doesn't, that element lacks conciseness.

To take a simple example, Fred's desire to put all the necessary information onto a single, highly portable sheet of paper was driven in part by a concern for conciseness. A piecemeal approach might have allowed him to include more details, but it would have obliged community center members to handle a whole sheaf of documents both before and during the meeting. So overall, conciseness won out for sound rhetorical reasons.

Frequently, conciseness decisions are complicated because they involve trade-offs—or balancing acts—with the other cognate strategies. For example, Fred decides not to use gridlines in his divided bar graphs showing expenses and membership trends. While that decision allows him to show the data without adding visual clutter, it entails a slight trade-off because adding gridlines might have enhanced clarity by enabling readers to compare more accurately the segments within the bars, as shown in Figure 1.13. As you can see, defining an appropriate level of conciseness usually depends on how it affects the other cognates.

FIGURE 1.13   Mapleton data display with gridlines

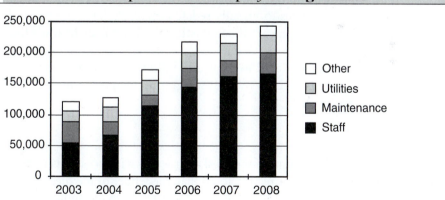

This same interdependence also occurs in screen design, but here two related issues arise. First, most readers are used to—and can effectively handle—more visual variety on their screen than they might be comfortable with in print. The visual clutter of stacked screens, pull-down menus, pop-up ads, and online help balloons may not be much of a conciseness issue. On the other hand, online readers might be particularly sensitive to visual conciseness in Web sites because there an elaborate design can reduce usability by slowing down readers who want to move quickly through the screens.

Tone

You know well that your word choices reveal your attitude toward your readers and your subject. Through your *tone* of voice, you can sound serious, humorous, excited, sincere, flippant, formal, glum, concerned, technical, and so on. You can also reveal the same range of voices through visual language—by your selection of typefaces, your use of space, your use of pictures and icons, and countless other design elements. Just as important, tone plays a crucial role in building ethos because your tone of voice—verbally or visually—tells that person a lot about your character (more on this below).

In Fred's Mapleton document the visual language projects a friendly and accessible yet businesslike and dignified tone. The familiar serif typeface humanizes the message and may provide a measure of sincerity, as does the warm beige paper stock. The simplicity of the drawings and floor plans in the options layout gives those two pages a nontechnical look that makes the information friendlier and more accessible to readers. The brochure-like quality of the document gives it a level of seriousness and formality while also suggesting a festive tone—the Jamison grant is certainly something extraordinary, something worth celebrating.

In screen design the variances in tone can be extreme, ranging from visually frenetic Web sites to visually sedate e-mail. Perhaps the most obvious incarnations of visual tone are the fantastic colors and backgrounds that appear in Web pages. In some cases it's serious and businesslike, while in others it's playful and boisterous, calculated to draw and hold the viewer's attention. By contrast, the visual tone projected by the typography of most e-mail is decidedly reserved and matter-of-fact.

Ethos

In any communication the speaker or writer tries to establish a trusting relationship with the listener or reader. To do that, the sender of the message needs to cultivate a sense of character or credibility that will appeal to the audience. Visual language also needs to build trust if it's going to respond adequately to the rhetorical situation.

In Fred's informational package, several of his design choices reflect his concern with establishing ethos with his audience. First and most obvious, Fred uses the Mapleton Community Center letterhead and logo, which have built-in credibility with his readers since they're already active members of the organization. Besides giving the document credibility, the logo (Figure 1.14) makes the message compelling and relevant to readers because, as the center's symbol, it speaks to their everyday concerns and hopes and those of others they know in the community.

FIGURE 1.14   Mapleton logo

Fred also builds ethos with his audience by putting everything into a single document that opens like a brochure, giving the whole message a measure of dignity without being overly formal or stodgy. At the same time, the use of line work at the top and bottom of the pages provides a framing device (Figure 1.15).

FIGURE 1.15   Ethos of the options pages

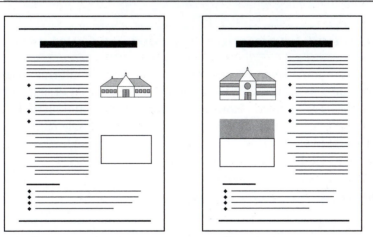

Finally, Fred's care in developing the parallel display of the two options contributes to the ethos of the document by persuading readers that the board isn't trying to sell them one of the options over the other. By giving the options equal visual treatment, Fred tries to convey to his readers that the plan isn't a "done deal" and that the board genuinely needs and wants their input on using the Jamison gift.

In general, ethos strategies employed in electronic communications function in the same way that they do for paper documents—certain design choices *reassure* users or fulfill their expectations. As with clarity strategies, however, some design choices calculated to build ethos for on-screen communications rely on the user's equipment for their full impact.

Interdependence of the Cognate Strategies

As you can see from the examples we've discussed, the designer can implement the six cognate strategies through a wide range of visual language. However, the six strategies don't work alone. They are closely related to each other, a tight-knit family, *interdependent.* They have to work in concert, not in isolation, balancing and complementing one another. And so when the designer implements one strategy, the impact on other strategies must be constantly monitored.

For example, Fred's use of the Mapleton building logo achieves strong emphasis because of its dark, bold design. At the same time, this emphasis strategy enhances ethos by giving the Mapleton documents an immediate identity; emphasis also enhances clarity because readers will easily recognize this image. In the document's overall design, conciseness and arrangement help ethos: By limiting his document to four pages and arranging the information in a brochure-like format, Fred gives the document credibility, making it look important and even a bit ceremonial.

We can isolate the six cognate strategies for discussion and analysis—and we will continue to do that throughout this book. However, as working strategies marshaled by the designer to solve a given rhetorical problem, the six cognates *are* thoroughly interdependent.

Process Example—Mapleton Center

Earlier in this chapter, you saw Fred's design for the informational package to be distributed to members of the community center. That design had to solve a specific rhetorical problem. However, like most document designs, Fred's represents a good deal of thought and planning, misfires and double takes—the same kind of messiness that writers experience as they work through a writing problem. Let's walk through Fred's process as he adapted his design to the rhetorical situation.

Understanding the Rhetorical Situation

As we saw earlier, Fred has to start by analyzing the audience, purpose, and context of his communication. He knows that his primary readers will be Mapleton residents—both young and old—who use or support the community center and thereby have a vested interest in the place. Fred also wants his document to empower his readers by objectively presenting facts and issues and thereby drawing readers into the decision-making process. The larger context of Fred's communication is the whole business surrounding the Jamison grant, but his most immediate contextual concern is that people will use the document both at home and at the meeting for review and decision making. Fred also realizes at least one important *ethical* concern: He doesn't want to develop a design so expensive that it undermines the spirit and tradition of the community center. In other words, given the Center's precarious budget, he wouldn't feel right about lavishing money on the document just because of the Jamison grant.

Although a communicator's grasp of the rhetorical situation will continue to evolve during the process of creating a message, a clear understanding of the audience, purpose, and context at the start is extremely important. That understanding will drive the design process, making it not only more effective and productive but more *efficient* as well. That's why Fred pays careful attention to these matters early on.

Just as in writing, Fred's design process includes several kinds of activities, beginning with invention, followed by revision, and ending with editing and fine-tuning. And like writing, the invention and revision phases are not lock-step but fluid and dynamic, with the designer sometimes inventing and revising in more than one cycle before starting to edit and fine-tune (Figure 1.16).

FIGURE 1.16   Cyclic nature of design

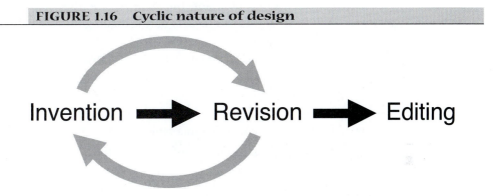

While the design process unfolds, the verbal text continues to evolve as well, though here we'll pay less attention to the writing so that we can concentrate primarily on visual language.

Invention

As Fred begins to think about his design problem, he realizes that he has three groups of information to work with:

1. An announcement of the Jamison gift and the meeting
2. The data about the Center's membership, operating expenses, and use
3. The information about the two options for using the Jamison gift

Initially, Fred has a simple and direct solution in mind: He envisions a package that contains the letter and a two-sided information sheet that can serve as an enclosure (Figure 1.17).

FIGURE 1.17   Fred's first plan for the information package

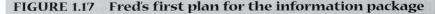

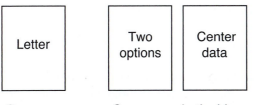

First, Fred drafts his letter. He decides to put the good news right up front, then to state the place, date, and time of the meeting. He next explains the issue of developing a plan, outlines the goals for the meeting, and refers readers to the attached flyer and data sheet, closing with "Hope to see you there." Visually, Fred uses the Center's letterhead stationery and follows the usual conventions of a letter—salutation, paragraphs in a single column, and signature. He also chooses a conventional typeface: Palatino in 11 point, the standard for this organization and a typeface that will seem familiar to readers on the mailing list. (Remember, Figures 1.2–1.5 were reduced in size.)

As Fred designs his letter, he also makes some important design choices to create emphasis.

- He centers the meeting time and place and enlarges and boldfaces the text.
- He puts the goals of the meeting in a bulleted list.
- He visually isolates the last sentence of the letter (the invitation to the meeting).

And, significantly, Fred decides to keep the letter to a single page, even though that constrains what he can say. For example, while he must explain the news of the grant, he realizes that he must exclude biographical information on Edna Jamison. He also decides that the letter does not need to discuss the less important terms of the grant. In the end, holding the letter to one page makes it more manageable for his readers—and more emphatic. Now Fred has a pretty good working draft of his page display (Figure 1.18).

FIGURE 1.18   Fred's letter design

Next, Fred assembles the data about the Center. From the file cabinet in the office he retrieves annual reports that contain data about memberships and yearly expenses. The data have never been graphed before, so he's curious about how the trends will look when he displays them visually. To do that, he uses multiple bar graphs because this conventional arrangement enables readers to compare lots of data categories over time. To show expenses, he creates the bar graph shown in Figure 1.19.

FIGURE 1.19   Fred's draft of the data display

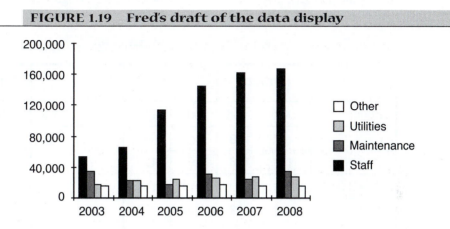

However, this chart looks cluttered and unprofessional, detracting from clarity, conciseness, and ethos. As he looks at his multiple bar graph, Fred becomes less convinced that readers will be able (or even want) to make precise comparisons between the different categories of expenses. So he decides to simplify things by using a divided bar graph instead (see Figure 1.20).

FIGURE 1.20   Fred's final version of the data display

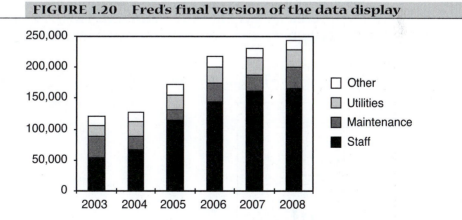

This conventional arrangement enables readers to see the big trends more quickly, while also giving them the option of comparing smaller units of data if they wish to examine the numbers more closely. Fred thinks few of them will, though.

Fred then turns to the data about the number of people who daily use the Center's various spaces. He doesn't think these data will be very clear if he places them in a chart, so he decides to use a table instead. He creates two levels of column headings to differentiate between 2007 and 2008, an arrangement and clarity decision. For the numerical data, Fred uses a sans serif typeface (Helvetica), partly because sans serifs have a high degree of clarity when they're surrounded with lots of space, partly because the sans serif gives the data a more objective tone (Figure 1.21).

FIGURE 1.21   Fred's draft of the data table

	January		April		July		October	
Rooms	2007	2008	2007	2008	2007	2008	2007	2008
Card/Game	67	138	54	145	21	47	62	174
Craft	110	178	90	123	27	58	123	195
Exercise	233	321	114	173	84	121	211	391
Meeting	37	59	22	72	11	32	41	98
Reading	53	77	49	65	13	38	54	83

Later, when Fred realizes that he has more space to work with on a landscape (horizontal) page format, he'll add another column of data to cover the average monthly use numbers for 2007 and 2008. But we're getting ahead of ourselves, so let's return to Fred's more immediate task of arranging his displays on a single page. As Fred organizes the displays—the two divided bar graphs and the table—his page begins to takes shape (Figure 1.22).

FIGURE 1.22   Portrait layout of the Mapleton data sheet

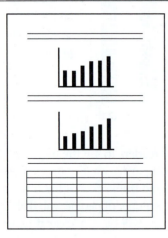

Next, Fred turns to the two options where he's written some text and made drawings of the renovated depot and the new building. Basing his drawings on those of a local architect who created some plans a few years earlier, Fred scales down and simplifies the drawings for this situation (see Figure 1.23).

FIGURE 1.23   Portrait layout of the options page

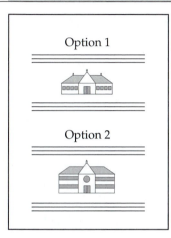

Revision

After putting the document aside for a day, Fred realizes that he has to make some large-scale adjustments in his design. The two options don't fit very well on one page, so to do them justice he'll have to add a page. That presents another problem: Now he has four pages instead of three. What should he do? Place the options on a double-sided page and the data on another sheet?

The overall arrangement of information is getting complicated, Fred thinks as he stares at his draft. Readers will now have to juggle three documents in the information package: the cover letter, the options sheet, and the data sheet. He envisions people at the meeting trying to sort through them all—losing their place, wondering if they even brought *all those documents.* Fred gets discouraged and starts to wonder if the Jamison grant is more a millstone than a blessing.

Fred puts the project aside for a few hours, then gets an idea—placing the data sheet on the back of the letter. That sounds promising, so he does a quick mock-up. Now his overall design looks like Figure 1.24.

Fred now begins to work more intensively with the options page, distributing the text and pictures across the front and back. Realizing that he doesn't have enough text to fill both sides, he creates a small table summarizing the two options and places it after option two on the back page.

FIGURE 1.24   Fred's revised plan for the information package

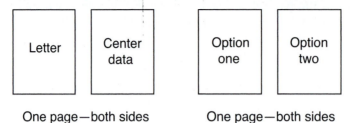

When Fred examines his design, however, he finds several flaws with respect to the rhetorical situation. First, the page design lacks conciseness because the centered picture takes up too much space. This also looks clumsy, diminishing the ethos of the document. More importantly, arranging the options on reverse sides of the same page limits the reader's ability to compare the two. Readers would be better served, Fred thinks, if the options appeared in closer proximity.

He quickly gets another idea: Place the four pages on a single 11" × 17" page folded in half. The letter can go on the front, the options in the center pages, and the data on the back. The new design, then, would look like Figure 1.25.

FIGURE 1.25   Fred's final plan for the information package

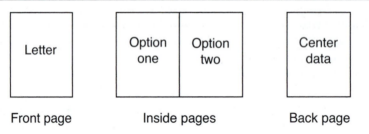

As Fred begins to arrange the option pages, he confronts another ethical issue: The board was adamant that *both* plans be considered—that community center members be given a real voice in the matter, as Edna Jamison stipulated in her gift. The document, therefore, can't give the impression that any course of action had already been chosen. The options pages have to be presented objectively; to do that, they need to be as visually parallel as possible. So Fred drops the comparative table and adds more textual details to fill out the page. He also splits the pages into two columns, one for text and the other for pictures, as shown in Figure 1.26.

As he studies these page displays, however, Fred isn't satisfied that his design has clarified the information: To compare the pictures, readers have to leap over a

FIGURE 1.26   Drafts of options pages

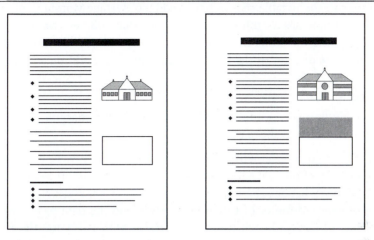

column of text. Therefore, he rearranges text and image for the second option page so that pictures appear on the inside, text on the outside, hoping that this arrangement will add clarity as well as enhance the credibility of the display. Readers need to trust that they will have a voice in the decision-making process; to earn their trust, Fred must be even-handed—that is, ethical—in his treatment, both visual and verbal, of the two options.

Now Fred goes back to his data page where he struggled to display all the information because he couldn't fit the bar charts side-by-side. After thinking about it awhile, he decides to arrange the information in landscape format instead of portrait (see Figure 1.27).

FIGURE 1.27   Mapleton data sheet—portrait versus landscape

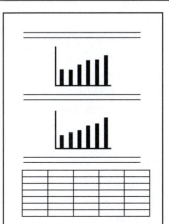
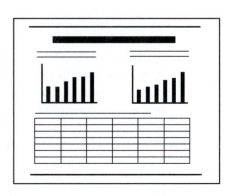

The change in page orientation gives Fred not only enough space for his charts but also more space for his table, so now he can add the "Average Monthly" column on the right.

Fred now has an information package that coheres visually, that is clear, and that projects the ethos that the occasion warrants. He'll run his design by Linda Verrips, the director of the Center, then begin some editing and fine-tuning.

Visual Editing

After Linda makes some helpful comments in the margins, Fred makes a list of things he needs to shore up.

1. Although the elements now hang together fairly well, he wants to unify the document into a single package and thereby give it greater cohesion and *ethos*. To create better cohesion, Fred uses an *arrangement* strategy, placing lines at the header and footer of the options pages and the data page. The lines tie these pages together as well as to the letterhead, which also uses the same line weight. Thus they enhance the *ethos* of the document by framing the pages and making them look more serious and professional, showing due respect and appreciation to Edna Jamison for her generous gift.
2. Fred chooses a birch paper stock to give the document a personal yet dignified *tone* appropriate for this occasion.
3. To ensure the parallelism of the options pages, Fred adds another item to the list of benefits for the build-new option so that now both options have four benefits. The parallelism enhances the objective *tone* of the information Fred's presenting.
4. Fred adds *clarity* to the document by the following decisions.

   - He places captions under the floor plans for each of the options.
   - Fred rearranges the textures on the bars, using black for the bottom of the bar and progressively lighter gray scales as they go up.
   - He boldfaces the row and column heads in the data table to make them more emphatic.
   - Fred places a gray scale in two alternating rows in the data table to guide the reader's eye across the long horizontal stretch.

Okay, that'll do it for now. Fred prints the document on the paper stock he's chosen and runs this version by Linda and some of his other co-workers. He'll also show it to some community center members to see if they understand the information and to gauge their reactions.

What Can We Learn from Fred's Process?

As you can tell, Fred's design process takes a number of twists and turns. Even though his document spans only four pages, he orchestrates a variety of design elements—text, pictures, two charts, a table, and so on. Just like writing, design is an unpredictable process that often involves risks and false starts. By having observed Fred's design process, then, we can extract three general principles.

1. *Like writing, design is a process of inventing, revising, and editing.* As Fred designs, he makes several discoveries, just as writers do as they draft and revise. Those discoveries redirect the process in ways he couldn't anticipate when the process began.

Take the two options pages. As Fred arranges the text, he discovers that he needs separate pages for each option so that readers can make quick, accurate comparisons. He also discovers that he needs (and that he now has space for) pictures that will spark reader interest and clarify the differences between the two options. So he develops pictures and rough floor plans of the two buildings. As he distributes the text on the two option pages, Fred clarifies the structure of the information. To help readers see this structure on both option pages, he uses a variety of visual cues—bullets, indentation, and run-in headings. As his design process unfolds, Fred continually invents, revises, and edits the visual language, redefining the design problem as he goes.

2. *Rhetorical concerns push the process ahead.* Fred's process isn't arbitrary or subjective but rather is driven by his conscious response to the rhetorical situation. He intends each design choice to make the document more appropriate for its audience, purpose, and context.

- When Fred ponders which typeface to use for the body text, he chooses one that he thinks will be clear and legible to his readers and that will make the tone of the document friendlier.
- When he decides to place the letter on a single page, the options on separate facing pages, and the data on the back page, he does so because he wants to simplify the readers' job and to reassure the readers that the information is accurate and important.
- When Fred creates the two bar graphs, he does so to draw readers into the data and give them quick access to the big picture. He tries to map the data in a way that will make his readers' exploration easy and interesting.

Virtually every decision Fred makes about his document—the color and texture of the page, the lines in the headers and footers, the diamond bullets, the page display—are driven by his understanding of the rhetorical situation.

3. *Visual and verbal design are interdependent.* Fred's design decisions affect the writing of his document, just as the writing affects his design. When he decides to give each option its own page, he creates additional space for text. In this way he goes back and forth between designing and writing so that the two blend together as a single package. This process continues from invention to editing.

But that's not the whole story—far from it. To result in a successful document, the visual and the verbal have to work together rhetorically. The verbal language of Fred's cover letter sets the tone for the document—an occasion to celebrate but one that also requires serious decision making. The visual language of the options and data pages reinforces this tone. In these ways the visual and the verbal support and extend one another rhetorically.

The visual and the verbal, however, don't always match each other rhetorically—sometimes the visual language has to carry the rhetorical moment alone. For instance, verbally, the options pages are plain and factual; however, the visual language—the paper stock, the lines, the diamond bullets—picks up the slack, giving the document energy and vitality.

Although the visual and verbal remain interdependent throughout the document design process, in the examples in Chapters 4 through 9 we'll focus almost exclusively on the visual. Keep in mind, though, when you develop a document, that the writing and design processes will usually unfold together.

Conventions—What Readers Expect

Long ago in a village by the sea, a young woman and her mother sat in the sunlight outside their house painting vases. The mother glanced over at her daughter's vase.

"Those flowers are too big," she said, frowning. "Wash them off before they dry, and make them smaller. No one in the market will buy a vase with flowers that big. Besides, they are too tall and too red."

The young woman looked up at her mother and replied, "I don't see what's wrong with my flowers. Large or small, tall or short, red or yellow—what difference does it make? They look like flowers, don't they? I've seen such flowers up in the hills."

Her mother moved toward her daughter, put her arm around her, and smiled. "You'll learn how to paint flowers. Just do what I say, and we'll sell every vase."

Part of successful communication is learning how to use *conventions*—the customary forms and configurations that members of an audience expect, whether that audience consists of vase buyers, users of a building, or readers of documents. Conventions are accepted ways of giving form to things—the templates, the guides, the well-worn paths. For most communication tasks, we identify relevant conventions (if any exist), find out how rigid or loose these conventions are, and decide how and if they apply to a particular situation. Virtually everything we communicate implicates verbal *and* visual conventions of one sort or another.

You're probably already familiar with many verbal conventions. Let's look briefly at some of those before we explore visual conventions.

Verbal Conventions

When you use verbal language, you usually draw on conventions to get the job done. For example, in creating your résumé, you would probably include sections on your job objective, education, and work experience. Using these categories is an example of a relatively rigid conventional practice because prospective employers who review your résumé for entry-level jobs will almost certainly look for such categories. Flouting this convention on a document as important as your résumé may be risky.

In many other kinds of documents, writers follow looser conventional patterns. For example, reports typically include introductions, methods, findings, discussions, and conclusions; but sometimes the findings and the discussion are rolled into one section, and some reports include recommendations while others don't—it depends on the rhetorical situation. Proposals usually include a problem statement, objectives, methods, qualifications, and costs; but some proposals combine the problem statement with the objectives, and some proposals have a separate section on benefits. Although we don't want to reinvent the wheel every time, when we write complex documents we need some flexibility within the conventional framework.

Using conventions helps you satisfy your readers' expectations and also helps readers understand the message—on a variety of levels. For example, on the sentence level, readers rely on conventional practices for punctuation, grammar, and spelling to move from one idea to the next. (And in many instances you need to conform to these conventions very carefully, unless you want to risk miscommunicating or sounding ignorant.) On a larger scale, including an abstract in a formal report or an article gives readers a glance at the big picture and also helps them decide whether to read the text.

Visual Conventions

Just as when you write or read a document, when you design a document or you read it "visually," you tap into a variety of conventions that govern its language (see Kostelnick and Hassett). Like those in the verbal realm, visual conventions can be described by many different criteria. For example:

- *Scope.* Some visual conventions are small scale, involving only minute marks on the page (superscript positioning for footnote numbers), while others are large scale, affecting much larger portions of the document (multiple columns for text in newsletters).

- *Degree of flexibility.* Some visual conventions are rigid and leave you little room for adaptation (italicizing book titles), while others are flexible and allow you some freedom (one-page résumés for entry-level jobs).

- *Size of the user group.* Some visual conventions will be expected and understood by a small group of readers (green paper for internal memos within a company), while others include a much larger range of readers (signs with a circle and a slash telling readers *not* to do something).

This last point about conventions has important implications for both designers and readers of visual language: You *learn* them; you acquire an understanding of conventions through your experience in the world—sometimes by observation, sometimes through formal training. Many visual conventions you've undoubtedly learned already; others you've probably observed in documents you've received but not yet used in documents you've created; still others you may not yet know about but will gradually acquire as you need them.

So what do visual conventions look like? Let's look at the résumé again, this time from the perspective of *visual* conventions (Figure 1.28a). Visually, the résumé will probably display headings on the left margin. If the résumé is for an entry-level job, it may be confined to just one page—a design convention that may affect the whole writing and design process.

Other genres you're familiar with have their own conventions as well. Take, for example, the page layout for a business letter—letterhead, date, inside address, salutation, body paragraphs, signature block (Figure 1.28b).

FIGURE 1.28   Conventional résumé and letter designs

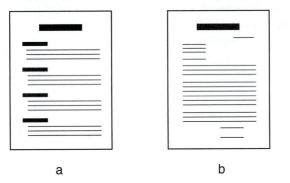

a   b

These design conventions are fairly common and vary slightly from one letter to another. An individual writer may prefer a certain conventional page layout, or a whole organization may have a uniform visual style to which all employees adhere. Communicators adapt visual conventions to their own needs and situations, sometimes choosing which ones, if any, to use or to flout, while other times having little choice in the matter.

Letter layout is just one of a host of visual conventions you'll encounter as you design. Instructions, brochures, business cards, annual reports, newsletters—all of these communications embody visual conventions that enable readers to make quick judgments about their type and purpose. "That looks like a report," or "That's obviously a brochure," or "That's a legal document," we say to ourselves—and when we do, visual conventions usually provide the clues that allow us to make these judgments. Conventions aren't an end in themselves but a *means* to an end—helping readers understand the document.

Visual Discourse Communities

Because conventions are learned and acquired, they depend entirely on the audience's familiarity with them to communicate the intended meaning. Depending on the convention, the audience may be large or small, with its members adhering to the convention within a discipline, an organization, or an entire culture. Whatever its size or makeup, an audience that understands certain conventions might be considered a *visual discourse community.*

In a small discourse community, a limited pool of users would readily understand the visual conventions—for example, architects, engineers, and contractors who know how to read a steel framing plan for a building. Often the visual conventions of specialized visual discourse communities are recorded in handbooks or manuals and sanctioned by professional organizations. Visual conventions with small discourse communities don't often give outsiders many clues about their meaning. Take the image in Figure 1.29.

FIGURE 1.29   Conventions/discourse communities

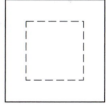

What is it? Let's say it's a plan of a kitchen table and the dotted line represents the stand that supports the table. The dotted line is a visual convention for displaying information behind the surface plane, a convention that engineers use all the time. Will all readers understand the convention? Many nonengineers will; some won't. Those in the know (inside the visual discourse community) will get it; others won't.

Not understanding visual conventions can inhibit meaningful communication. Often this problem occurs when we encounter conventions that have very specialized users—for example, scientific data displays, navigational maps, electrical circuit diagrams, medical charts, and the like. Like specialized jargon in writing, these conventions are too technical for lay readers. Pick up a technical journal or publication and you'll soon discover a host of design conventions you probably never knew existed.

On the other hand, sometimes the discourse community for a visual convention can be quite large, cutting across disciplines and cultures and virtually assuring that most readers will understand it. An example of a large visual discourse community would be automobile drivers (in North America, at least) who recognize a triangle as a warning sign. Perhaps an even larger visual discourse community would include readers who understand the image in Figure 1.30, which has a specific meaning but a very wide international audience.

FIGURE 1.30   Familiar design convention

You've probably seen many uses of this visual convention, particularly on roads and in public spaces like airports. Many other visual conventions also have large audiences. Some of these conventions have been formally adopted by discourse communities (e.g., italics or underlining for book titles). Other conventions, however, circulate informally and are imitated by document designers. Some of these more informal conventions include:

- Sans serif typefaces for headings
- Script typefaces for formal invitations
- Navigational bars for Web pages
- Initial letters to start articles in newsletters or annual reports

The discourse communities for these conventions are large and amorphous and probably determined as much by culture and geographic location as by professional discipline.

Fred Noonan's Use of Conventions

As Fred creates his document, he integrates a variety of conventions to shape his design. In the cover letter, for example, he uses some conventions that are genre-related (the basic visual structure of the letter) and others that derive from the organization he works for (Palatino typeface for text, the Mapleton letterhead). Fred also taps into several conventions on the options and data pages.

- *Options pages.* The lines in header and footer, the diamonds for bullets, the italicized run-in headings, the floor plan drawings—all of these are conventional ways of displaying information.

- *Data page.* The divided bar graphs are conventional forms of displaying data over time. The table has the conventional features of a matrix—row and column headings that direct readers vertically and horizontally to specific pieces of data.

Conventions don't back Fred into a corner, however; they help him to respond to the rhetorical situation. Based on the circumstances, Fred has to decide which conventions to use—and which ones to flout—and how to adjust them to meet his readers' needs. Let's look at some of the ways Fred uses and adjusts conventions to solve his design problem.

1. Fred's letter conforms to the typical Mapleton letter format—letterhead, Palatino font, and so on—which readers can quickly identify. On the other hand, he deviates from the convention by using birch paper stock and by embedding the letter in a brochure format.
2. On the options pages, Fred shows conventional floor plans of the two buildings. Most readers understand the convention of looking at a building from the top down. Fred adapts this convention to his needs by showing the plan at a high level of abstraction, hiding the windows, doors, closets, bathrooms, and other details that he believes would distract his readers in this situation.
3. Fred displays the information about expenses and memberships in conventional divided bar graphs; however, he decides against using horizontal gridlines because he fears that they would make the charts look too technical.

During his design process, Fred draws on many conventions to push the process ahead efficiently and to meet the needs and expectations of his readers. Most of these conventions are fairly flexible, and as he refines his design he adapts them to his needs.

Some Basic Principles of Conventions

Using conventions effectively, then, means gauging them to particular rhetorical situations—knowing when they are appropriate for a given audience, purpose, and context, and when they are adaptable or irrelevant. Below are some specific guidelines to help you use conventions.

1. *Identify relevant conventions for any design problem you're trying to solve.* Knowing the range of relevant conventions for a given design problem can save you time and make your solution more reader-sensitive. Virtually any area of visual design—from text design to data displays to pictures and symbols—conforms to some conventional codes, both in print and on computer screens. Though they just scratch the surface, the examples below illustrate the breadth of visual conventions.

- *Text design:* script typefaces for invitations and awards, superscripts for footnote numbers, double or triple columns for newsletters, sans serif typefaces for headings, bullets next to parallel items in a list
- *Data displays:* the x–y axes on bar charts and line graphs, gridlines and tick marks to clarify data points, slices in pie charts to show parts of the whole, lines to show trends, legends to code the data
- *Pictures:* cross hatching to show a cut through a surface, dotted lines to reveal planes beneath the surface, arrows to show motion, blowups to show details, exploded views to show the relationship of parts
- *Color:* red for stop, yellow for warnings in Western culture, green for ecologically friendly products

As a document designer, you'll continually need to identify the range of available conventions and decide how useful they are for a given design problem. Depending on the rhetorical situation, they may be irrelevant or they may save you lots of time.

  2. *Realize that some conventions are more rigid than others.* Sometimes you can choose to use a convention or ignore it; sometimes you have little choice in the matter; and other times you can adapt conventions to your own needs, as Fred does. How much choice you have in the matter depends on the nature of the convention and the rhetorical situation. You might imagine a continuum where rigid conventions stand on one end, flexible ones on the other, and all of the others somewhere in between.

Rigid  Flexible

  The rigid side of the spectrum would include the convention of italicizing titles of books or using an x and a y axis for a line graph; in either case, you have little choice in the matter. Also on the rigid side of the spectrum we could put the circle with a slash, which tells readers not to do something: "Don't drive here" or "Don't walk your dog." You could convey the same "Don't do" command by putting an "X" through the picture of a car or a dog on a leash, but that sign would be risky since it doesn't have the same conventional status as the circle with the slash.
  Although these conventions—italicizing titles of books, plotting a line graph on x–y axes, and using the slash through the circle—are relatively universal, rigidity has little to do with universality. Imagine that you work for the ABC Corporation, which always uses pale blue paper for invoices. Doing this may be a convention confined only to you and your colleagues within ABC, but none of you has a choice in the matter. Pale blue is what the boss and your colleagues expect—every time.
  Other conventions lean toward the flexible end of the spectrum, giving the designer more room for decision or variation. Using tabs for training materials in

three-ring binders, boxing off warnings in instructions, or using a tear-off return card in a brochure—all of these are common conventions, but the designer can choose to follow them or not depending on the situation.

On the Internet, conventions are still evolving as Web sites multiply and as the technology continues to develop. Although Web site designers often elect to use paper conventions—headings, initial letters, color—many Web conventions have emerged, such as navigational bars, highlighted text to signal links, pop-up menus, and a panoply of others that continue to emerge.

3. *Think of conventions in terms of your readers, who give them meaning and significance.* If your readers understand and expect certain conventions, then using them can enhance the clarity and ethos of your document. You've probably received documents that don't meet your expectations because they violated conventional design practices, leading to confusion and prompting you to question the writer's ethos: "Do these people know what they're doing?" Conventions are powerful templates, and when visual language doesn't conform, we notice.

However, not meeting the reader's expectations doesn't *always* have negative results. Flouting conventions can sometimes attract the reader's attention in a more positive way. If you get an annual report printed horizontally on an odd-size page, you'll notice immediately that it violates the conventions for annual reports. However, you might think, "This is interesting. I've never seen a report that looks like this one! I wonder what's inside." Flouting conventions may entail some risks, but designers have to measure those risks in relation to rhetorical situations; the potential gains may outweigh the losses. If one of the designers' main objectives was getting you to explore their annual report, the risk of an unconventional design paid off.

The most important principle to remember? Conventions are reader-oriented strategies. Use them or flout them where the rhetorical situation calls for it.

Acquiring the Language of Visual Conventions

Learning visual language conventions and integrating them in your own work will take time. But that's true of any language you learn. You have an advantage in learning visual conventions, however, because every day you're probably inundated with documents, both print and electronic. If you want to become familiar with the conventions, train yourself to study them. Observing and analyzing documents can go a long way toward helping you acquire visual language skills. Fluency in any language—visual or verbal—takes total immersion and practice!

Throughout this book, we'll help you identify design conventions in many different forms of visual language, from text design to pictures to data displays. In the exercises and assignments, we'll also ask you to identify, analyze, or use conventions. Because conventions derive from many different disciplines, organizations, and cultures, we'll just scratch the surface in this book. Still, we hope our examples will serve as a springboard for you to discover many more conventions on your own.

Conclusion

We began this chapter with the notion that visual design, like writing, *depends on* the rhetorical situation—audience, purpose, and context. To be successful, then, your communication's visual language must be tailored to its audience, enable the communication to fulfill its purpose, and be suitable for the context in which users actually interact with the communication. To meet the demands of the rhetorical situation, you can employ six strategies: arrangement, emphasis, clarity, conciseness, tone, and ethos. To help you implement these strategies, you have many ready-made guides in the form of visual conventions. Figure 1.31 represents the relationships among all of these elements. The actual design process, of course, isn't as neat, controlled, or static as this model may suggest. Rather, as we've shown in Fred's development of the Mapleton document, visual design is a dynamic process that entails invention, revision, and editing.

In the next two chapters, we'll continue to define elements of this model. In Chapter 2 we'll introduce two additional guides for implementing the cognate strategies: principles of perception and empirical research. Then in Chapter 3 we'll outline a system for describing the vocabulary of visual language itself.

Note

1. Visual rhetoric has become the focus of much scholarly work, both in the fields of writing and design. Studies of visual rhetoric have encompassed written communication (Bernhardt, "Seeing"; Tebeaux), historical and cultural analysis (Ong), screens (Bernhardt, "Shape"), data displays (Barton and Barton, "Modes"; "Toward a Rhetoric"; Tufte), semiotics (Ashwin; Barthes; Bertin; Killingsworth and Gilbertson), graphic and typographic design (Bonsiepe; Ehses; Kinross; Twyman; Waller), and product design (Buchanan). Together these works—and others, some of them by these same authors—have laid a foundation for studying visual rhetoric and have helped us develop the rhetorical approach outlined in this book for teaching visual design in professional communication. Since the first edition of this book, the study of visual rhetoric has greatly proliferated: Numerous valuable studies and collections (far too many to cite here) have appeared—for example, examining information design practices through a cultural lens (Brasseur), expanding the realm of visual rhetoric across many genres and sites (Hill and Helmers), applying visual rhetoric to Web and online design (Handa), and providing pedagogical guidance (David and Richards). And the influence of Gunther Kress and Theo Van Leeuwen's *Reading Images,* now in its second edition, has widened considerably.

FIGURE 1.31   Design process diagram

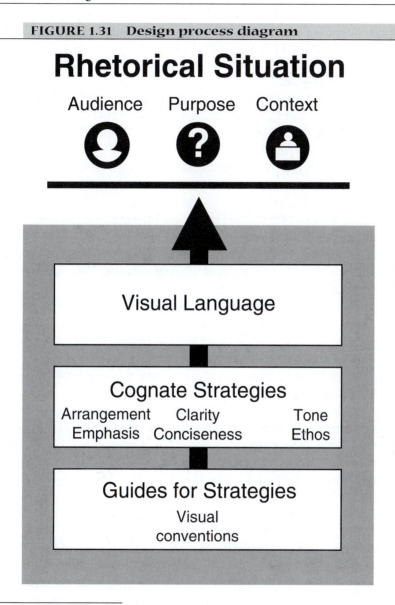

References

Ashwin, Clive. "Drawing, Design, and Semiotics." *Design Issues* 1.2 (1984): 42–52.

Barthes, Roland. "The Rhetoric of the Image." *The Responsibility of Forms: Critical Essays on Music, Art, and Representation.* Trans. Richard Howard. New York: Farrar, Straus and Giroux, 1985.

Barton, Ben F., and Marthalee S. Barton. "Modes of Power in Technical and Professional Visuals." *Journal of Business and Technical Communication* 7 (1993): 138–162.

————. "Toward a Rhetoric of Visuals for the Computer Era." *The Technical Writing Teacher* 12 (1985): 126–145.

Bernhardt, Stephen A. "Seeing the Text." *College Composition and Communication* 37 (1986): 66–78.

————. "The Shape of Text to Come: The Texture of Print on Screens." *College Composition and Communication* 44 (1993): 151–175.

Bertin, Jacques. *Semiology of Graphics.* Trans. William J. Berg. Madison: University of Wisconsin Press, 1983.

Bonsiepe, Gui. "Visual/Verbal Rhetoric." *Ulm* 14–16 (1965): 23–40.

Brasseur, Lee E. *Visualizing Technical Information: A Cultural Critique.* Amityville, NY: Baywood, 2003.

Buchanan, Richard. "Declaration by Design: Rhetoric, Argument, and Demonstration in Design Practice." *Design Issues* 2.1 (1985): 4–22.

David, Carol, and Anne R. Richards, eds. *Writing the Visual: A Practical Guide for Teachers of Composition and Communication.* West Lafayette, IN: Parlor Press, 2008.

Ehses, Hanno H. J. "Representing Macbeth: A Case Study in Visual Rhetoric." *Design Issues* 1.1 (1984): 53–63.

Handa, Carolyn, ed. *Visual Rhetoric in a Digital World: A Critical Sourcebook.* Boston: Bedford/St. Martin's Press, 2004.

Hill, Charles A., and Marguerite Helmers, eds. *Defining Visual Rhetorics.* Mahwah, NJ: Erlbaum, 2004.

Killingsworth, M. Jimmie and Michael K. Gilbertson. *Signs, Genres, and Communities in Technical Communication.* Amityville, NY: Baywood, 1992.

Kinross, Robin. "The Rhetoric of Neutrality." *Design Issues* 2.2 (1985): 18–30.

Kostelnick, Charles, and Michael Hassett. *Shaping Information: The Rhetoric of Visual Conventions.* Carbondale, IL: Southern Illinois University Press, 2003.

Kress, Gunther, and Theo Van Leeuwen. *Reading Images: The Grammar of Visual Design.* 2nd ed. London: Routledge, 2006.

Ong, Walter J. *Orality and Literacy: The Technologizing of the Word.* New York: Methuen, 1982.

Tebeaux, Elizabeth. "Developing a Heuristic Approach to Graphics." *Teaching Technical Writing: Graphics.* Ed. Dixie Elise Hickman. Anthology No. 5, Association of Teachers of Technical Writing, 1985. 28–39.

Tufte, Edward. *The Visual Display of Quantitative Information.* Cheshire, CT: Graphics Press, 1983.

Twyman, Michael. "The Graphic Presentation of Language." *Information Design Journal* 3 (1982): 2–22.

Waller, Robert H. W. "Graphic Aspects of Complex Texts: Typography as Macro-Punctuation." *Processing of Visible Language* 2. Ed. Paul A. Kolers, Merald E. Wrolstad, and Herman Bouma. New York: Plenum, 1980. 241–253.

Exercises

1. In each of the three cases below, consider how changes in the rhetorical situation can alter your approach to designing a document. Where you can, refer to the six cognate strategies in discussing your design approach.

   a. *Audience:* Suppose you are writing a short report to your new supervisor recommending that the company purchase a solar-powered heating system because of growing energy costs. Today you found out that your new supervisor prefers images to words. How might this insight about your audience affect the way you design your report?

   b. *Purpose:* Your city parks and recreation department has asked your communication design firm to update an informational brochure that maps walking trails in a popular wooded area. Proposals are now being floated, however, about rezoning the wooded area for residential or commercial construction, a prospect that alarms the parks and recreation board. To persuade readers to oppose the rezoning, how might you change the brochure design in response to this change in purpose?

   c. *Context:* As a technical communicator for a toy manufacturing company, you've been asked to redesign the instructions for assembling a child's toy airplane that flies via a rubber band motor. The instructions are currently on a 14" × 30" sheet of onionskin paper (Figure 1.32a) that shows the step-by-step assembly primarily with drawings. These instructions are used by people in their homes, garages, or yards.

   Marketing research has shown that more people might purchase the airplane if the instructions appear right on the cardboard backing of the package—people like to gauge the complexity of the assembly before buying. But this means that you must alter the instructions to fit a page that's about 9" × 14" (Figure 1.32b). It also means that people will now read (though not actually

---

FIGURE 1.32   Toy airplane instructions

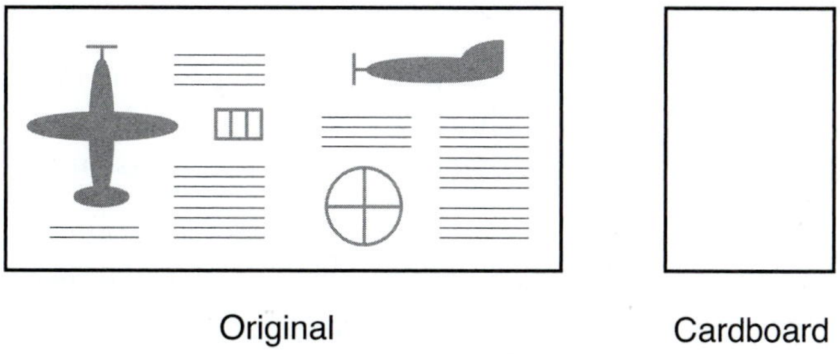

Original   Cardboard

use) the instructions standing in the aisle of a store, deciding how easily they—or their child—can build the model.

How will this change in context affect your redesign of the instructions? How might the new purpose, which now includes both instruction *and* persuasion, affect your redesign?

2. Figure 1.33 shows a draft of a Web site for the Giza Archeology Club, an organization for people interested in exploring antiquities throughout the world. Members include people from all walks of life—teachers, plumbers, doctors, professional archeologists, aspiring Indiana Joneses, retirees. The club updates members on the latest discoveries as well as enables them to share information about their own adventures. Currently, the club's main reporting medium is a quarterly printed newsletter. Now the club is developing a Web site so it can share information more quickly with members (and prospective members) throughout the world as well as enable them to interact with each other. One of the main goals of the site is to make the organization more international by attracting new members, particularly in Europe, the Middle East, and Asia.

   a. As you look over the initial page of the Web site mock-up, what *arrangement* and *emphasis* strategies are evident in its design? How do these strategies respond—or not respond—to the rhetorical situation outlined above? How conventional are these strategies? Are there any arrangement or emphasis conventions that readers in other cultures might not interpret the same way as readers in North America?

   b. How would you define the *tone* of the design? How well does the visual tone match the verbal tone and the subject matter? What visual elements build *ethos?* How could ethos be improved through visual language? How might readers from different cultures interpret the tone and ethos differently? Why?

   c. Finally, consider how well the Web site achieves visual *conciseness* and visual *clarity*. What design choices contribute to clarity? Do any diminish clarity? Could this Web page be more visually concise—that is, do all design elements do some rhetorical work? Are there any design elements that don't?

3. Visual conventions exist all around us in design objects we use—buildings, cars, furniture, stereos, children's toys, televisions, cooking utensils, dinnerware, and so on. Observe the design objects in the world around you and:

   a. Identify a convention that's no longer in use. (For example, fins on cars were very popular in the late 1950s and early 1960s, but then disappeared from use.) Why do you think the design convention faded from use?

FIGURE 1.33   Giza Archeology Club Web site

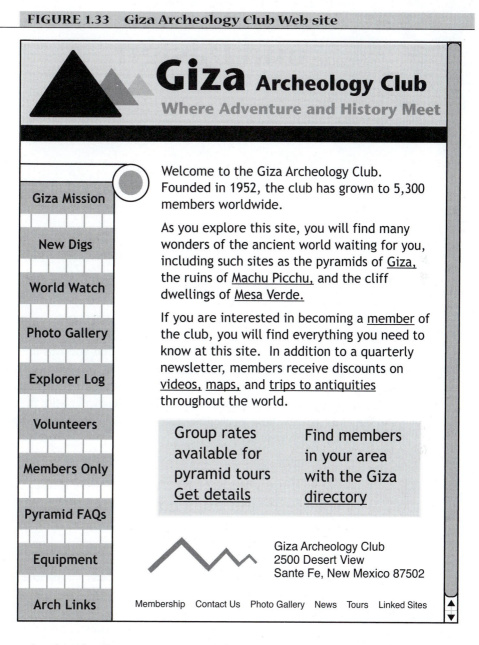

Giza Archeology Club
Where Adventure and History Meet

Giza Mission

New Digs

World Watch

Photo Gallery

Explorer Log

Volunteers

Members Only

Pyramid FAQs

Equipment

Arch Links

Welcome to the Giza Archeology Club. Founded in 1952, the club has grown to 5,300 members worldwide.

As you explore this site, you will find many wonders of the ancient world waiting for you, including such sites as the pyramids of <u>Giza,</u> the ruins of <u>Machu Picchu,</u> and the cliff dwellings of <u>Mesa Verde.</u>

If you are interested in becoming a <u>member</u> of the club, you will find everything you need to know at this site. In addition to a quarterly newsletter, members receive discounts on <u>videos,</u> <u>maps,</u> and <u>trips to antiquities</u> throughout the world.

Group rates available for pyramid tours <u>Get details</u>

Find members in your area with the Giza <u>directory</u>

Giza Archeology Club
2500 Desert View
Sante Fe, New Mexico 87502

Membership   Contact Us   Photo Gallery   News   Tours   Linked Sites

b. Identify a design convention that's currently popular for certain kinds of products—clothes, hairdos, cell phones, backpacks. Why do you think it's become the norm? How long has it been an accepted way of designing these products?

c. Identify a design convention that's making a comeback—that once fell out of fashion but is now becoming accepted again. Why do you think the convention has experienced a revival?

Perception

and Design

Introduction to Perception Issues

Up to this point we've discussed many strategies that you can use to adapt visual language to a given rhetorical situation. As you design a communication, however, you'll inevitably find yourself making assumptions about how readers will respond to visual language—assumptions about what readers will notice first, how well they can organize things, how easily they can read the text. For example, during the design process, you may say to yourself:

> "If I place this text in the center of the page, enlarge it, and put a box around it, I assume my readers will notice it."

But how can you be sure? How exactly *do* readers perceive the images on a page or a screen? How do they process the visual information—the typefaces, the pictures, the icons, the data displays, the Web sites?

Perceiving visual information is a complex process, and fully explaining that process is well beyond the scope of this book. Still, knowing some basic principles that underlie the perceptual acts your readers perform can help you immensely as a designer. The goal of this chapter is to give you that basic understanding.

In the first section we'll examine the relation between perception and thinking and the role of perceptual context in seeing images. Then we'll explore how some

Gestalt principles of perception apply to design and how you can use them to help solve rhetorical problems. Toward the end of the chapter we'll introduce empirical research and discuss how it can help you become a more effective designer.

Keep in mind that the perceptual principles outlined in this chapter are only a means to an end—adapting visual language to your audience, purpose, and context. You must decide how, or whether, to apply these principles in a given rhetorical situation.

Perception Requires Thinking

Perception is the process of comprehending the world around us: trees, faces, movies, cars in traffic, raindrops on the window, the page before you now. Our senses—sound, touch, smell, taste, and sight—provide the points of contact with the external world. Although our senses may initiate the perceptual process, perception entails more than a sensory response. It also requires lots of thinking, especially when it involves the sense of sight.

You may not be accustomed to associating visual perception with thinking. When we see something, we might assume that we're merely gathering in sensory material with our eyes. However, as Rudolf Arnheim shows in his book *Visual Thinking*, that sensory response tells only a part of the story. Perception is a thoughtful, not just a physiological, act. Using Arnheim as our main guide, let's examine a few of the ways in which thinking pervades visual perception.

1. *We search for focal points.* Perception is active and intense; when we look at the things around us, we work at it. As Arnheim explains (19–26), our eyes try to focus on something, to find a place on which to center their attention. That focal point could be a door across the room, an image on a PowerPoint screen, or a heading above a column of text. As perceivers of visual information, we constantly look for these focal points to give meaning to the perceptual act. When we gaze into a room, for example, we don't see everything equally. To do so would be impossible, and meaningless as well. Instead we choose a few things to focus on— a chair, an oak desk, a painting on the wall—and in the process we filter out much of the rest.

When we don't have something to focus on, perception breaks down because it ceases to stimulate thinking. Arnheim points out that this problem occurs when "the field is homogenous," when we are confronted with a "repetitious pattern" (25). For example, looking at the pattern in Figure 2.1 might catch our attention at first, but we are soon likely to get bored because the repetitive pattern gives us nothing to focus on, no place to pause and ponder or to explore. The image turns into a perceptual dead end because we naturally want to be in control, to find a focal point and get down to work.

FIGURE 2.1   Monotonous pattern

2. *We draw on past experience.* Searching for a focal point happens instantaneously whenever we confront a visual field. Perception is also active over the longer term: When we perceive something, we bring our past experiences to that perceptual moment, experiences that profoundly shape the images we see (Arnheim 80–96). For example, Figure 2.1 may remind some viewers of a rug or pattern that they've seen on a floor, or it may remind them of a trellis or some other kind of fence. Another viewer may associate the pattern with a weaving project or with a loom, and yet another with a board game, a coffee table, or a doormat. By constantly filtering our perception, past experience plays an active part in our seeing.

To understand how this works, consider the image in Figure 2.2. Because the image is fairly ambiguous, your prior experience will play a big part in creating meaning.

FIGURE 2.2   What is this image?

So what is it? A traffic signal? A head with one eye open, the other closed? A block with holes in it? To a large extent, what you think it is depends on what it literally "re-minds" you of, images you've stored in your mind from prior perceptual experiences and that you now call forth. In this way, your understanding of this image will rely largely on the experience you bring to the perceptual moment. That experience can be based on many things, including your education, your social life, and your cultural background. For example, if you grew up in Tokyo, no doubt Figure 2.2 would evoke different meanings than in if you grew up in Boston, Chicago, or rural Kansas.

The same process occurs when we encounter a document. We bring our stored knowledge to that perceptual moment. If the document, for example, displays conventional features of an annual report—and we have experience reading those visual conventions—that experience immediately shapes our perception. If we are used to seeing graphics that are highly ornate, as they are in some cultural traditions, that experience will shape our encounter with images in a Web site. In this way, our perception of documents actually begins before our eyes even meet the page or the screen.

3. *We use vision to complete the task at hand—and little more.* When we look at something we usually do so with an aim in mind (Arnheim 19–26), whether the subject of our attention is a building, a picture, or a book. That aim guides our viewing and filters out extraneous information. Think of a simple situation that you probably experience every day: entering a building—for example, an office, a store, a dorm, or an apartment building. If you're in a hurry, chances are you'll notice only the doorway because that's what the perceptual moment demands. (If you fail to notice the outer edges of the doorway, you'll be in big trouble!) In the process you'll probably ignore most of the other sensory data that you're taking in—windows, gutters, trees, people passing by, and so on. Likewise, if you walk into an auditorium you'll probably pay close attention to the seats because that's what you need to look for first. Initially, at least, you won't pay much attention to the curtain, the stage, or the lighting system.

Perception is goal-directed: We seek what we need from a field of images and largely ignore the rest. To experience how this search process works, look at the image in Figure 2.3 and quickly calculate the number of sides on the three shapes within the gray square.

FIGURE 2.3   Perception is goal oriented

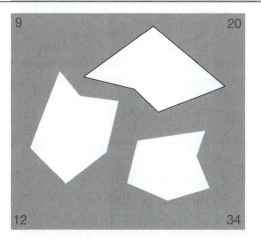

That's pretty easy, right? If you counted carefully, you came up with 17 sides in all. But in the process of doing that task you may have missed other features in the image. For example:

- Can you recite the numbers in the corners?
- Did you notice the fact that the object in the upper right of the square has a black border and the others have none?
- Did you realize that the objects on the left and the lower right have the same shape, with the one on the lower right smaller and rotated slightly?

Probably not. Why? Because the task we asked you to perform required you to pay attention to other things. The lesson? We usually see what we need to see in a given situation and filter out lots of other things.[1]

In most perceptual situations, we encounter too much information to process at one time and we gather only what we need—as purposefully and efficiently as we can. When we look up a name in a telephone book, for instance, we ignore almost everything else on the page. Likewise, when we go to a computer manual to answer a question, we look only at the text and pictures that are relevant to solving the problem. Even if we read a document from beginning to end, we may not notice everything on the page. For example, we probably won't pay much attention to the pagination or the page headers and footers, partly because we don't need them if we're turning pages consecutively.

Or if we're scrolling through screens in a Web site, we probably won't notice other options on the navigation bar or pull-down menus if we're immersed in reading text, data displays, or maps in front of us. Until we've finished reading the document at hand, we probably won't get the urge to explore elements outside our immediate field of vision. On the other hand, if we encounter links within the document, we might quickly jump from one screen to the next as we redefine the task.

Perception, then, is not confined only to our senses but rather entails various kinds of thinking, among them selecting a focal point, recalling stored images and experiences, and completing the task at hand. Understanding these thinking processes is important to you as a designer because the images you create will engage your readers in active decision making, not rote physiological responses. As a designer, you are stimulating your readers to think visually.[2]

We See Images within a Visual Field

When we perceive things in the world, we do so within a visual field—our range of vision that in any perceptual moment will likely include an array of shapes, lines, colors, patterns, and textures. The images we choose to focus on are situated within this visual field—in isolation or, more often, among many other visual elements. Consider the image in Figure 2.4—a square with a little shading.

FIGURE 2.4   Image in field

In isolation, the image dominates its space. However, when other images enter the visual field, things change. Arnheim shows in *Visual Thinking* (54–79) that as the visual elements around a given image change, our perception of the image also changes. Let's take a look at the same square in another perceptual context (see Figure 2.5). Does it look any different?

FIGURE 2.5   Effect of a different field on the same image

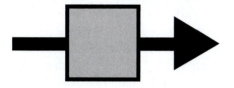

The square still claims the center of attention, but the arrow destabilizes it, giving it direction and movement. How about the visual field in Figure 2.6? Here the square no longer occupies the center of attention. Competing with several other images, it loses its singular status. Context again transforms it.

FIGURE 2.6   Effect of yet a different field on the same image

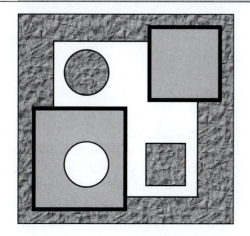

The perceptual principle? Whenever an image is taken from one perceptual context and placed in another, our perception of it changes. In other words, our perception of a given image depends on the visual field in which the image appears. When we transplant the same image into a new visual field, the image appears to change.

This perceptual principle has significant implications for designing pages or screens: If we transport a typeface, icon, or other visual element from one document to another, its new perceptual context transforms it. As designers we constantly have to take that into account.

Gestalt Principles of Design

Gestalt principles of perception can help us understand how readers see images in context—that is, in relation to a whole visual field. The term *Gestalt* itself means "form." As we've seen above, our perception of a form depends on its juxtaposition with other forms within a visual field. In other words, the *whole* form plays an essential role in understanding its parts.

Gestalt principles cover a wide range of perceptual experiences. Here we'll consider two of the most important principles: figure–ground contrast and grouping.[3] These two principles are virtually universal—that is, most readers will have similar perceptual responses to visual language that displays these principles, whether that visual language occurs on a sheet of paper, a computer screen, a billboard, a facade, or on a football field at halftime. In this way, figure–ground and grouping can apply to virtually any design. Learning to recognize and use these principles will go a long way toward helping you build your repertoire of design skills.

Although these principles apply to most perceptual situations, we need to make two important disclaimers right from the start. First, readers' perceptual responses aren't limited to Gestalt principles; as we've seen earlier in this chapter, prior knowledge and experience and completing the task at hand play powerful roles in any perceptual act. Second, you can measure the usefulness of Gestalt principles in relation only to the rhetorical situation. Gestalt principles are the *means* rather than the ends, perceptual tools that you can use to solve rhetorical problems visually.

Figure–Ground Contrast

One of the most basic and useful Gestalt principles is figure–ground contrast. Virtually everything we see relies on our ability to separate one image from another, to distinguish what stands in the front from what stands in the back. When you look at the image in Figure 2.7, you can see this principle at work. The white circles (the figure) stand out in stark contrast to the black square (the ground).

FIGURE 2.7   Figure–ground contrast

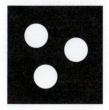

Of course, it's possible to switch the figure and the ground, to see the black square in front and the white dots in the back; however, at any given perceptual moment, we can see only one combination of figure and ground. The contrast between the two is the important thing.

The degree of figure–ground contrast can vary widely from one perceptual context to another. As a result, our ability to distinguish the figure from the ground can be less certain than in the previous example. Notice in the examples in Figure 2.8 how the figure–ground contrast diminishes from left to right as the circles get darker and the boxes lighter.

FIGURE 2.8   Variations in figure–ground contrast

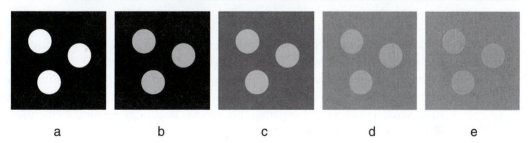

a   b   c   d   e

When we're given any field of images, we make the same figure–ground distinctions. Sometimes the figure–ground contrast is rather murky—like looking at a forest on a foggy morning where everything is gray and blends together. Sometimes the contrast is as sharp as an afternoon bathed in brilliant sunlight, where every leaf on a tree has crisp resolution.

Documents—whether in print or on screens—display the same range of contrast. When we look at a field of text, we immediately rely on the figure–ground contrast to decipher it. The print you're reading now depends on your ability to see the typefaces (the figure) as distinct from the paper (the ground). When we look at a whole page or screen (the Gestalt), we look for macro-variations across the entire visual field. In Figure 2.9, the sample text creates a general figure–ground contrast against the page of this book, but within that gray mass nothing stands out.

FIGURE 2.9   A homogeneous page of text

This page has lots of text and not much visual variation. As a result, readers won't be drawn to any particular place on this page. This page has lots of text and not much visual variation. As a result, readers won't be drawn to any particular place on this page. This page has lots of text and not much visual variation. As a result, readers won't be drawn to any particular place on this page. This page has lots of text and not much visual variation. As a result, readers won't be drawn to any particular place on this page. This page has lots of text and not much visual variation. As a result, readers won't be drawn to any particular place on this page. This page has lots of text and not much visual variation. As a result, readers won't be drawn to any particular place on this page. This page has lots of text and not much visual variation. As a result, readers won't be drawn to any particular place on this page. This page has lots of text and not much visual variation. As a result, readers won't be drawn to any particular place on this page. As a result, readers won't be drawn to any particular

And because nothing stands out, you have nothing to focus on, nothing to guide you visually. You're lost in a sea of gray, as if you were looking at that murky forest in the fog. Luckily, most document designers understand the debilitating effect of low-contrast pages on their readers. For that reason, most pages or screens have some visual variety—paragraph breaks, headings, graphic elements, icons, illustrations—that create contrast.

Examine, for instance, Figure 2.10. What textual elements stand out? Which elements recede? How does the contrast orient you visually? Unlike the gray mass in the first example, this page draws us to certain elements—the headings, the blocks of paragraphs, the numbered items in the list—by defining them as figures against the background. The page gives us some focal points, some places to begin exploring its contents.

The principle of figure–ground contrast applies to virtually any field we encounter, whether it contains text, data displays, or pictures. The images in Figure 2.11 show some of these possibilities.

- In a, the paragraph block in the center of the page with space around it stands out because of figure–ground contrast, which is enhanced by its darker tone against the large white field in the background.

FIGURE 2.10   A page of text with focal points

How Is This Page Better?

This page has lots of text and not much visual variation. As a result, readers won't be drawn to any particular place on this page. This page has lots of text and not much visual variation.

As a result, readers won't be drawn to any particular place on this page. This page has lots of text and not much visual variation.

How Is This Page Better?

As a result, readers won't be drawn to any particular place on this page. This page has lots of text and not much visual variation.

1. As a result, readers won't be drawn to any particular place on this page.

2. As a result, readers won't be drawn to any particular place on this page.

As a result, readers won't be drawn to any particular place on this page. This page has lots of text and not much visual variation.

- In b, the boxed paragraph stands out from the field of text around it because of its dark border. In fact, boxed text draws so much attention that designers often need to find ways to tone down its figure–ground contrast—by thinning the border or by using a lighter gray scale.

- In c, placing a gray-scale background on the same page will slightly diminish the figure–ground contrast of the paragraph blocks. However, if this page were inserted into a document with white pages, it would stand out from the rest—precisely because of figure–ground contrast.

- In d, the bars in the top data display stand out from the white background because of their darkness and spatial isolation. The lighter bars in the bottom display show less contrast with the page background, reducing the emphasis on their data.

- In e, the figure–ground contrast of the black bars diminishes with the gray background, while the white bars in the bottom display come to life. This reverse effect—white bars or text on a dark background—results entirely from figure–ground contrast.

- In f, the figure–ground contrast directs our eyes toward the dark square in the lower left. Grabbing the reader's attention through figure–ground contrast is often crucial in instructional pictures.

FIGURE 2.11   Figure–ground examples

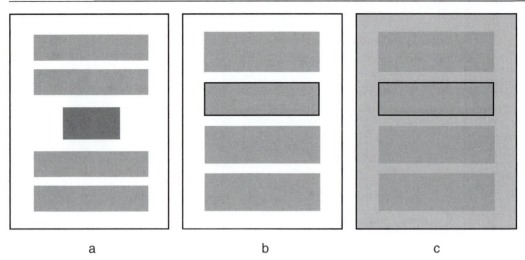

a   b   c

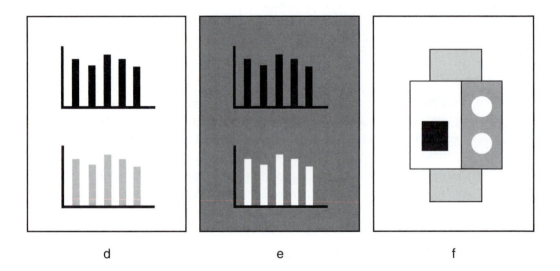

d   e   f

Degrading Figure–Ground with Visual Noise

The Gestalt principle of figure–ground contrast gives you a powerful tool to respond to a given rhetorical situation, particularly for developing emphasis and arrangement strategies. In this sense, you can selectively use figure–ground to achieve your rhetorical goals.

However, you also need to consider how the *absence* of figure–ground contrast affects your communications. Figure–ground contrast can easily be degraded by *visual noise,* diminishing the clarity of your document—as well as its conciseness and its ethos. Visual noise is anything that impedes our perceptual response to sensory stimuli: static in a telephone line, a boisterous crowd at a concert, fog that prevents us from seeing a highway sign, and so on.

So how does visual noise affect figure–ground contrast? In Figure 2.12 you can see that the figure–ground changes from left to right. In the middle example, the noisy gray background erodes the contrast between text and page. However, in the example on the right, a white box surrounds the text and contrasts with the gray background to enhance figure–ground. The white box filters out the noise.

FIGURE 2.12   Effects of visual noise

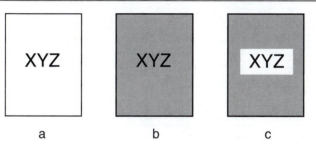

Noise happens frequently when designers use dark blue or red paper or textured backgrounds. Web sites that overuse color are vulnerable to noise. In some Web pages that blend colors for text and background, the perceptual problems can be so severe that users can't read the text at all.

Typefaces themselves can sometimes be noisy in their design or in their treatments. For example, the typeface below has lots of extra lines and strokes—design elements that give it character, to be sure, but that also add noise.

This is a noisy typeface.

Outlining, shading, and boldfacing a text can also create a noisy figure–ground effect.

This is a noisy typeface.

This isn't to say that these typefaces don't have their place, but the rhetorical situation must warrant the noise. For example, you might decide to use the ornate typeface for an award certificate or an invitation to boost the ethos, which could be well worth the trade-off in loss of clarity.

Noise can also occur in data displays: In Figure 2.13, the horizontal and vertical gridlines of the graph compete with the data lines for our attention. As a result, we can't see the data lines very clearly. Or take the picture of an office building in Figure 2.14. Readers can't see the windows very well because of the blurred shading, which degrades the lines marking the edges of the windows.

FIGURE 2.13   A noisy data display

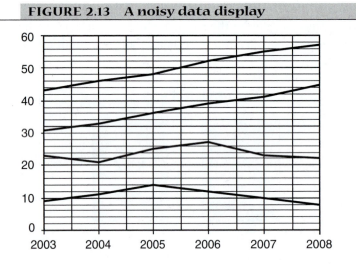

In virtually any design, you can spot some noise that challenges the figure–ground integrity of the visual language. Is visual noise always bad? It depends on the rhetorical situation. When a high degree of clarity is important, noise is definitely a problem; in these situations you'll want to filter it out. For example, in Figure 2.13 noise reduces our ability to comprehend the data, and if we can't comprehend the data, the display loses its value. The noise also adds visual complexity to the display, eroding conciseness.

The noise in Figure 2.14 also reduces its conciseness, but the degree to which the noise reduces clarity isn't as straightforward. Do readers need to see *exactly* where the edges of the windows are, or do they only have to see how many there are and get a general idea of their location? If the latter, noise might undermine conciseness but might not as seriously damage clarity. Indeed, it might enhance the tone of the image by evoking mystery.

Depending on the rhetorical situation, noise may not be much of a liability. In fact, in certain situations a little noise can enhance some rhetorical strategies even while it erodes clarity. For example, you might choose to use a gray card stock for the cover of a report, slightly degrading the figure–ground contrast of the text but at the same time adding ethos to the document. Or you might use light blue paper for pages in the appendix, an arrangement strategy that slightly

FIGURE 2.14   A noisy picture

degrades the clarity of the print on those pages but one that's worth the trade-off if it enables readers to grasp more readily the structure of the document. The real impact of following or flouting perceptual principles can be measured only in relation to the rhetorical situation.

Grouping: Making the Parts Cohere

Along with figure–ground, the Gestalt principle of grouping can greatly enhance your repertoire of design tools. While figure–ground pulls out images from a field, grouping organizes them into units and subunits. Grouping is a powerful tool for structuring the parts of a document—pieces of text, pictures, icons, lines, bullets, and so on. By threading these parts together into manageable units, grouping enables readers to sort through the parts of a document more efficiently. Grouping creates *visual cohesion;* it's the glue that holds the parts together.

Visual groups can be created in several ways. Three of the most important are likeness of form, spatial nearness, and division.[4] Figure 2.15a illustrates the first principle: When the forms are placed randomly on the page, our eye organizes them into groups based on the likeness of their forms—in this case, either circles or squares. We see the squares as one group, the circles as another. Figure 2.15b shows the grouping power of spatial positioning. Although the squares and circles still occupy the same visual field, their placement in mixed but spatially tight-knit groups competes with, and largely overrides, their grouping by shape. In Figure 2.15c, the lines between the forms divide them into groups by fencing off one group from another.

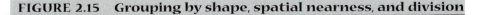

FIGURE 2.15   Grouping by shape, spatial nearness, and division

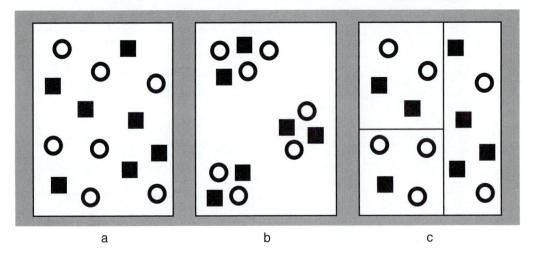

a   b   c

It's easy to see how these principles work in a field of abstract forms. Let's look at how the same principles might apply to text fields. In Figure 2.16a, the boldfaced, uppercase text divides into groups because of the likeness of form among these text units. In Figure 2.16b, the text divides into two vertical groups because of the spatial nearness of the text segments in two distinct columns. The text in Figure 2.16c divides into four horizontal groups, again because of close spatial positioning.

FIGURE 2.16   Grouping—columns and rows

xxx xxx x **XXX** x	xx xx	xx xx xx xx
xxxx xxx xxx xx	xx xx	
XXX xx xxxxx x	xx xx	xx xx xx xx
xx x xx xxxxx xx	xx xx	
xxx xx xxx **XXX**	xx xx	xx xx xx xx
xx xx xx xxxx x	xx xx	
XXX xxx xx xxx	xx xx	xx xx xx xx
xxx xxx xxx x x	xx xx	
xx xx xx xx **XXX**	xx xx	

a   b   c

Spatial positioning can't do the job alone, however, and sometimes we need other visual cues to define the groups. Here, division can help. In Figure 2.17, the lines define the groups as vertical units (a), horizontal units (b), and boxed groups with a separate row isolated in the middle (c). In each case, the closure of the text group creates cohesion among the units within the group. Of course, we could use graphic cues to regroup the text field in several other ways, as you can see in Figure 2.18. We could use lines to divide the text into six groups (a), or we could use shading to divide the text into columns (b), or to separate a center group from unshaded groups above and below it (c). In each case, shading or lines create spatial cohesion among the members in the group.

FIGURE 2.17   Grouping through linework

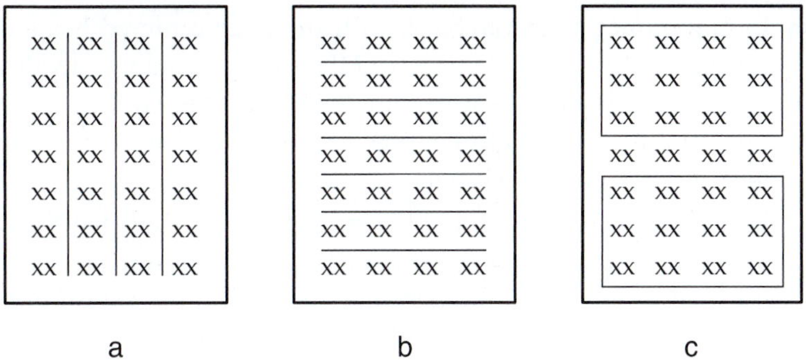

a   b   c

FIGURE 2.18   Grouping through shading

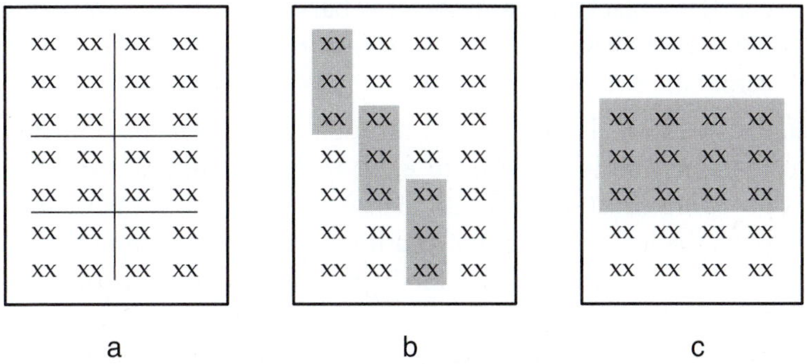

a   b   c

While the principle of division drives these grouping effects, likeness of form and spatial nearness also play a role. For example, in Figure 2.18b, the three columns of shaded text cohere as a group because of their likeness of form, and the units within each group bond together because they are near each other. Grouping, then, frequently results from a combination of principles rather than just one.

These examples only begin to describe the complex grouping and subgrouping that occur in text displays. When we look at a visual field—either a printed page or a computer screen—we immediately search for clues about its structure. Visually defined groups usually satisfy that need, whether the field contains text, pictures, or data displays—or a combination of textual and nontextual elements. In the six examples shown in Figure 2.19, you can see the principle of grouping at work in a variety of ways.

- In a, grouping occurs through the use of the headings, which divide the paragraphs into chunks. Because the two headings display like forms, readers will know that the text chunks beneath them are somewhat parallel as well. Positioning the headings nearer to the text below than the text above tells readers that the heading bonds with the text below it.

- In b, grouping is hierarchical, with the large centered heading serving as an umbrella over the whole page and the smaller headings dividing the page into subgroups. The size of the headings—not just their position on the page, which might reflect a conventional practice—tells us that the one on top claims the highest place in the hierarchy.

- In c, grouping occurs through a simple series, a bulleted list with several like items. Likeness of form suggests a parallel relationship among these items. The list itself is not hierarchical, though its indentation subordinates it to the text chunks above and below it.

- Data displays—bar graphs, line graphs, pie charts, and so on—also rely on grouping. In the bar chart at the top of d, we immediately see the likeness among the data bars, each of which is measured from the x axis. In the bottom chart, the black bars and the gray bars each create their own group, based on likeness of form, which helps us to compare data both within a subgroup and across the two subgroups.

- Pictures can also be unified through likeness of form, including image size, style, or framing device. In e, all three techniques are deployed to create a grouping effect: the likeness of size of the pictures, their simple line style, and their shaded backgrounds and line borders that frame them. Although these pictures vary in subject and shape, their likeness of form gives them strong cohesion as a group.

- Pages across an entire communication can be grouped through color, icons, or page texture or thickness. In f, the gray pages form a separate group; the gray pages may also function to divide key sections, creating grouping through closure from one section to the next. These global grouping strategies can be an important cohesive device in longer, more complex communications as well as shorter ones such as brochures.

FIGURE 2.19   Examples of grouping

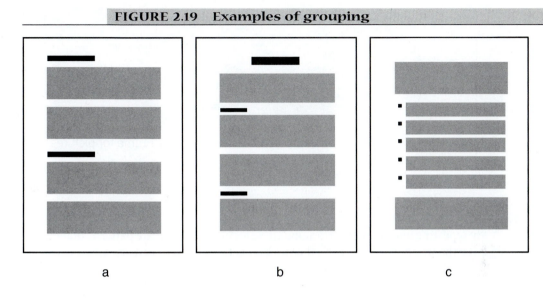

a   b   c

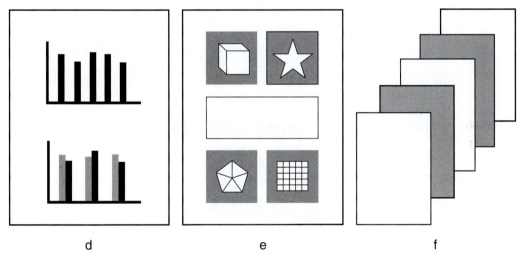

d   e   f

Patterns: Creating Groups across the Communication

A quick look at a page or screen can tell you a lot about how to structure the information. As groups of visual language form and repeat themselves over the span of a document, patterns emerge. These patterns can take many forms: type style and size, headings, boxes, shading, arrangement within the field, icons, color, and so on.

Visual patterns create an abstract language with a functional purpose—to help us sort through and structure information into groups and subgroups. A pattern can be built from a few simple forms like those in Figure 2.20.

FIGURE 2.20   Components of a visual pattern

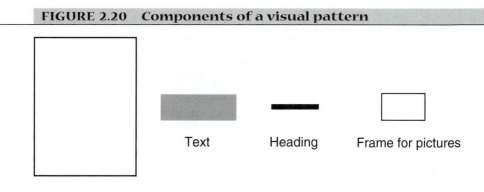

Page

By repeating and spatially arranging these forms, we can create patterns that extend over the whole document (see Figure 2.21). These patterns create cohesive groups through the repetition of any of the three grouping principles:

- Likeness of form (page size and vertical orientation, headings, boxed inserts)
- Nearness of spatial positioning (headings in the center and near the text below)
- Division (headings and boxed inserts that separate one element from another)

Or patterns can create cohesive groups through a combination of any of the three.

FIGURE 2.21   Visual pattern across a document

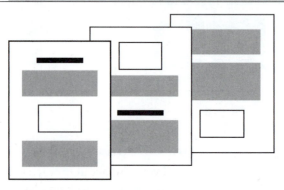

In longer documents these patterns may continue for hundreds of pages and may even continue in subsequent documents to create a set or a series. In hypertext documents or Web sites, patterns serve the same functions, creating cohesion across screens. In the mock-up Web site shown in Figure 2.22, grouping across screens results from the repetition of key visual elements: the Shopper's Paradise bar at the top of the screen, the navigational bar at the left with the links to shopping categories, and the repetition of the logo (the dollar sign on the tropical island).

FIGURE 2.22   Visual pattern in a Web site

Pattern-making as a grouping strategy will play a major role as you design functional documents. In most cases, those patterns will display any one, or a combination, of the principles of grouping through likeness of form, spatial nearness, and division.

Using Gestalt Principles to Respond to the Rhetorical Situation

You can find examples of the Gestalt principles of figure–ground and grouping in virtually any communication. They play a crucial role in helping readers to identify key information and to structure that information. Because responses to figure–ground and grouping are fairly consistent from one reader to another, you can apply these principles to achieve your rhetorical purposes—to emphasize information, to arrange it in a certain way, to clarify it, and so on. Although Gestalt principles bear upon almost any perceptual act, their application to document design can be gauged only within a particular rhetorical situation.

To see how Gestalt principles can be applied rhetorically, let's look again at the Mapleton document's letter, options pages, and data page.

Letter.   The letter (see Figure 2.23) displays figure–ground contrast beginning with the letterhead, which establishes a strong identity that readers will recognize

FIGURE 2.23   Gestalt effects in Fred's letter

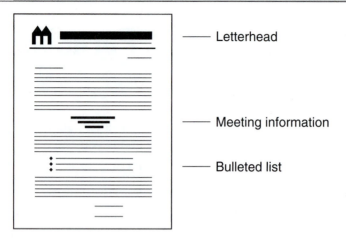

— Letterhead

— Meeting information

— Bulleted list

immediately. Figure–ground also emphasizes the meeting information that's centered on the page and set in larger, boldface type; emphasis through figure–ground contrast also enables readers to retrieve these facts quickly if they need to return to them later. Finally, toward the bottom of the page, the indented, bulleted list outlines the goals of the meeting, a strategy that helps persuade readers to participate. All three of these elements rely on the perceptual principle of figure–ground contrast to achieve their rhetorical effects.

Grouping also plays a role in the letter, beginning with the letterhead at the top of the page. The close arrangement of the Mapleton logo, the name and address, and the line beneath makes them cohere as a group. The arrangement of the meeting information and of the bulleted list also creates a group.

Options Pages.   The options pages (see Figure 2.24) display figure–ground in the headings, pictures, and bulleted lists. Figure–ground emphasizes each of these components (without having them compete for attention) and gives readers quick access to the facts—both in text and picture form. Grouping also plays a key role here by defining units of information that readers can quickly identify. For example, the bulleted lists tell readers that the items at the bottom of each page cohere as the benefits section. Equally important, the parallel arrangement of the two pages (creating a group with two units) suggests an even-handedness in the presentation of the two options, thereby enhancing the ethos of the document.

Data Page.   On the data page (see Figure 2.25), the dark bars on the graphs have strong figure–ground contrast, though figure–ground diminishes as the bars lighten at the top. By displaying the data with a divided bar graph, Fred makes a trade-off with clarity so he can maximize conciseness.

FIGURE 2.24   Gestalt effects in the options pages

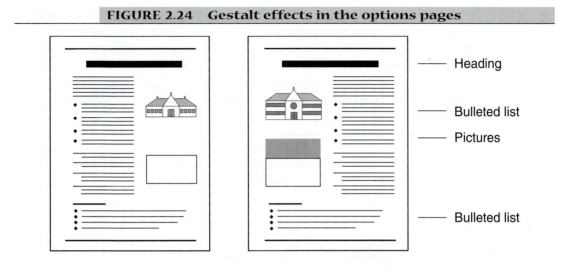

Heading

Bulleted list

Pictures

Bulleted list

FIGURE 2.25   Gestalt effects in the data sheet

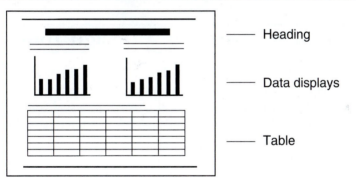

Heading

Data displays

Table

Grouping plays a critical role on this page by enabling Fred to implement arrangement and clarity strategies. In the bar charts, the like shading of bars in each data group (maintenance expenses, staff expenses, individual and family memberships) enables readers to compare values, enhancing clarity. In the table, arrangement is intrinsically tied to grouping, mostly through spatial positioning of the rows and columns. The lines on the grid divide the categories and numbers into groups and subgroups. Rhetorically, grouping gives the reader quick access to the data and in the process also creates credibility for the display.

Using Gestalt principles, then, is a means to an end—adapting visual language to a rhetorical situation. Fred continually draws on these principles as he adapts his document visually to his audience, purpose, and context.

Whenever you look at a communication, you should look for these perceptual principles while at the same time taking stock of the rhetorical work they do. You might look at a document and say, "Wow! That page has great figure–ground" or you might look at a Web page and say, "That screen lacks any sense of visual grouping. What a mess!" These observations are natural responses to the visual language in a field, but they are only a start. They become meaningful only when we also ask, "To what end does that communication display great figure–ground contrast?" Or, "Why does this screen have such poor grouping? Is the writer trying to conceal the structure of the information?"

> ## Remember, Gestalt principles are only a means to an end, not an end in themselves.

See the figure–ground contrast in this piece of text? See the grouping by division? Now you know the perceptual principles that made that sentence at the start of this chapter leap off the page. In both situations, we were trying to emphasize key points so you'd remember them! In both cases, perceptual principles served rhetorical ends.

Empirical Research as a Design Tool

Just as Gestalt principles can help you design your communication, design research can also help you address functional questions about how readers perceive information visually. For example, empirical research in visual communication might help you decide which of the three versions below is the most legible:

Which version is the most legible?

Which version is the most legible?

WHICH VERSION IS THE MOST LEGIBLE?

Research can answer that question fairly well: The middle version in 11-point Palatino in lowercase is the most legible (Tinker 57–73). It's useful to know that—partly because designing information with a high degree of clarity is usually a high priority in professional communication. Having the research to back up your decisions can also persuade others—for example, your co-workers, your boss, your client—that you know what you're doing.

Empirical research seeks to answer questions about how readers respond to design elements. Those questions can be very generic and broad. For example:

- Do readers perceive the same data more efficiently in bar graphs or in pie charts?
- To what extent do readers benefit from the presence of headings in text?

Or the questions can be generic but quite specific:

- Can readers comprehend text better in 8-point Palatino or in 12-point Palatino?
- Do close-up views in illustrations help readers?

Or the questions can pertain only to a single document:

- How well does the visual language of XYZ's annual report help its intended readers to grasp its structure?
- Do visual cues empower readers to find the information they want in the ABC Web site?

Answers to such questions can be obtained through a variety of methods: experiments, testing, observations, interviews, and focus groups. Some of the data that empirical research yields are quantitative, some qualitative. Below we'll outline two kinds of empirical research: universal and contextual. Universal research tends to be generic, quantitative, and nonrhetorical; contextual research tends to be document-specific, qualitative, and linked to a specific rhetorical situation (Kostelnick 108–110). As you'll see, both types have their benefits and their limitations.

Universal Research

Researchers have scrutinized many design elements used in professional communication—the layout of the text on the page, headings, data displays, diagrams, and pictures. Much of this research is what we'll call *universal* (Kostelnick 108). It measures, usually under controlled conditions, how quickly and efficiently people process various kinds of visual language. Sometimes it also measures people's preferences for one design variation over another. This kind of research can be extremely useful because it gives you a general barometer of what works perceptually and what doesn't. In many of the chapters ahead, we'll highlight some of this research, and we'll try to develop guidelines you can use in your own design. We'll also provide end-of-chapter references so you can consult this kind of research if you're interested in knowing more.[5]

As helpful as universal research may be, keep in mind that it alone will not necessarily lead to effective design. It's just one of many tools to help you develop a sound plan. When you consult universal research, keep in mind these two limitations:

1. *Universal research often focuses on one design element at a time, so translating findings to the perceptual context of your communication may be problematic.* For example, an empirical study might examine a certain kind of text display in isolation from the array of other design elements—type size and color, page size and texture—actually contained in your communication. Because perceptual context changes visual language, the findings of universal research may not be entirely reliable when you apply them to your design.

2. *Universal research is often nonrhetorical, or its rhetorical situation may be quite different from yours.* Universal research often measures reader performance without attention to who the readers are or what they'll actually do with the information. Even if a rhetorical situation is factored into the research, it may differ from the situation you're trying to address.

Let's look again at the three versions of this text:

Which version is the most legible?

Which version is the most legible?

WHICH VERSION IS THE MOST LEGIBLE?

Empirical research tells us that the middle version is more legible than the top or bottom ones. The type size (11-point) is more legible than the top version (8-point), and the lowercase is more legible than the all caps in the bottom version (Tinker 59–61, 71). However, even though the first and third versions might be perceptually inferior to the middle one, in some situations they might be more appropriate—the small text version for an insignificant note in a report, the all caps text for a warning in a set of instructions.

Or take the divided bar graphs that Fred Noonan uses to display data about the Mapleton Community Center. Because research says that readers have trouble comparing unequal scales (Cleveland and McGill 532–533; Cochran, Albrecht, and Green 27–29), divided bar graphs are *not* the optimal way to display data. So in Fred's bar graph, his readers can't compare some expenses (maintenance, utilities, other) very precisely from year to year. Still, Fred ignores the research because he needs a compact display, and he doesn't think making those minute comparisons is very important either to his readers or to the purpose of the document. For Fred's readers, getting just a general picture is rhetorically sound.

In the end, then, you'll need to consider perceptual and rhetorical context when you apply research findings to a given design problem. Universal research can help you prevent some design disasters, but it's only one of many tools you have at your disposal.

Contextual Research

Another way to use research in your design process is to test your document with your readers to see if it fulfills its purpose in the context in which your readers will actually use it. We'll call this kind of research *contextual* (Kostelnick 110). Unlike most universal research, contextual research enables your readers to test, evaluate, or offer feedback about your communication—part or all of it—in its rhetorical context. Contextual research can yield either quantitative or qualitative results, though the latter may be easier to generate, less costly, and more beneficial.[6] You can gather your readers' responses to your design through a variety of methods:

- *Observation.* You could observe readers as they interact with your document. For example, if you designed an informational document like Fred's, you could give it to prospective readers—or to friends or colleagues—and watch how they actually used it. You could observe which items caught their attention, which ones they studied the most, and which ones seemed to puzzle them. You could also tape-record your readers' moment-to-moment reactions.

- *Interviews.* You could interview your readers after they used your communication to discover their reactions to the design. For example, you might spend a few minutes with one of your readers asking about specific design elements: "How well do the headings structure the text?" "How well did you understand the illustration on page 2?" "Is the text design too busy?" Michael Floreak provides some good suggestions for gathering feedback like this in interviews.

- *Surveys.* You could survey your readers by having them fill out a questionnaire, either while or after they use your communication. Your questionnaire could ask them performance questions about how much information they can recall. Or you might ask preference questions about whether they liked a certain type style or page design. If you've designed a Web site, you could ask visitors to e-mail their feedback to you.

- *Focus groups.* You could have your readers meet in a small focus group in which they discuss specific design issues in your communication. You could lead the discussion and record their responses.

Gathering these kinds of feedback, of course, can be time consuming. However, you don't need to test very many readers to get some quality feedback about how your readers perceive your design—feedback you can cycle directly into your design process to improve your communication. Karen Schriver provides expert advice on how to gather and apply feedback from your readers. And that's the most important thing in contextual research, gathering feedback from your readers that you can use to improve your design.

Conclusion

To update our model, then, we now have two additional guides for implementing the cognate strategies:

1. Perceptual principles (the general principles we outlined early in this chapter) and Gestalt principles, including figure–ground and grouping
2. Empirical research, both universal and contextual

These two types of guides are now included in our diagram (Figure 2.26).

FIGURE 2.26   Update of the design process

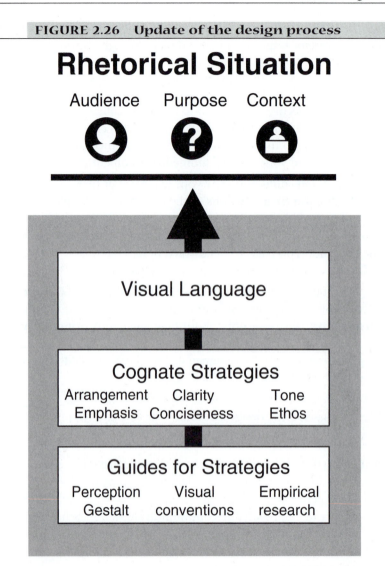

In the next chapter we'll expand on the visual language part of the diagram. We'll outline a system for describing the wide variety of visual language commonly used in professional communication, and we'll show you how to analyze that language rhetorically.

Notes

1. A. T. Welford refers generally to this phenomenon of seeing what we need to in a given situation as the "economy principle."

2. Eva Brumberger suggests a variety of pedagogical techniques from other disciplines to stimulate the visual thinking of designers.
3. Our application here of Gestalt principles to practical document design derives largely from Stephen Bernhardt and from Patrick Moore and Chad Fitz. You can find a more in-depth and technical explanation of Gestalt theories of perception in Leonard Zusne's *Visual Perception of Form.*
4. To simplify things, we've conflated into the concept of *grouping* three Gestalt principles: *proximity* (spatial nearness), *similarity* (likeness of form), and *closure* (division), all three of which are outlined by Moore and Fitz, and by Bernhardt. We describe all three as grouping principles because that's the common rhetorical effect of each of the three.
5. You can find summaries of research on the effects of different typography in Miles A. Tinker's *Legibility of Print* and in Herbert Spencer's *The Visible Word,* and a compact summary of typographical research in an article by Philippa Benson. James Hartley's *Designing Instructional Text* will introduce you to research-based guidelines for a wide range of document design issues.
6. In her *Dynamics in Document Design,* Karen Schriver narrates several case studies in document design that superbly illustrate contextual research in action.

References

Arnheim, Rudolf. *Visual Thinking.* Berkeley: University of California Press, 1969.

Benson, Philippa J. "Writing Visually: Design Considerations in Technical Publications." *Technical Communication* 32 (1985): 35–39.

Bernhardt, Stephen A. "Seeing the Text." *College Composition and Communication* 37 (1986): 66–78.

Brumberger, Eva R. "Making the Strange Familiar: A Pedagogical Exploration of Visual Thinking." *Journal of Business and Technical Communication* 21 (2007): 376–401.

Cleveland, William S., and Robert McGill. "Graphical Perception: Theory, Experimentation, and Application to the Development of Graphical Methods." *Journal of the American Statistical Association* 79.387 (1984): 531–554.

Cochran, Jeffrey K., Sheri A. Albrecht, and Yvonne A. Green. "Guidelines for Evaluating Graphical Designs: A Framework Based on Human Perception Skills." *Technical Communication* 36 (1989): 25–32.

Floreak, Michael. "Designing for the Real World: Using Research to Turn a 'Target Audience' into Real People." *Technical Communication* 36 (1989): 373–381.

Hartley, James. *Designing Instructional Text.* 2nd ed. New York: Nichols, 1985.

Kostelnick, Charles. "From Pen to Print: The New Visual Landscape of Professional Communication." *Journal of Business and Technical Communication* 8 (1994): 91–117.

Moore, Patrick, and Chad Fitz. "Using Gestalt Theory to Teach Document Design and Graphics." *Technical Communication Quarterly* 2 (1993): 389–410.

———. "Gestalt Theory and Instructional Design." *Journal of Technical Writing and Communication* 23 (1993): 137–157.

Schriver, Karen A. *Dynamics in Document Design: Creating Text for Readers.* New York: John Wiley & Sons, 1997.

Spencer, Herbert. *The Visible Word.* 2nd ed. New York: Hastings, 1969.

Tinker, Miles A. *Legibility of Print.* Ames, IA: Iowa State University Press, 1963.

Welford, A. T. "Theory and Application in Visual Displays." *Information Design: The Design and Evaluation of Signs and Printed Material.* Ed. Ronald Easterby and Harm Zwaga. New York: Wiley, 1984. 3–18.

Zusne, Leonard. *Visual Perception of Form.* New York: Academic, 1970.

Exercises

1. Perception requires mental energy—sometimes lots of it! Study the shape on the left in Figure 2.27. Which shape on the right (a, b, or c) represents the same image (1) whose top and bottom have been flipped (the north part is south, the south part north) and (2) that's then been rotated counterclockwise 90 degrees?

FIGURE 2.27   Exercise 1—Perception practice

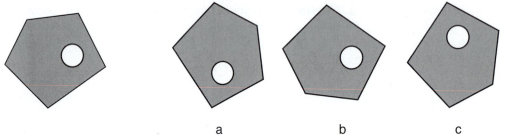

a   b   c

Before you arrive at an answer, you have to do some mental work to envision how the image changes.

2. What happens to figure–ground contrast when you boldface or italicize letters? Compare the plain, boldface, and italic letters below:

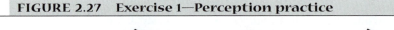

plain   **bold**   *italic*

Does boldfacing help or hurt figure–ground contrast? Why or why not? (Notice how boldfacing fills the inside space of the letters *b, o,* and *d.*) What effect does the use of italics have on the figure–ground contrast of the text? Are the letters thinner than plain text?

3. Find a document that has text printed on darker colored paper stock (blue, red, green, brown, gray, purple). Use the questions below to guide your analysis of figure–ground contrast and noise.

   a. How does the figure–ground contrast between text and paper affect the clarity of the text? In other words, how distracting is the noise created by the background color?

   b. Does color have any advantages for the rhetorical situation that compensate for the noise? For example, does the color enhance tone or ethos? Does it add emphasis?

   c. Overall, is the lack of optimal figure–ground contrast between text and background a good rhetorical trade-off here? Why or why not?

4. Locate a Web site with several linked screens and identify the kinds of grouping techniques it uses to create cohesion, both within individual screens and across several screens. Use the questions below as a guide:

   a. How does the Web site use likeness of form to group elements on a single screen and across several screens? Which like forms are used? Icons? Pictures? Lines, bars, colors, gray scales?

   b. How does the Web site use spatial nearness to create groups? Lists? Headings (as they relate to the text they introduce)? Text positioned beside pictures or data displays?

   c. How does the Web site use division to show the boundaries between groups of information on the screen? Frames, lines, shades of colors?

   d. Does the Web site repeat and/or combine any of these grouping effects to create consistent patterns that extend over several screens? If so, how successfully do the patterns create cohesion across the entire Web site? How do these grouping patterns help the Web site respond to the rhetorical situation?

5. Evaluate the *Client Update* 09 document (Figure 2.28) according to perceptual principles outlined in this chapter. For example, how well does the document display figure–ground contrast and grouping? How would you change the document so it better adhered to these perceptual principles? How would adherence to these principles enhance clarity, arrangement, or any other cognate strategies?

6. Collect a half dozen newsletters and compare the nameplates (the logo and title) for figure–ground contrast. What design aspects of the nameplates distinguish them? The typeface? Graphic elements? The size of the nameplate?

FIGURE 2.28   Evaluating perceptual principles

Fund Wrap-Up

Most of our funds turned in gains last year. Here's a fund-by-fund rundown of 2008 and brief predictions for next year.

Precious Metals

What a year! Precious metals growth turned in a gain of 16.4%, led by gold and silver. But that gain paled in comparison to the security that precious metals gave our clients, especially in this unpreditable and volatile market. Metals continue to be an extremely safe hedge against all of the other markets.

International Fund

Things were volatile on the international front this past year, with virtually all of our holdings down 30% or more. Fund manager Jill Jones, however, is optimistic about the future. "We're expecting the European stocks to rally this year," says Jill.

Aggressive Growth Fund

Not a great year for aggressive growth, but we held our own and experienced small gains in high-techs and medicals. About next year, fund manager Jim Charney III says, "We're still optimistic about solid growth in selected high-tech companies in the U.S. and abroad."

Bond Fund

The end of year rally pushed the bond fund up, resulting in a 4.3% return for the year. The outlook for next year? "It all depends on the Fed," says fund manager Patty Wiegel. "We don't anticipate any more interest rate cuts, so that should be good news for our clients."

New Online Service

Investment Web Site

Access our investment website and receive up-to-the-minute values on your portfolio. When you reach our main menu, you'll have the following choices:

1   Current values for all of our funds, including our money market and CDs.
2   Changes you want to make in your fund portfolio.
3   Withdrawing funds from your accounts.
4   Scheduling an appointment with an investment adviser.
5   Investment tips (changes weekly).
6   Retirement planning.

**Or call 1-800-000-0000
Day or Night**

New Investment Opportunity

Beginning in 2009, we will offer an entirely new investment option, a real estate fund that invests primarily in highly productive farm land. If you're interested in receiving a prospectus about this exciting opportunity, call our toll-free number. In just a few days you'll get the information you need to begin investing in high-grade farmland.

Assignments

1. Redesign the nameplate for the *Client Update* 09 page in Exercise 5 so that it has stronger figure–ground contrast. The nameplate needs to establish a strong visual presence on the page, so don't be timid!

2. Using the Gestalt principles of grouping outlined in this chapter, identify the visual grouping that occurs in an instructional document—for example, a VCR owner's manual or a how-to booklet on arranging flowers or building a deck. How are the steps in the instructions grouped visually? Are pages grouped? How are items such as warnings grouped?

   Make a chart that outlines all of the grouping patterns that you discover across the document. In your chart be sure to include the pictures and diagrams.

3

Visual

Analysis

Introduction to Visual Analysis

Analyzing design goes hand in hand with doing design. Just as athletes watch tapes to prepare for a game, painters imitate the masters, and lawyers dissect judicial cases to sharpen their courtroom skills, you can learn much by examining the design successes, and faux pas, of the practical communications swirling all around you—both in print and online. Sharpening your analytical skills will enlarge your visual vocabulary and help you see how that vocabulary responds to—or fails to respond to—a given rhetorical situation.

Analysis can also help you *while* you're designing communications. It can serve a reflective function, giving you a tool for in-process evaluation of your design decisions—a mental checklist of sorts to see if you're responding to the rhetorical situation. Just as good writers are able to evaluate their writing critically as they compose, and make adjustments along the way, good designers develop this same ability to examine their work during the design process.

The Visual Vocabulary of Professional Communication

Two keys to analyzing professional communications are learning to notice what's going on visually and learning how to categorize it all. Both take some concentration and skill because a communication often contains more design than first meets the eye—or than the brain is willing to acknowledge. As we saw in the last chapter, we tend to focus our attention on a few things and overlook the others.

Let's take a moment to go back to Fred Noonan's informational package designed for the Mapleton Community Center. We'll go through each item—the letter, the options, and the data sheet—and generate a list of visual design elements. Many of these elements are identified in Figures 3.1, 3.2, and 3.3.

FIGURE 3.1 Mapleton letter

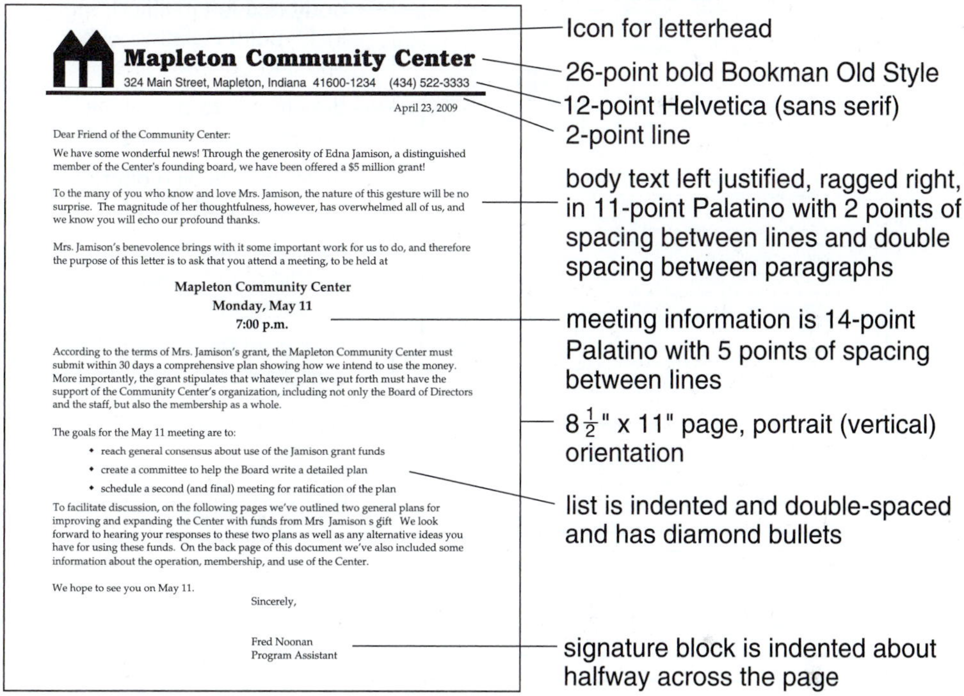
Mapleton Community Center
324 Main Street, Mapleton, Indiana 41600-1234 (434) 522-3333

April 23, 2009

Dear Friend of the Community Center:

We have some wonderful news! Through the generosity of Edna Jamison, a distinguished member of the Center's founding board, we have been offered a $5 million grant!

To the many of you who know and love Mrs. Jamison, the nature of this gesture will be no surprise. The magnitude of her thoughtfulness, however, has overwhelmed all of us, and we know you will echo our profound thanks.

Mrs. Jamison's benevolence brings with it some important work for us to do, and therefore the purpose of this letter is to ask that you attend a meeting, to be held at

Mapleton Community Center
Monday, May 11
7:00 p.m.

According to the terms of Mrs. Jamison's grant, the Mapleton Community Center must submit within 30 days a comprehensive plan showing how we intend to use the money. More importantly, the grant stipulates that whatever plan we put forth must have the support of the Community Center's organization, including not only the Board of Directors and the staff, but also the membership as a whole.

The goals for the May 11 meeting are to:

- reach general consensus about use of the Jamison grant funds
- create a committee to help the Board write a detailed plan
- schedule a second (and final) meeting for ratification of the plan

To facilitate discussion, on the following pages we've outlined two general plans for improving and expanding the Center with funds from Mrs Jamison s gift We look forward to hearing your responses to these two plans as well as any alternative ideas you have for using these funds. On the back page of this document we've also included some information about the operation, membership, and use of the Center.

We hope to see you on May 11.

Sincerely,

Fred Noonan
Program Assistant

Icon for letterhead
26-point bold Bookman Old Style
12-point Helvetica (sans serif)
2-point line
body text left justified, ragged right, in 11-point Palatino with 2 points of spacing between lines and double spacing between paragraphs
meeting information is 14-point Palatino with 5 points of spacing between lines
8 1/2" x 11" page, portrait (vertical) orientation
list is indented and double-spaced and has diamond bullets
signature block is indented about halfway across the page

Although Fred's Mapleton document may seem relatively plain at first, when you start to catalog the visual language as we've done above, things can get pretty complex. Like most documents, Fred's contains its own universe of visual forms—forms that parade across the pages in rapid succession, from columns of text to illustrations, from large type to small type, from lines to gray scales, from headings to bulleted lists. Some elements appear on several pages (type style, size, and spacing; lines framing top and bottom), while other elements appear on only a single page (bar charts). Even in a relatively short document like Fred's, visual language can take many twists and turns.

How do you cope with such complexity? How can you make sure you see everything? And if you're designing the document, how do you *manage* all the forms that comprise its visual universe? Whether you're analyzing a communication on paper or screen, whether the communication is someone else's or your own work in progress, a systematic scheme for describing visual language would help you account for everything, from local design decisions—say, italicizing a word—to larger-scale decisions—say, selecting page size, shape, and color.

FIGURE 3.2   Mapleton options pages

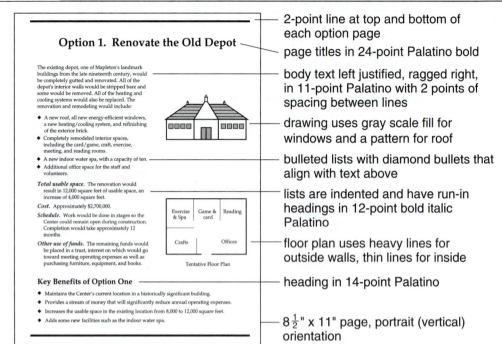

2-point line at top and bottom of each option page

page titles in 24-point Palatino bold

body text left justified, ragged right, in 11-point Palatino with 2 points of spacing between lines

drawing uses gray scale fill for windows and a pattern for roof

bulleted lists with diamond bullets that align with text above

lists are indented and have run-in headings in 12-point bold italic Palatino

floor plan uses heavy lines for outside walls, thin lines for inside

heading in 14-point Palatino

$8\frac{1}{2}$" x 11" page, portrait (vertical) orientation

FIGURE 3.3   Mapleton data sheet

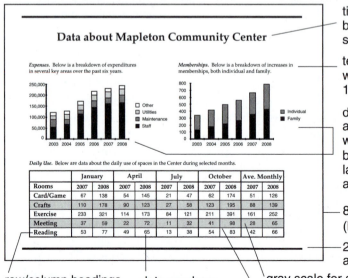

title in 24-point Palatino bold, centered, with white space above and below

text in 11-point Palatino with run-in headings in 12-point bold italic

divided bar charts are about the same size, with legends to the right; black and gray-scale bars; labels for legends and X/Y axes in 9-point Helvetica

$8\frac{1}{2}$" x 11" page, landscape (horizontal) orientation

2-point line at top and and bottom

row/column headings in 14- or 12-point bold Palatino

data numbers centered in 10-point Helvetica

gray scale for alternating rows

table boxed in by lines, some thicker than others

The following section outlines such a framework for describing visual language. This framework is simply a descriptive tool, not an end in itself. Its purpose is to help you chart the visual vocabulary of any document you encounter—to account for what's happening visually. After we've outlined this framework, we'll return to Fred's document and chart its visual language in a more systematic way.

A Taxonomy for Visual Vocabulary

One way of looking at the visual vocabulary of professional communication is to distinguish between *levels of design*—from local, minute design decisions such as using uppercase letters for a phrase to large-scale decisions about the size and shape of the communication. Below are four levels for examining visual language.

- Intra
- Inter
- Extra
- Supra

The first two levels, the intra- and inter-levels, pertain primarily to text design. The extra-level pertains primarily to nontextual elements such as data displays and pictures. The supra-level refers to the large-scale design of the whole communication.[1] The four levels are charted in Figure 3.4.

Each of these four levels, in turn, may contain design elements in three coding modes:

- textual
- spatial
- graphic

The coding modes supply the raw materials of design, the stuff that makes design visible—the words and numbers, the graphic elements (lines, textures, shading, etc.), and the spatial positioning of these elements on a page or screen. If we combine the four levels and three coding modes, we can display all their possible variations on a 12-cell matrix (Kostelnick, "Systematic"; "Visual Rhetoric"). The matrix (Table 3.1) serves as a framework for describing the visual language of a given document. Using the 12-cell matrix as our guide, let's look at each of the four levels, and each coding mode within each level.

FIGURE 3.4   Four levels for examining visual language

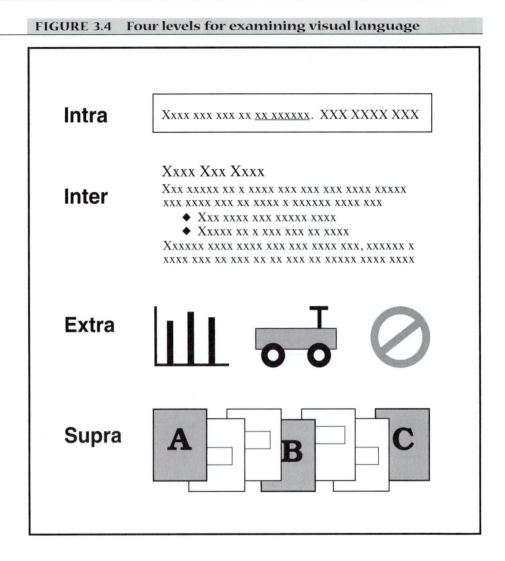

Intra-Level Design: Linear Components

Intra-level design controls the local variations of text, character by character, word by word, across a single line of text or a thousand lines. Intra-level design creates the building blocks, the atoms and particles, for the visible text. Individually, intra-level effects are small, even minuscule, but multiplied many times over they have a huge impact on the visual language of the document. Without intra-level design, most pages or screens would be invisible or have gaping holes in them. Like the other three levels, intra-level design operates in all three modes (see Table 3.2).

TABLE 3.1   Visual Language Matrix

	Textual	Spatial	Graphic
Intra	**1** type style: Palatino, Helvetica, Times type size: 10, 11, 12 point case: upper or lower treatment: italic, bold, shadow, outline	**2** spacing between characters: normal, condensed, expanded; kerning in/out spacing between words vertical spacing: superscript, subscript	**3** punctuation marks: periods, commas, parens., dashes symbols: dollar signs treatment: underline, strike through
Inter	**4** headings, levels of headings numbers or letters that signal items in lists Web links	**5** paragraphs, indentation, hanging indents, lists justified vs. unjustified, centered text line lengths, margins text arranged in tables, organizational charts, decision trees leading	**6** bullets and other listing devices gray scales highlighting text (e.g., boxed inserts) color for Web links line work in tables, organizational charts, decision trees
Extra	**7** labels, call outs, and captions for pictures and data displays numerical labels on x- and y-axes of data displays legends for data displays	**8** data displays: size of plot frame (x- and y-axes), orientation of plot frame (vertical or horizontal); space between bars, lines picture size, viewing angle, perspective	**9** line weights or shading on pictures or on data displays (bars or lines on graphs, gridlines, tick marks) details on pictures: line drawing vs. photograph use of color for pictures or data displays
Supra	**10** page headers or footers navigational bars major section or chapter headings or numbers tab labels–internal and external to the page titles on the cover or spine of the document initial letters signaling the start of an article or major text segment	**11** shape, thickness, and size of the page ($8\frac{1}{2}$" x 11", legal size, scrollable length of the screen) orientation of the field (portrait vs. landscape) section dividers embossing placement of data displays and pictures	**12** color or texture of paper page borders boxes, lines, or gray scales around pictures or data displays pictures or icons placed behind the text or spread over the whole document or Web site for cohesion lines in page headers or footers

Adapted from Kostelnick, "Systematic" (33), "Visual Rhetoric" (79). Courtesy of the Association of Teachers of Technical Writing.

TABLE 3.2   Intra-Level

	Textual	Spatial	Graphic
Intra	1	2	3
Inter	4	5	6
Extra	7	8	9
Supra	10	11	12

■ *Textual.* The textual mode (cell 1) includes the choice of a typeface (Palatino, Helvetica, Times) and type size (10-, 11-, 12-point) as well as its treatment.

Typeface selection—Palatino, **Helvetica**, Times

Type size—10-point, 11-point, 12-point

Italics, roman, **boldface,** UPPER CASE, shadow

■ *Spatial.* In the spatial mode (cell 2), intra-level choices include type size and local spacing between textual units, such as those shown below:

Text that's **widened** or condensed

Text that's set in ^superscript or in ~subscript

■ *Graphic.* In the graphic mode (cell 3), intra-level design involves punctuation marks (periods, commas, dashes, question marks, hyphens, and the like). It also includes a variety of other local marks, as those shown below:

Text that's underscored

~~Text with strike-throughs~~

Text with gray-scale or color background

In Chapter 4 we'll explore intra-level text design in depth. We'll refer to this kind of text design as *linear components*—variations of text design on a single line.

Inter-Level Design: Fields and Nonlinear Components

Inter-level elements help readers comprehend the text—line to line, paragraph to paragraph, column to column—within a given field. Through headings, through the spatial distribution of the text across the page or screen, and through a variety of graphic treatments (bullets, lines, shading), inter-level elements make text accessible to readers. Inter-level design (see Table 3.3) often divides the text into discrete units so readers can structure it.

TABLE 3.3   Inter-Level

	Textual	Spatial	Graphic
Intra	1	2	3
Inter	4	5	6
Extra	7	8	9
Supra	10	11	12

■ *Textual.* In the textual mode (cell 4), headings and numbers divide the text into units and often signal a hierarchy among these units. Variations in the size and position of headings create a skeletal outline of the text, as Figure 3.5 shows.

FIGURE 3.5   Inter-level, textual mode

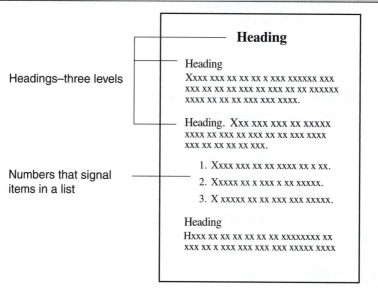

Headings–three levels

Numbers that signal items in a list

■ *Spatial.* In the spatial mode (cell 5), the text is divided into units and distributed across the page. Figure 3.6 shows some of the spatial elements in the text we just examined.

FIGURE 3.6   Inter-level, spatial mode

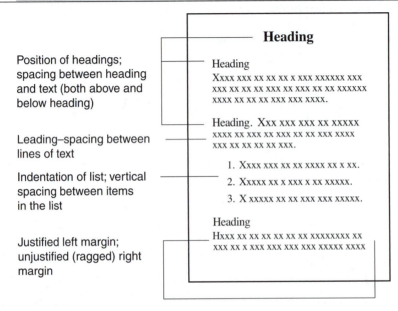

The spatial mode also includes sculpting the text into columns (Figure 3.7a) or dividing it into small pieces and organizing it into tables (Figure 3.7b), flow charts, or decision trees.

■ *Graphic.* In the graphic mode (cell 6) the designer can further help readers structure the text through a variety of cues—bullets in lists, lines between columns, and gray scales to enclose text (Figure 3.8a). In tables like spreadsheets, graphic elements include horizontal and vertical lines (Figure 3.8b). Inter-graphic elements also include boxes around text in organizational charts (Figure 3.9), the gray scale that fills each box, and the lines that connect the boxes. Graphic elements also include arrows and other directional signals in flowcharts and diagrams (Figure 3.10).

In Chapters 5 and 6 we'll explore inter-level text design in more depth: In Chapter 5 we'll examine variations in *text fields,* while in Chapter 6 we'll examine what we call *nonlinear components:* text structured as tables, organizational charts, decision trees, and other kinds of diagrams.

FIGURE 3.7   Inter-level, spatial mode

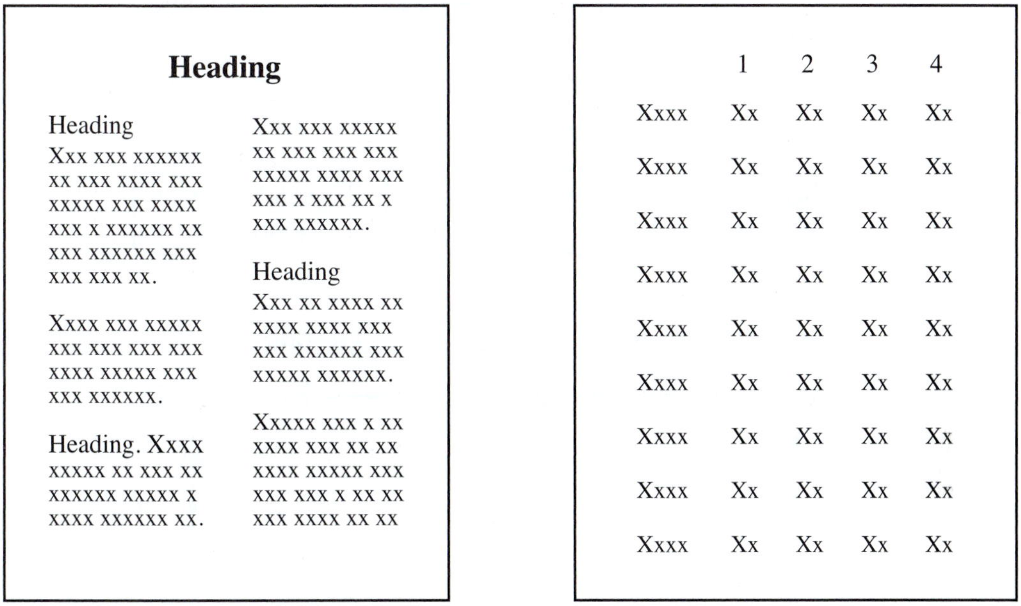

Heading

Heading
Xxx xxx xxxxxx xx xxx xxxx xxx xxxxx xxx xxxx xxx x xxxxxx xx xxx xxxxxx xxx xxx xxx xx.

Xxxx xxx xxxxx xxx xxx xxxx xxx xxxx xxxxx xxx xxx xxxxxx.

Heading. Xxxx xxxxx xx xxx xx xxxxxx xxxxx x xxxx xxxxxx xx.

Xxx xxx xxxxx xx xxx xxx xxxx xxxxx xxxx xxx xxx x xxx xx x xxx xxxxxx.

Heading
Xxx xx xxxx xx xxxx xxxx xxx xxx xxxxxx xxx xxxxx xxxxxx.

Xxxxx xxx x xx xxxx xxx xx xx xxxx xxxxx xxx xxx xxx x xx xx xxx xxxx xx xx

	1	2	3	4
Xxxx	Xx	Xx	Xx	Xx
Xxxx	Xx	Xx	Xx	Xx
Xxxx	Xx	Xx	Xx	Xx
Xxxx	Xx	Xx	Xx	Xx
Xxxx	Xx	Xx	Xx	Xx
Xxxx	Xx	Xx	Xx	Xx
Xxxx	Xx	Xx	Xx	Xx
Xxxx	Xx	Xx	Xx	Xx
Xxxx	Xx	Xx	Xx	Xx

a   b

FIGURE 3.8   Inter-level, graphic mode

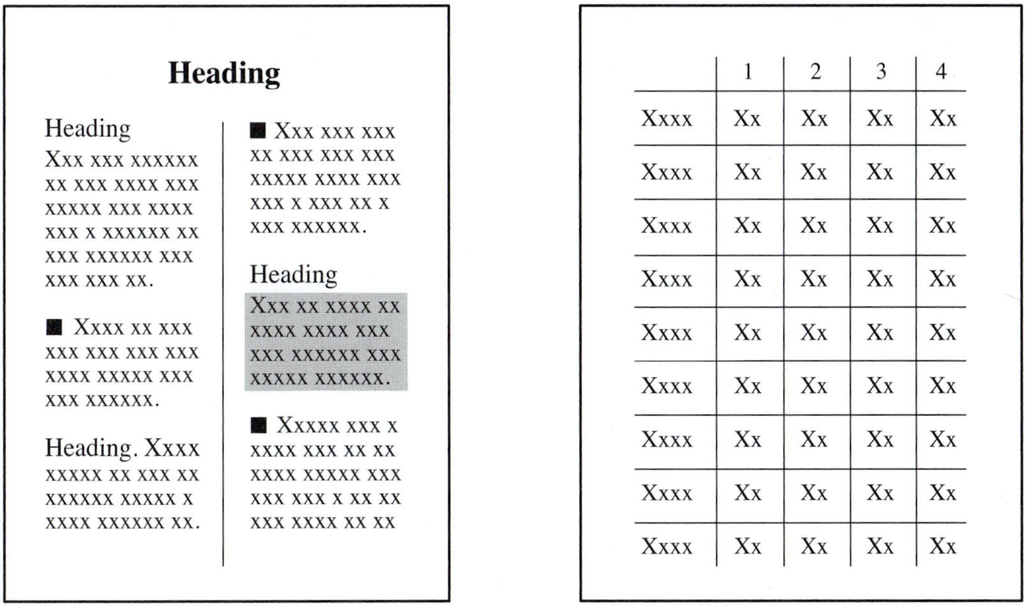

Heading

Heading
Xxx xxx xxxxxx xx xxx xxxx xxx xxxxx xxx xxxx xxx x xxxxxx xx xxx xxxxxx xxx xxx xxx xx.

■ Xxxx xx xxx xxx xxx xxx xxx xxxx xxxxx xxx xxx xxxxxx.

Heading. Xxxx xxxxx xx xxx xx xxxxxx xxxxx x xxxx xxxxxx xx.

■ Xxx xxx xxx xx xxx xxx xxx xxxxx xxxx xxx xxx x xxx xx x xxx xxxxxx.

Heading
Xxx xx xxxx xx xxxx xxxx xxx xxx xxxxxx xxx xxxxx xxxxxx.

■ Xxxxx xxx x xxxx xxx xx xx xxxx xxxxx xxx xxx xxx x xx xx xxx xxxx xx xx

	1	2	3	4
Xxxx	Xx	Xx	Xx	Xx
Xxxx	Xx	Xx	Xx	Xx
Xxxx	Xx	Xx	Xx	Xx
Xxxx	Xx	Xx	Xx	Xx
Xxxx	Xx	Xx	Xx	Xx
Xxxx	Xx	Xx	Xx	Xx
Xxxx	Xx	Xx	Xx	Xx
Xxxx	Xx	Xx	Xx	Xx
Xxxx	Xx	Xx	Xx	Xx

a   b

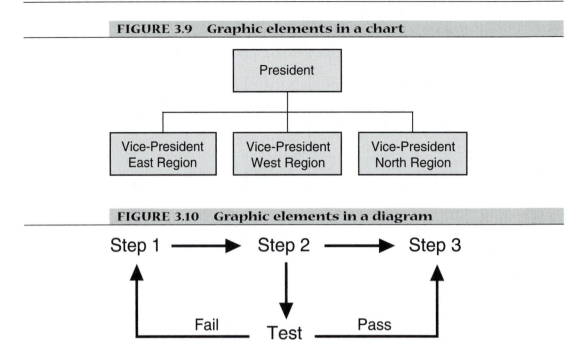

FIGURE 3.9   Graphic elements in a chart

FIGURE 3.10   Graphic elements in a diagram

Extra-Level Design: Data Displays, Pictures, Icons, and Symbols

The extra-level includes pictures, data displays (e.g., bar charts, line graphs, pie charts), icons, and symbols. These elements operate outside the main text (if there is any) as autonomous entities with their own visual vocabulary and conventional forms. Extra-level elements (see Table 3.4) may include some text to help readers understand them (a caption, label, or legend), but text plays mostly

TABLE 3.4   Extra-Level

	Textual	Spatial	Graphic
Intra	1	2	3
Inter	4	5	6
Extra	7	8	9
Supra	10	11	12

a supporting role. To describe extra-level design, we'll look at data displays first, then pictures.

■ *Textual.* In data displays, text (cell 7) plays primarily a descriptive role—pointing to, tagging, occasionally adding bits of information to clarify the data. Textual elements include labels, titles, legends, and the like, some of which are noted in the bar graph shown in Figure 3.11.

FIGURE 3.11   Data display, textual mode

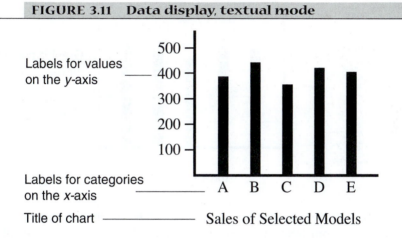

■ *Spatial.* In the spatial mode (cell 8), extra-level design often begins with the choice of a conventional configuration—pie chart, vertical or horizontal bar chart, line graph, and so on. Another key spatial decision involves selecting the size and shape of the area in which to plot the data—in our sample bar chart, the height of the y axis and the width of the x axis (see Figure 3.12).

FIGURE 3.12   Data display, spatial mode

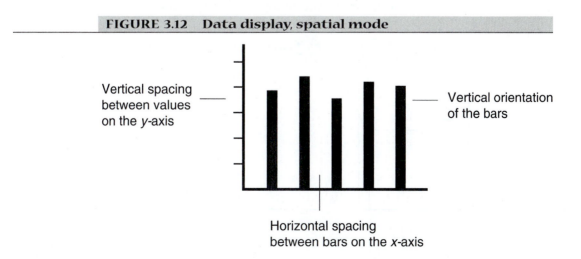

The spatial mode also includes the use of perspective—for example, to give the bars or other graphical elements a three-dimensional effect.

- *Graphic.* The graphic mode (cell 9) includes the visible stuff of the display—the shading, textures, and colors of the bars; the *x*- and *y*-axis lines, the tick marks, and the gridlines behind the bars, as shown in Figure 3.13.

FIGURE 3.13   Data display, graphic mode

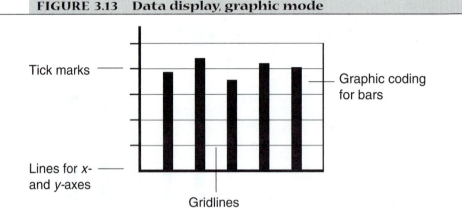

Tick marks

Graphic coding for bars

Lines for *x*- and *y*-axes

Gridlines

Extra-level elements also include pictures—of objects, scenes, and people—that range from freehand sketches to computer-aided drawings to photographs. Like data displays, pictures use all three coding modes, though the spatial and graphic modes dominate.

- *Textual.* The textual mode includes descriptive information in the form of labels, call-outs, or captions, like those below the drawings in Figure 3.14.

- *Spatial.* In the spatial mode you can select the angle for looking at the subject—for example, the front, side, or top of the garage in Figure 3.14.

FIGURE 3.14   Pictures, textual and spatial modes

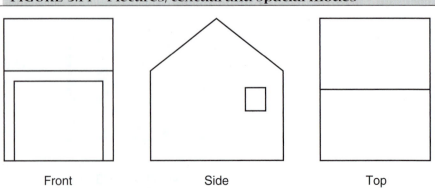

Front   Side   Top

Also in the spatial mode, you can represent the garage from more than one angle at a time, as in the perspective drawings in Figure 3.15.

FIGURE 3.15   Pictures, spatial mode

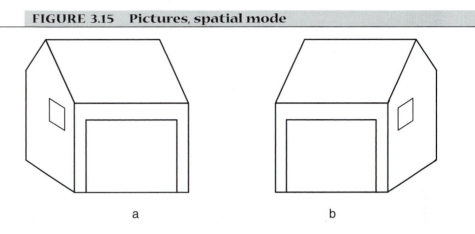

a   b

■ *Graphic.* In the graphic mode, you can give the garage texture by shading the walls and roof (Figure 3.16a). And you can use graphic coding to add more details—window frames, door texture, shingles, and so on (Figure 3.16b).

FIGURE 3.16   Pictures, graphic mode

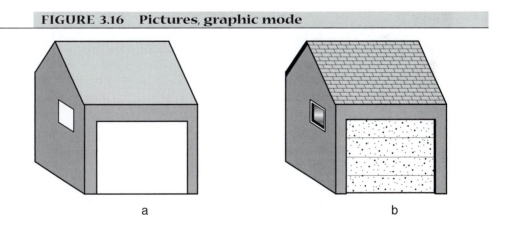

a   b

Supra-Level Design: The Whole Communication

The supra-level includes top-down design elements that visually define, structure, and unify the entire communication, whether print or electronic. Because supra-level design is so obvious and pervasive, it often influences design decisions on the other three levels. And like those other levels, the supra-level includes textual, spatial, and graphic modes (see Table 3.5).

TABLE 3.5   Supra-Level

	Textual	Spatial	Graphic
Intra	1	2	3
Inter	4	5	6
Extra	7	8	9
Supra	10	11	12

■ *Textual.* In the textual mode (cell 10), supra-level design includes title pages, chapter and section titles, numbers, and tabs that signal major breaks in the document (Figure 3.17a). Textual coding at the supra-level also includes page headers or footers and pagination (Figure 3.17b).

FIGURE 3.17   Supra-level, textual mode

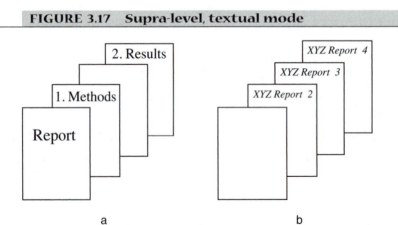

a   b

■ *Spatial.* In the spatial mode (cell 11), supra-level design includes the arrangement of extra-level elements within the document (Figure 3.18a) as well as the orientation of the page—portrait or landscape (Figure 3.18b). Supra-spatial elements also include page size and shape, which can vary from U.S. standard 8½" × 11" and legal size to European standard sizes and half sheets (Figure 3.19). Supra-level variations in the spatial mode can also include the paper thickness, folds, flaps, pockets, and the like. In an electronic environment, supra-spatial variations include the size of the computer screen, the scrollable length of the document, and links (Figure 3.20).

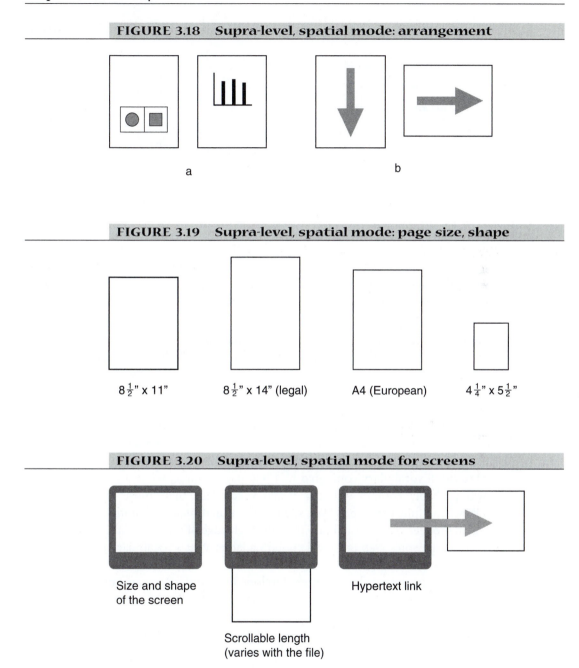

FIGURE 3.18   Supra-level, spatial mode: arrangement

a   b

FIGURE 3.19   Supra-level, spatial mode: page size, shape

$8\frac{1}{2}$" x 11" $8\frac{1}{2}$" x 14" (legal)   A4 (European) $4\frac{1}{4}$" x $5\frac{1}{2}$"

FIGURE 3.20   Supra-level, spatial mode for screens

Size and shape
of the screen

Hypertext link

Scrollable length
(varies with the file)

■ *Graphic.* In the graphic mode (cell 12), supra-level design includes marks, icons, color, linework, and logos that unify pages, sections, or screens of the document (Figure 3.21a) or that create major divisions (Figure 3.21b).

FIGURE 3.21   Supra-level, graphic mode

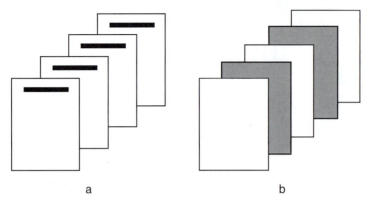

a   b

Each Communication Uniquely Combines Elements from the Matrix

The twelve-cell matrix of levels and coding modes is a tool for describing the visual vocabulary of a given communication, whether in print or on screen. Like a communication's range of words, its visual vocabulary will differ from that of others. Each contains its own universe of visual language that uniquely combines the cells on the matrix, even if that identity relies only on minute variations in type style, punctuation marks, or the ragged right margin. However large or small the variations, each communication has its own visual signature and footprint.

Some communications, of course, employ a much broader visual vocabulary than others. An annual report from a Fortune 500 company has a relatively complex visual vocabulary compared to a one-page résumé, while a one-page résumé will probably contain a richer visual vocabulary than most routine memos. Likewise, a fully developed Web site for a multinational corporation will display a much broader visual vocabulary than the Web page of one of its salespersons, while that salesperson's Web page will contain a larger visual vocabulary than will an e-mail message to a customer.

Some documents have a more developed vocabulary in some of the levels and individual cells than in others. A newsletter may have lots of variations in its intra- and inter-level text design (cells 1–6) but contain only a few pictures or data displays (cells 7–9). On the other hand, a set of instructions may rely more heavily on pictures than text and have only light activity in cells 1–6. And sometimes documents are entirely inactive in some of the cells: A short memo with no data displays or pictures will be inactive in all three extra-level cells (7–9).

Any communication can be charted on the matrix. To show how, we've charted in Table 3.6 much of the visual language of Fred Noonan's Mapleton document. As you can see, the visual language of Fred's document ranges widely across the matrix.

TABLE 3.6   Matrix Applied to Mapleton Document

	Textual	Spatial	Graphic
Intra	1 all text type 11-pt. or 12-pt. Palatino data in table 12-point Helvetica 14-pt. bold Palatino for meeting information	2 normal spacing between all local textual units single spacing after periods	3 periods, commas, exclamation points dollar signs slashes parentheses
Inter	4 bold, 14-pt. Key Benefits headers bold, italic headers for key features lists bold 12-pt. headers for chart & table intros.	5 unjustified text (except in table) centering of meeting information in letter list of meeting goals in letter; list of key features and benefits on options pages spacing between headings and text leading, margins	6 all five sets of bullets are black diamonds gray scale in two rows of the tables line work in table, heavier lines outside, lighter lines dividing individual cells
Extra	7 captions beneath floor plans labels within floor plans numerical labels on x- and y-axes of bar charts legends for bar charts	8 size of bar chart plot frame, which creates horizontal and vertical spacing and viewing angles size of elevations and floor plans size of Mapleton logo	9 line weights for various parts of the floor plans shadings for windows, roofs, garden area details in drawings shading of bars tick-marks on x- and y-axes black Mapleton logo
Supra	10 page headers 24-pt. Palatino no page numbers text in the Mapleton letterhead	11 document printed on 11" x 17" sheet with one fold letter and options sheets in portrait orientation, data sheet in landscape drawings on options pages on inside of page placement of bar charts above table on data sheets	12 top and bottom framing lines on options pages and data sheet birch paper

Although the matrix allows us to describe this vocabulary systematically, it shouldn't be applied lock-step. For one thing, as we mentioned above, some communications will be visually intensive in some cells and relatively passive in others. Also, keep in mind that the cells on the matrix aren't rigid, airtight boxes, and the lines that separate them are often gray and fuzzy. If something doesn't fit neatly into a cell, or you don't know where it fits, place it where you think it makes the most sense.

Analyzing Visual Vocabulary Rhetorically

The matrix is primarily a descriptive tool that helps you identify and classify the visual language of a given communication. *Analyzing* visual rhetoric means examining *how well* this visual vocabulary helps a communication respond to its rhetorical situation. In other words, the overarching question for visual analysis is:

> How well does the visual vocabulary of this communication match its audience, purpose, and context?

For a given communication, its visual language at any level of the matrix should do *some rhetorical work,* however subtle or conspicuous. Depending on the rhetorical situation, visual language on any level of the matrix can develop any of the cognate strategies—arrangement, emphasis, clarity, conciseness, tone, or ethos. In a certain rhetorical situation, for example, supra-level elements might be critical to arrangement and ethos, while in a different rhetorical situation, supra-level elements might be more crucial for emphasis and conciseness. Also, depending on the rhetorical situation, visual elements in any of the cells may conform to conventional practices that help the document meet readers' expectations. *The important thing is that each visual element does some rhetorical work that enables the document to respond appropriately to the rhetorical situation.* Visual elements that don't do any rhetorical work, or that actually run counter to the rhetorical situation, need to be edited, revised, or thrown out altogether.

To illustrate how visual language responds to rhetorical situations, we'll analyze a printed document explaining how to assemble a bunk bed. The analysis is preceded by a brief explanation of the rhetorical situation, followed by an analysis of the rhetorical work that the visual language does for this instructional document.

Analysis of the Visco Manufacturing Bunk Bed Instructions

The Visco bunk bed instructions (Figure 3.22) are included in the box with either of two tubular steel bunk beds when they are purchased. Here's the rhetorical situation for the instructions:

■ *Audience:* Users of the document will be the purchasers themselves, probably parents of young children, or people the parents have persuaded, hired, or bribed to put the bed together. Their skill level probably varies, with many readers having little or no experience constructing an object this large.

FIGURE 3.22   Visco bunk bed instructions

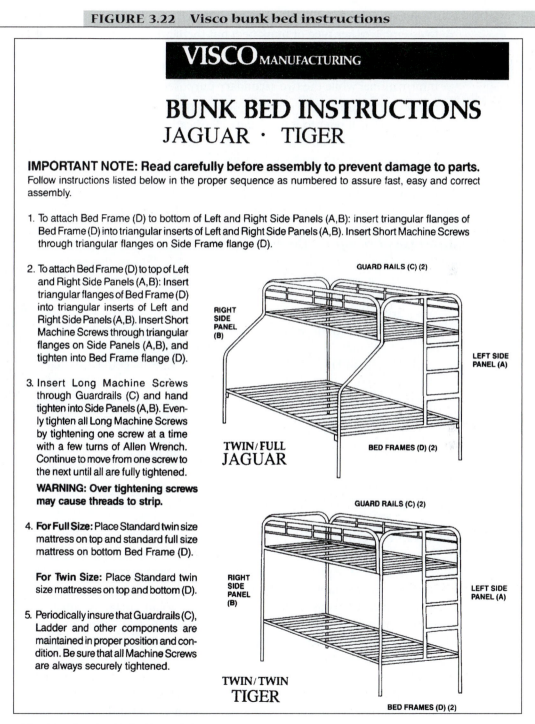

VISCO MANUFACTURING

BUNK BED INSTRUCTIONS
JAGUAR · TIGER

IMPORTANT NOTE: Read carefully before assembly to prevent damage to parts.
Follow instructions listed below in the proper sequence as numbered to assure fast, easy and correct assembly.

1. To attach Bed Frame (D) to bottom of Left and Right Side Panels (A,B): insert triangular flanges of Bed Frame (D) into triangular inserts of Left and Right Side Panels (A,B). Insert Short Machine Screws through triangular flanges on Side Frame flange (D).

2. To attach Bed Frame (D) to top of Left and Right Side Panels (A,B): Insert triangular flanges of Bed Frame (D) into triangular inserts of Left and Right Side Panels (A,B). Insert Short Machine Screws through triangular flanges on Side Panels (A,B), and tighten into Bed Frame flange (D).

3. Insert Long Machine Screws through Guardrails (C) and hand tighten into Side Panels (A,B). Evenly tighten all Long Machine Screws by tightening one screw at a time with a few turns of Allen Wrench. Continue to move from one screw to the next until all are fully tightened.
   WARNING: Over tightening screws may cause threads to strip.

4. **For Full Size:** Place Standard twin size mattress on top and standard full size mattress on bottom Bed Frame (D).

   For Twin Size: Place Standard twin size mattresses on top and bottom (D).

5. Periodically insure that Guardrails (C), Ladder and other components are maintained in proper position and condition. Be sure that all Machine Screws are always securely tightened.

GUARD RAILS (C) (2)

RIGHT SIDE PANEL (B)

LEFT SIDE PANEL (A)

TWIN/FULL
JAGUAR

BED FRAMES (D) (2)

GUARD RAILS (C) (2)

RIGHT SIDE PANEL (B)

LEFT SIDE PANEL (A)

TWIN/TWIN
TIGER

BED FRAMES (D) (2)

- *Purpose:* The primary purpose of the instructions, of course, is to enable users to assemble either type of bunk bed; but there are at least two secondary purposes: (1) to minimize potential damage to the product and (2) to convince readers that they've purchased a good product. The primary purpose, then, is informational while the two secondary purposes are largely persuasive.

- *Context:* The context for using the document will probably be a table or floor, where users will refer to it for details, clarification, or the next step in the procedure. Or perhaps an assistant will read the instructions aloud to the assembler as he or she proceeds with the work.

Let's examine the visual vocabulary from the top down, from supra-level to the intra-level, and examine how the visual language does its rhetorical work.

Supra-Level Design. The document consists of a single page, an important conciseness factor because it will simplify physical handling by the user(s). The page is marked at the top with the company's name on a white-on-black bar running across the right two-thirds of the page. (Assembly instructions for other Visco products are marked with the same identifier.) The white all-caps type on the black bar emphasizes the name of the manufacturer, and the strong figure-ground contrast of the bar itself enhances the ethos of the document by creating an official look. The main title, BUNK BED INSTRUCTIONS, and the subtitle (JAGUAR • TIGER) are also emphasis strategies. Both titles contribute to both clarity and ethos by assuring the user that the instructions match the product itself and not some other bunk bed or product in the VISCO line.

The placement of the two pictures on the page is also a supra-level decision. Arranging the pictures on right side of the page will help readers relate the text to the appropriate drawing (Jaguar or Tiger model) in an uninterrupted movement from left to right. The placement on the right half of the page also allows nearly equal space for both without giving one priority over the other.

Extra-Level Design. The pictures of the Jaguar and Tiger models contribute to clarity by making the text instructions more usable; in fact, the reader depends almost entirely on the pictures to understand how the parts fit together. The level of realism in the pictures, even down to the slats in each bed frame, contributes to clarity and ethos, as users will have accurate-looking details against which to check their own work during assembly. Also, showing the pictures in perspective is both a clarity and a conciseness strategy: Readers will find the perspective drawings nontechnical and easy to decipher, and perspective saves space by showing the object partially from the front, side, and top views all at the same time.

The captions and the labels are also clarity strategies, helping readers correctly identify the parts (even though the orientation seems backward, with the "right side panel" appearing on the left side of the drawings and the "left side panel" on the right side). All-caps typography in the labels and captions is an emphasis strategy. The consistent arrangement of captions and the labels (they all match spatially) contributes enormously to clarity, and perhaps to ethos as well since the consistency itself boosts reader confidence.

Inter-Level Design.   The instructions use a variety of inter-level cues that serve clarity, emphasis, arrangement, tone, and ethos functions. In the textual mode, the run-in headings for the Important Note at the top, the warning, and the full- and twin-size options in step 4 emphasize key information. The boldfacing of these cues heightens the serious tone of the instructions, and the contrast with the other text enhances clarity. The arrangement of the steps in a numbered list, the indentation of the text, and the spacing between them emphasize each step so that readers can find their place on the page as they shuttle between the task and the instructions.

The arrangement of the text columns—with step 1 running across the top of the document and the other steps down the left side—frames the pictures. This framing effect and the justified text (the smooth right margin) add to the professional look of the instructions, enhancing ethos. Notice also that the column widens slightly below the warning in step 3, closing the gap between the bottom drawing and the text column—a subtle ethos-building strategy.

Intra-Level Design.   Visual elements here include the overall typographic pattern of a sans serif font for the steps and the picture labels, and a serif font for the titles and picture captions. The fact that only two fonts appear in the document is a conciseness strategy. The contrast between the fonts contributes to clarity as well as to emphasis. Using sans serif type for most of the written material establishes a technical, professional tone. Use of capitals for the first letter of all part names is a clarity strategy, though it also perhaps adds unnecessary formality—a trade-off in tone.

In the graphic mode, the consistent use of parentheses throughout the text instructions and the drawing labels serves an important clarity function. Anything in parentheses denotes a part (side panel, guard rail, bed frame) and never anything else. This consistency also builds ethos.

Summary of the Rhetorical Analysis.   Even in this short, ordinary, matter-of-fact set of instructions we can find design elements in virtually every cell of the grid, which collectively make up the unique visual language of the document. As we've shown above in our brief analysis, that language does important work by responding to the rhetorical situation—the document's audience, purposes, and context—through all six of the cognate strategies.

Conclusion

In this chapter we've outlined a system for describing the rich and complex visual vocabulary of professional communications, ranging from a single italicized word, to an illustration, to the size, shape, and texture of the page or screen. We've also explored how you can analyze the visual vocabulary of a given communication systematically, a skill that will prepare you to make smart decisions while you're designing your own document.

On our diagram outlining the design process, we'll now define the vocabulary of visual language to include four levels and three coding modes (Figure 3.23). The

FIGURE 3.23   Update of the design process

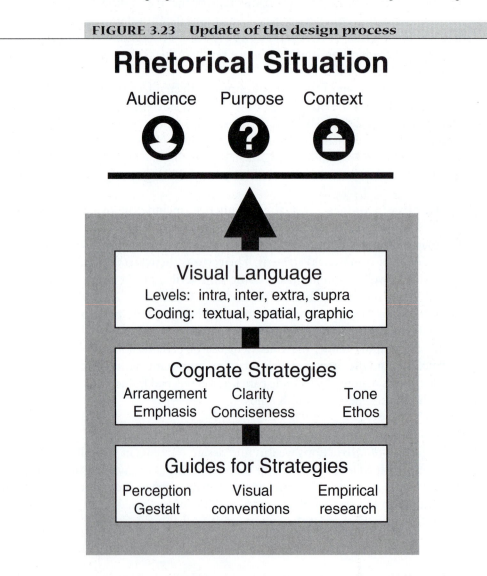

remainder of this book will show how the elements on the diagram are enacted on the four levels of visual language outlined in this chapter. Specifically,

- Part Two will cover the intra- and inter-level design of text, from linear components (Chapter 4), to field design (Chapter 5), to nonlinear components (Chapter 6).
- Part Three will cover extra-level elements, including data displays (Chapter 7) and pictures (Chapter 8).
- Part Four will cover supra-level elements, the large-scale design of the whole communication and how it enhances usability (Chapter 9).

In each of these chapters, you'll continually discover how the rhetorical situation shapes all forms of visual language—from a boldface word to a warning icon to a home page. To benefit from these chapters, you'll need to remain flexible in your thinking about the elements on the design process diagram, which vary from one design opportunity to another like the shifting sands on a beach.

Note

1. This taxonomy was outlined by Charles Kostelnick ("Systematic"; "Visual Rhetoric"). Related taxonomies of visual language have been outlined by Stephen Bernhardt, Michael Twyman, and Robert H. W. Waller.

References

Bernhardt, Stephen A. "Seeing the Text." *College Composition and Communication* 37 (1986): 66–78.

Kostelnick, Charles. "A Systematic Approach to Visual Language in Business Communication." *The Journal of Business Communication* 25.3 (1988): 29–48.

———. "Visual Rhetoric: A Reader-Oriented Approach to Graphics and Designs." *The Technical Writing Teacher* 16 (1989): 77–88.

Twyman, Michael. "A Schema for the Study of Graphic Language." *Processing of Visible Language*. 2 vols. Ed. Paul A. Kolers, Merald E. Wrolstad, and Herman Bouma. New York: Plenum, 1979–80. 1: 117–150.

Waller, Robert H. W. "Graphic Aspects of Complex Texts: Typography as Macro-Punctuation." *Processing of Visible Language 2*. Ed. Paul A. Kolers, Merald E. Wrolstad, and Herman Bouma. New York: Plenum, 1980. 2: 241–253.

Exercises

1. Pictured in Figure 3.24 is a page from a document written and published by the Office of Institutional Research, Iowa State University. The document is printed on

FIGURE 3.24   Page with data produced by the Iowa State University Office of Institutional Research

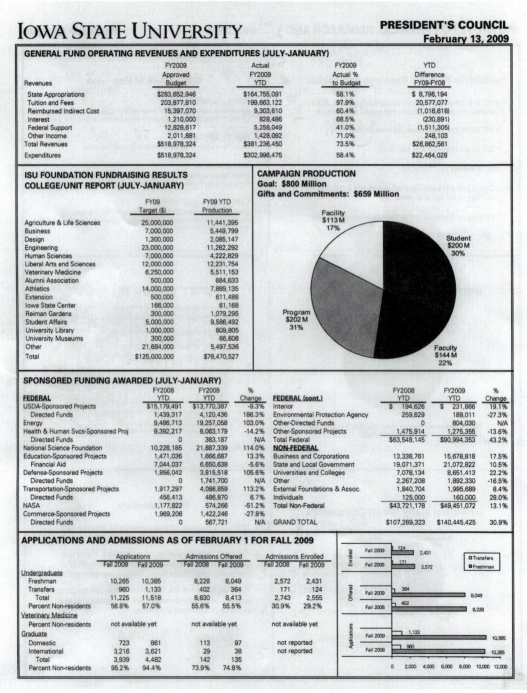

both sides of an 8½" × 11" sheet. Copies of the document are distributed at a monthly meeting of the Iowa State University president with campus administrators.

Shown below (Table 3.7) is a blank analytical grid. Using the page displayed in Figure 3.24, fill in the grid as completely as you can, listing specific visual elements in their appropriate cells.

TABLE 3.7   Blank Analytical Grid

	Textual	Spatial	Graphic
Intra	1	2	3
Inter	4	5	6
Extra	7	8	9
Supra	10	11	12

2. Figure 3.25 is an excerpt from a business letter denying credit to the reader. The reader, JoAnn Smith, recently applied for the credit card and obviously will find the news disappointing.

FIGURE 3.25   Credit rejection letter

```
DEAR MS. SMITH:

THANK YOU YOUR REQUEST FOR AN XYZ CARD ACCOUNT. WE HAVE CARE-
FULLY CONSIDERED YOUR APPLICATION BUT REGRET WE ARE UNABLE TO
APPROVE YOUR REQUEST AT THIS TIME. FEDERAL LAW ENTITLES YOU TO
A STATEMENT OF THE SPECIFIC REASONS(S) FOR OUR DECISION. AS PART
OF OUR CONSIDERATION, WE MAY HAVE OBTAINED A COPY OF YOUR CREDIT
REPORT. IF WE OBTAINED INFORMATION FROM A CONSUMER REPORTING
AGENCY, ITS NAME AND ADDRESS ARE SHOWN BELOW.

CREDIT INFORMATION COMPANY
222 SOUTH GEORGE STREET
MIDDLETON, MO 52502
```

a. Identify the *intra-level* design elements in the letter: typefaces, sizes, treatments, and so on.

b. Discuss the effects of these elements upon the following cognate strategies: emphasis, clarity, and tone.

c. Overall, how does intra-level design help or hinder the purpose of the letter?

3. Find a newsletter from a business or an organization and focus on the *extra-level* design elements that appear throughout the document.

a. Thumb through the newsletter and identify the extra-level design elements—pictures, data displays (pie charts, bar graphs, line graphs), and icons, logos, or symbols. If the newsletter is packed with these elements, choose just one kind—for example, data displays or pictures.

b. Discuss how well these elements implement the following cognate strategies: clarity, conciseness, and tone.

c. How do these strategies help or hinder the newsletter in responding to its rhetorical situation?

4. Find a short handbook, report, owner's manual, or other instructional document and focus on its *supra-level* design elements.

a. Identify as many supra-level design elements as you can—page size and orientation, visual divisions between major sections, headers and footers, cover page, method of binding, and so on.

b. Discuss how well these design elements implement the following cognate strategies: arrangement, tone, and ethos.

c. How do these strategies help or hinder the document in responding to its rhetorical situation?

Assignments

In this assignment your goal is to analyze the visual rhetoric of a communication—that is, you are to evaluate how effectively the communication's visual design strategies respond to the rhetorical situation. You will first describe the visual language, then analyze its rhetorical impact. Below are some specifics.

1. *Select a sample communication.* To begin the assignment, you'll need to find a business or technical document. Below are a few possibilities:

   - A manual or a set of instructional materials—for example, for a computer, household device, recreational equipment
   - Informational materials—a bus timetable, a schedule of meetings or classes, a directory, a fact sheet
   - A home page for a business, educational institution, park, or museum
   - A brochure—for a product or service, a company or nonprofit organization—or some other promotional material

   The concern is quality, not quantity, so if you pick a longer communication, you should plan to analyze only a portion of it.

2. *Summarize the rhetorical situation.* The rhetorical situation, of course, consists of the audience, the purpose, and the context. Here are some of the questions you should address:

   - *Who are the readers and what do they expect?* How much do readers already know about the subject? What can you assume about readers' design preferences or their previous experience using this kind of communication?
   - *What is the writer/designer's purpose?* To what extent is the communication intended to inform, to persuade, or to stimulate interest? What issue, question, or task generated the communication?
   - *What is the context?* How will readers use the communication? Will they read it from beginning to end? Search for information? Will they use it at a desk, at a computer terminal, in the field?

3. *Describe the visual language.* Look closely at the visual language of your communication—everything from typefaces to the size and shape of the pages. Here are some things to keep in mind as you scrutinize the visual design choices in your sample:

   - What typefaces are used? How do typeface sizes and treatments vary?
   - What textual, spatial, or graphic cues are used to structure the communication?
   - What kinds of extra-level elements are included—icons, logos, illustrations, data displays?
   - What is the page size and orientation? How about color, paper stock, or supra-level unifiers? If you're analyzing a Web site, how long are the scrollable screens? How are the links organized visually?

4. *Discuss the rhetorical impact of the document's visual language.* Analyze how the visual language responds (or doesn't respond) to the rhetorical situation. Use the six cognates as the basis for your discussion. Here are some questions about the cognates to guide you:

   - Which visual elements implement *arrangement* strategies? How effectively do these elements map the communication and show the relationships among its various pieces?
   - Which visual elements implement *emphasis* strategies? How successfully do these make the important things stand out?
   - How well does the communication's visual language achieve *clarity?* How well does visual language enable readers to get through the message smoothly and unambiguously?
   - How well does the visual language achieve *conciseness?* Do all of the visual elements in the communication do some rhetorical work?
   - What *tone* do the visual elements project? Is the tone appropriate for the rhetorical situation?
   - Which visual elements contribute to *ethos?* To what extent do these develop the communication's credibility or character?

   Also, consider the extent to which the communication follows the *Gestalt principles* of figure–ground contrast and grouping and how its adherence to—or violation of—these principles affects the cognate strategies. Finally, assess the role of *visual conventions,* the degree to which they are (or are not) followed in the communication and the impact these conventions have on the visual rhetoric.

5. *Write your analysis as a memo report to members of the class.* Attach an original of your document to your report; if you analyze a Web page, print out the screen and include the URL.

4 Linear

Components

Introduction to Linear Components

Linear components are the most basic elements of text design—the letters, words, numbers, and other intra-level forms that are visible to the eye but often taken for granted. While linear components tend to be physically small, they can have significant—even striking—rhetorical effects.

Take the word *stop*. Without the conventional shape of an octagon surrounding it, *stop* may not have much impact. But few readers would deny that STOP looks more insistent simply because of the capital letters. Change the typeface from Palatino to Chicago or Peignot Demi, and **STOP** looks still more demanding and authoritative. Bold the type and enlarge it, and you'll almost surely grab the viewers' attention:

STOP

You could also add space between characters:

S T O P

or use a graphic treatment:

<u>STOP</u>

—but perhaps the rhetorical point is already made.

To some extent, focusing on linear elements is artificial because most professional communications contain more than a character, a word, or a single line of text. Nevertheless, it's important to recognize two things:

- Readers frequently process messages one piece at a time and therefore even small swatches of text can have significant functional value. For example, a single *italicized* word will stand out clearly in a line of type, as will a footnote number (such as[x]).

- Linked together, linear components have a *cumulative* effect on the overall visual language of the document. For example, the selection of a type style and size can profoundly shape the texture of a page or screen.

Seen one piece at a time or as a textual fabric woven together from many bits and pieces, linear components have visual impact.

Like other forms of visual language, however, that impact can be measured only in terms of the rhetorical work that linear components perform. You design linear components to respond to rhetorical situations, in the process implementing each of the six cognate strategies. To demonstrate this process, we'll start by watching a designer in action.

Process Example—Linear Components

Jill Salome works in the computer documentation section of her company, where she edits and designs manuals and other kinds of documents. Recently, Jill found a note on her desk from her manager, Bernie Briggs, asking her to create a sign from the message shown in Figure 4.1.

FIGURE 4.1   Text for Jill's design problem

```
If your pages are faded or streaked, remove the
toner cartridge and shake it. Place the cartridge
back in the printer and try printing again. If the
print quality is still poor, replace the toner
cartridge. Follow the directions on the inside panel
of the laser printer. If you need help, see Cheryl.
```

Bernie wants Jill to create 20 such signs, each of which will be taped onto the tops of all the laser printers in the office complex. Many of the laser printers have recently sat idle because the cartridges have run dry or haven't been shaken. That's created havoc around the office because employees route their work to the few remaining printers. Employees from all parts of the complex now line up before the few operating printers, waiting for their documents to appear, glancing nervously at their watches as deadlines come and go.

Analyzing the Rhetorical Situation

Jill's job is straightforward: to design this message so users will take responsibility to maintain the printers. How should she design this simple message? What factors should she consider? First, Jill briefly appraises the rhetorical situation—audience, purpose, and context.

- ■ *Audience.* Other employees, including office workers and managers, all ages. Many of them are reluctant to change the toner cartridge because they don't know how or are afraid they'll break the printer. They'd rather let the printer sit idle than make an embarrassing mistake.
- ■ *Purpose.* The message has to get the reader's attention, so it must be clear, emphatic, and concise. It also has to be friendly and reassuring because readers have a negative attitude toward this task. The message should motivate readers to shake the cartridge, change it, or seek help to change it.
- ■ *Context.* Readers will see the message attached to the top of the laser printer. At that moment they'll decide whether or not to comply. The next time readers encounter the message, it will simply serve as a reminder.

Invention

In analyzing the rhetorical situation, Jill realizes that the message must catch the employees' attention, so it must be highly visible and readable without appearing overwhelming. Aware of those needs and constraints, Jill sits down in front of her computer and begins designing the text. At first, she's concerned mostly with clarity: If readers can't easily see her message, it won't stand a chance of fulfilling its purpose. So she designs her first draft to look like Figure 4.2.

FIGURE 4.2   Jill's draft

If your pages are faded or streaked, remove the toner cartridge and

shake it. Place the cartridge back in the printer and try printing again.

If the print quality is still poor, replace the toner cartridge. Follow the

directions on the inside panel of the laser printer. If you need help,

see Cheryl.

Jill chooses Helvetica type because it's clean, simple, and direct. It also conforms to the conventional language of her workplace. Her manager prefers Helvetica for their manuals, and Jill herself uses it in most of her work. She selects 10-point type, assuming that her readers will be comfortable with it because they read her manuals in the same type size all the time. So far so good. She has a pretty good idea about what she's trying to accomplish. Now that she has a design draft, she can begin revising.

Revision

After printing her message, Jill discovers that the text is too small to attract her readers' attention or to enable them to read it comfortably in the context in which they'll encounter it: standing in front of the laser printer. In other words, the message is too visually concise for this rhetorical situation. So in her revision Jill increases the point size from 10 to 16 and adds some space between lines. The new message looks like Figure 4.3.

FIGURE 4.3   Jill's first revision

If your pages are faded or streaked, remove the toner cartridge and shake it. Place the cartridge back in the printer and try printing again. If the print quality is still poor, replace the toner cartridge. Follow the directions on the inside panel of the laser printer. If you need help, see Cheryl.

Although it takes more space, now the message is clear and legible without being overwhelming. However, as Jill studies it, she finds the text dull and a bit cold and off-putting. Posting this message, she thinks, would make her manager seem demanding and authoritarian, a tone Jill knows he doesn't want to project. Jill also knows that the employees in the office are afraid of changing the printer cartridge, so she tries to personalize the text—first by changing the font to a script typeface, Zapf Chancery (Figure 4.4). A script font, Zapf Chancery has a gentler, more humane look than Helvetica. But Jill finds its tone too formal for this situation. Readers might mistake the message for an invitation or announcement. Worse yet,

FIGURE 4.4   Jill's second revision

If your pages are faded or streaked, remove the toner cartridge and shake it. Place the cartridge back in the printer and try printing again. If the print quality is still poor, replace the toner cartridge. Follow the directions on the inside panel of the laser printer. If you need help, see Cheryl.

the Zapf Chancery erodes the visual clarity of the message because the slanting text will slow their reading. Many will simply ignore it, Jill thinks. So she tries another typeface, New Century Schoolbook (Figure 4.5).

FIGURE 4.5   Jill's third revision

If your pages are faded or streaked, remove the toner cartridge and shake it. Place the cartridge back in the printer and try printing again. If the print quality is still poor, replace the toner cartridge. Follow the directions on the inside panel of the laser printer. If you need help, see Cheryl.

The message now looks less severe and formal. Jill's satisfied that her design will do the job because it has good *clarity,* it's still reasonably *concise,* and the *tone* is serious yet friendly.

Visual Editing

Jill puts her message aside to work on a manual for the rest of the morning. After lunch and an afternoon meeting, where Bernie Briggs again mentions the laser printer problem, she returns to her document to do some quick visual editing.

1. She realizes that the message lacks *emphasis.* Everything runs together because the text lacks figure–ground contrast. So she decides to vary the message a bit. Jill knows that employees are worried about changing the cartridge correctly, so she decides to emphasize the fact that they can find instructions inside the printer. Her message now looks like Figure 4.6.

FIGURE 4.6   Jill's edited version

If your pages are faded or streaked, remove the toner cartridge and shake it. Place the cartridge back in the printer and try printing again. If the print quality is still poor, replace the toner cartridge. Follow the directions on the inside panel of the laser printer. If you need help, see Cheryl.

2. The figure–ground contrast doesn't work particularly well; moreover, emphasizing this part of the text seems demanding and patronizing. Everyone's always telling everyone else to "follow the directions"! The *tone,* she thinks to herself, is trite and belittling. Instead, Jill decides to emphasize that employees can get help from Cheryl if they need it. She also will emphasize the importance of shaking the cartridge first, since she knows that this measure alone often alleviates the problem.

3. Jill thinks the shadow text looks a bit unprofessional, an *ethos* problem. So she does a quick visual edit—changing the shadow text back to normal text. Her edited version appears in Figure 4.7.

Good enough, Jill thinks to herself. She places a copy on Bernie Briggs's desk and awaits some feedback before she makes copies for the 20 laser printers.

FIGURE 4.7 Jill's final edited version

FIGURE 4.7   Jill's final edited version

If your pages are faded or streaked, REMOVE THE TONER CARTRIDGE AND SHAKE IT. Place the cartridge back in the printer and try printing again. If the print quality is still poor, replace the toner cartridge. Follow the directions on the inside panel of the laser printer. IF YOU NEED HELP, SEE CHERYL.

Vocabulary of Linear Components

As you can see from Jill's process, designing linear components entails lots of decisions. While individually these decisions may not seem very complex—a type style here, a type size there, boldface for this text, italic for that—when you consider the combinations of potential variations over a line of text and over all the lines of an entire document, the possibilities can multiply in a hurry. To get some perspective on this rich vocabulary, let's walk systematically through the three coding modes—textual, spatial, and graphic—developing a working lexicon of linear components as we go.

Textual Elements

Textual elements at the intra-level include the visual qualities of the typeface itself: the shape of its design and the possible variations within this basic shape—size, italics, uppercase, shadow, and so on. Every time you read a line of text—on a billboard, a screen, or a bus schedule—you're absorbing the visual language of type.

Yet identifying typefaces based on their design features can be tricky: The differences in form among the hundreds, perhaps thousands, of typefaces in use today are relatively small. To understand the visual language of type, you have to train yourself to notice minute details. So what do you look for?

Let's start by examining several design qualities that group typefaces with other typefaces and that also give them their distinct traits.[1] These include:

- Serifs
- X-height
- Width
- Line quality

Then we'll examine some of the design choices you can make to transform a given typeface.

Serifs. Serifs are the finishing strokes on the ends of letters. Some typefaces have them, some don't. Although the origin of serifs remains a mystery, stone carvers have traditionally used serifs to square off the ends of letters with their chisels. Whatever their origin, serifs today come in many forms, as the examples below show:

Palatino   Bookman   Times   Zapf Chancery   Courier

Many typefaces, especially modern ones, don't have serifs; hence, they're called *sans serifs* (literally "without serifs"). Below are some examples:

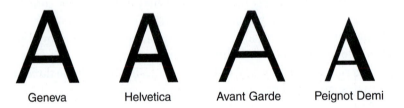

Geneva   Helvetica   Avant Garde   Peignot Demi

Serifs, or the lack of them, can affect the clarity of the text as well as its tone. However, depending on the resolution of your computer screen, serifs may be less visible on a screen than in print.

X-Height. Typefaces differ in their geometry. One significant aspect of this geometry is the x-height—the vertical height of a typeface at its center line. For example, compare the height of the round part of the three letter *d*'s shown in Figure 4.8. Even though all three typefaces are set at the same point size, each x-height becomes progressively higher. Notice how much lower the round part of the Times typeface (on the left) is, compared to Bookman (center) and Helvetica (right). Because of these differences in x-height, 12-point Times will appear to take up less space than 12-point Bookman.

FIGURE 4.8   The effects of x-height

x-height

Times   Bookman   Helvetica

Across a line of text, the x-height establishes an invisible boundary. Notice in the word *party* below (Figure 4.9) how the letters *p* and *t* cross the x-height boundary, below and above it respectively. The part of a letter that rises above the x-height line is called an *ascender;* the part below the x-height line is called a *descender.*

FIGURE 4.9   Ascenders and descenders

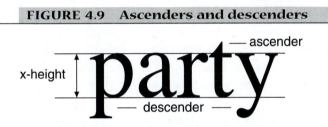

A key geometric trait of any typeface is the ratio between the x-height and the relative length of the ascenders and descenders. Examine the typefaces in Figure 4.10: Palatino on the left, Avant Garde in the center, and Helvetica on the right:

FIGURE 4.10   Relation between x-height and ascenders/descenders

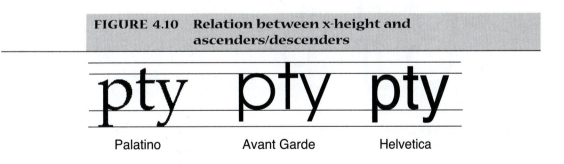

Palatino   Avant Garde   Helvetica

Notice how the x-heights and the lengths of the ascenders and descenders vary. This variation causes one typeface to look like it takes up more space than another typeface, even when both are set at exactly the same point size.

Width of Typeface.   Typefaces differ not only in their vertical height but also in the horizontal space they occupy. Notice the differences in length among the alphabet lines of the five typefaces in Figure 4.11, all set at 12 points.

FIGURE 4.11   Varying widths of typefaces

Times	abcdefghijklmnopqrstuvwxyz
Helvetica	abcdefghijklmnopqrstuvwxyz
Palatino	abcdefghijklmnopqrstuvwxyz
Bookman	abcdefghijklmnopqrstuvwxyz
Avant Garde	abcdefghijklmnopqrstuvwxyz

Times is a narrow typeface, Avant Garde a relatively wide one. Overall, Avant Garde and Bookman have broader letters than Times, Helvetica, or Palatino. Multiply these differences over several pages and they add up: Four pages of text set in Bookman will take only about three pages if the same text is set in Times.

You can see these differences in width more clearly when you examine typefaces up close. In Figure 4.12 you can see that Avant Garde and Palatino have comparatively large O's, especially Avant Garde. Other letters, however, tell slightly different stories: The *T*'s set in Palatino and Times are wider than the *T* set in Avant Garde, while the *P*'s in all three typefaces vary less than the O's and the *T*'s.

FIGURE 4.12   Typeface widths

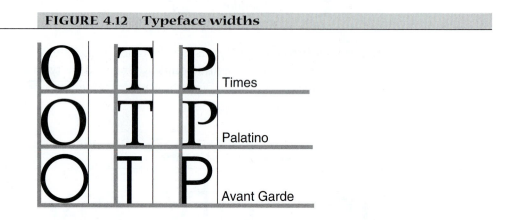

Line Quality.   A fourth way to distinguish typefaces is according to the qualities of the line work in the letters themselves—(1) how thick or thin they are and (2) whether the lines vary in width or have a constant width. Let's look at thickness first.

Geneva   Courier   Times

Although all three letters are set at 72 points, notice how much thicker the lines in the Geneva typeface are compared to those in Courier. And notice how in Times the angled line on the right is thicker than the angled one on the left as well as the horizontal cross stroke. The thick line in Times is about the same as those in the Geneva *A*, while the thin one matches the lines in the Courier *A*.

Typefaces whose lines don't vary in width are called *monoline* typefaces. Common monolines include Avant Garde, Helvetica, and Geneva—though even in these you might be able to detect a *slight* variation between the vertical and horizontal lines:

Avant Garde   Helvetica   Geneva

Typefaces with line variations are fairly easy to spot, especially when you enlarge them. In the Times text shown in Figure 4.13, you can see how the curved lines frequently change their width.

FIGURE 4.13   Varying widths of curved lines in typefaces

In any given typeface, then, you can find several distinguishing characteristics: in the serifs (if it has any), in the x-height, or in the thickness and consistency of the lines. Let's say we want to compare the typefaces below:

Palatino   Bookman   Times   Helvetica   Courier

Using the criteria we've outlined above, we've charted each of these typefaces in Table 4.1. As you can see, some of the typefaces sort into groups according to their shape. For example, Palatino, Bookman, Times, and Courier have serifs; in terms of x-height, Times and Courier have short x-heights, Times and Helvetica are narrow,

TABLE 4.1 Typeface Characteristics

	Serifs	X-height	Width	Lines
Palatino	square ends, small brackets	moderate	moderate	moderate variation
Bookman	square ends, large brackets	moderate	slightly wide	moderate variation
Times	square ends, medium brackets	short	narrow	strong variation
Helvetica	none	tall	narrow	monoline
Courier	square ends, no brackets	short	wide	slight variation

and Bookman and Courier are wide; and in terms of line quality, Bookman and Palatino display moderate variations while Helvetica and Courier don't.

Up until now we've examined intrinsic design traits that distinguish one typeface from another. Now let's look at some of the possible textual variations *within* a given typeface design. We'll divide these additional visual characteristics into two categories:

- Type size
- Treatments—from all caps to boldface

Type Size. We've already seen type set at various sizes. Type is measured in points, with each point equal to ½₂ of an inch. Figure 4.14 shows several point sizes and their equivalents in inches:

FIGURE 4.14 Type size in points

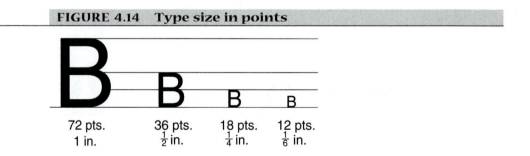

72 pts.	36 pts.	18 pts.	12 pts.
1 in.	½ in.	¼ in.	⅙ in.

Remember too that the actual vertical size of a typeface in a given point size will vary slightly among typefaces because of their differences in design (i.e., their x-height and the extension of their ascenders and descenders from that x-height). Compare these typefaces all set at 60 points.

B B B B B

Birch	Peignot Light	Helvetica	Bookman	Times

Even though it's set in the same point size, a tall typeface such as Birch looks larger than a short typeface such as Peignot Light. Obviously, when choosing a type size, you need to consider the typeface design.

Point size also affects horizontal space, which you can see by comparing the samples in Figure 4.15. If you increase the type size by only a point, the horizontal space it consumes on a given line will increase, which adds up quickly over a page of text.

FIGURE 4.15   Effect of point size on line length

6	Typography is a form of visual language
7	Typography is a form of visual language
8	Typography is a form of visual language
9	Typography is a form of visual language
10	Typography is a form of visual language
11	Typography is a form of visual language
12	Typography is a form of visual language
13	Typography is a form of visual language
14	Typography is a form of visual language

Treatments.   In addition to changes in size, typefaces can undergo other transformations. Figure 4.16 shows some of these variations with 12-point New Century Schoolbook.

FIGURE 4.16   Typeface treatments

all caps	TYPOGRAPHY IS A FORM OF VISUAL LANGUAGE
small caps	TYPOGRAPHY IS A FORM OF VISUAL LANGUAGE
italics	*Typography is a form of visual language*
boldface	**Typography is a form of visual language**
outline	Typography is a form of visual language
shadow	Typography is a form of visual language

You can make these variations quickly from the pull-down menu of virtually any word processing program. In some programs, you can also customize your own variations by stretching and compressing the typeface, as we've done in Figure 4.17, starting with a 72-point Adobe Caslon.

FIGURE 4.17   Stretching and compressing type

G → G G G

So once you've selected a typeface, you can vary its size and you can transform it in several ways—everything from adding italics, boldface, and shadow to stretching and compressing it.

Conventions.   The typefaces you use will probably be influenced by conventions, which may derive from the kind of document you're producing, the organization you work for, or even your cultural background. For example, some typefaces are conventional for certain kinds of documents—Zapf Chancery for invitations, Times Roman for newsletters, or Monaco or Geneva for e-mail messages. Although these conventions aren't written in stone, through practice they have attained a certain status as norms.

You may also adhere to typeface conventions if you work for an organization that specifies a typeface for all of its documents. Adhering to the convention enables an organization to achieve cohesion across its documents, to maintain its visual identity, and to build professional ethos.

On a broader scale, you might follow the typographical conventions that have developed within the country or the culture in which your documents will be used. For instance, Europeans such as the French, Swiss, and Dutch prefer sans serifs more than the Americans or the British do. Cultural influences on typeface selection extend beyond the Western world: Taiwanese are more likely to use traditional Chinese typefaces than the mainland Chinese; Egyptians typically use traditional Arabic fonts for religious text, modern fonts for commercial text.[2] Because cross-cultural text design is occurring more frequently in professional communication, you'll need to be on the lookout for type conventions influenced by culture.

Spatial Elements

Spatially, linear components govern the flow of letters and words in a line of text. This includes the direction of the text itself, which we largely take for granted because it's bound to conventions deeply rooted in our reading habits. Most of you are accustomed to contemporary Western lineation—left to right, as you're reading now. Like other aspects of type, however, line direction can vary across cultures and time (see Figure 4.18).

FIGURE 4.18   Conventions for directing a line of text

| Western | Arabic & Hebrew | Ancient Greek (boustrophedon, as the ox plows) | Traditional Chinese |

Assuming that left-to-right text flow is a given for your design, you still have many spatial choices at the local level, though some of these can be fairly subtle. We'll look at three variations:

- Horizontal spacing between characters and words
- Vertical spacing between characters and words
- Special treatments

Horizontal Spacing between Characters and Words.   In a running line of text, you have some choices about spacing between words—for example, whether to place one or two spaces after a period. If you want your document to have a typeset quality, you'll insert just one space, though that may take some getting used to.

But individual character spacing is only a small part of the story. Most software programs give you some options for adjusting the spacing between characters. For example, Microsoft Word allows you to choose among three spacing options: condensed, normal, and expanded. Within these, you can control the expansion and contraction by a fraction of a point, as shown below:

condensed	Typography is a form of visual language.
normal	Typography is a form of visual language.
expanded	Typography is a form of visual language.

These minute differences can add up quickly: Take four lines of text and you can quickly condense it to three or expand it to six, a 100 percent variation in space.

You can also custom control the spacing between individual letters or words by using a technique called *kerning*. When you kern letters, you pull them closer together or space them farther apart in tiny increments. Notice in Figure 4.19 how the letters *W* and *A* are pulled apart in the pair at the right and pulled closer together in the pair at the left. Kerning can be quite useful for packing words in, or stretching them out, to fit a set line length.

FIGURE 4.19   Kerning letters

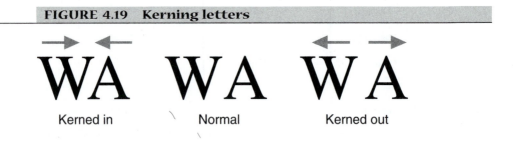

Kerned in   Normal   Kerned out

Sometimes spacing between characters and words is affected by other design elements—for example, a justified right margin. Notice how the words in the justified version shown in Figure 4.20 spread out to fit the right margin. This can create a clean right edge, but sometimes it can also create gaps between words.

FIGURE 4.20   Unjustified versus justified text

Unjustified. In a running line of text, you have some choices about spacing between words—for example, whether to place one or two spaces after a period. Choosing a justified or an unjustified right margin will also affect the spacing between words. Notice how the words in the justified version are spread out to accommodate the right margin.

Justified. In a running line of text, you have some choices about spacing between words—for example, whether to place one or two spaces after a period. Choosing a justified or an unjustified right margin will also affect the spacing between words. Notice how the words in the justified version are spread out to accommodate the right margin.

Vertical Spacing—Superscript/Subscript.   You can also adjust the vertical spacing of letters by using superscripts (above the line) and subscripts (below the line). These mini-spatial adjustments are often governed by conventions such as footnotes and scientific notations.

The institute was founded in 1890 by John Smith.[15]

Fill the container with H_2O and heat it on the stove.

The new XYZ™ generator will cut your fuel bills in half.

Special Treatments. Ordinarily, you'll design text that flows in straight, even lines. However, on the occasions that you want to be more expressive with type—for example, in a marketing or promotional document—you might decide to do something a little different. For example, to add novelty to the message, you might bend a line of text into a shallow arc.

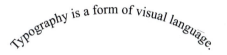

Text design options like WordArt (in Microsoft Word) give you lots of flexibility to improvise with type size, shape, and flow.

Graphic Elements

Linear components also have graphic elements—small lines, marks, and other cues. Some of these graphical forms, like punctuation marks, are highly conventional; others, like iconic letters, can be very original and expressive.

Punctuation Marks. Punctuation is a visual signal system that conducts the linear flow of text. Commas, semicolons, colons, dashes, periods, apostrophes, quotation marks, parentheses, brackets—all are conventional marks of standard English usage. Some of these marks have slight variations in their design, though. For example:

- An em dash is slightly longer than an en dash, and both are longer than a hyphen.

  —   em dash

  –   en dash

  -      hyphen

- Sexed quotation marks curl into the quoted words, a graphical effect that you can see more clearly when it's bigger:

"quote"

While most of these conventional marks are fairly consistent in meaning, some marks adhere to the conventions of disciplines or other discourse communities. For example, to accountants a number that's double underlined means a total, while a number in parentheses means a loss.

155,323.34   (155,323.34)

In European currencies, the conventions differ from those in the United States. The British, for example, use the pound symbol, and use a comma to signify a decimal:

£155,323,34

These illustrate only a few of the many micro-level variations in graphic coding from different disciplines and countries.

Line Work and Shading.   Underlining text, placing a box around text, striking through the text—these are also part of the linear vocabulary of design, as you can see in Figure 4.21. Line work is most often used for emphasis, but in some contexts it can help clarity and contribute to visual tone. Shading selected text also emphasizes it, even while it somewhat degrades clarity. Shading also tends to make text look slightly more sophisticated, particularly in linear contexts.

FIGURE 4.21   Intra-level graphic cues

Please use <u>Type B</u> cleaner in this machine.

Please use │ Type B │ cleaner in this machine.

~~Please use Type B cleaner in this machine.~~

Please use ▒Type B▒ cleaner in this machine.

Iconic Letter Forms.   For special purposes, designers sometimes create letters that suggest, or actually look like, the subject matter of the verbal message—letters that look like ice, wood, metal, animals, whatever. For example, a decorative title for a hotel and convention center in the Upper Peninsula of Michigan might have a woodsy, outdoor look, while the nameplate for a construction company in the Washington D.C. area specializing in Georgian brick masonry might be constructed from, well, lots of bricks (see Figure 4.22).

FIGURE 4.22   Iconic typefaces

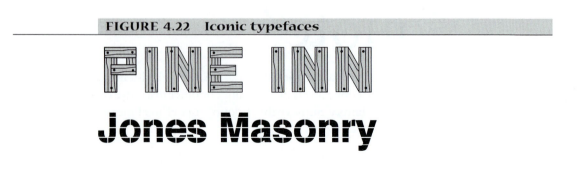

Synergy of the Coding Modes

When you design with type, all three coding modes come into play, with one design choice affecting another. For example, you might begin with a statement that looks like this:

To shut off the heat, turn the valve 90° clockwise.

Then in the *textual* mode, change it to 12-point Helvetica:

To shut off the heat, turn the valve 90° clockwise.

Then in the *spatial* mode, change it to condensed:

To shut off the heat, turn the valve 90° clockwise.

Then in the *graphic* mode, underline selected text:

<u>To shut off the heat,</u> turn the valve 90° clockwise.

Or you can change it in all three modes simultaneously: boldface Bookman, slightly expanded, and double underlining for emphasis.

To shut off the heat, turn the valve 90° <u>clockwise.</u>

As you can see from these variations of this simple line of text, linear components have an extremely rich and flexible vocabulary. And the visual impact of these variations has rhetorical consequences, as we shall now see.

Applying the Cognate Strategies

How do we apply this rich visual vocabulary to a given line of text—whether in print or on a Web site, a PowerPoint presentation, or a road sign? We need to think about how the design of linear components will affect readers. We can do that by considering the six cognate strategies.

Arrangement

Arranging linear components can show relationships among groups of text—individual words and phrases or whole chunks of text. For example, varying the type style in a page of text creates a grouping effect through the perceptual principle of likeness of form (Figure 4.23).

FIGURE 4.23   Text groups through type-style variation

Arranging linear components can show relationships among groups of text–individual words and phrases or whole chunks of text. **Arranging linear components can show relationships among groups of text–individual words and phrases or whole chunks of text.** *Arranging linear components can show relationships among groups of text–individual words and phrases or whole chunks of text.* **Arranging linear components can show relationships among groups of text–individual words and phrases or whole chunks of text.** *Arranging linear components can show relationships among groups of text–individual words and phrases or whole*

Varying the type *size* can also define groups, suggesting a hierarchical relation between the large text and the fine print, as shown in Figure 4.24. The larger size dominates the smaller one because of its stronger figure–ground contrast, which is

FIGURE 4.24   Text groups through type-size variation

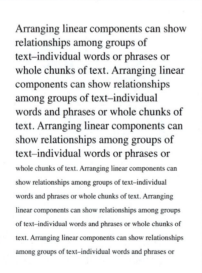

Arranging linear components can show relationships among groups of text–individual words or phrases or whole chunks of text. Arranging linear components can show relationships among groups of text–individual words and phrases or whole chunks of text. Arranging linear components can show relationships among groups of text–individual words or phrases or whole chunks of text. Arranging linear components can show relationships among groups of text–individual words and phrases or whole chunks of text. Arranging linear components can show relationships among groups of text–individual words and phrases or whole chunks of text. Arranging linear components can show relationships among groups of text–individual words and phrases or also an emphasis strategy. Using type styles and sizes as an arrangement strategy is quite conventional. For example, fine print text is usually reserved for notes and minor clarifications and often buried at the bottom of the page or the end of a major text segment. On the other hand, large text usually gets first priority, often at the top of the page, as titles and high-level headings.

Besides the use of typefaces to reveal text structure, arrangement includes spatial choices at the local level—for example, the use of kerning to fit text on a given line. The text below doesn't quite fit the box intended for it, leaving open space on the left and the right:

Tech Notes

Spreading out the letters will fill in the box with textual material.

Tech Notes

Arranging the text this way uses the available space, a conciseness issue, and makes the text look more comfortable within its border, which perhaps adds ethos to the message as well.

Emphasis

As we've seen above, varying the size of the typeface can emphasize text set in large type and deemphasize text set in small type. The degree of emphasis results from the principle of figure–ground contrast. If you browse a magazine, a Web site, or even a newsletter, you'll see a wide range of type sizes that create varying degrees of emphasis within the text, from bold headline type to meek, almost microscopic notes.

Creating emphasis *within* a line of text also relies on the perceptual principle of figure–ground contrast. For example, if you send an e-mail message and you want your readers to get the point, you might capitalize a few words for emphasis.

Thanks for your message this morning. I agree we need more time to prepare for our meeting. Let's meet instead NEXT WEDNESDAY AT ONE. If you have a conflict, let me know right away.

In print you'll have many more options for creating textual contrast. Suppose you want to draw your readers' attention to the warning below, which will appear in an instructional manual for a grinder:

Warning! Unplug the grinder before oiling.

You can use a variety of strategies to create emphasis, ranging from subtle to extreme. We can change the typeface to Helvetica and boldface it.

Warning! Unplug the grinder before oiling.

We can enlarge the type size to 14 point:

Warning! Unplug the grinder before oiling.

And add space between the letters:

Warning! Unplug the grinder before oiling.

Or create a hierarchy, emphasizing the warning first, the specific instructions second.

Warning! Unplug the grinder before oiling.

Of course, these effects are hard to gauge because we don't have the full perceptual context—how the warning contrasts with other text and images on the page. We also don't know the specifics about the rhetorical situation—the context in which readers will actually encounter this message (e.g., in a workshop while servicing the grinder), how likely readers are to leave the grinder plugged in, and the consequences if they do so while oiling the machine. This last issue—the potential physical harm from not doing the task correctly—has ethical and legal implications. *Careful attention to emphasis can help prevent your readers from injuring themselves. Lack of emphasis can result in disaster.*

Emphasis within a line of text also causes subtle psychological shifts from one part of the message to another, just as we raise or lower our voice to shift the emphasis in our speech. Let's say this sentence appears in a brochure selling custom-made furniture:

All of our pieces are crafted by hand from the finest-quality materials.

What should we emphasize and how? We could start by underlining the two most important selling points.

All of our pieces are crafted <u>by hand</u> from the <u>finest-quality materials.</u>

And if we think that's not emphatic enough, we could add boldface:

> All of our pieces are crafted **<u>by hand</u>** from the **<u>finest-quality materials.</u>**

As well as small caps:

> All of our pieces are crafted <u>BY HAND</u> from the <u>FINEST-QUALITY MATERIALS.</u>

But that might look as if we're gloating, damaging our ethos. So let's save face and choose *one* of the three treatments:

> All of our pieces are crafted **by hand** from the **finest-quality materials.**

Or if we want a more subtle look, a softer sell, we might settle for simple italics:

> All of our pieces are crafted *by hand* from the *finest-quality materials.*

But this isn't necessarily the best design choice for implementing our emphasis strategy: It depends on how subtle or obvious we want to be with our readers as well as how much visual emphasis occurs across the whole message. If we emphasize too much text—line to line, across the whole page—the figure–ground contrast will evaporate and nothing will stand out. Excessive emphasis can undermine the ethos of our message because readers will cease to believe that anything is important. They'll think we're visually "crying wolf."

Clarity

Clarity pertains to the ease with which readers can pick up information in the text. Research on legibility has examined how well readers can process text in various type sizes and fonts. Several factors determine legibility: type style, type size, upper-/lowercase, boldface, and italics—to name some of the most important. Below are some findings from well-known sources, including Miles A. Tinker's *Legibility of Print*. As we pointed out in Chapter 3, universal research can provide important but limited guidelines for design. The rhetorical situation may call for something different, leading you to flout rather than follow the research findings.

Type Style.   Commonly used typefaces (Tinker studied ten) have roughly equal legibility. Only a typeface with a marked difference (such as Old English) significantly reduces legibility (Tinker 51; 64). In other words, readers can comprehend text about as easily with one typeface as with another.

Of course, that doesn't mean that readers will prefer all typefaces equally; as Burt (8) showed, they'll probably process text most comfortably in a typeface they're used to. On the other hand, if one of your purposes is to grab your readers' attention, you might choose a less familiar typeface, even though it might not be as legible.

In some situations, then, using a novel typeface—on a limited basis—might be preferable to using a more legible one.

Sans Serif versus Serif.   Research has shown no significant difference between the legibility of serif and sans serif type (Tinker 64). Some designers, like Jan White (14, 26), however, claim that serifs have a functional value because they carry your eye across the line and therefore make the text more legible. You can see this effect in Figure 4.25; look at the line of serif text and the isolation of the serifs

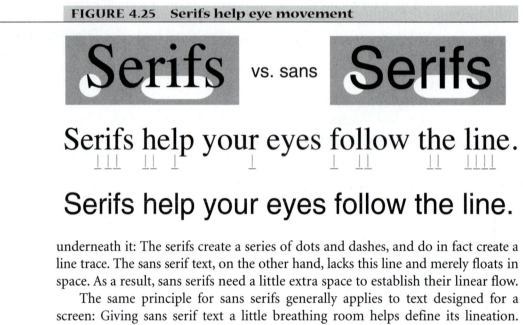

FIGURE 4.25   Serifs help eye movement

underneath it: The serifs create a series of dots and dashes, and do in fact create a line trace. The sans serif text, on the other hand, lacks this line and merely floats in space. As a result, sans serifs need a little extra space to establish their linear flow.

The same principle for sans serifs generally applies to text designed for a screen: Giving sans serif text a little breathing room helps define its lineation. However, serif text can lose its linear effect on the screen. Depending on its size and style and on the resolution of your computer screen, serif type may create noise— eroding rather than enhancing the clarity of your text. More on that in Chapter 5.

Type Size.   Type sizes can make a big difference in legibility. For body text, 10-, 11-, and 12-point type are generally the most legible. Overall, readers prefer 11-point type first, followed by 10-point, then 12-point (Tinker 72). In Figure 4.26 you can see the erosion in legibility in type sizes smaller and larger than these optimal sizes.

FIGURE 4.26   Type size affects legibility

6   Typography is a form of visual language

7   Typography is a form of visual language

8   Typography is a form of visual language

9   Typography is a form of visual language

10   Typography is a form of visual language

11   Typography is a form of visual language

12   Typography is a form of visual language

13   Typography is a form of visual language

14   Typography is a form of visual language

15   Typography is a form of visual language

16   Typography is a form of visual language

On screens, this erosion in clarity will be much more dramatic for small type sizes. While you can probably still read 9-, 8-, and even 7- or 6-point type in print, on screen these small sizes will be nearly impossible to read because the resolution is generally poorer than in print.

Of course, the clarity of a type size depends on the rhetorical situation. If the audience consists of elderly persons, you'll probably want to use a larger typeface—maybe as large as 14- or 16-point. The context in which readers encounter your message may also affect clarity. For example, if your readers examine a set of instructions posted on a workplace wall, 12-, 14-, or even 16-point type may be way too small. On the other hand, if you're dealing with limited space—ingredients on a small food package—you may have little choice but to use a small typeface.

Upper- versus Lowercase.   For most reading situations, words in lowercase letters are more legible than those in uppercase. This difference is due to the distinctiveness of lowercase letters, evident in the external shape of words (Tinker 42, see also Benson 37).

For example, compare the shape of the word *party* in uppercase versus lowercase (Figure 4.27). The lowercase version creates a more distinct word form, while the letters in the uppercase version tend to run together because they're all the same height.

FIGURE 4.27   Word shapes in all caps and lowercase

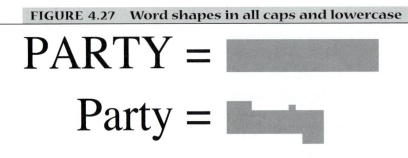

UPPERCASE TEXT ISN'T MUCH OF A PROBLEM FOR A WORD OR TWO, BUT DESIGNING TEXT IN CONTINUOUS UPPERCASE CAN ANNOY YOUR READERS BECAUSE THEY HAVE TO WORK HARDER TO PROCESS THE MESSAGE. SOME READERS MAY GET FRUSTRATED AND EVEN QUIT READING. YOU'RE PROBABLY TEMPTED TO DO THAT ABOUT NOW, SO WE WON'T TEST YOUR PATIENCE ANYMORE!

Is it ever appropriate to sacrifice clarity with continuous uppercase text? One possibility might be a message that needs a very formal tone—for example, an invitation, or a collection letter.

Boldface.   Although boldface type can be read at the same rate as ordinary lowercase, readers don't prefer it (Tinker 65). Therefore, you should use boldface very selectively. Reading boldface over long stretches of text can be tiring and irritating. Why? At first glance, boldface text appears to have stronger figure–ground contrast than normal text—and it does, on the outside edges of the words. However, when you look at an enlargement of a boldfaced word, you can see that the figure–ground actually diminishes because the boldface fills the internal spaces of the letters:

group   group

As a result, 10-point Palatino in boldface actually appears smaller than normal.

As a result, normal 10-point Palatino actually appears smaller in boldface.

As a result, normal 10-point Palatino actually appears smaller in boldface.

Italic.   Italic text is less legible than normal text (Tinker 65). Italicizing text will slightly thin out the lines in a typeface, as you can see below:

italic   *italic*

As a result, italic type has less figure–ground contrast than normal type; across a line of text, italic takes less space. Compare this same text to the italic version below.

As a result, italic type has less figure–ground contrast than normal type; across a line of text, italic takes less space. Compare this same text to the italic version below.

While empirical research can give us some general guidelines about how to achieve clarity, ultimately clarity depends on what readers are used to. For example, it's likely that readers will process normally spaced text better than expanded text.

While empirical research can give us some general guidelines about how to achieve clarity, ultimately clarity depends on what readers are used to. For example, it's not likely that readers will process expanded text as easily as they will process normally spaced text.

But then again, what readers are used to can vary across disciplines, cultures, national borders, and time. For example, Gutenberg printed books in a Gothic script that imitated the manuscript writing that readers were used to but that today's readers would find nearly illegible. Gestalt principles notwithstanding, clarity depends heavily on the reader's previous experience. On the other hand, as we've seen above, optimal clarity isn't always the best option either; sometimes you might sacrifice some clarity to enhance one or more other strategies.

Conciseness

When you design linear components, you'll often find a close connection between conciseness and clarity. Take serifs, for example. A simple way to achieve conciseness is to replace a serif typeface (here Cheltenham)

message

with a sans serif typeface (here Helvetica).

message

Removing serifs from typefaces was a hallmark of 20th-century modernism, which aimed to make design lean and functional by eliminating ornament. Today, modernism still influences many aspects of design, including what we regard as functional and ornamental. However, as we've seen earlier, serifs do have some functional value—in a print medium at least—so eliminating them purely as a conciseness strategy may actually compromise the clarity of the message.

Another conciseness issue pertains to the space that type consumes. If you use a small typeface, you can shrink the message way down, saving lots of space.

> How much space should the message take? If you use a small typeface, you can shrink the message way down, conserving lots of space. How much space should the message take? If you use a small typeface, you can shrink the message way down, conserving lots of space.

But then again, hardly anyone will read 6-point text—unless it's in high-resolution print, the readers have excellent eyesight, *and* they're highly motivated. Small print may also raise ethical and legal issues: Instructions set in very fine print will conserve space but in some situations—for example, directions for taking a drug—may put readers, especially older ones, at risk. Such a conciseness strategy would fail to meet the rhetorical situation because, in the most basic sense, it might jeopardize the reader's well-being.

On the other hand, most readers aren't likely to appreciate the other extreme, continuous stretches of large text.

> How much space should the message take? If you use a large typeface, you can expand the message, using lots of space. How much space should the message take? If you use a large typeface, you can expand the message, using lots of space.

However, they'll probably be more tolerant of large text on a PowerPoint screen rather than in print. Readers aren't likely to find compressed or expanded text very appealing either; the first is too spatially concise, the latter not spatially concise enough:

> How much space should the message take? If you use a condensed typeface, you can shrink the message way down, conserving lots of space. How much space should the message take? If you use a condensed typeface, you can shrink the message way down, conserving lots of space.

> How much space should the message take? If you use loosely spaced type, you can expand the message, using lots of space. How much space should the message take? If you use loosely spaced type, you can expand the message, using lots of space.

Nor, as we've seen above, are readers likely to be comfortable reading pieces of bulked-up boldface:

How much space should the message take? If you use a bold typeface, you can give the message visual bulk. How much space should the message take? If you use a bold typeface, you can give the message visual bulk.

And they probably won't find skinny italic very pleasing either, especially if they have to read italic text on a screen:

How much space should the message take? If you use an italic typeface, you can conserve space. How much space should the message take? If you use an italic typeface, you can conserve space.

In most instances, conciseness directly influences clarity—too much or too little conciseness may result in less legible text.

Tone

Tone can change immensely from one typeface to another—though it's often hard to explain exactly how or why. Researchers have been puzzling over this problem for decades, trying to pin down the "atmosphere value" of typefaces (Spencer 29–30). Still, we know intuitively that when we design a statement to look like this:

Please attend the weekly staff meeting next Monday.

it sounds different than the same message that looks like this:

Please attend the weekly staff meeting next Monday.

or like this:

Please attend the weekly staff meeting next Monday.

So how do we select a typeface to express the right tone? We can begin by considering two key issues: degree of formality and level of technicality.

Formality.   What makes a typeface look formal? Convention probably dictates some of our responses. We're used to seeing uppercase in rhetorical situations where formality is the accepted protocol: uppercase for titles of universities, preambles to charters, and on inscriptions on memorials and friezes of buildings. Partly because of convention, partly because of its square, chiseled look, uppercase type tends to look serious and formal.

UPPERCASE AND SCRIPTS TEND TO LOOK FORMAL.

Scripts like Old English and Zapf Chancery also derive their formality from convention because they're frequently used for certificates, awards, announcements, and invitations.

𝔘𝔭𝔭𝔢𝔯𝔠𝔞𝔰𝔢 𝔞𝔫𝔡 𝔰𝔠𝔯𝔦𝔭𝔱𝔰 𝔱𝔢𝔫𝔡 𝔱𝔬 𝔩𝔬𝔬𝔨 𝔣𝔬𝔯𝔪𝔞𝔩.

Uppercase and scripts tend to look formal.

Among these three we can further distinguish levels of formality: The uppercase text looks authoritarian and rather cold, perhaps because of its blocky, uniform appearance. The two scripts, on the other hand, look more festive and personal, perhaps because they appear to be hand-made, as if the writer carefully formed each stroke. Of the two scripts shown above, the first, Old English, looks more serious and traditional, perhaps because of its cultural identity with the past—though non-Western readers might not make the same association.

At the other end of the spectrum, some typefaces have an informal, expressive, or even playful look. The first typeface below, Twang, is informal and projects a carefree tone. The second typeface, Avant Garde, is a also light, but its geometric design makes it look more modern and a little less personal.

Some typefaces have an informal or even playful look.

Some typefaces have an informal or even playful look.

Formal or informal, serious or playful—a type style isn't necessarily limited to one tone or another simply because of its basic design. We can take a relatively serious typeface like Helvetica and lighten it up a bit by inflating the letters with an outline treatment:

Some typefaces have an informal or even playful look.

Level of Technicality.   Some typefaces look cool and objective, others personal, humane, and empathetic. Why? Sans serifs like Univers display the clean, machinelike look of modernism. Perhaps that's why it looks technical and objective.

Sans serifs like Univers display the clean, machinelike look of modernism.

The OCRA typeface takes the level of technicality to the extreme.

```
The OCRA typeface takes the level of
technicality to the extreme.
```

On the other hand, a serif typeface like Times tends to look less technical and more personable, probably because it's more delicate, bookish, and traditional looking.

On the other hand, a serif typeface like Times tends to look less technical and more personable.

But all of these explanations about the tone of a typeface are based on subjective impressions as well as on conventional practices—which typefaces people actually use in certain situations. Research can take some of the mystery out of this. Peter Walker, Sylvia Smith, and Alan Livingston had subjects rate selected typefaces according to "multimodal" features such as "cool/warm," "bright/dull," and "heavy/light." They found that the multimodal features that subjects associated with the typeface and with certain professions (chemist, doctor, florist, etc.) correlated with the subjects' selection of an "appropriate" typeface to represent that profession. In other words, they successfully measured the subjective elements of a typeface by cross-checking its multimodal qualities with those of the things it might represent.[3]

Beyond the research and the generalizations about levels of formality and technicality, you'll have to use your rhetorical radar to guide your typeface decisions. So which typeface matches the tone of this text?

a   The 57 hp. engines have two cylinders.

b   The 57 hp. engines have two cylinders.

c   *The 57 hp. engines have two cylinders.*

About all you can do is make some rhetorical hunches: (a) is too stodgy for this subject, (b) looks appropriately technical, and (c) is too personal. Gauging the right typeface to suit the tone of a given situation is a rhetorical art, and we need to know much about the rhetorical situation before we can judge.

Ethos

Linear components can engender ethos, reflecting the credibility or character of the writer/designer as well as the organization as a whole. Like tone, however, ethos can be a slippery concept, because building trust with linear components requires rhetorical judgment, one situation at a time. However, in most of the situations you'll encounter, two design guidelines for building trust will probably apply: matching the typeface with the subject, and creating a professional look.

Matching the Typeface with the Subject.   Text designed in a style that doesn't match the message may quickly alienate readers. The following messages probably won't engender much credibility because of the mismatch between the message and the typeface:

> *The defective bridge beams, which buckled because of the intense live loads, must be replaced immediately.*

> The defective bridge beams, which buckled because of the intense live loads, must be replaced immediately.

A similar credibility problem occurs in the text below. In all caps, boldfaced, and underlined, the text screams at readers, suggesting a false sense of urgency.

> <u>AFTER YOU HAVE GATHERED THE REQUIRED TOOLS</u>
> <u>AND MATERIALS, YOU ARE READY TO INSTALL YOUR</u>
> <u>NEW MAGICPANE WINDOW. FIRST, CAREFULLY REMOVE</u>
> <u>THE WINDOW FROM THE CARDBOARD BOX.</u>

This design may have doubly negative consequences: It might erode the ethos of this message as well as that of other text elements in the document, which the reader may consider frivolous if they have less visual emphasis than this one.

Creating a Professional Look.   Linear components lead readers to form impressions about the character and competence of the designer or the organization the text represents. For example, a design that's too busy, like the one below, can quickly diminish the reader's confidence:

> After you have gathered the required tools and materials, you are ready to install your new Magic-Pane window. First, carefully remove the window from the cardboard box.

For instructions, this text looks clumsy, overwrought, and hollow. Will readers make similar judgments about the company that makes MagicPane windows? Trust can also be eroded through inattention to editing details:

> THe new procedure is outlined in a recent issue of the Jour*nal of Biochemistry.*

Just as with tone, gauging ethos can be done most effectively with respect to the rhetorical situation. Take the statement below:

> *We sincerely appreciate the hard work you've put in this past month. Without your cooperation we couldn't have reached our goal.*

In one rhetorical situation the Kaufmann® typeface might build ethos, whereas in another it might undermine it. For example, if readers in a car manufacturing plant had to work overtime under duress, they might find such a personal message from the plant manager disingenuous. On the other hand, if this message were written from the director of a nonprofit organization to a cadre of dedicated volunteers, the readers might find the typeface believable and sincere.

Interdependence of the Cognate Strategies

For analysis or teaching purposes we can talk about the cognate strategies individually, but within a given rhetorical situation all six must work together. In the example and discussion that follow, you'll see how design decisions that bring one strategy into play can affect other strategies.

Dennis Murphy is president and CEO of Kray-Com, a manufacturer of semiconductor products. A reformed heavy smoker, Murph (as his employees call him) has wanted to make Kray-Com smoke-free for some time, but he's a savvy enough executive to know that an imperious order from the boss might have more negative repercussions than the same order coming from a group of employees. Therefore, over many weeks Murph has skillfully guided the discussions of the Management–Employee Advisory Work group as they addressed the smoking issue.

That group voted overwhelmingly to make Kray-Com a smoke-free work environment. But even in this moment of private victory, Murph knows that the memo announcing the work group's decision, which will go out over his signature as president and CEO, must be written and designed carefully in order to maximize cooperation and minimize potential bad feelings. Although Murph knows that the no smoking policy is the right thing to do, he has to express the health benefits as sincerely and positively as possible through the visual and verbal language of his memo. After going through several drafts, the memo finally appears (Figure 4.28).

The choice of ITC Bookman type for the message results from *clarity, tone,* and *ethos* strategies. Conventionally, Kray-Com internal memos appear in Helvetica or Univers, both technical-looking sans serif fonts. The significantly different look of the Bookman type will grab readers' attention, telling them this is more than a routine announcement. The serifs themselves will make the lines of text a tad easier on the eye, enhancing *clarity*. At the same time, Bookman has a calm, humane, and reassuring look.

Murph achieves *ethos* by using the Lithos Black type style for the Kray-Com name throughout the body of the memo. Because readers are used to seeing the Kray-Com logo in this font, repeating it in the memo will tell readers that the new smoke-free policy was a group decision that has the full authority of Kray-Com

FIGURE 4.28   Kray-Com memo (reduced in size)

Internal memorandum

Date: May 29, 200-
To: All **KRAY-COM** Employees
From: Dennis Murphy, President and CEO
Subject: Smoke-free workplace

On behalf of the Management-Employee Advisory Workgroup, I am
sending this memo to personally notify you that starting August 1, 200-,
KRAY-COM will be a totally smoke-free workplace.

As you know, this issue has been controversial and divisive. **KRAY-COM**
has always tried to promote employee health and well-being, yet we also
make every effort to respect individual rights. I want to assure you that
the MEA Workgroup has worked very hard to hear all points of view, to
gather as much information as possible, and to develop a workable plan.

The implementation plan features a phased-in schedule and a series of
free quit-smoking clinics (to be held during work hours). In addition, we
have negotiated with our group health insurance carrier a modest
reduction in premiums for non-smoking employees, including any
current smokers who can successfully quit within the next six months.

For the period of June 1 through July 31, **KRAY-COM** will establish
special, isolated smoking rooms for use during work breaks. A map
showing these designated areas will be sent out within the week.
Employees who choose to smoke may also do so outside the buildings, in
those areas where smoking is now permitted. Beginning August 1, only
outside smoking will be allowed.

The free quit-smoking clinics–to be offered by RAMSEY HEALTH
ASSOCIATES–will consist of two one-hour sessions per week for four
weeks. Clinics will start June 3, with a new group starting every other
week. To join, contact Mandy Rodrigues in the Personnel Office.

Information on qualifying for the non-smoker reduction in health
insurance premiums can be obtained from Dennis Cjakowski in the
Payroll Office. If you have any questions, please feel free to contact me by
phone (5-1100) or by e-mail (dmurph).

behind it. The logotype for Ramsey Health Associates enhances the ethos of the memo by assuring readers that the nonsmoking clinics will be run by respected professionals.

The primary *arrangement* issue for Murph was choosing a type style and size that ensured that his memo fit on a single page but at the same time used all the available space within the visual field. If the memo spilled onto another page, Murph might lose some credibility ("another long-winded statement from the powers-that-be!"), but if the memo were only half a page long it might not look substantive enough. A minor *conciseness* issue entails Murph's choice of parentheses for his phone number and e-mail address. He could have used em dashes or commas or even made a separate notation at the bottom of the page.

Murph's simple but important memo is designed for its specific rhetorical situation, which is rather delicate here, both politically and personally, because the news will have a major impact on the lives of its readers. The design decisions he makes to execute the cognate strategies involve some trade-offs and compromises, but this occurs in virtually any professional communication.

Notes

1. Two excellent resources for more detailed explanations about the technical aspects of typography are Wendell Crow's *Communication Graphics* and Jan White's *Graphic Design for the Electronic Age.*
2. The information about Chinese typeface conventions came from Yong-Kang Wei; the information about Egyptian conventions came from Lee Tesdell. Both Wei and Tesdell completed Ph.D.s in rhetoric and professional communication at Iowa State University.
3. Other research on the "atmosphere value" of typefaces is summarized in Herbert Spencer. Eva Brumberger has conducted research on the "persona" of typefaces ("Persona") and on their rhetorical fit for a given verbal text ("Awareness"); Jo Mackiewicz has devised a system for evaluating typeface "personality" by correlating her research with design features of the letters *J, a, g, e,* and *n.* See also Camille L. Rowe for research on the "connotative" elements of typefaces.

References

Benson, Philippa J. "Writing Visually: Design Considerations in Technical Publications." *Technical Communication* 32 (1985): 35–39.

Brumberger, Eva R. "The Rhetoric of Typography: The Awareness and Impact of Typeface Appropriateness." *Technical Communication* 50 (2003): 224–231.

Brumberger, Eva R. "The Rhetoric of Typography: The Persona of Typeface and Text." *Technical Communication* 50 (2003): 206–223.

Burt, Cyril L. *A Psychological Study of Typography*. Cambridge: Cambridge University Press, 1959.

Crow, Wendell C. *Communication Graphics*. Englewood Cliffs, NJ: Prentice-Hall, 1986.

Mackiewicz, Jo. "How to Use Five Letterforms to Gauge a Typeface's Personality: A Research-Driven Method." *Journal of Technical Writing and Communication* 35 (2005): 291–315.

Rowe, Camille L. "The Connotative Dimensions of Selected Display Typefaces." *Information Design Journal* 3.1 (1982): 30–37.

Spencer, Herbert. *The Visible Word*. 2nd ed. New York: Hastings, 1969.

Tinker, Miles A. *Legibility of Print*. Ames, IA: Iowa State University Press, 1963.

Walker, Peter, Sylvia Smith, and Alan Livingston. "Predicting the Appropriateness of a Typeface on the Basis of Its Multi-Modal Features." *Information Design Journal* 5 (1986): 29–42.

White, Jan V. *Graphic Design for the Electronic Age*. New York: Watson-Guptill, 1988.

Exercises

1. Below are several different versions of a *danger* warning.

   a. Informally catalog the differences among the versions with respect to the following visual design categories:

      - Serif versus sans serif
      - Type size
      - Graphic options (punctuation, background shading)
      - Treatments (bold, italics, shadow)

   b. In what contexts might some of these versions be more credible than the others? Less credible? How do clarity and emphasis affect ethos in these examples? For instance, are the most legible and most emphatic versions the ones readers are most likely to *believe*?

2. Below are letterhead names for three small businesses, shown in 24-point Palatino. Kathy's Klip Korner is a hairstyling salon for women; Custom Car Stereos designs and installs automobile sound-systems; Grover's Donuts & Rolls is a pastry shop (not a full-fledged bakery—they don't do bread).

   Select a font that will be likely to align visually with each business's purpose and clientele. If appropriate, tweak the look of the letterhead by using typographical treatments such as italics or bold, spacing techniques such as widening or condensing, or graphic treatments such as underlining or gray scale.

Kathy's Klip Korner

Custom Car Stereos

Grover's Donuts & Rolls

3. Below are four different versions of a brief internal memo sent by a department manager to her subordinates. The typeface design in each of the four versions establishes a visual tone. Your job is to describe as precisely as you can the tone of each sample, then apply your description to the rhetorical situation.

   a. To help you describe the visual tone of each sample, we've created five continua below. Decide where each of the four versions fits on each continuum—toward the left, the right, or somewhere in between (center would be neutral). When you're done, you should have four numbers on each continuum.

formal	_____	informal
serious	_____	relaxed
technical	_____	nontechnical
authoritative	_____	tentative
friendly	_____	unfriendly

   1) We need to meet next Wednesday afternoon at 3:00 to discuss the results of last month's customer survey. Please come prepared to justify your area's request for additional marketing expenditures. We must finish our quarterly forecast before Thursday morning's general staff meeting.

   2) We need to meet next Wednesday afternoon at 3:00 to discuss the results of last month's customer survey. Please come prepared

to justify your area's request for additional marketing expenditures. We must finish our quarterly forecast before Thursday morning's general staff meeting.

3) We need to meet next Wednesday afternoon at 3:00 to discuss the results of last month's customer survey. Please come prepared to justify your area's request for additional marketing expenditures. We must finish our quarterly forecast before Thursday morning's general staff meeting.

4) *We need to meet next Wednesday afternoon at 3:00 to discuss the results of last month's customer survey. Please come prepared to justify your areas request for additional marketing expenditures. We must finish our quarterly forecast before Thursday morning's general staff meeting.*

b. When you're finished, you'll probably have very different tone profiles for each of the four versions. Based on your profiles, which version do you think best fits the rhetorical situation? Why? What assumptions have you made about the rhetorical situation that influenced your choice? What changes in your assumptions might make any of the other versions more appropriate than the one you chose?

4. Find a Web site that offers a product or service for sale. Use the questions below to guide your analysis of the linear components in the site.

a. How many different typeface variations can you identify in the site? If more than one typeface is used, how do the typefaces differ (serifs, x-heights, line quality)? How do the typefaces vary in their *treatments* (size, italics, underlining, boldface, etc.)?

b. The typefaces you see on your screen may depend on selections you (or someone else) made in the software. For example, you (or someone else) may have chosen Helvetica as the main display type for your screen when you access Web sites.

  ▪ If you *can't* change the typefaces on your screen, how appropriate are the type styles and sizes for this rhetorical situation? What effect do they have on clarity and conciseness? On tone and ethos?

  ▪ If you *can* change the typefaces on your screen, which type style and size do you think best matches this site? Why? What effect does your typeface choice have on clarity and conciseness? On tone and ethos?

5. The following text has several inconsistencies in linear components that undermine both its clarity and its ethos. Note each of the visual editing problems. You should find at least ten.

The experimental field plot used in the research was located in Alcorn county, five miles west of Granger. Six hybrid seed corn types were used in the study - - three of them variations of GoldleafTM, three of them variations of Circle 200™. results showed that Goldleaf™ outperformed Circle 200 ™ in pest resistance, while both had ab*ove average yields*. A follow—up study on a plot in Jackson county is planned for next year ,contingent on funding .

Assignments

1. The president of the local student chapter of the Society for Technical Communication (STC) has composed the text below announcing the first meeting of the semester. The text will be a single-page 8½" × 11" flyer distributed in writing and communication classes to majors, as well as to all interested faculty. The flyer will also be taped to the walls and doors in selected campus locations where lots of people will see it.

   As a member of STC, you've been asked to produce a finished flyer from this text. The goal of your flyer is to get students (and faculty) to come to the first meeting, especially students who are interested in professional communication and who have never attended a meeting before. So your flyer should grab the attention of your readers and persuade them to attend the meeting.

   In designing your flyer, you may select any typefaces or type sizes, arrange the text as you wish, or use graphic elements that you think appropriate for this situation. You can make minor editing changes to accommodate your visual choices, but the verbal text should remain essentially intact. Your document will be reproduced at a campus copy center, so your design will have to conform to the paper and printing options available there.

Text for the flyer:

```
Want to meet students outside your classes?
Interested in becoming a professional writer?
Clueless about the job market?
Thinking about going to graduate school?
If you answered yes to any of these questions, or if
you're just curious about what technical communicators
do, join us for the first STC meeting.
Guest speaker: Amy Stevens, Web designer, Cape
Technologies, Greenville, NC
Topic: Designing Web sites That Sell
Friday, September 22, 4:00, Chapman Hall
Munchies and soft drinks provided
```

2. Minor league baseball is coming to the Passamaquoddy River Valley! The Passamaquoddy Polecats are joining the New York–Penn League.

The new team has a name (and a dandy mascot that looks like a giant deranged weasel), but the owners need some help developing a corporate identity for the ball club, in particular a logotype representation of *Passamaquoddy Polecats* that can be used on letterhead stationery, on business cards, on posters and other forms of advertisements, on the team's Web site, and even on the ballplayers' uniforms.

Your communication design firm has been hired to create the necessary logotypes for the Polecats, and you've been named to spearhead the project. The first thing you need to do is some research on logotypes so you'll have a sense of what's already out there. The second thing you'll need to do is check out some Web sites of minor league baseball teams. Doing this will help you understand how baseball logotypes actually function.

Once you've created a logotype that you believe will work, lay it out on a mock-up page of letterhead stationery, at least one marketing document (e.g., brochure, flyer, or poster), a business card, and a T-shirt or jacket. Be prepared to share your logotype layouts with the class and discuss the rhetorical decisions that drove your design.

5 Text

Fields

Introduction to Text Fields

Ordinarily, when you think about business or technical communications, you probably envision text—lines and lines of it sprawling across a page or some other surface such as the panels of a brochure or a computer screen. You saw in the previous chapter that the lines of text themselves—*the linear components*—provide lots of design opportunities for adapting your communication to your audience, purpose, and context. In this chapter you'll examine text design in a larger domain, something we'll call a *field*.

What is a field of text? In traditional terms, you might think of paragraphs, lists, or other chunks of text. Or if you're browsing the Web, you might think in terms of menus, navigational bars, or pop-up ads. Despite the differences among these types of fields, all of them share one essential trait: *a distinguishable area of visual interest or attention.* Fields, then, whether they occur as ink on paper or pixels on a screen, can be defined by our immediate attention to textual information on a two-dimensional surface.

In recent years, technology has transformed field design in professional communication, giving us new and exciting tools to design text. Where a communication might have once looked like one big chunk (Figure 5.1a), we now have the capability, even for the most ordinary message, to make design choices such as multiple columns (Figure 5.1b) or text that wraps around pictures or illustrations (Figure 5.1c). We have at our disposal design tools for shading behind text (Figure 5.2a), using white-on-black text (Figure 5.2b) or color, or employing spacing, line work, and other nontextual cues (Figure 5.2c).

FIGURE 5.1   Text layout possibilities

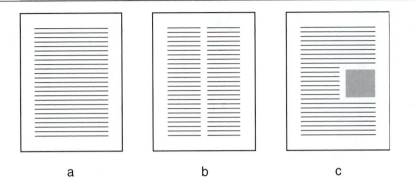

FIGURE 5.2   Nontextual design cues

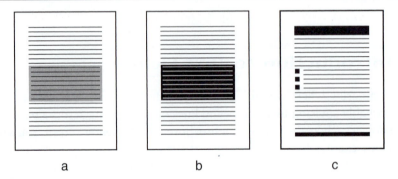

When we have all of these options, the term *page* becomes quite relative. For instance, a newsletter may physically consist of a single page but be divided into separate visual chunks, or subfields, as shown in Figure 5.3a. Likewise, one side of a brochure may consist of a single sheet of paper but be visually divided into three panels (Figure 5.3b).

FIGURE 5.3   Subfields and panels

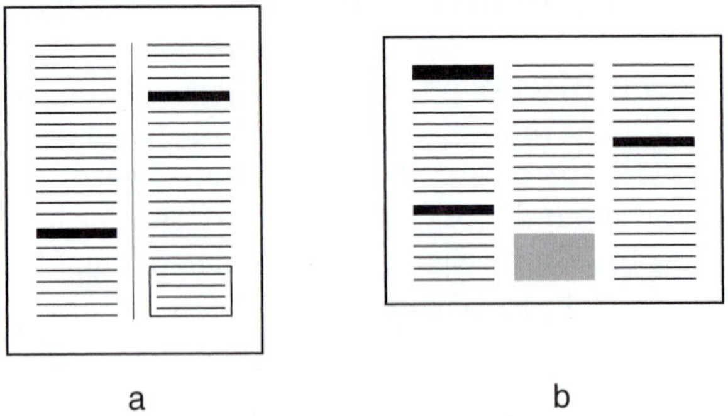

On the other hand, a multiple page layout may contain elements that run *across* two or more pages (Figure 5.4), or may comprise a single visual entity, such as the options display in Fred's Mapleton document (Figure 5.5).

FIGURE 5.4   Multiple page layout with unifying element

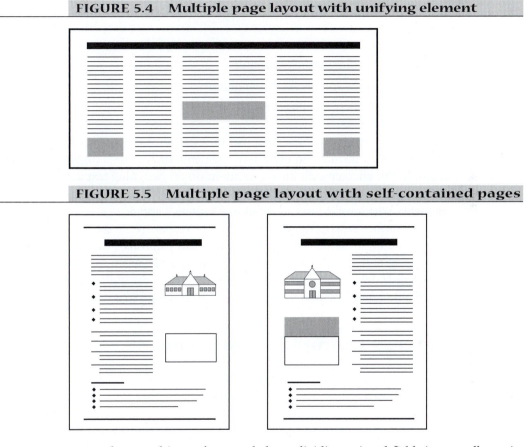

FIGURE 5.5   Multiple page layout with self-contained pages

Nearly everything we've noted about dividing printed fields into smaller units also applies to computer screens. Like the printed page, screens can display text and images in a variety of configurations such as the one in Figure 5.6.

FIGURE 5.6   Sample screen display

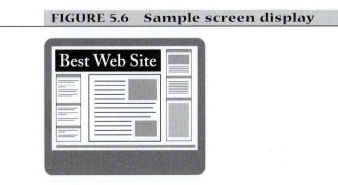

Fields, then, can be extremely flexible, ranging from a large physical surface—a fold-out page that opens into a poster, a double-page computer screen—to smaller units, or subfields, that exist within a larger field—for example, a boxed insert in a newsletter or a navigational bar on a Web page. Whether in print or on screen, our access to information within a field can be enhanced by visual cues in all three modes:

- Textual: headings, numbers, letters
- Spatial: paragraph blocks, lists, columns
- Graphic: bullets, shading, lines

In the context of professional communication, a field may often consist of a *combination* of textual and extra-level elements such as data displays, pictures, or icons. In this chapter we'll focus our attention on designing text within a field—in the textual, spatial, and graphic modes—and simply "box out" areas for extra-level elements, which we'll cover in detail in Chapters 7 and 8.

As in other areas of design, fields must be responsive to the rhetorical situation in which they are actually going to be used. Text columns, headings, bullets, boxes, and paragraph breaks—these are meaningful only when readers use them to accomplish some end. Before we explore the visual vocabulary of text fields, let's watch a designer in action as he adapts his field design to a rhetorical situation.

Process Example—Text Fields

Matt Reisner, a freelance document designer, has been asked to develop a one-page fact sheet for Prescott and Associates Engineering and Development. As Prescott has grown, many people—clients, investors, and employees—visit the office or inquire about the company, and staff members have nothing to give them. The fact sheet will at least temporarily meet this need.

While at Prescott working on a larger project, Matt gathered the information he needed for the fact sheet. The office manager, Jean Sullivan, also gave him a brief note from Joe Prescott, president of the company and son of its founder. After drafting the remainder of the text from his notes, Matt realizes that writing any more would be useless until he begins to see his text take shape on the page. Here's what he has to work with.

```
From the President:

Welcome to Clyde Prescott and Associates Engineering and
Development. Whether you are a developer, prospective
homeowner, or investor, Prescott is pleased to outline
our services for you. At your request, our staff will be
```

pleased to give you additional information or to answer
your questions. Thanks for your interest in our company.
Joe Prescott

History. Prescott was founded in 1968 by William
Prescott, an engineer and builder whose innovations in
foundation and soil design received national recognition. By 1980 Prescott grew from three employees to over
fifty. Today Prescott has two hundred employees with
branch offices in Milwaukee and Denver and building
projects that span from coast to coast, to Europe, and
to the Middle East.

Recent Projects. Heirloom Community. This state-of-the-
art retirement center includes a variety of residential
structures, including individual units, townhouses, and
apartments. Heirloom Community was recently recognized
as an outstanding design for senior citizens.

Shoreline Harbor. This waterfront development on Lake
Michigan houses over 100 business and professional
offices. It has been recognized as one of the best historical designs in the Midwest.

Plateau Irrigation. This unique irrigation system
provides a reliable, year-round source of fresh water
for farmers and ranchers in southern Montana. It has
been recognized as the most cost-efficient system in
the area.

Employees. Prescott's professional staff includes over
100 engineers and designers. Engineering specialties
include civil, mechanical, environmental, structural,
and electrical. Design specialties include residential,
historical preservation, interior, and landscape.

Offices. Main office at 125 W. Jackson, Chicago, IL.
Branch offices at 310 N. Oak, Milwaukee, WI, and 5577
Mountain View, Denver, CO.

Projects completed in 2008. 11 in the U.S., 3 international; net worth of building projects in 2008:
$24,500,000.

Management. Joe Prescott, President; Jean Sullivan,
Office Manager; Frank LaVesta, Chief Engineer; Allan
Perch, Chief Designer.

Matt has done a few consulting jobs for Prescott before, so he knows something about who their clients are and the image they want to portray. Jean Sullivan wants something simple but professional that Prescott can use to introduce people to their organization.

Analyzing the Rhetorical Situation

As Matt begins to envision some possible designs, he assesses the rhetorical situation—audience, purpose, context.

- *Audience.* The main readers will be potential clients who visit the office or inquire in writing; they'll use the fact sheet to get a quick first impression of the company. Other readers will include prospective investors, home buyers, and employees. Because Prescott has begun contracting work overseas, part of the audience will also consist of international readers from Europe, the Middle East, and Asia.

- *Purpose.* The fact sheet must enable readers to get a quick picture of the company, so clarity will be foremost. Ethos will also play a major role since the document needs to project a professional look. Although the piece needs to be persuasive by creating a positive first impression, it should look professional, objective, and technical rather than promotional or glitzy.

- *Context.* Readers will receive the fact sheet in the reception area at one of the Prescott offices, at a client meeting in a conference room, as an enclosure in a response to inquiry, or as a PDF attached to an e-mail. They won't take much time to examine it, so the content has to be very accessible and legible.

Invention

The first thing that Matt wants to do is to create a format that will enable his readers to scan the document quickly for key information. He'd like to get all the information on a single page, so he starts by estimating how much space he has to work with. He has no model or conventional format to guide his work, so he thinks of the fact sheet as a kind of company résumé that highlights their key accomplishments.

He distributes the text across the page, using headings to map each segment. In his initial plan, headings are his main signaling device, and he uses bold and italics to make them stand out from the body text. He chooses Avant Garde because he wants the cool, factual look of a sans serif. He also wants a font that looks contemporary and a bit elegant, enhancing the ethos of the fact sheet. The Avant Garde not only looks contemporary but also has an international flavor, which might help the document appeal to readers outside North America. Initially, Matt uses 11-point because he wants to spread the text over the whole page. (Note: Figures 5.7 through 5.10 show the fact sheet reduced to approximately 70 percent of its actual size.)

For the main heading he chooses 30-point Avant Garde, and he decides on 18-point Avant Garde for the subhead. He centers this text on the page to give it a formal look. Satisfied that he's made some headway, Matt hits the print button, sits back with a cup of coffee, and waits for his fact sheet to roll out of the laser printer (see Figure 5.7).

FIGURE 5.7   Matt's draft of the Prescott Engineering fact sheet

Clyde Prescott and Associates
Engineering and Development

From the President:

Welcome to Clyde Prescott and Associates Engineering and Development. Whether you are a developer, prospective homeowner, or investor, Prescott is pleased to outline our services for you. At your request, our staff will be pleased to give you additional information or to answer your questions. Thanks for your interest in our company.

Joe Prescott

History. Prescott was founded in 1968 by William Prescott, an engineer and builder whose innovations in foundation and soil design received national recognition. By 1980 Prescott grew from three employees to over fifty. Today Prescott has two hundred employees with branch offices in Milwaukee and Denver and building projects that span from coast to coast, to Europe, and to the Middle East.

Recent Projects. *Heirloom Community.* This state-of-the-art retirement center includes a variety of residential structures, including individual units, townhouses, and apartments. Heirloom Community was recently recognized as an outstanding design for senior citizens.

Shoreline Harbor. This waterfront development on Lake Michigan houses over 100 business and professional offices. It has been recognized as one of the best historical designs in the Midwest.

Plateau Irrigation. This unique irrigation system provides a reliable, year-round source of fresh water for farmers and ranchers in southern Montana. It has been recognized as the most cost-efficient system in the area.

Employees. Prescott's professional staff includes over 100 engineers and designers. Engineering specialties include civil, mechanical, environmental, structural, and electrical. Design specialties include residential, historical preservation, interior, and landscape.

Offices. Main office at 125 W. Jackson, Chicago, IL. Branch offices at 310 N. Oak, Milwaukee, WI, and 5577 Mountain View, Denver, CO.

Projects completed in 2008. 11 in the U.S., 3 international; net worth of building projects in 2008: $24,500,000.

Management. Joe Prescott, President; Jean Sullivan, Office Manager; Frank LaVesta, Chief Engineer; Allan Perch, Chief Designer.

Revision

When Matt returns to his computer with the printed page in hand, he immediately spots some problems with clarity and emphasis. The text looks jumbled together, line by line, which makes it hard to read and uninviting. The text also looks too flat and homogeneous, lacking emphasis to draw readers in. So Matt turns to his computer screen and takes some steps to make the document more legible and emphatic.

1. He adds two points of leading (three points total) to the sans serif typeface; this is an especially important spatial decision because Avant Garde is a large typeface and needs some extra "breathing room."
2. He decreases the text to 10 points to give him more space to work with. However, he keeps the bold headings in 11 point so they'll look larger than the surrounding text, increasing their emphasis.
3. He indents the list of recent projects and adds diamond bullets to give them emphasis and enhance the professional tone.

Matt also makes adjustments in the heading at the top, bolding the main heading and adding more space (8 points) between it and the subheading, increasing its emphasis through figure–ground contrast. He also changes the font for the president's name to Kaufmann so it looks like a signature, giving it a more personal tone. Matt discovers, however, that he has to enlarge the typeface to 16 points and boldface it to make it comparable to the 10-point Avant Garde. (*Script* typefaces often need a boost in point size.) Figure 5.8 shows Matt's revised document. Do you agree that it's more legible, emphatic, and professional looking than his first version? Why or why not?

When Matt returns to the fact sheet a few hours later, he decides that he has satisfactorily addressed the clarity problem, but now he thinks that the document lacks interest. It's still too text heavy, too bland. So he tries a different arrangement, pulling the headings into the margin so they're more emphatic. That way readers can scan the margin, find what they're interested in, and enter the text to the right. At the same time, Matt makes several other adjustments to enhance other cognate strategies (see Figure 5.9).

1. He uses Kaufmann for "From the President" and increases the point size to 18 so it and the signature are more emphatic.
2. He changes the font for the marginal headings to 16-point Helvetica; because Helvetica is narrower than Avant Garde, it allows more flexibility in horizontal spacing even at a larger point size. Helvetica will also give the document some variety.
3. He alters the "History" heading to "The First Half Century" to make it more interesting and to expand the horizontal line. By creating better balance at the top of the heading column, this arrangement decision also contributes to ethos.

FIGURE 5.8 Matt's first revision of the fact sheet

Clyde Prescott and Associates
Engineering and Development

From the President:
Welcome to Clyde Prescott and Associates Engineering and Development. Whether you are a developer, prospective homeowner, or investor, Prescott is pleased to outline our services for you. At your request, our staff will be pleased to give you additional information or to answer your questions. Thanks for your interest in our company.

Joe Prescott

History. Prescott was founded in 1968 by William Prescott, an engineer and builder whose innovations in foundation and soil design received national recognition. By 1980 Prescott grew from three employees to over fifty. Today Prescott has two hundred employees with branch offices in Milwaukee and Denver and building projects that span from coast to coast, to Europe, and to the Middle East.

Recent Projects.

◆ *Heirloom Community.* This state-of-the-art retirement center includes a variety of residential structures, including individual units, townhouses, and apartments. Heirloom Community was recently recognized as an outstanding design for senior citizens.

◆ *Shoreline Harbor.* This waterfront development on Lake Michigan houses over 100 business and professional offices. It has been recognized as one of the best historical designs in the Midwest.

◆ *Plateau Irrigation.* This unique irrigation system provides a reliable, year-round source of fresh water for farmers and ranchers in southern Montana. It has been recognized as the most cost-efficient system in the area.

Employees. Prescott's professional staff includes over 100 engineers and designers. Engineering specialties include civil, mechanical, environmental, structural, and electrical. Design specialties include residential, historical preservation, interior, and landscape.

Offices. Main office at 125 W. Jackson, Chicago, IL. Branch offices at 310 N. Oak, Milwaukee, WI, and 5577 Mountain View, Denver, CO.

Projects completed in 2008. 11 in the U.S., 3 international; net worth of building projects in 2008: $24,500,000.

Management. Joe Prescott, President; Jean Sullivan, Office Manager; Frank LaVesta, Chief Engineer; Allan Perch, Chief Designer.

FIGURE 5.9   Matt's second revision of the fact sheet

Clyde Prescott and Associates

Engineering and Development

From the President

Welcome to Clyde Prescott and Associates Engineering and Development. Whether you are a developer, prospective homeowner, or investor, Prescott is pleased to outline our services for you. At your request, our staff will be pleased to give you additional information or to answer your questions. Thanks for your interest in our company.

Joe Prescott

The First Half Century

Prescott was founded in 1968 by William Prescott, an engineer and builder whose innovations in foundation and soil design received national recognition. By 1980 Prescott grew from three employees to over fifty. Today Prescott has two hundred employees with branch offices in Milwaukee and Denver and building projects that span from coast to coast, to Europe, and to the Middle East.

Recent Projects

◆ *Heirloom Community.* This state-of-the-art retirement center includes a variety of residential structures, including individual units, townhouses, and apartments. Heirloom Community was recently recognized as an outstanding design for senior citizens.

◆ *Shoreline Harbor.* This waterfront development on Lake Michigan houses over 100 business and professional offices. It has been recognized as one of the best historical designs in the Midwest.

◆ *Plateau Irrigation.* This unique irrigation system provides a reliable, year-round source of fresh water for farmers and ranchers in southern Montana. It has been recognized as the most cost-efficient system in the area.

Employees

Prescott's professional staff includes over 100 engineers and designers. Engineering specialties include civil, mechanical, environmental, structural, and electrical. Design specialties include residential, historical preservation, interior, and landscape.

Offices

Main office at 125 W. Jackson, Chicago, IL. Branch offices at 310 N. Oak, Milwaukee, WI, and 5577 Mountain View, Denver, CO.

Productivity

Projects completed in 2008: 11 in the U.S., 3 international; net worth of building projects in 2008: $24,500,000.

Management

Joe Prescott, President; Jean Sullivan, Office Manager; Frank LaVesta, Chief Engineer; Allan Perch, Chief Designer.

Visual Editing

Satisfied with the overall concept and running out of time, Matt now spends a few minutes visually refining the fact sheet, adapting it more precisely to the rhetorical situation (see Figure 5.10).

1. He replaces "and" in the main heading at the top with an ampersand so that he can enlarge the text to 36 points, giving it greater *emphasis* on the page.
2. He uses italics for the Helvetica headings to make their *tone* less severe and more humane.
3. He enlarges the Kaufmann script font to 20 points so it has greater *emphasis* and isn't overpowered by the marginal headings below. The large script font further highlights the personal *tone* of the fact sheet.
4. He puts a light gray scale behind the logo to emphasize it and create interest.

Matt's not convinced that he's found the ideal solution, but he at least has something he can show Jean Sullivan when he meets with her later that day. Also, a group of college students is visiting the Prescott office in the morning, so maybe Matt can test his design with them.

Vocabulary of Text Fields

As you can see from Matt's design process, the vocabulary of text fields includes a variety of elements from each of the three coding modes—textual, spatial, and graphic. And Matt blends these elements as he creates, and re-creates, his fact sheet. Let's go through the three coding modes one by one so you can get some perspective on the range of visual language at your disposal when you're designing text fields. Along the way, we'll point out some conventions that can help you adapt your design to your audience as well as simplify your design process.

Textual Elements

Textual elements in fields include primarily headings, numbers, and letters that signal text groups, ranging from several paragraphs (or even pages) to a single item in a list. Let's focus on headings first since they play such an important role in text design.

Headings. Headings give readers a road map. They allow readers to scan text to find what they want, they tell readers what comes next, and they help them return to text groups later on. Headings are highly conventional, and they come in a variety of configurations, as shown in Figure 5.11.

FIGURE 5.10 Matt's edited fact sheet

Clyde Prescott & Associates
Engineering and Development

From the President

Welcome to Clyde Prescott and Associates Engineering and Development. Whether you are a developer, prospective homeowner, or investor, Prescott is pleased to outline our services for you. At your request, our staff will be pleased to give you additional information or to answer your questions. Thanks for your interest in our company.

Joe Prescott

The First Half Century

Prescott was founded in 1968 by William Prescott, an engineer and builder whose innovations in foundation and soil design received national recognition. By 1980 Prescott grew from three employees to over fifty. Today Prescott has two hundred employees with branch offices in Milwaukee and Denver and building projects that span from coast to coast, to Europe, and to the Middle East.

Recent Projects

◆ *Heirloom Community*. This state-of-the-art retirement center includes a variety of residential structures, including individual units, townhouses, and apartments. Heirloom Community was recently recognized as an outstanding design for senior citizens.

◆ *Shoreline Harbor*. This waterfront development on Lake Michigan houses over 100 business and professional offices. It has been recognized as one of the best historical designs in the Midwest.

◆ *Plateau Irrigation*. This unique irrigation system provides a reliable, year-round source of fresh water for farmers and ranchers in southern Montana. It has been recognized as the most cost-efficient system in the area.

Employees

Prescott's professional staff includes over 100 engineers and designers. Engineering specialties include civil, mechanical, environmental, structural, and electrical. Design specialties include residential, historical preservation, interior, and landscape.

Offices

Main office at 125 W. Jackson, Chicago, IL. Branch offices at 310 N. Oak, Milwaukee, WI, and 5577 Mountain View, Denver, CO.

Productivity

Projects completed in 2008: 11 in the U.S., 3 international; net worth of building projects in 2008: $24,500,000.

Management

Joe Prescott, President; Jean Sullivan, Office Manager; Frank LaVesta, Chief Engineer; Allan Perch, Chief Designer.

FIGURE 5.11   Conventions for designing headings

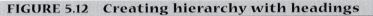

Centered   Flush left   Run-in   Marginal   Column

All of the headings in Figure 5.11 divide the text at a single level, from one unit to the next, creating parallelism among these units. Headings are often also arranged hierarchically to help readers structure text. All three coding modes can be used to convey this hierarchy, as shown in Figure 5.12.

- *Textual:* strong or weak figure–ground contrast depending on the type size, boldface, and uppercase.
- *Spatial:* location with respect to the text—centered, flush left, indented, and so on. Hierarchy based on location is highly conventional.
- *Graphic:* underlining, bullets, gray scales, and other cues that enhance emphasis through figure–ground contrast.

FIGURE 5.12   Creating hierarchy with headings

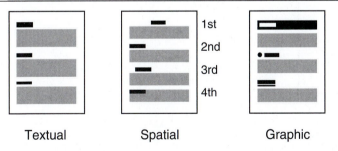

Textual   Spatial   Graphic

In his fact sheet, Matt uses two levels of headings: large marginal headings (the first level) and small italic run-in headings (the second level) that introduce three recent Prescott projects. Although levels of headings are highly conventional, often designers will mix and match levels in a given situation, as Matt does, assuming that readers will understand the code.

Web Links.   While headings provide clues about sequencing and the relative importance of chunks of text, Web links function like footnotes on steroids. That is, instead of referring to some additional information that would inappropriately interrupt the text, or citing a bibliographical source, Web links actually whisk the reader away (at least temporarily) to whole other communications. Visually, Web links are very conventional, usually appearing in underlined type and often in color and as pull-down menus with sublinks.

Numbers and Letters*.*   Like headings, numbers and letters can break text into discrete units—frequently items in lists. A simple numbered list signals parallel items of text, with the numbers typically hanging in the margin (more on this below). Likewise, initial letters, as the name suggests, can *initiate* parallel text units in a visual field. For example, newsletters often use initial letters (or drop caps, a variation) to signal the beginning of a new article.

Numbers and letters can also organize text hierarchically. Some schemes use numbers alone, while others use numbers (including roman numerals) and letters together. For example, in a scheme using numbers and letters, section I might be followed by section A, then 1, then a, and so on.

In many kinds of scientific and technical writing, numbers alone signal hierarchical relations among text units. Section 1.0 is followed by 1.1, then 1.11, and so on—the only visual cue the numbering system itself (Figure 5.13). A highly conventional numbering system like this would likely be used by a relatively specialized discourse community that bridges countries and cultures around the globe. It is also used in most military manuals and many government reports.

FIGURE 5.13   Conventional numbering system

```
1

1.1

1.11
```

Spatial Elements

Distributing text across a field is one of the most crucial tasks a designer can undertake—it can make the difference between a field that's dull and unusable and one that's interesting, legible, and professional-looking. Some of the spatial elements used most frequently in field design include breaking text into lists, spacing between lines of text (leading), and justifying text. More complex spatial elements include dividing the text field into columns and using grids to structure the field.

Lists*.*   Many documents, both on paper and on screen, call for lists—of steps in instructions, of jobs on a résumé, or of content on PowerPoint slides. Lists break up the text, making it more accessible and emphasizing each item. Take the text in the PowerPoint slide in Figure 5.14, for example.

FIGURE 5.14   Text chunk

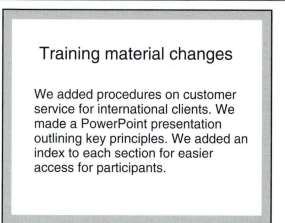

If we break this into a list, as in Figure 5.15, readers will gain quicker access to the information, which is particularly important if they must refer to the slide to search for something.

Of course, the writer could configure this list in other ways—for example, by using bullets instead of numbers—which would create a different rhetorical effect.

FIGURE 5.15   Text chunk broken into a list

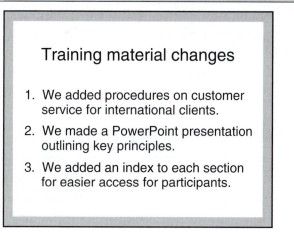

Leading.   Spacing between lines can make a big difference in how a field looks. When Matt was designing his fact sheet, he adjusted the leading when he realized that the text was packed too tightly for the typeface he selected.

Figure 5.16 shows blocks of text, set in 10-point Times, each with a 1-point increase in leading. Amazingly, the eye can easily detect these increments of $\frac{1}{72}$ of an inch.

FIGURE 5.16   Leading in 1-point increments

1-point   Prescott was founded in 1968 by William Prescott, an engineer
                and builder whose innovations in foundation and soil design
                received national recognition. By 1980 Prescott grew from three
                employees to over fifty. Today Prescott has two hundred
                employees with branch offices in Milwaukee and Denver and
                building projects that span from coast to coast, to Europe, and to
                the Middle East.

2-point   Prescott was founded in 1968 by William Prescott, an engineer
                and builder whose innovations in foundation and soil design
                received national recognition. By 1980 Prescott grew from three
                employees to over fifty. Today Prescott has two hundred
                employees with branch offices in Milwaukee and Denver and
                building projects that span from coast to coast, to Europe, and to
                the Middle East.

3-point   Prescott was founded in 1968 by William Prescott, an engineer
                and builder whose innovations in foundation and soil design
                received national recognition. By 1980 Prescott grew from three
                employees to over fifty. Today Prescott has two hundred
                employees with branch offices in Milwaukee and Denver and
                building projects that span from coast to coast, to Europe, and to
                the Middle East.

4-point   Prescott was founded in 1968 by William Prescott, an engineer and
                builder whose innovations in foundation and soil design received
                national recognition. By 1980 Prescott grew from three employees
                to over fifty. Today Prescott has two hundred employees with
                branch offices in Milwaukee and Denver and building projects that
                span from coast to coast, to Europe, and to the Middle East.

5-point   Prescott was founded in 1968 by William Prescott, an engineer
                and builder whose innovations in foundation and soil design
                received national recognition. By 1980 Prescott grew from
                three employees to over fifty. Today Prescott has two hundred
                employees with branch offices in Milwaukee and Denver and
                building projects that span from coast to coast, to Europe, and
                to the Middle East.

Justified/Unjustified.   Justified text blocks have smooth, even edges; unjustified text blocks have rough, ragged edges. Technically, either side of a text column can be justified, but in the Western world, most justification decisions have to do with the right margin, as shown in Figure 5.17.

FIGURE 5.17   Justified versus unjustified text

Right justified   Prescott was founded in 1968 by William Prescott, an engineer and builder whose innovations in foundation and soil design received national recognition. By 1980 Prescott grew from three employees to over fifty. Today Prescott has two hundred employees with branch offices in Milwaukee and Denver and building projects that span from coast to coast, to Europe, and to the Middle East.

Ragged right   Prescott was founded in 1968 by William Prescott, an engineer and builder whose innovations in foundation and soil design received national recognition. By 1980 Prescott grew from three employees to over fifty. Today Prescott has two hundred employees with branch offices in Milwaukee and Denver and building projects that span from coast to coast, to Europe, and to the Middle East.

Columns.   Most of the time we organize text into a single column: It's simply easier to write, edit, and revise that way, and in many cases that's what our readers expect. Multiple columns, however, have certain advantages. For example, the eye can pick up information quickly in narrow (3- to 4-inch) columns, and dividing text into columns offers many new design options, as you can see in Figure 5.18.

FIGURE 5.18   Text organized into columns

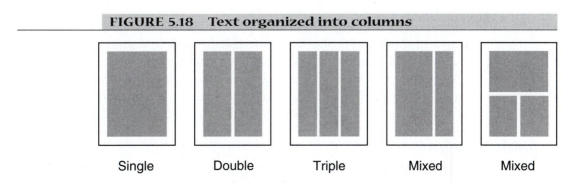

Single   Double   Triple   Mixed   Mixed

Field grids.   Designing a field with text columns is the first step toward structuring the field as a grid. Imagine a workspace on a field that extends up to the margins (Figure 5.19a). You can then divide this workspace vertically into, let's say, two units (Figure 5.19b). Those two vertical units provide the spatial framework for organizing text—and images—in the field. In the examples that follow, we've simply boxed out places for pictures and data displays, which we'll examine in later chapters. The examples in Figure 5.19 are only a few of the many spatial variations possible with a simple two-column grid.

FIGURE 5.19   Two-column grids

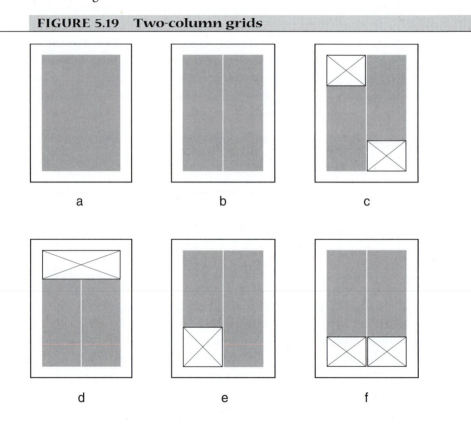

| a | b | c |
| d | e | f |

With additional columns, the possible spatial variations increase proportionately. Figure 5.20 shows three-, four-, and five-column grids and some of their spatial variations. Obviously, the more column units you use, the more spatial flexibility you allow yourself. However, you should also remember that narrower columns exaggerate the raggedness of unjustified right edges, while fully justified text in narrow columns can open up internal gaps in the text field. More on this later.

Graphic Elements

The third mode of field design consists of graphic elements, which can shape the text in a variety of ways—bullets and other highlighting cues, line work, and shading.

FIGURE 5.20   Three-, four-, and five-column grids

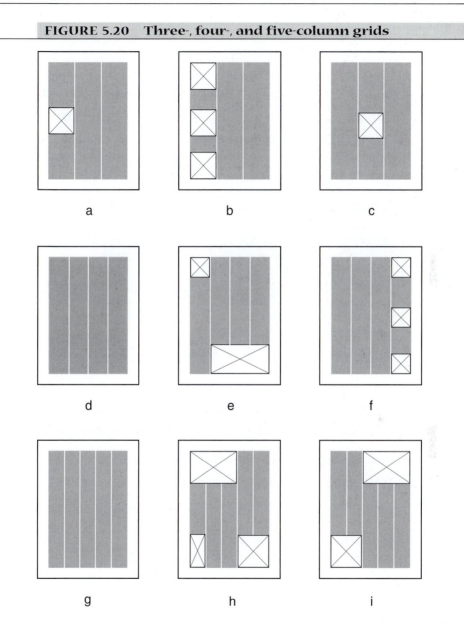

Bullets and Other Highlighting Cues.   Bullets come in all shapes and sizes, from circles and squares to stars, pointing hands, and icons. Zapf Dingbats, a popular icon and symbol font, contains an array of graphic cues that you can use for bullets or other points of emphasis in the text. Many of the Zapf Dingbats (set at 12 points) are shown in Figure 5.21.

Bullets can be configured on the field as markers that highlight items in a vertical list (Figure 5.22a), structure a list internally within the text (Figure 5.22b), or signal the start of paragraphs (Figure 5.22c).

FIGURE 5.21   A sampling of Zapf Dingbats

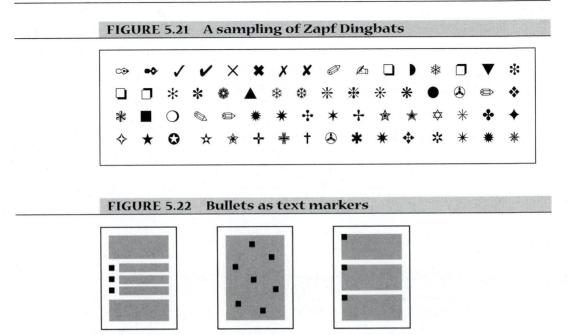

FIGURE 5.22   Bullets as text markers

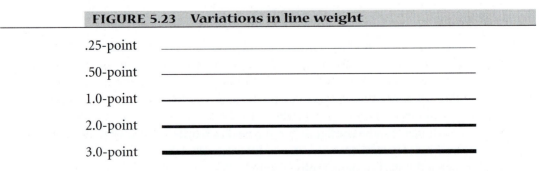

a   b   c

Emphatic bullets like those in Figures 5.21 and 5.22—whether they're dark squares or one from the assortment of Zapf Dingbats—are not necessarily appropriate for all lists in all documents. The convention in Europe is quite low-key:

- Brussels, technical headquarters for the West Region

- Hamburg, business headquarters for the Central Region

- Moscow, production headquarters for the East Region

Line work.   Lines can come in a variety of thicknesses—from thin "hairlines" to thick rules. Figure 5.23 shows some variations in line weight.

FIGURE 5.23   Variations in line weight

.25-point   _____

.50-point   _____

1.0-point   _____

2.0-point   _____

3.0-point   _____

Lines can come in different styles—for example, with dashes at various intervals (Figure 5.24).

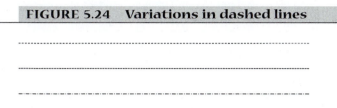

FIGURE 5.24   Variations in dashed lines

Lines can be used in a variety of ways to segment and accent the text (Figure 5.25). Lines can also box off text, emphasizing it by dividing it from the rest of the field (Figure 5.26).

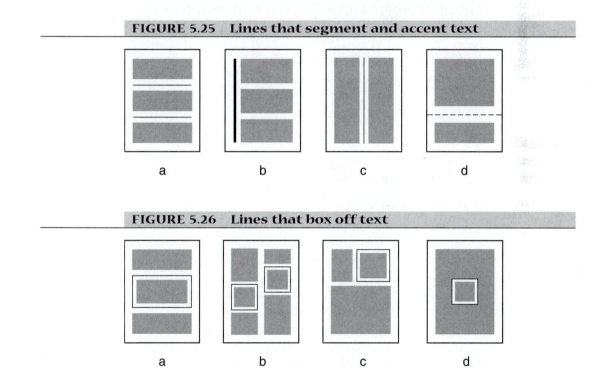

FIGURE 5.25   Lines that segment and accent text

a   b   c   d

FIGURE 5.26   Lines that box off text

a   b   c   d

Shading.   Shading is usually measured as a gray-scale percentage, ranging from 1 percent to 100 percent. Figure 5.27 shows a range of gray scales, beginning with 15 percent and increasing in 5 percent intervals. The 15 percent gray scale is repeated at the end of the row so you can compare the highest and lowest percentages shown. As the gray scale increases, notice how the figure–ground contrast with the text progressively diminishes.

FIGURE 5.27   Gray-scale percentages

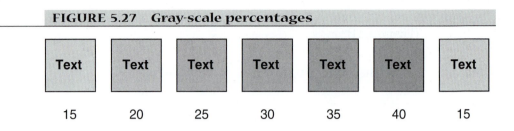

As shown in Figure 5.28, gray scales can be used in a variety of ways in field design to accent text, including headings, whole paragraphs (within a wide or narrow column), and quotations set in large type, often referred to as *pull quotes.*

FIGURE 5.28   Using gray scales to accent text

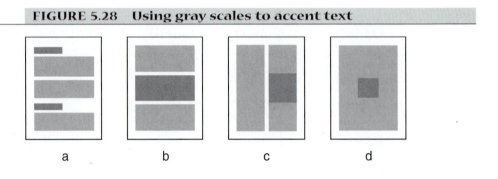

Synergy of the Coding Modes

The rich vocabulary of the three coding modes—textual, spatial, graphic—enables you to give your text field structure and texture. When you're designing a document, remember that the coding modes are interdependent and must work together. To review, we can change the text field seen in Figure 5.29a by inserting *textual* cues in the headings, which have immediate *spatial* implications because they break up the text and extend it beyond a single page (Figure 5.29b).

In Figure 5.30a we introduce spatial elements by breaking some of the text into a list and by indenting the paragraph in the center of the field. We also include *graphic* elements by adding the bullets and by boxing the indented paragraph. Finally, in Figure 5.30b, we add elements in all three modes: textually, we supply numbers for the list and reverse the type for the headings; graphically, we shade the box and add heading bars; and spatially, we run the bars across the page, separating the main text segments. As a field design unfolds, none of the coding modes develops in a vacuum. Just as when you use your verbal vocabulary to build sentences, building a text field requires a variety of visual elements that interact with each other.

FIGURE 5.29   Transforming the field with textual and spatial cues

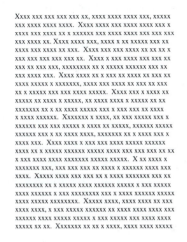

a

b

FIGURE 5.30   Cues that further transform the field

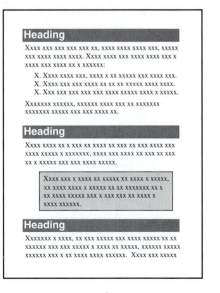

a

b

Applying the Cognate Strategies

Given this rich and complex vocabulary, designing text fields can be an exciting, creative—and daunting—task. However, if you let the rhetorical situation drive the process, you'll focus your creative energy where it counts most—helping your readers find what they need in your text field. Like any communication, then, you can adapt your design to your rhetorical situation by implementing the cognate strategies.

Arrangement

In fields, arrangement strategies operate within the size and orientation of a given surface—standard or legal, portrait or landscape, a brochure panel, computer landscape, or computer portrait (Figure 5.31). Within this framework, a variety of textual, spatial, and graphic cues enact arrangement strategies.

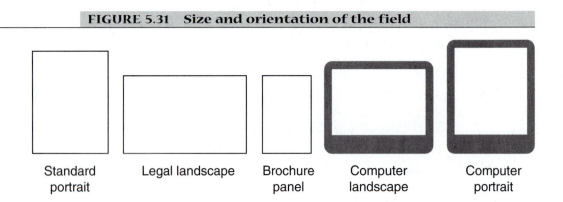

FIGURE 5.31   Size and orientation of the field

Standard portrait   Legal landscape   Brochure panel   Computer landscape   Computer portrait

Textually, for example, headings not only order and chunk information, but also help control readers' access to it. In the process example earlier in this chapter, recall how the arrangement of Matt's fact sheet changes as he revises and edits. In the early versions readers access information by having to leap over blocks of text to get to the next heading. In the later versions, however, which isolate the headings in the left margin, the information flows from left to right and readers have the freedom to select what they want to read.

Web links are an essential online arrangement strategy because they enable readers to navigate complex sites. As David Farkas and Jean Farkas point out, links can be effective navigational tools when they are cued explicitly (e.g., with underlining, as lists), they are clearly visible on the screen, and they adequately describe where they are taking readers (342–345).[1]

Spatially, using lists and columns to arrange information within the field's framework can have significant rhetorical impact (see Kostelnick). For example, if we use a list for the information below, readers are likely to respond favorably.

Before you begin assembling the playground equipment you need to complete the following steps:

1. Lay out the plan on the outside area you want to use.
2. Gather all of the tools listed on the tool sheet.
3. Make sure you carefully read the safety information on page 4.

But if we also arrange the following information in a list, readers may *not* respond so favorably. In fact, they may be quite offended.

We were impressed by your workshop proposal for next year's convention, but we were not able to approve it because:

1. The committee received an unusually high number of quality workshop proposals this year.
2. The convention site in Miami can accommodate only the number of sessions we had last year, and far fewer than we would have liked to accept.
3. We had to distribute acceptances across all specialties, ensuring a balanced program attractive to the broad spectrum of members in our organization.

While none of this information may be personally hurtful to the readers, arranging it in a list overemphasizes it and makes it too negative. In some Asian cultures, such as the Japanese, where business writing is often ambiguous, especially about negative news, such visual directness would be particularly offensive. Listing can also have serious drawbacks in PowerPoint presentations: Edward Tufte vehemently argues that PowerPoint lists can undermine the presenter's thinking and greatly diminish the audience's experience.

Similar to lists, a designer's choice of column arrangement can affect the way readers access information. For instance, Figure 5.32 shows a field of text—with headings—in a single column.

In a two-column arrangement (Figure 5.33), the same text is easier to scan, and the shorter line lengths also contribute to clarity and to a somewhat more official and authoritative tone, enhancing the ethos of the text.

Graphically, we can also create arrangement strategies by inserting bullets in lists and by boxing off text, placing lines between columns, shading text, and so on. Many of these cues divide the text into subfields—for example, boxed or shaded text that stands apart from other text in the field. Matt did something like this in his fact sheet when he inserted a line between the marginal headings and the text.

FIGURE 5.32   Text in a single column

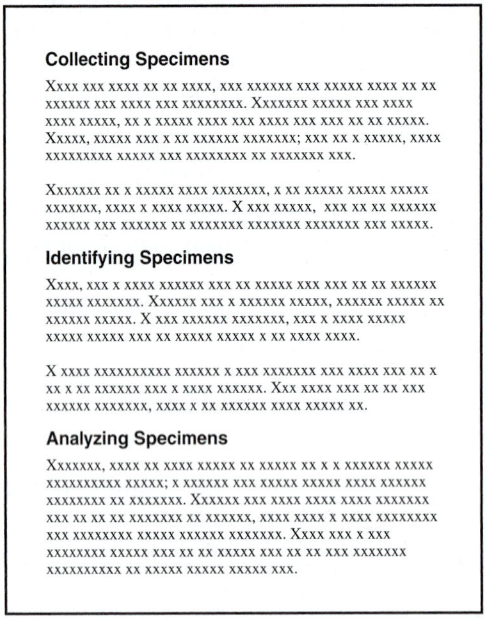

Collecting Specimens

Xxxx xxx xxxx xx xx xxxx, xxx xxxxxx xxx xxxxx xxxx xx xx
xxxxxx xxx xxxx xxx xxxxxxxx. Xxxxxxx xxxxx xxx xxxx
xxxx xxxxx, xx x xxxxx xxxx xxx xxxx xxx xxx xx xx xxxxx.
Xxxx, xxxxx xxx x xx xxxxxx xxxxxxx; xxx xx x xxxxx, xxxx
xxxxxxxxx xxxxx xxx xxxxxxxx xx xxxxxxx xxx.

Xxxxxxx xx x xxxxx xxxx xxxxxxx, x xx xxxxx xxxxx xxxxx
xxxxxxx, xxxx x xxxx xxxxx. X xxx xxxxx, xxx xx xx xxxxxx
xxxxxx xxx xxxxxx xx xxxxxxx xxxxxxx xxxxxxx xxx xxxxx.

Identifying Specimens

Xxxx, xxx x xxxx xxxxxx xxx xx xxxxx xxx xxx xx xx xxxxxx
xxxxx xxxxxxx. Xxxxxx xxx x xxxxxx xxxxx, xxxxxx xxxxx xx
xxxxxx xxxxx. X xxx xxxxxx xxxxxxx, xxx x xxxx xxxxx
xxxxx xxxxx xxx xx xxxxx xxxxx x xx xxxx xxxx.

X xxxx xxxxxxxxxx xxxxxx x xxx xxxxxxx xxx xxxx xxx xx x
xx x xx xxxxxx xxx x xxxx xxxxxx. Xxx xxxx xxx xx xx xxx
xxxxxx xxxxxxx, xxxx x xx xxxxxx xxxx xxxxx xx.

Analyzing Specimens

Xxxxxxx, xxxx xx xxxx xxxxx xx xxxxx xx x x xxxxxx xxxxx
xxxxxxxxxx xxxxx; x xxxxxx xxx xxxxx xxxxx xxx xxxxxx
xxxxxxxx xx xxxxxxx. Xxxxxx xxx xxxx xxxx xxxx xxxxxxx
xxx xx xx xx xxxxxxx xx xxxxxx, xxxx xxxx x xxxx xxxxxxxx
xxx xxxxxxxx xxxxx xxxxxx xxxxxxx. Xxxx xxx x xxx
xxxxxxxx xxxxx xxx xx xx xxxxx xxx xx xx xxx xxxxxxx
xxxxxxxxxx xx xxxxx xxxxx xxxxx xxx.

FIGURE 5.33   Text presented in two columns

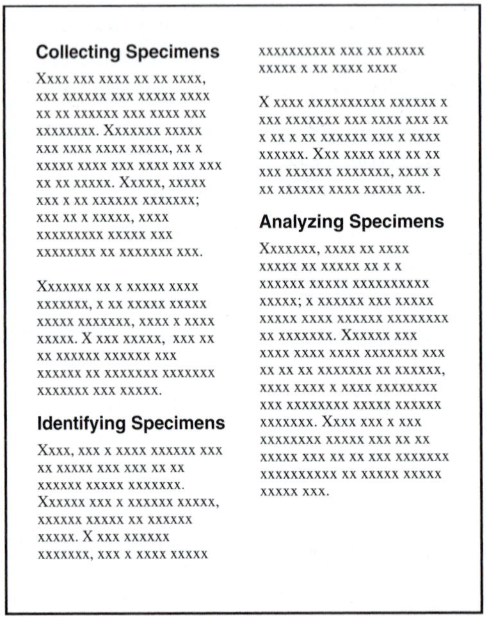

Collecting Specimens

Xxxx xxx xxxx xx xx xxxx,
xxx xxxxxx xxx xxxxx xxxx
xx xx xxxxxx xxx xxxx xxx
xxxxxxxx. Xxxxxxx xxxxx
xxx xxxx xxxx xxxxx, xx x
xxxxx xxxx xxx xxxx xxx xxx
xx xx xxxxx. Xxxx, xxxxx
xxx x xx xxxxxx xxxxxxx;
xxx xx x xxxxx, xxxx
xxxxxxxxx xxxxx xxx
xxxxxxxx xx xxxxxxx xxx.

Xxxxxxx xx x xxxxx xxxx
xxxxxxx, x xx xxxxx xxxxx
xxxxx xxxxxxx, xxxx x xxxx
xxxxx. X xxx xxxxx, xxx xx
xx xxxxxx xxxxxx xxx
xxxxxx xx xxxxxxx xxxxxxx
xxxxxxx xxx xxxxx.

Identifying Specimens

Xxxx, xxx x xxxx xxxxxx xxx
xx xxxxx xxx xxx xx xx
xxxxxx xxxxx xxxxxxx.
Xxxxxx xxx x xxxxxx xxxxx,
xxxxxx xxxxx xx xxxxxx
xxxxx. X xxx xxxxxx
xxxxxxx, xxx x xxxx xxxxx

xxxxxxxxxx xxx xx xxxxx
xxxxx x xx xxxx xxxx

X xxxx xxxxxxxxxx xxxxxx x
xxx xxxxxxx xxx xxxx xxx xx
x xx x xx xxxxxx xxx x xxxx
xxxxxx. Xxx xxxx xxx xx xx
xxx xxxxxx xxxxxxx, xxxx x
xx xxxxxx xxxx xxxxx xx.

Analyzing Specimens

Xxxxxxx, xxxx xx xxxx
xxxxx xx xxxxx xx x x
xxxxxx xxxxx xxxxxxxxxx
xxxxx; x xxxxxx xxx xxxxx
xxxxx xxxx xxxxx xxxxxxxx
xx xxxxxxx. Xxxxxx xxx
xxxx xxxx xxxx xxxxxxx xxx
xx xx xx xxxxxxx xx xxxxxx,
xxxx xxxx x xxxx xxxxxxxx
xxx xxxxxxxx xxxxx xxxxxx
xxxxxxx. Xxxx xxx x xxx
xxxxxxxx xxxxx xxx xx xx
xxxxx xxx xx xx xxx xxxxxxx
xxxxxxxxxx xx xxxxx xxxxx
xxxxx xxx.

Emphasis

Like visual magnets, emphasis strategies draw the reader's attention to key elements within a visual field. You can emphasize text with a variety of visual cues—textual, spatial, and graphic.

Textually, one way to create emphasis is to strengthen figure–ground contrast by enlarging selected pieces of text. In Matt's fact sheet, for example, he emphasizes his marginal headings by increasing their point size. Initial letters also create strong figure–ground contrast, drawing readers to selected points in the field where they can begin reading. Pull quotes, which repeat phrases from the text in a large type size, are yet another emphasis technique, as shown in Figure 5.34.

FIGURE 5.34   Pull quote

Spatially, as we've already seen, breaking text into a list can create emphasis by isolating each item. The location of information in the field and the placement of headings can also help achieve emphasis. In general, the most emphatic places in a visual field—at least in Western culture—are the left and upper part, as illustrated in Figure 5.35. If you want Western readers to notice something, placing it in this area will probably help.

FIGURE 5.35   Placement affects emphasis

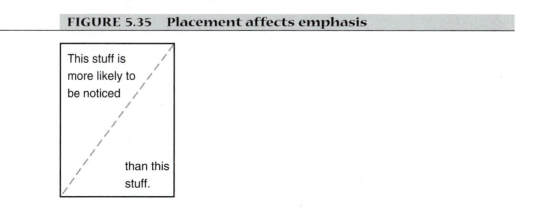

Using marginal headings, where lots of space isolates the heading, can emphasize an idea or a text group, as Matt does in his fact sheet. On the other hand, in
more complex communications that require several levels of headings, creating a
hierarchy in a marginal format (Figure 5.36a) can be difficult because the higher-
level headings lose some emphasis. Placing the headings flush left (Figure 5.36b)
restores the emphasis—and the hierarchy.

FIGURE 5.36   Marginal headings (a) versus flush (b)

a   b

Graphically, you can use a variety of cues to create emphasis in a text field. For
example, compare the following solid paragraph with the one below it that uses
bullets to highlight key information (Figure 5.37). Of course, spatially distributing
part of the text into a list accounts for some of the emphasis here; however, it's the
bullets that have the magnetic power to focus the eye on each item. Shading (either
gray scale or color) is another technique that focuses the reader's attention on
selected text—such as quantitative data in a technical description (Figure 5.38).
Shading creates emphasis by producing figure–ground contrast with the entire
field; however, you need to be careful to shade lightly so that you don't erode the
clarity of the text. You can achieve similar graphical emphasis within a field by boxing off text or placing vertical lines next to the text.

Clarity

A well-designed field enables readers to glide effortlessly through the text; a poorly
designed one makes their work hard, like climbing a steep and stony path, and may even
discourage them from reading at all. You can achieve clarity of field design through
several forms of visual language, so let's again look at the three modes separately.

FIGURE 5.37   Emphasis through listing

Sample text   The seminar will focus on the six most commonly used inspection methods: visual, liquid penetrant, ultrasonic, magnetic particle, eddy current, and x-ray. Participants will learn the basic principles, advantages, limitations, and common applications of each method. Demonstrations of basic inspection techniques will be performed for all methods except x-ray, and participants will have some hands-on opportunities with state-of-the-art equipment as time allows.

———————————————————— *or* ————————————————————

Same text with list   The seminar will focus on the six most commonly used inspection methods:

- Visual
- Liquid penetrant
- Ultrasonic
- Magnetic particle
- Eddy current
- X-ray

Participants will learn the basic principles, advantages, limitations, and common applications of each method. Demonstrations of basic inspection techniques will be performed for all methods except x-ray, and participants will have some hands-on opportunities with state-of-the-art equipment as time allows.

Note: Seminar description is from "Introduction to Nondestructive Evaluation (NDE)," courtesy of the Center for Nondestructive Evaluation, Iowa State University.

FIGURE 5.38   Emphasis through gray-scale shading

X-ray energy dispersive detectors and data analysis methods have been developed for a wide range of materials characterization applications, including detection and measuring corrosion products in aluminum airframe structures, porosity, and fiber resin ratio in graphite composite structure.

Measurements of aluminum 2% skin metal loss can be made in the presence of paint and sealant. Porosity measurements in graphite composites can be made to 1% by volume.

A prototype of an array energy dispersive detector is being developed in cooperation with Lockheed for production inspection.

Note: Text is from the Federal Aviation Administration Center for Aviation Systems Reliability, Iowa State University.

As we've already seen, headings are an effective *textual* cue to enhance clarity because they provide a road map for the text. Headings not only help readers remember information they've read but also help them go back to the text and retrieve information later on (Hartley and Trueman 107, 117).

Spatially, clarity of text design often depends on decisions about line length and leading.[2] Other decisions about line breaks (ragged right versus justified right) and visual clutter can also affect clarity.

Line length.   Line lengths that are too short or too long can erode clarity.[3] You can see this principle by comparing the three versions of the text in Figure 5.39.

FIGURE 5.39   The effects of line length on clarity

Prescott was founded in 1968 by William Prescott, an engineer and builder whose innovations in foundation and soil design received national recognition. By 1980 Prescott grew from three employees to over fifty. Today Prescott has two hundred employees with branch offices in Milwaukee and Denver and building projects that span from coast to coast, to Europe, and to the Middle East.

a

Prescott was founded in 1968 by William Prescott, an engineer and builder whose innovations in foundation and soil design received national recognition. By 1980 Prescott grew from three employees to over fifty. Today Prescott has two hundred employees with branch offices in Milwaukee and Denver and building projects that span from coast to coast, to Europe, and to the Middle East.

b

Prescott was founded in 1968 by William Prescott, an engineer and builder whose innovations in foundation and soil design received national recognition. By 1980 Prescott grew from three employees to over fifty. Today Prescott has two hundred employees with branch offices in Milwaukee and Denver and building projects that span from coast to coast, to Europe, and to the Middle East.

c

The version in Figure 5.39a probably isn't very comfortable to read because the lines are very short (e.g., less than two inches) and your eye has to keep jumping from one line to the next. Research shows that very short line lengths can reduce legibility (Tinker 74–86). Version b has longer lines and is probably more comfortable to read because of that. Version c has the same width, but because it's right justified, the spacing between words is a little irregular in places, leaving holes in some of the lines. These holes also create an ethos problem because they can be distracting.

Leading.   In general, the longer the line length, the more attention you should pay to leading, and this holds true for both print and screen fields. Longer lines in typefaces 10-point or smaller without leading can be hard to read (Tinker 90–97; 106–107). The following example is a long 8-point text passage without leading.

Prescott was founded in 1968 by William Prescott, an engineer and builder whose innovations in foundation and soil design received national recognition. By 1980 Prescott grew from three employees to over fifty. Today Prescott has two hundred employees with branch offices in Milwaukee and Denver and building projects that span from coast to coast, to Europe, and to the Middle East.

Adding two points of leading makes each line a little more distinct, which helps readers' eyes find a path to the right margin:

Prescott was founded in 1968 by William Prescott, an engineer and builder whose innovations in foundation and soil design received national recognition. By 1980 Prescott grew from three employees to over fifty. Today Prescott has two hundred employees with branch offices in Milwaukee and Denver and building projects that span from coast to coast, to Europe, and to the Middle East.

However, an even better solution for a typeface this small would be to shorten up the lines. Then we could give back a point of leading:

> Prescott was founded in 1968 by William Prescott, an engineer and builder whose innovations in foundation and soil design received national recognition. By 1980 Prescott grew from three employees to over fifty. Today Prescott has two hundred employees with branch offices in Milwaukee and Denver and building projects that span from coast to coast, to Europe, and to the Middle East.

So in general, the shorter the line, the less you need to worry about adding leading. However, even short lines of sans serif type can create perceptual problems because the letters don't have the tiny feet to help your readers' eyes follow the line of text, a problem Matt faced in using a sans serif for his fact sheet. Increasing the leading for a sans serif, as Matt did, often creates a clearer, more unified line. Notice the difference in legibility between the two examples of Helvetica text in Figure 5.40, the first with 1-point leading, the second with 3-point leading.

FIGURE 5.40   Extra leading makes sans serif more readable

1-point   Prescott was founded in 1968 by William Prescott, an engineer and builder whose innovations in foundation and soil design received national recognition. By 1980 Prescott grew from three employees to over fifty. Today Prescott has two hundred employees with branch offices in Milwaukee and Denver and building projects that span from coast to coast, to Europe, and to the Middle East.

3-points   Prescott was founded in 1968 by William Prescott, an engineer and builder whose innovations in foundation and soil design received national recognition. By 1980 Prescott grew from three employees to over fifty. Today Prescott has two hundred employees with branch offices in Milwaukee and Denver and building projects that span from coast to coast, to Europe, and to the Middle East.

Did you find the 3-point leading more readable than the 1-point? Notice too that the additional leading brings out the design features of the sans serif typeface, softening its hard edges. In terms of tone, the sans serifs will look more humane and elegant with thicker leading.

Justified text.   Some experts believe that left-justified, ragged-right text may be easier to read because the human eye prefers variation in the linear point where it returns to the left and moves down to the next line. Densely packed, justified text is not only visually monotonous but also, when set in narrow columns, sometimes creates odd spacing between words, as we saw above. On the other hand, justified text can have a highly formal and polished visual tone that is quite appropriate in many rhetorical situations.

Visual clutter.   A field that's arranged haphazardly can distract and confuse readers as well as damage its ethos. The page in Figure 5.41 doesn't do much to help readers get a clear idea of how to process its contents because novelty takes precedence over structure. Develop a visual pattern for your page and stick to it: Readers will appreciate your consistency. (Of course, the scattered approach might work in some situations; can you think of one?)

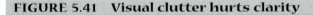

FIGURE 5.41   Visual clutter hurts clarity

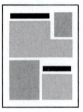

Visual clutter can be particularly problematic in Web sites, where links, buttons, and animations can distract readers, drawing them away from the text and reducing clarity even while these elements enhance interest.

Conciseness

Obviously, you can pack a lot of information on a page or screen if you want to—line upon line of text with little relief—but that won't do much for clarity. Dense text fields often obscure the structure of the ideas because everything blends together. Let's look at some of the most common ways you can address visual conciseness.

For example, the pattern of headings that you choose, and the arrangement of those headings in the field, will influence how much text can fit on the page. The page shown in Figure 5.42a, which you also saw earlier in the chapter, loses some of

FIGURE 5.42 Headings affect conciseness

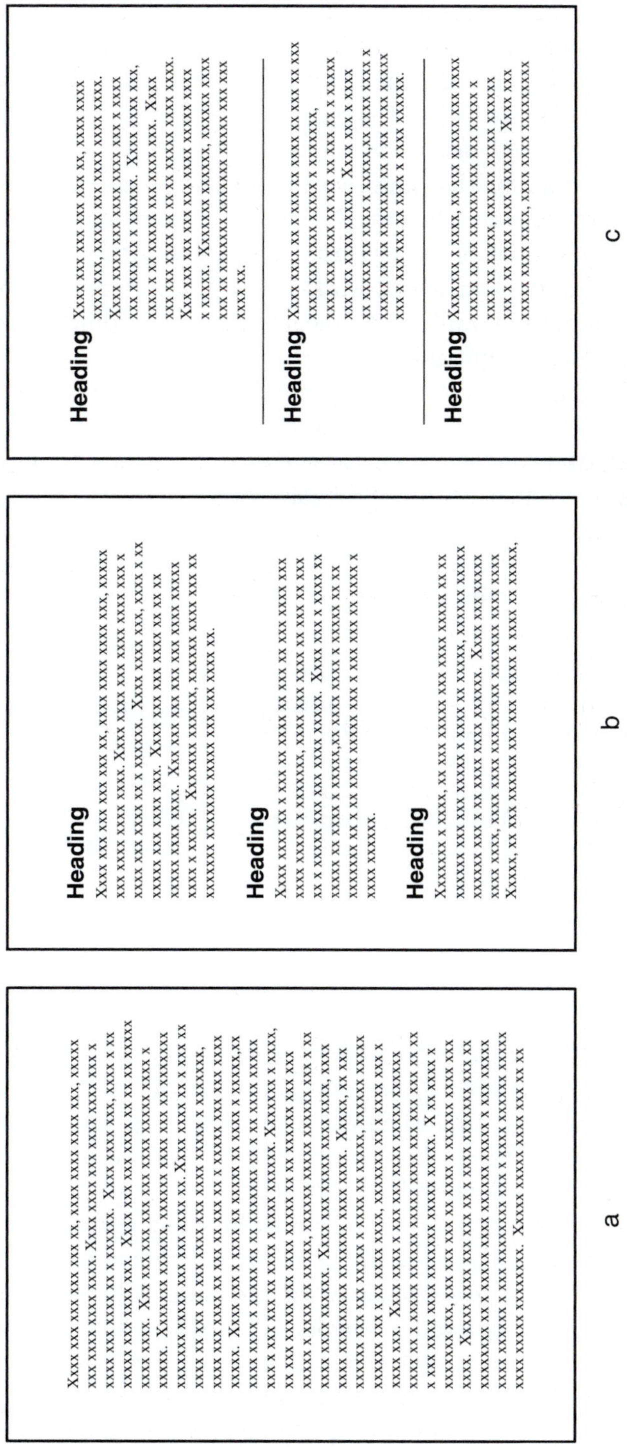

its visual conciseness when headings are added (Figure 5.42b). Most readers, however, would consider the headings a wise investment in text and space. Using marginal headings reduces the space for text even further, as you can see in the page shown in Figure 5.42c. If you compare it with the original text, you can see that we've lost a good deal of text in this field.

Are marginal headings worth the loss of space for text? It depends on the rhetorical situation. If readers need quick access to information, the trade-off can easily be justified both in terms of clarity *and* conciseness because the headings do some significant rhetorical work. Other heading configurations can also affect the amount of space available for the text. Run-in headings, for example, are more efficient but less emphatic.

Leading will also play a significant role in the spatial conciseness of a field. Compare the two chunks of text in Figure 5.43. The one on the left takes less space than the one on the right because it doesn't have any leading. Would readers prefer the more concise version? Probably not.

FIGURE 5.43   Leading affects visual conciseness

Obviously, you can pack a lot of information on a page or screen if you want to—line upon line of text with little or no relief—but that won't ensure that it's clear. Dense text fields often obscure the structure of the ideas because everything blends together.

Obviously, you can pack a lot of information on a page or screen if you want to—line upon line of text with little or no relief—but that won't ensure that it's clear. Dense text fields often obscure the structure of the ideas because everything blends together.

So can the impact of *widows*—short pieces of text that dangle at the end of a paragraph. Editing out some of the widows can save precious lines of space, which is particularly critical when you're working in narrow columns (e.g., a newsletter). On the other hand, eliminating all of the widows, especially in wide columns of text, can make the field look text-heavy.

The width of your columns can also affect spatial conciseness. As you can see in Figure 5.44, if you use two columns rather than one, for example, you'll probably forfeit some space; you'll forfeit even more with three columns. These losses are caused by the shorter line lengths and the alleys between columns.

In some multicolumn fields, however, you'll get some of this space back because of room saved when short headings fit in fewer columns. On page 174 we showed you two examples of a field, one in a single column and the other a

FIGURE 5.44   Conciseness and columns

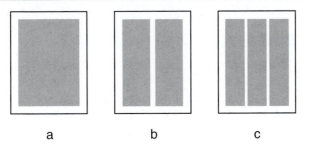

a   b   c

double column (Figures 5.32 and 5.33). Because of the placement of the headings, the double-column field was a little more concise than the single-column version.

Margins can also determine the level of conciseness of a field. You can use most of the field, as in Figure 5.45a, or comparatively little of it, as in Figure 5.45c, which uses less than half the available space.

FIGURE 5.45   Conciseness and margin width

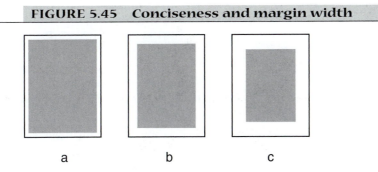

a   b   c

What's most appropriate—small margins or generous margins? From a legibility standpoint, it doesn't make much difference (Tinker 114). From a conventional standpoint, your communication may have to follow certain standards—for example, a minimum of one-inch margins. However, for documents like formal certificates or invitations, very generous margins will be more appropriate, largely to ensure ethos. Once again, conciseness depends on other cognate strategies and their response to the rhetorical situation.

Text fields can also be assessed for *graphical* conciseness. The field in Figure 5.46a contains several graphic elements: the three bars across the headings, the bullets, the box around the indented paragraph along with the gray scale. Does it make sense to use all of these? From a purely perceptual standpoint, probably not. The field in Figure 5.46b is a more graphically concise version.

FIGURE 5.46   Conciseness of graphic elements

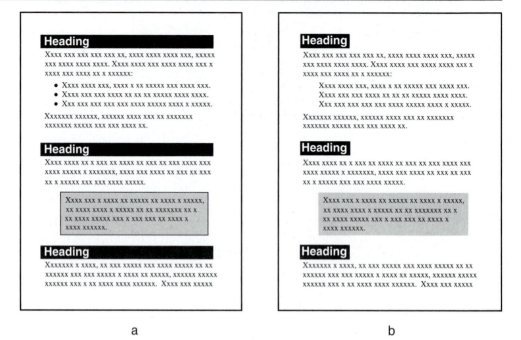

a   b

Still, we need to know more about the document to decide finally whether or not these graphical elements do enough rhetorical work to justify their presence. For example, maybe headings in subsequent text fields run across the entire page; if that were the case, the margin-to-margin heading bar might make sense to preserve consistency. Once again, we can't judge conciseness in a vacuum.

Tone

Text fields speak in many different voices: formal, informal, serious, playful, authoritative, low-key, and so on. How do we know one from another? For example, what gives a visual field a formal or an informal tone?

Textually, the style of headings can project a certain voice, as Figure 5.47 illustrates. Using a sans serif typeface for the heading will give the text a serious, objective look; italicizing the heading will project a warmer, more informal tone. You can also signal tone by the letters or numbers you choose for listing and outlining text. Lists with letters (A, B, C; a, b, c) will look slightly more formal than lists with arabic numbers (1, 2, 3); roman numerals (I, II, III) and decimals (1.00, 1.10, 1.11) will look even more formal and authoritative.

Spatially, field design can instantly establish the tone of the document. If you want to create a formal tone, right justifying the text and centering the headings

FIGURE 5.47   Headings and tone

Headings Affect Tone

Using a sans serif typeface for the heading will give the text a low-key, objective look; italicizing the heading will project a warmer, more informal tone.

Headings Affect Tone

Using a sans serif typeface for the heading will give the text a low-key, objective look; italicizing the heading will project a warmer, more informal tone.

will send some strong signals to your reader. As you can see in Figure 5.48, the visual language immediately reveals the tone of the document—formal and official.

FIGURE 5.48   Centering creates a formal tone

Of course, we're basing our assessment of tone here on North American conventions; some cultures may not associate a smooth right margin and centered headings with a formal tone.

Graphically, readers can pick up additional signals about the tone of a text field. A line a half point thick will have a different tone than a line that's 3 points thick, as you can see in Figure 5.49. The thin line may seem subtle and cautious, the thick line assertive and even overbearing.

FIGURE 5.49   Examples of tonal differences

- Lay out the plan on the outside area you want to use.
- Gather all of the tools listed on the tool sheet.
- Make sure you carefully read the safety information on 4.

✔ Lay out the plan on the outside area you want to use.
✔ Gather all of the tools listed on the tool sheet.
✔ Make sure you carefully read the safety information on 4.

Even something as simple as a bullet can express a certain voice. The square bullets in Figure 5.49 look serious, reserved, even a bit ponderous, especially for such a simple task as putting together playground equipment. The check marks in the second example are more informal, friendlier, and perhaps more appropriate for the rhetorical situation.

The preceding examples point to an important aspect of visual tone: consistency. Just as your writing voice needs consistency, so does your visual voice. The examples in Figure 5.49 lack that consistency: The "laid-back" check mark bullets don't match the assertive 3-point box; and for that matter, the elegant thin line doesn't exactly match the square, ponderous bullets. In both examples, readers might sense some misdirection in visual tone.

Ethos

Ethos in field design depends partly on how professional the document looks. For example, we can weaken our credibility by configuring text as in Figure 5.50.

FIGURE 5.50   Text configuration affects ethos

> Prescott was founded in 1968 by William Prescott, an engineer and builder whose innovations in foundation and soil design received national recognition. By 1980 Prescott grew from three employees to over fifty. Today Prescott has two hundred employees with branch offices in Milwaukee and Denver and building projects that span from coast to coast, to Europe, and to the Middle East.

Why? Because most U.S. readers aren't used to reading left unjustified text; it jolts their sense of what looks right. It looks—well—ragged! What looks correct, however, can vary from one reader to another; for example, readers from the Middle East might find the ragged left margin quite conventional. For them, ragged left might build ethos rather than erode it.

The type of document can also influence the effect of text design on ethos: If you wrote a letter of application or a short story with several levels of headings, the design probably wouldn't look right. Including headings in such texts might well erode your credibility with your readers. Or take the examples of a memo and a newsletter in Figure 5.51. A memo with three columns might lead the boss to suspect the employee's motives or to wonder if the employee were wasting time. On the other hand, a corporate newsletter with a single column of text might lead readers to think that the designer—and the corporation—were inept.

FIGURE 5.51   Relation among genre, text design, and ethos

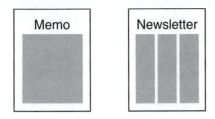

To a large extent, then, building ethos in a field design means satisfying readers' expectations about what constitutes a professional-looking document in a given situation. In most situations, sloppy or inconsistent presentation of the text—headings in various positions and type sizes, gray scales that reduce figure–ground contrast with text, unaligned columns and indents—all will diminish credibility. Careful visual editing can help you avoid these problems.

However, a document that looks professional might still lack ethos. Although both of the pages in Figure 5.52 look reasonably professional, Figure 5.52a, with its marginal headings and its lines demarcating section breaks, sends a more sophisticated, interesting, and probably credible message to the reader. Figure 5.52b, while quite conventional, is also exceedingly plain. The information is the same in both examples, but the one on the left would build more ethos in many rhetorical situations.

FIGURE 5.52   Heading design affects ethos

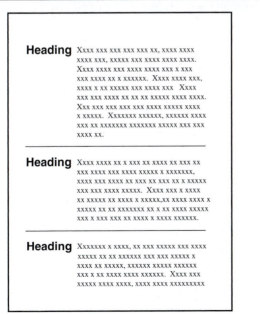

a   b

Of course, sophistication of design doesn't guarantee credibility. Far from it. A CEO who handwrites a letter to a customer will probably engender more trust than a CEO whose words are designed with a computer and laser printer. Similarly, a sales letter that looks like a full-blown newsletter may initially grab the reader's attention, but ethos may quickly wane once the reader catches on.

Interdependence of the Cognate Strategies

For a text field to succeed, all six of the cognate strategies have to work together to meet the demands of the rhetorical situation. That may mean that one strategy enhances another, or it may mean that the designer has to make trade-offs among cognates to adapt them to the situation. Let's examine how this works in a simple field design for a Web site.

Genealogy Service Web Page

Armand Killeen met Scottie Grayson six years ago at an international genealogical convention in Buenos Aires. They hit it off both personally and professionally, and after a few successful freelance consulting projects they have decided to form a business, Int-Gen Research Services, Inc., and to use the World Wide Web to attract customers. After planning their new venture for several weeks, Armand and Scottie have created the mock-up for their Web design, shown in Figure 5.53.

- *Arrangement.* The key arrangement strategy in Armand and Scottie's design is the division of the material into three subfields: the Int-Gen nameplate that runs across the top, the left-hand column listing (and offering links to) the services their company offers, and the wider column of text on the right. Such an arrangement clarifies the functions of each of the three text subfields: identification (nameplate), navigation (services/links), and information (text and bulleted descriptions). By representing Int-Gen as a well-organized and comprehensive service, this three-part division also builds ethos and helps to establish a professional tone.

- *Emphasis.* The gray scale in the nameplate, the title topping the left-hand column, and the bold run-in headings all create emphasis. Although you may have little control over the typography of a Web page, you *can* employ linear components such as type size and boldface. The bulleted list, of course, also creates emphasis as well as enhances clarity by making information more accessible to site visitors. The use of penlike bullets gives the Web page a more formal and professional tone than plain bullets, contributing to ethos as well.

- *Clarity.* Separating the Featured Services column with the shaded scroll executes both emphasis and clarity strategies. The scroll suggests the historical and

FIGURE 5.53   Int-Gen Research Service web page

Int-Gen Research Services, Inc.
International Genealogy Consulting & Assistance

Curious to know your story? We can help . . .

Featured Services

Custom research reports

Family tree charts

Family group spreadsheets

Family legislative reference indexes

Graves registration maps

Photocopies of archival documents

Property abstracts

Baptismal records

Resource videos & CDs

Special gift books

Our Story. Founded by Armand Killeen and Scottie Grayson in 1990, Int-Gen Research Service combines state-of-the-art technology with unmatched professionalism to offer fast, reliable, and confidential information about your family tree.

Our Services. We provide genealogical backgrounds for families with primary roots in North America as well as for those with ancestral ties to:

- Great Britain
- Continental Europe
- Scandinavia
- Australia and New Zealand

Our Fees. Int-Gen Research Services offers flexible fee structures, including a free trial package that will tell you if our capabilities meet your needs and preferences. All of our consultations are completely confidential.

E-mail contact: intgen@usa.com   Fax requests: 01-950-924-3716

Credentials   Privacy Policy   Genealogical Research   Contact Us   Testimonials   Links

research-oriented nature of the service while defining the navigational bar. Users of the Web around the world will be quite familiar with this design convention, which will also build ethos in this context. The underlined links and the links along the bottom of the screen are conventions that will also enhance clarity and ethos.

■ *Conciseness.* Armand and Scottie achieve conciseness by using restraint with design choices such as line work and shading, avoiding visual noise and enhancing clarity. That's the hallmark of a concise field design, and conciseness usually works hand-in-hand with clarity. They also chose to be visually concise because they are appealing to a large audience that spans many cultures and national boundaries, and they want to be careful not to include graphic elements that readers might misinterpret.

■ *Tone.* As suggested previously, the tone of the site is low-key and functional.

■ *Ethos.* The simple, straightforward design is intended to build confidence in readers by talking plainly and directly with them about a subject they take seriously.

All of the cognate strategies work together as Armand and Scottie adapt their design to their rhetorical situation. This is their first effort to advertise on the Web. Later they may decide to add pictures to their site, but for now their Web page contains a simple field that complements the verbal text.

Notes

1. Jan Spyridakis, Kathryn Mobrand, Elisabeth Cuddihy, and Carolyn Wei have experimented with several Internet linking techniques to measure user comprehension and exploration.

2. Miles Tinker provides summaries of a wide range of research on the spatial organization of text. Other excellent sources include Cyril Burt and James Hartley. A briefer summary of research can be found in Philippa Benson.

3. In general, Tinker (74–87) reports that line lengths for text set in common type sizes should be less than about 36 picas (about 6 inches). Although Tinker generally found that smaller type sizes (e.g., 6 or 8 point) require somewhat shorter line lengths for optimal legibility, a consistent correlation between type size, line length, and legibility was not established. Tinker did find, however, that increased leading improved the legibility of type that was set in longer line lengths.

References

Benson, Philippa J. "Writing Visually: Design Considerations in Technical Publications." *Technical Communication* 32 (1985): 35–39.

Burt, Cyril L. *A Psychological Study of Typography.* Cambridge: Cambridge University Press, 1959.

Farkas, David K., and Jean B. Farkas. "Guidelines for Designing Web Navigation." *Technical Communication* 47 (2000): 341–358.

Hartley, James. *Designing Instructional Text.* 2nd ed. New York: Nichols, 1985.

Hartley, James, and Mark Trueman. "A Research Strategy for Text Designers: The Role of Headings." *Instructional Science* 14 (1985): 99–155.

Kostelnick, Charles. "The Rhetoric of Text Design in Professional Communication." *The Technical Writing Teacher* 17 (1990): 189–202.

Spyridakis, Jan H., Kathryn A. Mobrand, Elisabeth Cuddihy, and Carolyn Y. Wei. "Using Structural Cues to Guide Readers on the Internet." *Information Design Journal* 15 (2007): 242–259.

Tinker, Miles A. *Legibility of Print.* Ames: Iowa State University Press, 1963.

Tufte, Edward R. *The Cognitive Style of PowerPoint: Pitching Out Corrupts Within.* 2nd ed. Cheshire, CN: Graphics Press, 2006.

Exercises

1. Figures 5.54 and 5.55 show two different field designs for instructions on how to jump-start a car. Readers will be younger people who've never done this task before; they'll probably use the instructions outside, often in very cold weather. Use the guidelines below to compare the rhetorical impact of these two designs.

   a. *Visual vocabulary.* List the differences in the visual vocabulary of the two versions. You should be able to find at least six significant ones.

   b. *Arrangement.* Which version structures the steps more effectively? Which visual elements make the most difference between the two versions?

   c. *Emphasis.* Which version emphasizes critical information more effectively? Does the warning have enough emphasis? What are the legal and ethical implications of ineffective emphasis?

   d. *Clarity.* Which version is the most legible? Why? How will the context affect clarity, assuming that readers will use the instructions outside in cold weather?

   e. *Conciseness.* Does either version contain design elements that don't do any rhetorical work? Does either version contain too few design elements (i.e., it's too concise)?

   f. *Ethos.* Which of the two versions builds the most ethos? Why?

   Note: The two versions of the jump-start instructions (Figures 5.54 and 5.55) are intended solely to illustrate and stimulate discussion of design elements.

2. To announce the opening of her tea garden and craft store, Joan Bernini would like to send a postcard to selected residents in her area. The postcard will invite readers to drop by her store, sip some tea in her intimate courtyard garden, and

FIGURE 5.54   Jump-start instructions—version 1

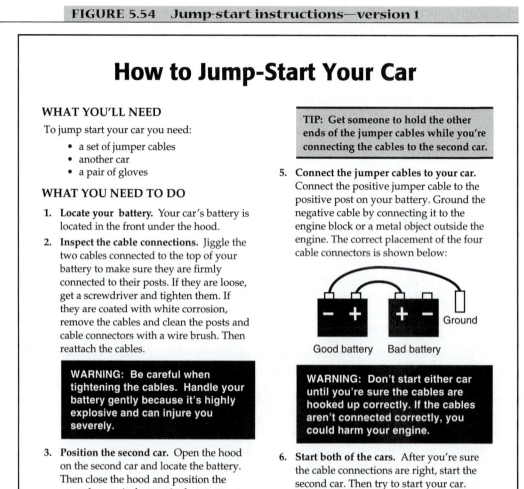

How to Jump-Start Your Car

WHAT YOU'LL NEED

To jump start your car you need:

- a set of jumper cables
- another car
- a pair of gloves

WHAT YOU NEED TO DO

1. **Locate your battery.** Your car's battery is located in the front under the hood.

2. **Inspect the cable connections.** Jiggle the two cables connected to the top of your battery to make sure they are firmly connected to their posts. If they are loose, get a screwdriver and tighten them. If they are coated with white corrosion, remove the cables and clean the posts and cable connectors with a wire brush. Then reattach the cables.

> **WARNING: Be careful when tightening the cables. Handle your battery gently because it's highly explosive and can injure you severely.**

3. **Position the second car.** Open the hood on the second car and locate the battery. Then close the hood and position the second car so its battery is close to your car's battery. When you have the second car in place, turn off its engine.

4. **Connect the jumper cables to the second car's battery.** Locate the negative (–) and positive (+) posts on the second car's battery. Then attach the jumper car's negative connector to the negative post of the second car's battery and the positive connector to the positive post.

> **WARNING: Be careful that the unattached connectors of the jumper cables don't touch or you'll get a shock!**

> **TIP: Get someone to hold the other ends of the jumper cables while you're connecting the cables to the second car.**

5. **Connect the jumper cables to your car.** Connect the positive jumper cable to the positive post on your battery. Ground the negative cable by connecting it to the engine block or a metal object outside the engine. The correct placement of the four cable connectors is shown below:

Good battery   Bad battery   Ground

> **WARNING: Don't start either car until you're sure the cables are hooked up correctly. If the cables aren't connected correctly, you could harm your engine.**

6. **Start both of the cars.** After you're sure the cable connections are right, start the second car. Then try to start your car.

> **TIP: Turn the key on your car for 10–15 seconds. If it doesn't start, wait a minute or two before trying again. This will give your battery some time to charge.**

7. **Disconnect the jumper cables.** After your car starts, remove the cables. Be careful not to touch the ends of the cables together until you've removed them from both cars.

FIGURE 5.55   Jump-start instructions—version 2

How to Jump-Start Your Car

WHAT YOU'LL NEED

To jump start your car, you need (1) a set of jumper cables, (2) another car, and (3) a pair of gloves.

WHAT YOU NEED TO DO

1. **Locate your battery.** Your car's battery is located in the front under the hood.

2. **Inspect the cable connections.** Jiggle the two cables connected to the top of your battery to make sure they are firmly connected to their posts. If they are loose, get a screwdriver and tighten them. If they are coated with white corrosion, remove the cables and clean the posts and cable connetors with a wire brush. Then reattach the cables.

    > **WARNING: Be careful when tightening the cables. Handle your battery gently because it's highly explosive and can injure you severely.**

3. **Position the second car.**   Open the hood of the second car and locate the battery. Then close the hood and position the second car so its battery is close to your car's battery. When you have the second car in place, turn off its engine.

4. **Connect the jumper cables to the second car's battery.** Locate the negative (–) and positive (+) posts on the second car's battery. Then attach the jumper cable's negative connector to the negative post of the second car's battery and the positive connector to the positive post.

    > **WARNING: Be careful that the unattached connectors of the jumper cables don't touch or you'll get a shock!**

    > **TIP: Get someone to hold the other ends of the jumper cables while you're connecting the cables to the second car.**

5. **Connect the jumper cables to your car.** Connect the positive jumper cable to the positive post on your battery. Ground the negative cable by connecting it to the engine block or a metal object outside the engine. The correct placement of the four cable connectors is shown below:

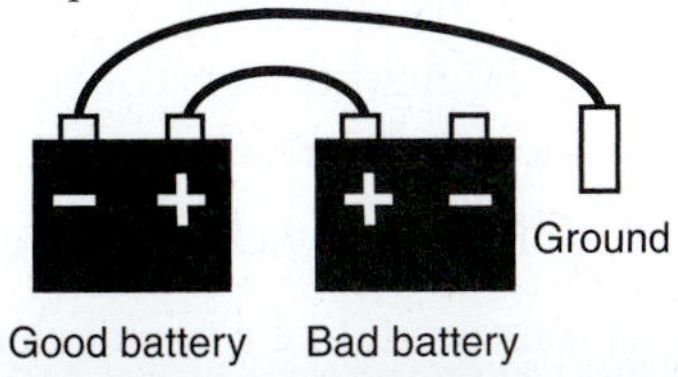

    > **WARNING: Don't start either car until you're sure the cables are hooked up correctly. If the cables aren't connected correctly, you could harm your engine.**

6. **Start both of the cars.** After you're sure the cable connections are right, start the second car. Then try to start your car.

    > **TIP: Turn the key on your car for 10–15 seconds. If it doesn't start, wait a minute or two before trying again. This will give your battery some time to charge.**

7. **Disconnect the jumper cables.** After your car starts, remove the cables. Be careful not to touch the ends of the cables together until you've removed them from both cars.

stroll through the aisles of crafts and collectibles. Design Joan's postcard, which will measure 4 inches by 5 inches, with the text below.

Your design should be clear and direct so that readers can immediately understand that they are invited to a grand opening. It should be persuasive, of course; and toward that end, your design should be tasteful and aesthetically pleasing, but without being gaudy or flashy, which would undermine Joan's ethos.

```
Grand opening! Joan's Tea Garden and Craft Emporium.
You're invited to celebrate the grand opening of Joan's
Tea Garden and Craft Emporium. Come browse among the
tables of potpourri, the baskets of dried flowers, and
the shelves of books and collectibles. Whether you're
shopping for a special gift or you enjoy doing your own
crafts, you'll love the selection. Saturday, May 17,
9-5. 125 South Main. Free croissants! Free tea! Free
potpourri!
```

3. Visit the personal Web pages (e.g., Facebook, MySpace, etc.) of some people you know and analyze the rhetorical impact of their field design. If the personal Web pages have links to more than one screen, analyze only the first screen. Use the questions below to guide your evaluation.

   a. *Emphasis.* How well does the field design emphasize important information about this person? Knowing what you do about this person, does this emphasis create an accurate picture of the person?

   b. *Tone.* How well does the tone of the design express this person's voice? Is the visual voice on the Web the same one you're familiar with? Does it ring true visually?

   c. *Conciseness.* Is the field design concise? Does each design element do some rhetorical work? If not, which ones can be deleted or modified?

   d. *Ethos.* How well does the field design enhance the ethos of the Web page?

4. Bullets for lists may seem like a trivial element in text design, but even a bullet can do some rhetorical work—for example, setting the tone and creating ethos. Decide which of the bullets below would best fit the tone and ethos of the rhetorical situations described.

   ✔   ■   ❄   ●

   a. A list of ingredients for making burritos; the checklist will appear in a cookbook sold by a local high school booster club.

   b. A list of recommendations in the executive summary of a 50-page report from a legislative task force to the governor of your state.

    c. A list of troubleshooting problems in a set of instructions for maintaining the ventilation system for a nuclear power plant.

    d. A list of seven "dates to remember" in a one-page winter newsletter for a ballet school; parents of enrolled children will probably hang it on the refrigerator.

    e. A list of budget cuts in a PowerPoint presentation at a staff meeting.

5. Using the content on jump-starting a car (from Exercise 1 in this chapter), construct a three- to five-slide PowerPoint presentation that covers the basics of this process. Assume that your audience is comprised of members of a Chautauqua-type class on "Auto Mechanics for Dummies." The purpose is to help automotively challenged people be better prepared for minor emergencies and other roadside issues.

    In designing your PowerPoint slides, remember that the goal is to cite key words and phrases to help the presenter make his or her points, not to provide text that the audience simply reads. Also remember principles of effective chunking of information, including visual strategies for showing subordination (as in major point versus secondary point).

Assignments

1. A friend who works for Desert Food Emporium has brought you some informational material about a new service his employer is offering. It's called Personal Shopping Express, and it's intended for the store's customers who need groceries in a hurry but are short on time or capability (e.g., elderly, disabled). Your friend's boss wants to develop an attractive fact sheet or brochure that can be mailed or handed out to prospective users of the new service.

    The document needs to fit on one 8½" × 11" sheet that's (a) unfolded, (b) folded once in a "treasure chest" format, or (c) folded twice into a six-panel brochure. Designing this communication represents an excellent opportunity for you to snag some additional business with the store—if you do a good job they may be willing to let you design (or redesign) other materials for them.

    You should devote most of your time to designing the appropriate visual elements, and on making sure that verbal and visual strategies work together to respond to the document's rhetorical situation. If you believe that the verbal elements need some editing changes, go ahead and make them; however, be careful not to alter the meaning. The information itself may be arranged in whatever order makes the best sense to you. Here's the text you have to work with:

```
Desert Food's Personal Shopping Express
To widen the convenient food shopping services we
provide, Desert Food Emporium is proud to announce
```

the kickoff of our Personal Shopping Express. Here's
how it works. Perhaps you're in the midst of preparing
a gourmet dinner for some special friends and discover
to your dismay that you've run out of some crucial
ingredients. What do you do? Or, suppose your houseguests
arrive a day early and you suddenly have extra meals
to prepare. What do you do? Or, maybe you're just
finding it difficult to make regular trips to buy
groceries because of all the ice and snow. What
do you do?

Just call Desert Food Emporium's Personal Shopping
Express (555-6789). We'll deliver your order right to
your door. The Express is open seven days a week from
7 a.m. to 11 p.m. There is a minimum charge of $25, and
we guarantee delivery within one hour to any place within a 5-mile radius of our store. For your security, our
delivery personnel will carry DFE identity badges and
will recite a special confirmation code.

You can order any quantity of groceries, beverages,
supplies, or sundries through the Personal Shopping Express,
with the exception of the customary limits on special
sale items.

We will bring you fresh fruits and vegetables right
off our supply trucks; we'll bring you the finest cuts
of meat, ready for the broiler or the barbecue grill;
we'll bring you lightbulbs and cellophane tape; we'll
bring batteries for your boombox and toothpicks for
your shish kebabs. If you desire prepared items from
DFE's excellent catering service, give us just a few
hours lead-time. (Did you forget to buy a birthday
cake? We can help, and that special someone will be
none the wiser.)

For your convenience, all Personal Shopping Express
orders will be billed once a month, and automatic
checking withdrawal payments are available through most
area banks.

The best part of DFE's Personal Shopping Express is
that you'll earn double frequent shopper points on all
orders, which will mean quicker access to rewards and
discounts, including promotion to Premier status. As a
Premier DFE Shopper, you'll be eligible for our special
drawing that will reward some lucky shopper with an
all-expenses-paid vacation to Costa Rica.

2. Many organizations use newsletters to keep in touch with their members: to
update them on current events, to give them facts and other information, and

to establish an identity for the group. In this assignment you'll design a short newsletter for the Student Mountain Club. The SMC has not published a newsletter before, so yours will be the first in the series. Here's a quick overview of the rhetorical situation:

- *Audience.* SMC members—students who enjoy hiking in the mountains; the students (both undergraduate and graduate) are from your state, across the country, and around the world (the club has attracted many international students in the past few years); also, the audience includes prospective SMC members. Some of the intended readers, then, will have little previous knowledge about the club, while others will know a great deal.
- *Purpose.* To tell members about club activities as well as to give them hiking tips and ideas; it should also get them interested in (or increase their interest in) mountain hiking. In addition to informing existing members about club activities, one of the main goals of the newsletter is to attract new members.
- *Context.* The newsletter will be distributed by mail to members as well as at booths at university events; readers will read for details or to retrieve important information (times and dates of activities).

As you design your newsletter, think about how you can implement all six of the cognate strategies—arrangement, emphasis, clarity, conciseness, tone, and ethos—to meet the rhetorical situation. Each visual element you include in your newsletter should do some rhetorical work—that is, each element should implement one or more of the cognate strategies. To satisfy the rhetorical situation, your newsletter should be inviting (have a friendly tone), should give readers easy access to the information (have good arrangement, emphasis, and clarity strategies), and should look professional (project good ethos; be concise by not looking cluttered).

In designing your newsletter, you'll have to do some careful supra-level planning to get your document to fit on both sides of one 8½" × 11" page. Within these two fields, you may arrange textual units any way you wish and make minor editing changes to accommodate your visual choices. Some thumbnail sketches with a pencil and paper would be a good way to get started. Once you've decided on the preliminary layout, you can start working on the computer.

You can use any typeface, point size, or graphic element that helps give readers access to the information or that adds interest to your document. Your newsletter should include a nameplate at the top—Thin Air—that creates a strong identity for your document (also contributing to its ethos). Your nameplate might also include graphic elements or a logo, though logos can take a good deal of effort to create. You should probably design the text first, then return to the nameplate in the remaining time you have.

Text for the Newsletter:

Thin Air
The Student Mountain Club Newsletter
Spring XXXX
Volume 1, No. 1

From the President
   Welcome to the first edition of the SMC Newsletter! We
hope it will create a reliable resource for you about club
activities and events. In this newsletter you'll find
announcements about club activities as well as other information we hope you'll find interesting, useful, and inspiring.
   Our officers have exciting programs and trips planned
for this year. I hope you'll enjoy all of them!
   Chris Jones, President

Fall Trip to Mount Washington
   During the Thanksgiving break several club members
drove to the Presidential Range in New Hampshire to climb
Mount Washington and surrounding peaks. The conditions
were excellent—clear skies, above-freezing temperatures,
and wind velocities under 50 mph. That was quite a pleas-
ant surprise: Mount Washington holds the wind velocity
record, and snow starts to fly in early fall.
   Club members camped in tents in a nearby national forest. They hiked to the summits of Madison, Adams, and
Jefferson, following the Appalachian Trail for nearly 40
miles. All members of the group spotted moose along the
trail. The club will definitely consider the Presidential
Range for future trips.

Trail Volunteers Needed
   Volunteers for clearing trails are needed in several
state and national forests and parks. This is a great way
to learn about a mountain ecosystem while preparing the
trails for the summer season for your fellow hikers. Spend
your spring break in the Rockies or the Appalachians where
the streams run clear, the trees open their canopies, and
the rhododendrons bloom. Housing is provided free, and car
pooling is available. Contact Steve at 782-5555 for details.

Dressing for the Climb
   Climbing a "fourteener" in Colorado can be an exhilarating experience—if you're prepared. Most novices, however, make the mistake of underestimating the brute force
of nature above the timberline. That can be a big—even
fatal—mistake.

At this February's monthly meeting, Fred Carlson will conduct a seminar on dressing for the climb. Fred, who worked for the National Park Service the past three summers, has lots of experience outfitting backpackers and climbers. Join us and let Fred help you plan your next mountain adventure.

Spring Trip to the Big Horn Mountains

The Big Horn mountains in northern Wyoming are one of the best kept secrets in the West—uncrowded, challenging, and rugged. That's why we've chosen them as the destination for this year's spring trip.

Here's our itinerary: We'll leave from the Union on Monday, March X, and stay overnight in Sheridan, Wyoming. Tuesday afternoon we'll be on the trail in the Big Horns, heading southwest. We'll camp four nights, then return on Saturday from Buffalo. The approximate cost for members will be $175. Sign up soon so we can line up transportation and supplies.

Congratulations to Jerry, Brenda, and Fred

In June Jerry Smith, Brenda Sikes, and Fred Carlson climbed Mount Rainier in Washington State. Although they were caught in a snowstorm on their descent, they made it back safely. "We had a clear view at the top," said Jerry. "It was worth every step-an incredible experience! I can't wait to go back."

Welcome New Members and Officers

Last fall we've had nearly 20 new members from around the country and the globe. Welcome!

This year's officers include:
President, Chris Jones
Vice President, Sally Smith
Secretary, Al Foster
Treasurer, Karl Neuberg
Field Trip Coordinator, Brenda Sikes

Annual Fundraiser

We'll be selling mountain T-shirts, mugs, and calendars for our annual fund-raiser. These items make great gifts any time of the year. We need volunteers for our booth displays. Contact Sue at 782-2222.

Planning the Summer Break Tour

Our annual summer tour (the week before classes begin) is still in the planning stages. Scotland, Norway, Switzerland, Chile, and Hawaii are just of few of the many

destinations under consideration. Give us your ideas and
input. We need to finalize our plans by the end of March
so we can get you the airfare discounts you need. Call
Joe (782-4593) with your ideas and preferences—soon!

Mountain Lectures

Thursday, February 12, Jim Spitzer, "Which Mountain
Will Be the Next St. Helens?" Find out about the geology
of the Cascades and how it's likely to change within the
coming decades.

Wednesday, March 17, Mary Ann Woodling, "High Terrain
Mammals." Learn about the amazing adaptive qualities of
bears, marmots, and other mountain creatures.

Monday, April 21, Liu Chang, "The Mountain People of
Tibet." Discover this unique culture from an anthropology
graduate student who has lived and worked in Tibet.

Club Meeting Schedule—Spring Semester

We'll meet every other Tuesday evening at 7:00 in the
Student Union Lounge. Bring your friends!

6 Nonlinear Components

Introduction to Nonlinear Components

Sometimes a rhetorical situation requires textual information—words, numbers, or both—to appear in a form that differs significantly from the linear, line-by-line layout of paragraphs. We'll refer to this other form of text design as *nonlinear*. For nonlinear design to occur, one of two conditions must be present:

1. Readers can more easily or accurately access the textual information in a non-linear form rather than in paragraphs of continuous text.
2. The relations among the textual elements call for a schematic rather than a literal, line-by-line expression.

Let's look at these conditions one at a time. Consider a baseball lineup for an all-star game where the players and managers come together for one game against another all-star team. The manager and his two assistants don't know all of the players that well, so they need a reference that gives them some quick facts about their lineup on the day of the game. Here's what such a lineup might look like in linear form:

1. Nick, shortstop, bats left, throws right, hits .294 (.267 against right-handed pitching, .311 against left-handed) with 14 home runs and 67 RBIs and 24 stolen bases in 32 attempts;
2. Matt, right field, bats right, throws right, hits .341 (hit .287 against righties, .372 against lefties) with 17 home runs and 95 RBIs and 41 stolen bases in 45 attempts.

and so on through the rest of the lineup. Even with only nine primary chunks of information, the text lacks accessibility, which will certainly frustrate the manager and his coaches. In this form the information is not very accessible, especially considering that they'll use it during the flow of the game when time is precious and they have to make quick decisions.

Placing this information in tabular form, however, gives the manager and coaches the access they'll need, as you can see in Figure 6.1.

FIGURE 6.1   Batting lineup in table format

		Pos	B	T	Ave.	Rt.	Lft.	HR	RBI	St.–At.
1	Nick	SS	L	R	.294	.267	.311	14	67	24–32
2	Matt	RF	R	R	.341	.287	.372	17	95	41–45
3	R.D.	C	S	R	.322	.274	.366	38	94	3–4
4	Pete	1B	L	L	.328	.359	.276	34	122	15–20
5	John	CF	R	R	.317	.297	.338	27	107	15–21
6	Chris	2B	R	R	.312	.306	.322	8	53	17–24
7	Joseph	3B	L	R	.284	.315	.259	24	102	7–15
8	David	LF	L	R	.293	.294	.289	20	89	22–29
9	Isaac	P	R	R	.292	.313	.270	2	33	9–11

Now they can easily find information that they'll want during the game when they decide whether to bunt, steal, sacrifice, or swing away in a given situation.

For the second condition, textual information that calls for a schematic representation, consider a family tree. Certainly a nuclear family is easy enough to envision, but beyond that, relationships can get complex, particularly if the family history includes lots of wars, diseases, beheadings, and second families after remarriages. Below is a linear description of the British royal family tree during the time of the Wars of the Roses (14th and 15th centuries).

> Edward III was born in 1312 and ruled from 1327 to 1377. He had seven sons, five of whom survived to adulthood. The eldest was Edward, known as the Black Prince. He was born in 1330 and died in 1376. Edward's son, Richard (1376 to 1399) became King Richard II upon the death of his grandfather, Edward III. The second son was Lionel of Antwerp, Duke of Clarence, who lived from 1338 to 1368. His daughter, Philippa, married Edmund Mortimer, Earl of March. Edward's third son was John of Gaunt, Duke of Lancaster, 1340 to 1399. John's eldest son became King Henry IV,

father of Henry V and grandfather of Henry VI, these three being known as Lancastrian kings. Edward III's fourth son was Edmund, Duke of York, who was born in 1341 and died in 1402. His great-grandsons became Edward IV and Richard III, known as Yorkist kings. Finally, the fifth son was Thomas of Woodstock, Duke of Gloucester, 1355 to 1397. . . .

The varied and often abstract relationships outlined here will be much more easily understood if we put the text into a nonlinear form, as we've done in Figure 6.2. In the chart version, readers can quickly visualize some of the complex relationships that would take many paragraphs to explain and even then would be impossible to hold in short-term memory. The family tree *reveals* relationships instead of explaining them.[1]

Nonlinear displays of text include a variety of genres, including tables, flowcharts, organizational charts, decision trees, and concept charts. All contain nonlinear text, all use nonlinear spatial formats, and many contain lines, borders, or other graphic elements so readers can access their information. In the process example that follows you'll see a professional communicator grappling with a nonlinear design problem related more to business than to baseball or genealogy.

Process Example—Nonlinear Components

Teresa Paolodudine works in the communication department of a sporting goods manufacturer. Today she finished collecting pricing data for a new line of camping tents that her company has developed. Her manager wants her to design a display that salespeople can use in figuring costs for their customers—large retail stores across the United States and Canada—quickly and efficiently. Although the table is intended primarily for sales staff and company management, customers can also receive copies upon request. Because of changes in cost, interest rates, and the business climate, the table will have to be revised periodically. So it will need to be flexible enough for a member of the clerical staff to type in the new numbers.

Teresa has several types of tents to include in her display:

- The Mountaineer—a four-person model and a two-person model
- The Galaxy—a six-person model and a deluxe eight-person model
- The Pathfinder—a four-person model and a deluxe four-person model

Each tent varies in price depending on the quantity ordered and the method of payment. For example, here's what her data look like for the Mountaineer:

Four-person tent: quantities of 1–5 each cost $65 (cash), $70 (90 days), and $75 (160 days); quantities of 6–10 each cost $60 (cash), $65 (90 days), and $70 (160 days); more than 10 each cost $55 (cash), $60 (90 days), and

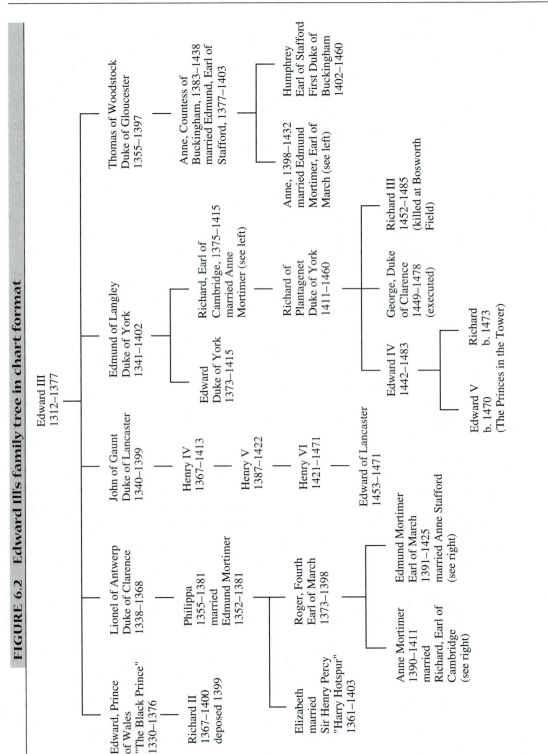

FIGURE 6.2   Edward III's family tree in chart format

$65 (160 days). Two person tent: quantities of 1–5 each cost $55 (cash), $60 (90 days), and $65 (160 days); quantities of 6–10 each cost $50 (cash), $55 (90 days), and $60 (160 days); more than 10 each cost $45 (cash), $50 (90 days), and $55 (160 days).

That's a lot of variables, she thinks—and that's data for just *one* of the three new tents models! How do I get all the data into the same table so users can easily find what they need?

Analyzing the Rhetorical Situation

Before she invests any of her time designing the data, Teresa mulls over the rhetorical situation.

- ■ *Audience.* The main readers will be 30 salespeople, who need to look up the costs as customers place orders. Most people in the sales force are younger males who have been with the company for fewer than two years. Other readers will include prospective customers, who may use the table to make purchase decisions.

- ■ *Purpose.* The price sheet has to help readers look up information based on several variables (for example, a customer who wants to buy eight Mountaineer tents and pay in 90 days), so clarity will be foremost. Mistakes could be costly and embarrassing to the company and the customer, undermining goodwill. Ethos will also play a role, since the document needs to project a professional image, especially if customers see it.

- ■ *Context.* Salespeople will use this sheet while meeting face-to-face with customers or talking to them on the phone. Although the salespeople are conscientious about their work, Teresa knows that they sometimes make mistakes when they figure up their orders while chatting with customers. The price sheet might later be included in promotional materials for the tent, so it has to be relatively compact.

Invention

Teresa begins by setting up a table with the tent models at the top and the price variables on the left. She guesses that the salespeople will look up information by first identifying the type of tent and then scanning the row headings to find the appropriate quantity and method of payment.

To accommodate this reading pattern, Teresa sets up a table with seven columns and ten rows, enough for each piece of information. She has some difficulty squeezing in the column heads, so she uses 9-point Times to conserve space. She uses the same font for the row headings—just to keep everything parallel—and uses 10-point

Times to make the numbers clear (mistakes can be costly). Teresa's first attempt is shown in Figure 6.3.

FIGURE 6.3   Teresa's draft of the tent price table

	Galaxy 6-person	Galaxy 8-person deluxe	Mountaineer 2-person	Mountaineer 4-person	Pathfinder 4-person	Pathfinder 4-person deluxe
1–5—cash	135	170	55	65	70	80
1–5—90 days	145	180	60	70	75	85
1–5—180 days	155	190	65	75	80	90
6–10—cash	125	160	50	60	65	75
6–10—90 days	135	170	55	65	70	80
6–10—180 days	145	180	60	70	75	85
11 or up—cash	115	150	45	55	60	70
11 or up—90 days	125	160	50	60	65	75
11 or up—180 days	135	170	55	65	70	80

Another issue Teresa must confront at this stage of her design is the order in which the three different families of tents are presented. Her arrangement strategy needs to address an ethical question: Does placing the higher-priced Galaxy line nearest the row headings *push* those more costly products? Teresa decides not, since both tents in the Galaxy series are, from company marketing surveys, likely to be as popular as the other two lines.

Revision

After looking at her table Teresa worries that it looks too bland. Nothing stands out. It lacks the visual structure users need to extract the information they want quickly and effortlessly. It also doesn't look very professional, especially considering that customers will occasionally receive it. So she goes to work revising.

First she needs to do some rearranging to give the table more structure. She begins by grouping the column headings according to the three types of tents. She also changes the headings to 12-point Times and bolds them to give more emphasis. Second, Teresa groups the row headings into three units based on quantity and changes the font to emphasize them. She also increases the subheads to 10 points to make them more legible. Figure 6.4 shows her revision.

Having addressed the structure problem, Teresa now realizes that the table still lacks clarity and ethos. The text looks too dense and crowded, so she changes the typeface for the numerical cells to Helvetica to give the data a cleaner, more professional look (Figure 6.5).

Teresa also adds five points of leading before and after the column headings and adds two points before and after each row. Now the column headings and

FIGURE 6.4   Teresa's first revision of the price table

quantity	terms	Galaxy 6-person	Galaxy 8-person deluxe	Mountaineer 2-person	Mountaineer 4-person	Pathfinder 4-person	Pathfinder 4-person deluxe
1–5	cash	135	170	55	65	70	80
	90 days	145	180	60	70	75	85
	160 days	155	190	65	75	80	90
6–10	cash	125	160	50	60	65	75
	90 days	135	170	55	65	70	80
	160 days	145	180	60	70	75	85
11+	cash	115	150	45	55	60	70
	90 days	125	160	50	60	65	75
	160 days	135	170	55	65	70	80

FIGURE 6.5   Teresa's second revision of the price table

quantity	terms	Galaxy 6-person	Galaxy 8-person deluxe	Mountaineer 2-person	Mountaineer 4-person	Pathfinder 4-person	Pathfinder 4-person deluxe
1–5	cash	135	170	55	65	70	80
	90 days	145	180	60	70	75	85
	160 days	155	190	65	75	80	90
6–10	cash	125	160	50	60	65	75
	90 days	135	170	55	65	70	80
	160 days	145	180	60	70	75	85
11+	cash	115	150	45	55	60	70
	90 days	125	160	50	60	65	75
	160 days	135	170	55	65	70	80

data have some breathing room. She also centers the data in each cell, increasing the figure–ground contrast of each number. To give the table additional structure, she adds a heavier line between the major row groups, which she hopes creates better continuity as the user's eye travels from left to right.

Visual Editing

Teresa thinks she's getting closer to a solution. She puts the price table aside for a few hours to attend a monthly staff meeting. On her way back to her office she talks briefly with the sales manager, then sits down before her computer and does some visual editing. Teresa makes several changes as she edits, changes that she hopes will make the display more accessible to her readers as well as enhance its ethos (see Figure 6.6).

FIGURE 6.6 Teresa's edited tent price table

Price Factors		Galaxy		Mountaineer		Pathfinder	
Quantity	Terms	6-person	8-person deluxe	2-person	4-person	4-person	4-person deluxe
1–5	cash	135	170	55	65	70	80
	90 days	145	180	60	70	75	85
	160 days	155	190	65	75	80	90
6–10	cash	125	160	50	60	65	75
	90 days	135	170	55	65	70	80
	160 days	145	180	60	70	75	85
11+	cash	115	150	45	55	60	70
	90 days	125	160	50	60	65	75
	160 days	135	170	55	65	70	80

Note: All prices are expressed in dollars. Prices are subject to change quarterly.

1. She shades the cells containing the column and row headings to give them more emphasis. The shading, she thinks, also enhances the ethos of the display by adding variety and interest.
2. She adds heavy vertical lines to separate divisions between the three tent models; she hopes this will help clarity by enabling users to locate the numbers more quickly and accurately.
3. She changes the column and row headings to Helvetica for greater emphasis and adds the column heading Price Factors to fill in the column stub, an arrangement strategy.
4. She vertically centers the column subheads that take only one line (e.g., Quantity) and adds space below the other column subheads so that they don't look so

crowded. Both of these visual moves make the table look more professional, enhancing its ethos.

5. She adds a note to the bottom of the table to ensure that users, both salespeople and customers, understand that the prices are in U.S. dollars and that they remain in effect only until the end of the quarter.

Although Teresa has added many features to her design, the table is still flexible enough for staff members to change the numbers in the future. Teresa is now ready to present this version of the table to the sales manager for his feedback. During the next few days she'll also test it with some salespeople to see how well they can use it.

Vocabulary of Nonlinear Components

As you can see from Teresa's experience designing her price table, the vocabulary of nonlinear displays includes a variety of textual, spatial, and graphic elements, which she continually orchestrates during her design process, from invention to revision to editing. Let's step back for a moment and isolate the three modes—textual, spatial, and graphic—so we can survey the expansive vocabulary that you can draw from as you create tables and other nonlinear displays such as flowcharts, organizational charts, and decision trees.

Textual Elements

Nonlinear design dislodges text from its verbal cadence by dividing it into fragments, distributing it across a field, and often reconnecting it with lines, boxes, or arrows. While linear text is sheltered visually within the smooth terrain of continuous lines, nonlinear text stands out like islands, keys, and archipelagoes. Nonlinear text has greater visual presence because we see each text fragment—each word, number, or phrase—distinctly, both in print and on screens.

Consider the text fragments in Figure 6.7 that describe the client services performed by a financial planner. Because of their isolation, these five text units have

FIGURE 6.7   Isolated text fragments have strong figure-ground contrast

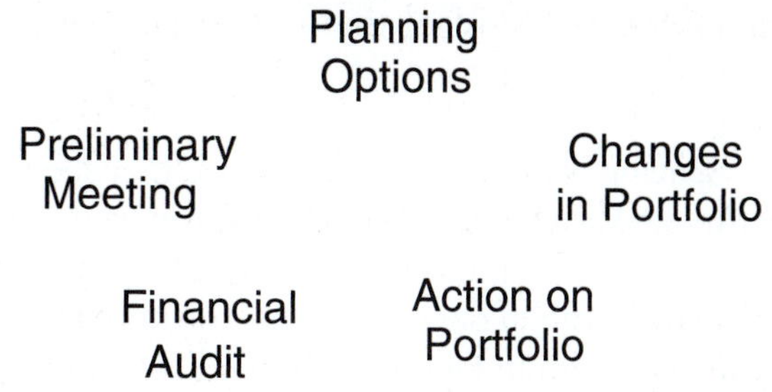

Planning
Options

Preliminary
Meeting

Changes
in Portfolio

Financial
Audit

Action on
Portfolio

strong figure–ground contrast, which highlights their typography. As a result, nonlinear text is often set in sans serif type; its clean, minimalist design is enhanced by the surrounding space.

Of course, the textual elements themselves need spatial and graphic coding to complete the message, as you can see in the new version shown in Figure 6.8. We'll return to these other coding modes in the next two sections.

FIGURE 6.8   Text fragments with spatial and graphic coding

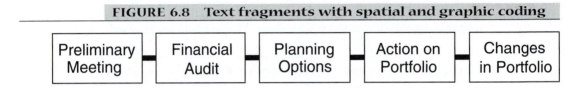

While text elements provide the raw materials of nonlinear displays, they also play an important role as headings, organizing the text units in columns and rows. Table headings might consist of only one level, emphasized in Figure 6.9 through the larger point size and the boldfacing.

FIGURE 6.9   Textual elements—column and row headings

	2005	**2006**	**2007**	**2008**
East Region	432	231	595	619
Central Region	723	542	738	871
West Region	241	381	982	951

Or headings might be hierarchical, as in Teresa's table, where both column and row headings have two levels.

Spatial Elements

The spatial mode of nonlinear design includes three spatial systems—strings, matrices, and branching displays. Most of the conventional genres of nonlinear design employ one of these three systems.

Spatial Systems.   Spacing creates a visual sequence that shows how one text unit relates to another to construct a visual statement. You can create visual statements out of text units with strings, matrices, and branching displays.

Strings create statements through one-directional tracks of text units, arranged vertically or horizontally, as shown in Figure 6.10.

FIGURE 6.10   Spatial elements—strings

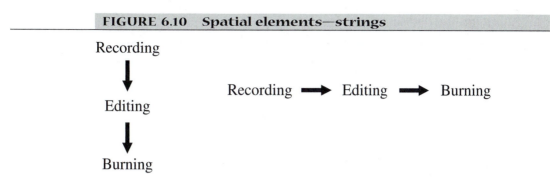

Because the flow of text is directional, strings usually narrate a sequence of events. The syntax of the visual language in the example above creates a coherent statement that reads: "First recording occurs, followed by editing, followed by burning." The arrows ensure that readers will interpret the three-part statement from top to bottom or from left to right.

While strings arrange text spatially in one direction, a *matrix* organizes text both vertically and horizontally *at the same time.* For example, let's say Figure 6.11 displays the annual number of employees in each region over a four-year period. The vertical arrangement of the 2005 column intersects with the West Region row to create the statement, "In 2005 the West Region had 241 employees."

FIGURE 6.11   Spatial elements—matrices

	2005	2006	2007	2008
East Region	432	231	595	619
Central Region	723	542	738	871
West Region	241	381	982	951

As you can see, a table can be very prolific—and efficient—at creating visual statements.

Branching displays structure text into hierarchical layers. They begin with one (or a few) text units and then multiply, layer by layer, like the limbs of a tree. Branching displays include a variety of genres, including organizational charts and decision trees (like the one in Figure 6.12 that enables the reader to select the correct paint type for different weather conditions).

Branching displays typically read, "If this, then that," from one set of circumstances to another, until the reader's needs are satisfied. So in the display above, one if/then statement might read, "If the temperature is above 60° F, and if rain is not in the forecast, then use type A20 paint." Another might read, "If the temperature

FIGURE 6.12 Spatial elements—branching displays**

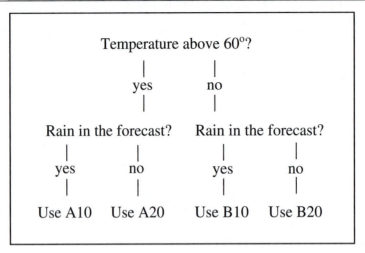

is below 60° F, and rain is in the forecast, then use type B10 paint." Using a visual display to make these statements gives readers a quick path through the relevant information that they can adapt to their own needs. And for international audiences with limited English skills, a branching display can help clarity because it translates much of the statement into visual language, which can bridge language barriers sometimes more easily than text. (That doesn't mean we can ignore the verbal text: Before an international audience used the paint tree, we'd have to translate degrees from Fahrenheit to Celsius.)

Conventional Genres. The three spatial systems—string, matrix, and branching—provide the building blocks for a variety of conventional genres, such as flowcharts, tables, organizational charts, decision trees, and concept diagrams, each of which is represented in Figures 6.13 to 6.17. The arrow(s) in the figures show how readers navigate each genre.

Flowcharts and diagrams are strings that narrate processes and usually move from left to right (see Figure 6.13). They may have some branching above or below the main track, but these typically merge at the end.

FIGURE 6.13 Conventional genres—flowcharts/diagrams

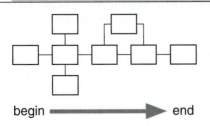
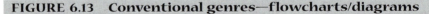

Tables usually take the form of matrices, with row headings defining the horizontal (x) variable, and column headings defining the vertical (y) variable. These variables intersect at a cell (z) within the matrix (see Figure 6.14).

FIGURE 6.14   Conventional genres—tables

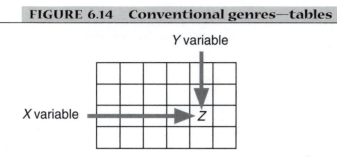

Organizational charts are branching displays that locate people within groups, as we saw earlier in the family tree of Edward III. Organizational charts tend to be hierarchical, with power (presidents, CEOs, kings, and queens) typically located at the top. You can see why these kinds of displays can be highly rhetorical (see Figure 6.15).

FIGURE 6.15   Conventional genres—organizational charts

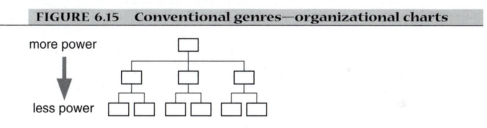

Decision trees are also branching displays that, like flowcharts, narrate a process. However, in decision trees users actually carry out the process, as they do with the paint tree, making decisions along the way according to various contingencies—if this, then that; if that, then this, and so on—until the user achieves the appropriate result (see Figure 6.16).

FIGURE 6.16   Conventional genres—decision tree diagrams

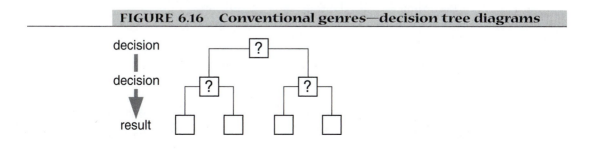

Concept diagrams are primarily branching displays and show relations between ideas, things, and other entities (Figure 6.17). They connect one concept to another at nodes (here the circle in the center) that can, in turn, connect to other nodes in a network.

FIGURE 6.17   Conventional genres—
concept/relationship diagrams

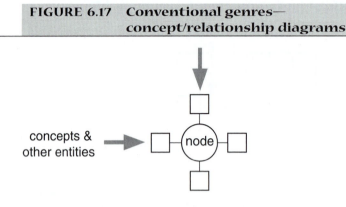

Graphic Elements

A third mode of nonlinear design consists of graphic elements that can serve as *framing devices,* which further isolate text into discrete units, and *linking devices,* which connect both text and framing devices, creating a visual sequence.

Framing Devices.   Text units can be framed in a variety of ways, further isolating them as discrete units and at the same time creating a grouping effect through likeness of form. Below, the three identical rectangles create a group by framing each text unit.

Of course, framing devices can appear in many different graphic forms—the lines of the border can be changed or the border itself can be reshaped:

Text can be framed with many other shapes—circles, diamonds, and the like, some of which bear conventional meanings. For example, in a decision tree, a diamond shape typically means a question or a decision point; a circle indicates a place where the reader takes action:

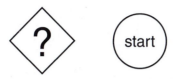

Text units can also be framed by shading, which further draws attention to the text unit by creating figure–ground contrast with the field behind it:

Or the lines can be erased so that the shading does all the work:

Framing devices for text are especially prominent in hypertext documents, such as Web sites. There designers also can use various borders, shapes, shading, and color to isolate small text units, and furthermore can make the frames—or the text units themselves—blink on and off.

Linking Devices.   In the examples above, the relationships between the text units are implied; linking devices—for example, lines and arrows—make those relationships more explicit by directing the flow of traffic, telling readers how to connect text units. Linking devices can connect framing devices or, as in our original example, the text units themselves:

Recording ⟶ Editing ⟶ Burning

The arrows create syntactic links between the text units, telling us in effect that "Recording occurs first, then editing, and finally burning. It can't happen the other way around, only in this sequence." If we reintroduce the framing devices, we can use simple lines as links, though here we run the slight risk that some readers won't understand the flow from left to right:

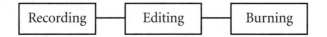

So we can insert the arrows to direct the text units in the flowchart, though the gray scale makes these links a bit more subtle.

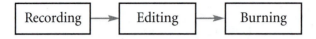

In tables, lines can act as linking devices by guiding the eye across the row (Figure 6.18a), or down the column (Figure 6.18b), or both down and across (Figure 6.18c), where they act as both linking and framing devices.

FIGURE 6.18   In tables, lines act as linking devices

	A	B	C			A	B	C			A	B	C
X	22	26	43		X	22	26	43		X	22	26	43
Y	12	41	52		Y	12	41	52		Y	12	41	52
Z	37	54	28		Z	37	54	28		Z	37	54	28

a   b   c

Synergy of the Coding Modes

To review, then, we can begin with several textual units, such as a series of 12 numbers (Figure 6.19), and spatially arrange those units in a matrix.

FIGURE 6.19   A simple table

432	231	595	619
723	542	738	871
241	381	982	951

To this we can add textual elements in the form of column and row headings (Figure 6.20). And we can add graphic coding to link and frame the text units, guiding users down and across the column and row headings so they can read the 12 different visual statements (Figure 6.21).

And we can activate all three coding modes (Figure 6.22) by changing the text to a sans serif and enlarging the headings (textual), increasing the spacing between rows and above and below the row headings (spatial), and thickening the border as well as shading selected boxes (graphic).

FIGURE 6.20   Table with textual elements added

	2005	2006	2007	2008
East Region	432	231	595	619
Central Region	723	542	738	871
West Region	241	381	982	951

FIGURE 6.21   Table with graphic coding added

	2005	2006	2007	2008
East Region	432	231	595	619
Central Region	723	542	738	871
West Region	241	381	982	951

FIGURE 6.22   Table transformed in all three modes

	2005	2006	2007	2008
East Region	432	231	595	619
Central Region	723	542	738	871
West Region	241	381	982	951

As you can see from these transformations, the coding modes have to work together because they depend on the perceptual context they create for each other. For example, enlarging the row headings increases the space above and below the numbers in their cells and increases the overall height of the table. And because the larger headings overpowered the outside border, we beefed up the border so it would better complement this textual change. You see once again that changing one design element often means that another change is likely to follow.

Applying the Cognate Strategies

As you can see, the text fragments in a nonlinear display rely heavily on visual language to give them form and meaning. While we have conventional genres—tables, decision trees, organizational charts—to help us shape these displays, we have lots of flexibility to adapt them to the rhetorical situation. The six cognate strategies can act as our guides.

Arrangement

How you arrange textual units can make a big difference in how readers respond to the display, whether it appears in print or on screen. Although different conventional genres typically follow certain spatial patterns (string, matrix, branching, or a combination of these), arranging text units across a visual field opens up many possibilities for rhetorical adaptation. Let's look, for example, at the simple organizational chart in Figure 6.23.

FIGURE 6.23   Simple organizational chart

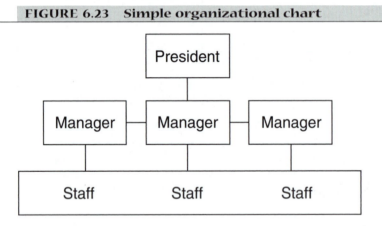

How readers create meaning from this display depends on what they expect.[2] If the audience consists of stockholders, they may be reassured that the organization has a clear hierarchy, a distinct chain of command. Stockholders might say to themselves, "The president runs a tight ship, everything's in order, and our investments are secure." On the other hand, if the audience consists of employees, the staff members may have a different response—perhaps seeing themselves as powerless and unappreciated. Presidents might have a variety of responses, ranging from those who value their authority to those who advocate a teamwork philosophy.

A different arrangement of the display, however, might engender very different reader responses (Figure 6.24). Placing staff in a more important position through textual, spatial, and graphic coding might alter the way that staff members, as well as the president and the managers, envision themselves in the organization.

Rather than towering over them, the president is now encompassed by the managers and the staff, who have a greater visual presence with the large boldface text.

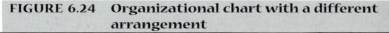

FIGURE 6.24   Organizational chart with a different arrangement

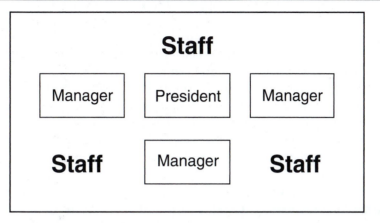

Arranging concepts, ideas, and other entities requires rhetorical thinking because their placement in the composition as text units will inevitably suggest relationships—either parallel or hierarchical—among these units. Consider the concept diagram in Figure 6.25 of a college engineering curriculum that shows the relationship among the three major groups of the student's coursework: engineering, general education, and electives. In this diagram engineering courses clearly dominate the curriculum.

FIGURE 6.25   Engineering curriculum chart

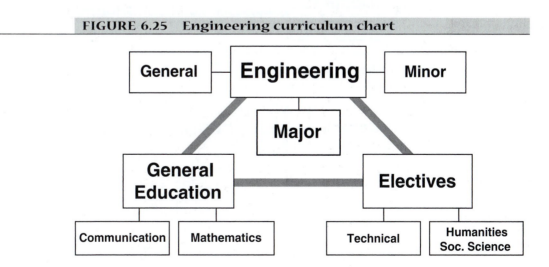

Placing engineering at the top of the pyramid—and the major at the very center of the diagram—recognizes the highly specialized nature of engineering education. If engineering faculty are part of the audience for this diagram, they'll probably think that it accurately describes the curriculum, though faculty who teach general education courses might feel that their efforts get short shrift.

Emphasis

Because nonlinear text is often isolated in fragments, arranged in space, and framed and linked by boxes and lines, you can readily select which elements to emphasize. For example, in the engineering curriculum diagram, enlarging the type size of the text and placing the engineering components at the top emphasizes these components, giving them greater status than the others. The humanities and social science components, on the other hand, lack emphasis because of their smaller type size, their peripheral position (below and to the side), and their small frame, which they have to share.

Some quick revision of the diagram, however, can shift the emphasis away from engineering and towards the other parts of the curriculum. In the revision shown in Figure 6.26, engineering still maintains its foremost position, but now the general education and electives components have greater emphasis, both because of their position at the top and the parallel shading of their frames. Through spatial and graphic coding, the diagram democratizes the curriculum by distributing the emphasis.

FIGURE 6.26   Curriculum chart with different emphasis

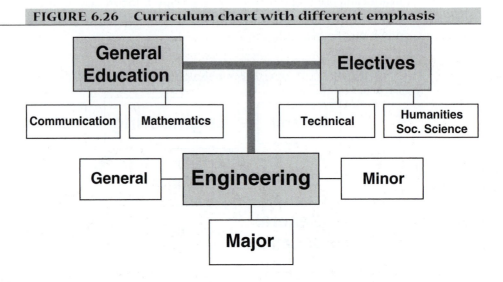

Do these changes improve the diagram? How will it play with readers now? Faculty who teach general education and elective courses might applaud the changes, but engineering faculty might not. So if the audience includes *both* engineering and non-engineering faculty, let's try one more revision (Figure 6.27) to restore the rightful centrality of engineering coursework.

FIGURE 6.27   Curriculum chart with still different emphasis

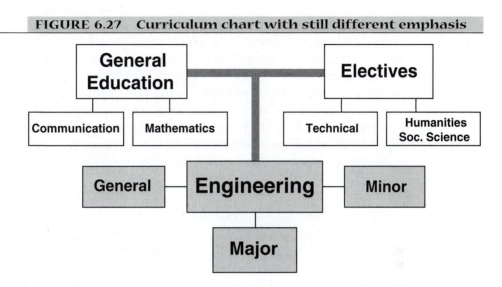

Shading all of the engineering components places the spotlight back on that curriculum. As in this case, emphasis strategies are often less a matter of selecting one design element over another than of *subtly managing the emphasis across a variety of elements.*

This juggling act can be illustrated in the organizational chart we saw earlier in Figures 6.23 and 6.24. In our revision in Figure 6.28, we've shaded the staff area, which subtly shifts the emphasis back to the president and managers by creating strong figure–ground contrast for the president and manager frames and slightly reducing figure–ground contrast for the staff text.

FIGURE 6.28   Organizational chart with shift in emphasis

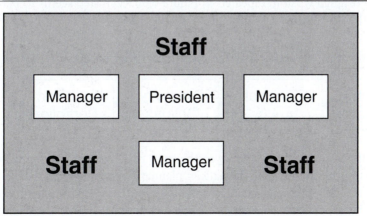

If we intended this chart for both internal and external audiences, the latest version might strike a good balance: Stockholders would see the key management people assuming their rightful position in the foreground, while staff would see their supporting but pervasive role behind these people. Without the staff in the background, the president and managers would lack definition. By playing off each other's strengths, they make the organization run smoothly.

Emphasis in tables can be created in similar ways—for example, by shading cells to highlight key data. Let's say that the data in Figure 6.29 represent unit sales in thousands, with the shaded cells representing the highest annual growth in the three regions.

FIGURE 6.29   Sales chart with key cells shaded for emphasis

	2005	2006	2007	2008
East Region	432	231	595	619
Central Region	723	542	738	871
West Region	241	381	982	951

Here this emphasis gives readers a quick perspective on where the most significant sales growth occurred. Depending on the rhetorical situation, the emphasis strategy may please some readers (salespersons in the Central and West Regions who are proud of their achievements) or embarrass others (salespersons in the East concerned about lagging behind). Emphasis choices almost always have rhetorical consequences, which you have to anticipate during the design process.

You can see rhetorical tension develop as we choose an emphasis strategy for our flowchart showing the sequence of services provided by a financial planner. In the original version, repeated in Figure 6.30, each step seems to play an equal part in the process.

FIGURE 6.30   Financial planning flowchart—all steps equal

Without any emphasis, however, the steps run together, begging the question about what's important. From a financial planner's perspective, the whole purpose of the investment process is to take action—both for the sake of the client, who sees that step as the opportunity to make profitable investments, and for the planner, who expects a percentage of the returns. Both audiences are driven by a desire to act, and so the flowchart could visualize that mutual desire by emphasizing action (Figure 6.31).

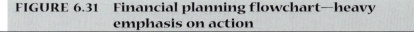

FIGURE 6.31   Financial planning flowchart—heavy emphasis on action

We need to be careful here, however, because emphasizing action too boldly may raise an ethical question: Is the planner motivated only to close a sale? If the client suspects that, the flowchart might seriously undermine ethos, however sincere the planner may appear. To avoid that ethical dilemma, let's erase the gloating action frame and manage the emphasis more carefully (see Figure 6.32).

FIGURE 6.32   Financial planning flowchart—less emphasis on action

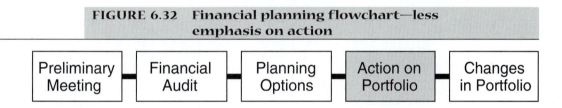

Instead of shading the action box, emphasis could also be achieved by adding color, and—if this display appeared in a Web site—by making the action box blink on and off, though that might actually worsen things rhetorically (even more gloating!). In both print and screen, the judicious use of shading or color would work better.

Clarity

Because nonlinear displays often conform to the spatial conventions outlined earlier, the clarity of a given display may depend largely on the reader's understanding of those conventions. For example, readers using Teresa's tent price table have to know how to use a matrix—how to connect the variables in the columns and rows—to translate the text units into meaningful visual statements.

If we assume that readers know these conventions, we still have much to do in all three coding modes to achieve optimal clarity. For example, the bus schedule in Figure 6.33, a simple matrix, needs revision: The headings are hard to distinguish from the text, the lines are crowded together, and readers don't have much visual direction to move across the rows. These perceptual problems are especially critical because readers will often be in a hurry (or standing under a street light) when they use the schedule.

FIGURE 6.33   Bus schedule lacking clarity

Route	1	2	3	4	5	6	7	8
Red	9:00	9:22	9:27	9:34	9:59	10:07	10:34	10:47
Blue	9:00	9:17	9:25	9:43	9:58	10:03	10:25	10:41
Green	9:00	9:32	9:54	10:01	10:17	10:39	10:46	11:05
Yellow	9:00	9:22	9:31	9:50	10:02	10:28	10:42	10:57
Purple	9:00	9:12	9:43	9:58	10:12	10:28	10:41	10:54

Through a combination of textual, spatial, and graphic coding, we can improve the perceptual clarity of the table. With more emphatic (and perhaps color coded) row and column headings, additional vertical spacing, and lines framing each cell, users can more easily find the time for a given route and stopping point (Figure 6.34).

FIGURE 6.34   Bus schedule revised for better clarity

Route	1	2	3	4	5	6	7	8
Red	9:00	9:22	9:27	9:34	9:59	10:07	10:34	10:47
Blue	9:00	9:17	9:25	9:43	9:58	10:03	10:25	10:41
Green	9:00	9:32	9:54	10:01	10:17	10:39	10:46	11:05
Yellow	9:00	9:22	9:31	9:50	10:02	10:28	10:42	10:57
Purple	9:00	9:12	9:43	9:58	10:12	10:28	10:41	10:54

Space can be particularly useful in clarifying paths to the data. The table in Figure 6.35 has little spacing between lines: this, together with the wide column spans, impedes the reader's movement across the rows. In the table in Figure 6.36, the columns have been pulled together and lines inserted under the rows, design changes that help the eye move horizontally across the display. Figure 6.37 keeps the wide span of the original display but uses shading on alternate lines to establish horizontal flow. Readers can follow the shaded row or they can use it to follow the line above or below it. Notice also the change in font—from Palatino to Helvetica. Sans serif type is a good choice for tables with lots of space; it also maintains good figure–ground contrast against the shading.

Although many clarity strategies work the same in print or on screen, size can present some special problems in screen design. This is particularly true of large tables where scrolling hides column and row headings, requiring readers to zoom in and out. Small screens that require horizontal scrolling can also be problematic (Kim and Albers).

In the end, the best way to ensure clarity—in print or on screen—is to test the display with the intended users. Deborah Keller-Cohen, Bruce Ian Meader, and

FIGURE 6.35 Clarity problems caused by wide column spacing

Region	2002	2003	2004	2005	2006	2007	2008
East	548	319	337	432	231	595	619
Central	831	893	721	723	542	738	871
South	379	351	406	395	371	442	410
West	205	333	371	435	381	982	951

FIGURE 6.36 Improving clarity with horizontal lines

Region	2002	2003	2004	2005	2006	2007	2008
East	548	319	337	432	231	595	619
Central	831	893	721	723	542	738	871
South	379	351	406	395	371	442	410
West	205	333	371	435	381	982	951

FIGURE 6.37 Improving clarity with gray scale

Region	2002	2003	2004	2005	2006	2007	2008
East	548	319	337	432	231	595	619
Central	831	893	721	723	542	738	871
South	379	351	406	395	371	442	410
West	205	333	371	435	381	982	951

David W. Mann did just that with telephone bills they redesigned (1990). While performance remained about the same, they found that readers nevertheless *preferred* their redesigned bill, which was significant because the company wanted to improve customer relations.

Conciseness

In using visual language to shape nonlinear displays for a given rhetorical situation, we often reach a point where additional design ceases to help. Identifying that point is what conciseness is all about. For example, adding some textual and spatial coding to the table in Figure 6.38 to create the table in Figure 6.39 is certainly justified because the additional design elements—the enlarged, bolded headings and the vertical spacing between cells—enhance clarity.

FIGURE 6.38   A very concise table

	2005	2006	2007	2008
East Region	432	231	595	619
Central Region	723	542	738	871
West Region	241	381	982	951

FIGURE 6.39   Table with additional design to improve clarity

	2005	**2006**	**2007**	**2008**
East Region	432	231	595	619
Central Region	723	542	738	871
West Region	241	381	982	951

We could add more design elements—a larger type size in the cells, more space between cells, light lines framing each cell, gray scales to column and row headings, and a heavy line framing the entire table, as we've done in Figure 6.40. But that may be more design than the reader needs to use this simple display. In most rhetorical situations, the first revision defines the point at which additional design becomes mere embellishment.

In some displays, however, visual repetition can be justified because it enhances clarity. In our bus schedule (Figure 6.41), repeating the row headings on the right gives readers easier access to the information. Readers can look from either the left or the right as they scan the times—an access feature that might come in handy in

FIGURE 6.40   Table that's probably overdesigned

	2005	2006	2007	2008
East Region	432	231	595	619
Central Region	723	542	738	871
West Region	241	381	982	951

FIGURE 6.41   Redundancy helps clarity

Route	1	2	3	4	5	6	7	8	Route
Red	9:00	9:22	9:27	9:34	9:59	10:07	10:34	10:47	Red
Blue	9:00	9:17	9:25	9:43	9:58	10:03	10:25	10:41	Blue
Green	9:00	9:32	9:54	10:01	10:17	10:39	10:46	11:05	Green
Yellow	9:00	9:22	9:31	9:50	10:02	10:28	10:42	10:57	Yellow
Purple	9:00	9:12	9:43	9:58	10:12	10:28	10:41	10:54	Purple

the contexts in which they'll use the display—walking to the bus stop, standing under an umbrella, sitting in a crowded bus. It would also be helpful for a large spreadsheet on a screen.

Repetition can also help in a matrix that requires readers to juggle two numerical variables, such as in Figure 6.42. Let's say that farmers who bring their grain to market get 10 euros for each bushel of rye, 5 for each bushel of wheat. They can look up the number of euros they'll get for each transaction.

Crossing the numbers in a matrix is fairly efficient but may be problematic for readers in a hurry, who might easily make a mistake. A simpler table that lists each variation might work better, even though it's very redundant:

```
1R      1W      15
1R      2W      20
1R      3W      25
1R      4W      30
and so on . . .
```

FIGURE 6.42   Conciseness can challenge readers

Wheat										
Rye	**1**	**2**	**3**	**4**	**5**	**6**	**7**	**8**	**9**	**10**
1	15	20	25	30	35	40	45	50	55	60
2	25	30	35	40	45	50	55	60	65	70
3	35	40	45	50	55	60	65	70	75	80
4	45	50	55	60	65	70	75	80	85	90
5	55	60	65	70	75	80	85	90	95	100
6	65	70	75	80	85	90	95	100	105	110
7	75	80	85	90	95	100	105	110	115	120
8	85	90	95	100	105	110	115	120	125	130
9	95	100	105	110	115	120	125	130	135	140
10	105	110	115	120	125	130	135	140	145	150

Some testing with the users might reveal whether the repetition actually improves their performance.[3] Even if it doesn't improve their performance, maybe they'll like the redundant table better, which would also justify using it.

Decision trees often contain redundant questions and responses that help readers locate the correct information. We could delete some of the redundant textual coding in the paint display, shown in Figure 6.43, but in doing so we'd have to enlarge the questions so they overarched the yes/no options. Even though we've also deleted "Use" from the commands at the bottom (see Figure 6.44), the text units crowd together; clarity suffers from the added efficiency.

Designing concise displays for Web pages can be particularly difficult because of the large visual vocabulary—colors, buttons, animated elements—available in the medium. You may find it hard not to overindulge. However, as some of these elements attain the status of conventions, and readers begin to *expect* them in Web documents, the conciseness problem may dissolve.

Tone

Like other forms of visual language, tables, flowcharts, schedules, and decision trees have a voice, ranging from formal and serious to friendly and relaxed. How does the display in Figure 6.45 sound?

Formal? Rigid? Perhaps a bit authoritarian? The textual, spatial, and graphic coding don't leave much room for negotiation here. This process is a done deal, and

FIGURE 6.43   Decision tree—right paint for the weather

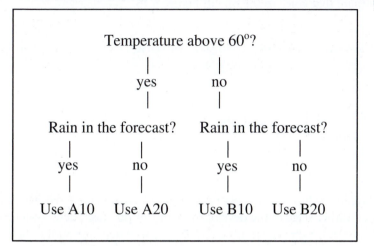

FIGURE 6.44   Decision tree without redundant text

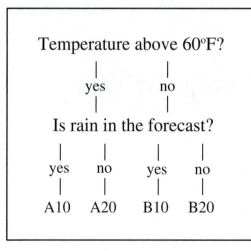

FIGURE 6.45   How does this display sound?

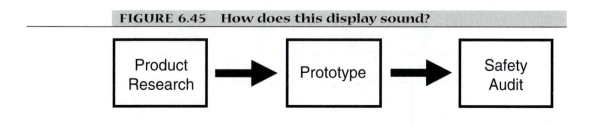

for readers wanting that assurance, this display will project an appropriate voice. Compare that voice to the one in Figure 6.46.

FIGURE 6.46   How does this tone compare to that of Figure 6.45?

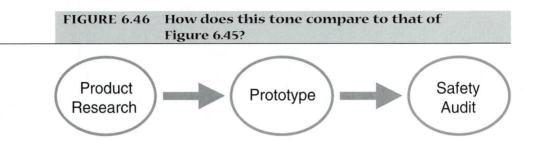

Its graphic coding looks informal, relaxed, and tentative—even vulnerable—suggesting an earlier stage in the development of this process. There's still room for negotiation here. Which version is better? As always, it depends on the rhetorical situation. Do we want readers to think there's room to negotiate, that things are still up in the air, or not? Only a designer who has defined the rhetorical situation can say.

Graphic coding, in particular, can transform tone very quickly from informal and low-key to serious and authoritarian—or vice versa. The original paint tree (Figure 6.43), which was fairly sedate and undemanding, can assume a more aggressive, authoritarian tone with the addition of large arrows and boxes around the action text, as shown in Figure 6.47. Some quick alterations in graphic coding,

FIGURE 6.47   Branching display with more authoritarian tone

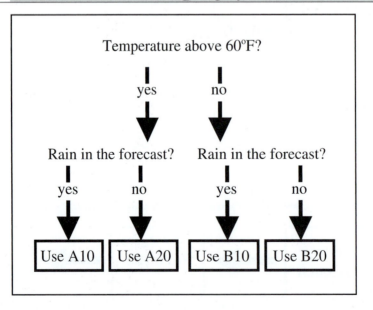

however, can again transform the tone. Applying a gray scale to all of the lines in the display, including the arrows, and adding light shading to the background (see Figure 6.48) can make the paint tree look less demanding and perhaps friendlier and more accessible. When designing on-screen communications, remember that colors will all look slightly different than they will in print, so you may have to make some adjustments for tone.

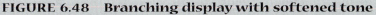

FIGURE 6.48   Branching display with softened tone

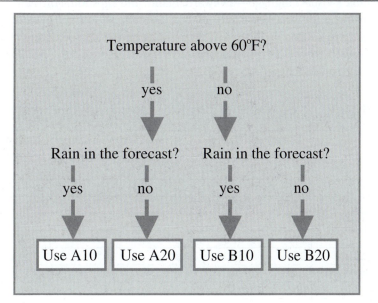

Ethos

Like other forms of visual language, the ethos of a nonlinear display derives from its character—from the readers' sense that the display can be trusted, that it's believable, that they can take it seriously. Based on that standard, readers will probably trust the paint tree display as it leads them logically through the decision-making process. Simplicity itself might engender trust, especially in strings and branching displays where visual language links together a narrative or a logical sequence. Consider the simple, unadorned display in Figure 6.49.

FIGURE 6.49   An unadorned display can be credible

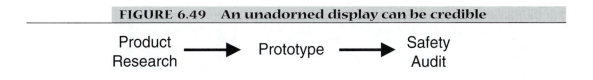

In a technical or scientific report that relies on precise facts and logical reasoning, where the readers want language to lay the truth bare without any hint of distortion or embellishment, this no-frills display might attain a high level of credibility.

The character of a display, however, becomes more problematic when it must persuade as well as inform. Consider again Teresa's first draft of her display, repeated here as Figure 6.50. This simple, functional table will perhaps look credible enough to the salespersons, who will use it daily to perform their jobs, but it may lack credibility for potential customers, whose image of the company will partly be shaped by the table's visual language—awkward, bland, and slipshod. For them, the table's tentative and unfinished look may suggest disorganization and uncertainty—as if the prices were negotiable instead of firm—putting the salesperson in an awkward and defensive position. Teresa's final edited version (Figure 6.6, page 208) avoids these pitfalls because it has more credibility.

FIGURE 6.50   Teresa's first draft of the price table

	Galaxy 6-person	Galaxy 8-person deluxe	Mountaineer 2-person	Mountaineer 4-person	Pathfinder 4-person	Pathfinder 4-person deluxe
1–5—cash	135	170	55	65	70	80
1–5—90 days	145	180	60	70	75	85
1–5—180 days	155	190	65	75	80	90
6–10—cash	125	160	50	60	65	75
6–10—90 days	135	170	55	65	70	80
6–10—180 days	145	180	60	70	75	85
11 or up—cash	115	150	45	55	60	70
11 or up—90 days	125	160	50	60	65	75
11 or up—180 days	135	170	55	65	70	80

That doesn't mean, however, that a more developed and complex design always has a more persuasive ethos than a simple no-frills design. A few customers might find Teresa's original display more persuasive because it suggests low company overhead—and low tent prices. Remember our financial planning diagram, where we rejected the version shown in Figure 6.51 because its overemphasis on action made the financial planner look too eager to make a sale. We preferred the

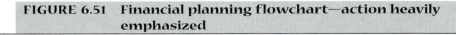

FIGURE 6.51   Financial planning flowchart—action heavily emphasized

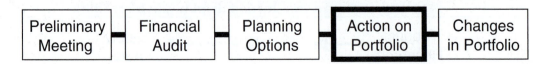

Preliminary Meeting — Financial Audit — Planning Options — **Action on Portfolio** — Changes in Portfolio

display in Figure 6.52 instead because its simplicity and plain-spokenness were more likely to engender the client's trust. Sometimes underdesigning a display can have a powerful effect on readers' trust.

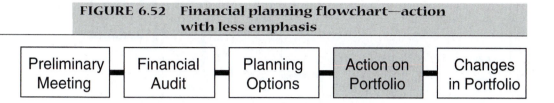

FIGURE 6.52   Financial planning flowchart—action with less emphasis

| Preliminary Meeting | Financial Audit | Planning Options | Action on Portfolio | Changes in Portfolio |

While in some situations conciseness can bolster the ethos of nonlinear displays, Internet users expect tables, flowcharts, and the like to have a certain amount of flash, glitter, and visual chic. If your designs don't, you may lose credibility with some members of your audience.

Interdependence of the Cognate Strategies

As we saw with linear components in Chapter 4 and fields in Chapter 5, for nonlinear components the six cognate strategies work together, influence each other, and must sometimes be balanced against one another as the design process unfolds. To demonstrate the interdependence of the cognates in nonlinear design, let's look at a rhetorical situation that calls for a decision tree.

Corporate marketing for Donovan's, a national chain of building materials and home improvement stores, has developed a document to enable store employees to process credit applications from local building contractors. Many of these businesses are new, and Donovan's wants to help their stores tap into this market without subjecting themselves to unnecessary risk.

If new businesses survive the first two years, they have a much better chance of prospering. Donovan's wants to develop good business relationships with these fledgling operations. These new businesses, however, won't survive two years without a decent credit line. Therefore, corporate accounting created a procedure that local stores can use to approve—or sometimes deny—credit to new local businesses. Figure 6.53 shows the decision tree, Credit Check B, that the communications department created. (A slightly different tree, Credit Check A, is used for customers in business longer than two years.)

Before they begin using the decision tree, employees in each store will be shown a short video explaining credit approval procedures and defining terms in the decision boxes. When employees use the decision tree, they'll start by answering a question that ensures they are following the correct version (B rather than A). Next comes a question about the amount of credit sought; it makes sense that

FIGURE 6.53 Donovan's credit check B

Credit Check B for Donovan's

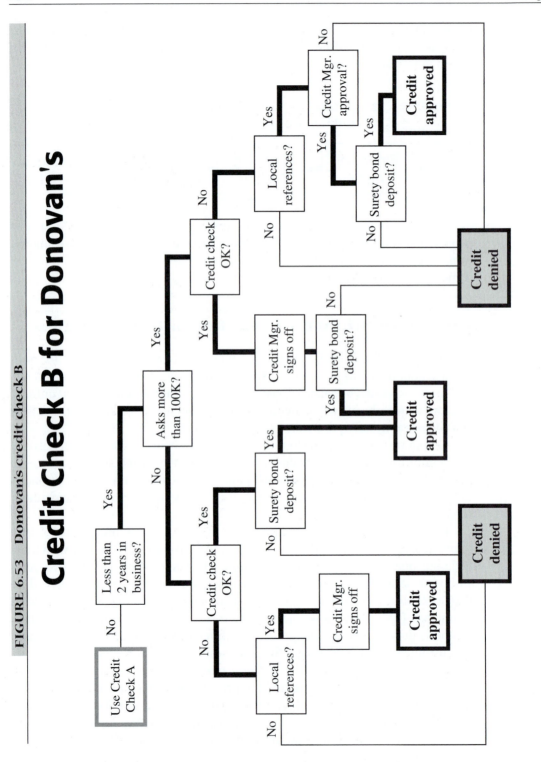

a contractor requesting only a few thousand dollars of credit would undergo a different procedure than one applying for a quarter of a million dollars.

The *arrangement* of this decision tree is fairly conventional: The user moves through the tree by answering questions, navigating from top to bottom. The bottom-most boxes—approval or denial—represent the final decision. The employee begins by determining the amount of credit the applicant is requesting and by performing a standard credit check. The procedures then branch out, with higher-risk applicants encountering more decision points and lower-risk ones fewer decision points. The stair-step alignment of the boxes also affects the *tone* because it gives the chart a formal, precise, and authoritative look—no bending the rules here. The arrangement is also fairly complex, which contributes to *ethos* because it suggests that the designers have covered all of the contingencies.

The most visible *emphasis* strategies in the decision tree are implemented with graphic elements—the heavier frames of some boxes and the shading of others. The placement of those boxes at the bottom emphasizes the vertical orientation of the chart—that is, credit decisions flow from top to bottom. Another emphasis strategy is the heavier lines along some of the branches, which also reveals a *clarity* strategy because the heavier lines indicate the paths customers take to reach the approval boxes.

Another clarity strategy is reflected in the choice of 10-point Times type because it's readable even with minimal leading. The designers wanted to keep the size of the display to a single sheet (a decision reflecting *conciseness* and ethos concerns), so they had to use small question boxes, which in turn required small but readable type. Clarity is also achieved with the low-key Yes/No text that prompts the decision flow.

Conciseness and clarity generally enhance one another. Having branches share the middle Credit Approved box and the two Credit Denied boxes at the bottom unclutters the lower half of the display. The small size of the question boxes as well as their consistent shape also contributes to conciseness. The clean line-work connecting the boxes further enhances conciseness, though this is perhaps a trade-off with clarity because arrows might have accentuated the top-down flow.

Ethos may be less important here than if the tree were intended for an external rather than an internal audience. Nevertheless, the designers want Donovan employees to believe that the home office has their welfare in mind. The decision tree builds ethos because, even though it's a tool for implementing corporate guidelines, it's designed to give stores control over their own credit decisions.

The marketing department could have created a flashier design, but they had to balance conciseness with clarity and emphasis in order to meet the needs and expectations of their readers. They also had to understand how their arrangement choices would affect tone and clarity if the chart is to fulfill its purpose. As always, the six cognate strategies work together to respond to the rhetorical situation.

Notes

1. As David Sten Herrstrom puts it, diagrams have the capacity to "surface" the structure among the textual units (229), to show clearly the logical relationships among the facts.
2. Their interpretations may also be influenced by their experience reading organizational charts. Research by Henk Pander Maat and Gemma Bierman shows that experienced and inexperienced readers sometimes have different interpretations of some elements in organizational charts.
3. Patricia Wright tested exchange rate tables and found that users had problems using a matrix as opposed to a simple table that included a separate entry for each combination of variables.

References

Herrstrom, David Sten. "Technical Writing as Mapping Description onto Diagram: The Graphic Paradigms of Explanation." *Journal of Technical Writing and Communication* 14 (1984): 223–240.

Keller-Cohen, Deborah, Bruce Ian Meader, and David W. Mann. "Redesigning a Telephone Bill." *Information Design Journal* 6 (1990): 45–66.

Kim, Loel, and Michael J. Albers. "Presenting Information on the Small-Screen Interface: Effects of Table Formatting." *IEEE Transactions on Professional Communication* 46 (2003): 94–104.

Pander Maat, Henk, and Gemma Bierman. "How Lay Readers and Experts Understand Organization Charts: A Study of Diagrammatic Literacy." *Information Design Journal + Document Design* 13 (2005): 118–132.

Wright, Patricia. "Using Tabulated Information." *Ergonomics* 11 (1968): 331–343.

Exercises

1. On page 237 are two versions of a table (Figures 6.54 and 6.55) that could be used in a college chemistry text. Assume that the table is part of a review chapter that includes several similar tables outlining key properties of chemical elements.

   a. Catalog the visual design differences between the two tables—you should be able to find significant differences in all three modes.

   b. Explain how the differences in design affect the cognate strategies. Does one version have better arrangement and emphasis strategies? Is one clearer than the other? Which one is more concise? How does the tone of the two tables differ? Which will have more ethos for the students?

FIGURE 6.54   Chemistry table—version 1

Some Properties of Group VIA Elements

	Oxygen	Sulfur	Selenium	Tellurium
atomic number	8	16	34	52
atomic weight	15.999	32.064	78.96	127.6
atomic vol., ml/mole	14.0	15.5	16.5	20.4
density, g/ml	1.27	2.06	4.82	6.26
melting point, °C	−218.9	119.0	220	450
boiling point	−183	440.6	688	1390
electronegativity	3.46	2.66	2.76	2.34

FIGURE 6.55   Chemistry table—version 2

Some Properties of Group VIA Elements

	Oxygen	Sulfur	Selenium	Tellurium
atomic number	8	16	34	52
atomic weight	15.999	32.064	78.96	127.6
atomic vol., ml/mole	14.0	15.5	16.5	20.4
density, g/ml	1.27	2.06	4.82	6.26
melting point, °C	−218.9	119.0	220	450
boiling point	−183	440.6	688	1390
electronegativity	3.46	2.66	2.76	2.34

c. Which design more closely adheres to the visual conventions for scientific tables? What effect, if any, will the less conventional display have on the readers, given this rhetorical situation?

2. Figure 6.56 shows a draft design for a price list from a stamp dealer's catalog. The price list is not as readable as it might be, and it certainly doesn't build the kind of ethos that it should. As you can see from the prices, the dealer caters to advanced collectors who have considerable money to spend on their hobby and who are very particular about the quality of the stamps they purchase.

FIGURE 6.56		Stamp dealer's price list			

LOT.#	CAT. #	COND.	DESCRIPTION		PRICE
1	13	XF/S	A RICH BLUE, SHARP PERFS.	$	185.00
2	24	SUPERB	POST OFFICE FRESH; NO GUM SKIPS	$	460.00
3	38	VF/XF	SMALL THIN UPPER LEFT CORNER	$	225.00
4	53	XF	NICE COPY OF HARD-TO-GET NUMBER	$	385.00
5	78	F/VF	GOOD CENTERING FOR THIS ISSUE	$	150.00
6	112	XF/S	BRIGHT & CLEAN; SMALL GUM SKIP	$	500.00
7	116	SUPERB	A VERY PRETTY STAMP	$	440.00
8	221	VF	HORIZONTAL PAIR	$	360.00
9	241	VF/XF	EX-WHITLOW COLLECTION; 07 PFC	$	1150.00
10	255	SUPERB	THE FINEST EXAMPLE WE HAVE SEEN	$	1740.00
11	318	XF/S	VERTICAL PAIR, WIDE MARGINS	$	295.00
12	343	VF	SLIGHT BEND LOWER 2 LEFT PERFS.	$	180.00
13	408	VF/XF	IMPERF. PAIR; BRILLIANT COLOR	$	400.00
14	416	SUPERB	POST OFFICE FRESH; 05 PFC	$	625.00
15	438	XF/S	A WONDERFUL EXAMPLE	$	345.00
16	490	XF/S	LARGE MARGINS, FRESH	$	710.00
17	511	VF/XF	PART OF ONE TOP PERF. MISSING	$	145.00
18	527	SUPERB	ENORMOUS MARGINS; 03 PFC	$	1000.00

Revise the price list to make it more readable, appealing, and professional. Be aware that in philatelic circles it's conventional to use all caps for the abbreviated condition of stamps. That is, Very Fine is always abbreviated VF, never Vf or vf.

After you've finished revising the price list, compare your version and the original with respect to the cognate strategies. How do the arrangements differ? How do the displays differ in their emphasis? Which version is clearer? More concise? How do tone and ethos differ? Identify the specific design choices that drive the strategic differences you listed.

3. The Office of Student Financial Aid at a state university is working on a set of documents intended to help students manage the procedures involved in receiving financial aid. One of the documents is to be titled, "How Much Does a College Education Really Cost?" One side of the document explains the two major kinds of costs, "direct" and "other." Direct costs include tuition ($5,550 in-state; $13,520 out-of-state); room and board ($5,600); books & supplies ($1,670); and required fees ($374). Other costs include personal expenses ($2,500); medical/dental ($600); and transportation (in-state $600, out-of-state $1,400). These are typical costs for undergraduates enrolled full-time in the College of Liberal Arts and Sciences and living in residence halls with a 20-meal-per-week food plan.

Your job is to design a chart that will present the information in an effective and accessible form. Do not use a table. This chart is intended to give a visual representation of the actual dollar amounts, leaving the other side of the document to define in text paragraphs the various expenses and the way they were calculated. Your chart should include a grand total (one for in-state, one for out-of-state), along with direct cost totals and other costs (in- and out-of-state for both).

4. Locate a Web site that displays numbers in tables or spreadsheets. Evaluate these displays for clarity, using the questions below as your guides.

- How well do column and row headings enable you to locate numerical values? Can you always see the column and row headings on your screen, or do you need to scroll to find them? Are the headings emphatic enough?
- How well does the display guide your eye across rows and down columns? Can you think of any spatial or graphic elements that might guide you more effectively through the rows and columns?
- How legible is the typeface? Would a different type size or style increase legibility?
- How does color affect the clarity of the display? For example, does the background erode figure–ground contrast?

Assignments

1. Design a decision tree for an on-the-job procedure that has some contingencies. The purpose of your decision tree will be to enable a beginner to follow the decision-making path through the task quickly and efficiently. Your decision tree will be laminated and placed in a conspicuous location (taped on a service counter, placed next to a telephone, mounted on a wall) where users can readily access it. Below are some procedures you might use for your decision tree.

- Taking returns from customers at a store
- Processing an application
- Performing a lab experiment
- Responding to a call at a crisis hot-line
- Handling an emergency (flood, power outage, etc.)
- Performing first-aid or some other health procedure
- Requesting money on the telephone for a worthy cause
- Screening volunteers for a nonprofit organization

2. You've been hired by a cable TV company, New Visions, to design a schedule for their new station. Located in a nearby city, New Visions is a growing company that produces educational shows that it previously sold to other cable stations. Now New Visions is developing its own station and is aggressively trying to carve a niche in the educational TV market. New Visions will begin by introducing the new station across your state. Here's an overview of the rhetorical situation.

- *Audience.* Mostly people within your state or region; readers will be interested in quality programs with an educational component; readers will mainly include parents (and their children) and senior citizens who are interested in travel, crafts, and health.

- *Purpose.* Mainly, the schedule will tell the new subscribers about times they can watch the programs on the NVTV channel (75). However, in addition to being usable for existing subscribers, who need to find out what to watch and when, your schedule should be *persuasive* by *selling* NVTV to potential new customers.
- *Context.* Subscribers will receive the schedule with their subscription materials; potential subscribers will receive it at marketing locations throughout the region (malls, schools, county fairs, etc.). Subscribers will probably put the schedule on their TVs and refer to it when wondering what to watch; potential subscribers will glance at it where they receive it, then take it home and examine it in more detail.

As you design your schedule, think about how you can implement all six of the cognate strategies—arrangement, emphasis, clarity, conciseness, tone, and ethos—to meet the rhetorical situation. Each visual element you include in your schedule should do some rhetorical work—that is, each element should implement one or more of the cognate strategies.

To satisfy the rhetorical situation, your schedule should be clear, concise, and well arranged, allowing readers quick access to information. Your design should also communicate an image of quality and creativity (tone and ethos). As an organization, New Visions prides itself on its innovative shows that expand the horizons of its viewers, young and old alike, and it wants to convey this sense of quality and creativity in its documents. Conveying a positive, credible image is important because NVTV will have to attract lots of subscribers to ensure that this new (and somewhat risky) venture is successful.

Below is the information you'll need to include in your schedule. You can organize it any way you want, as long as the display is usable, interesting, and persuasive. Your final design should fit on a single page no larger than 8½" × 11". Your design will be printed on a card stock (both sides) in your choice of color.

Text for the New Visions Schedule:

```
    Monday: 6-7, Wake Up with Nature; 7-8, Starting Your
Business; 8-9, Basic Physics; 9-10, Jazzercise; 10-11,
Thelma's Kitchen; 11-12, Classic Game Shows; 12-1,
Alphabet Lunch; 1-2, Geo-Travel with Bob Florida; 2-2:30,
Underworld Adventure; 2:30-3, Great Historical Moments;
3-4, Children's Classics; 4-5, Brain Teasers; 5-6, Who's
News?; 6-6:30, Local Programming; 6:30-7, Sky's the
Limit; 7-8, Medical Update; 8-9, World Art; 9-10,
Political Landscape; 10-11, Local Programming; 11-12,
Poetry Workshop
    Tuesday: 6-6:30, Early Birds; 6:30-7, Rural Tapestry;
7-9, Investor's World; 9-10, Jazzercise; 10-10:30,
```

Woodworker's Bench; 10:30-11, Pottery Studio; 11-12, Classic Game Shows; 12-1, Alphabet Lunch; 1-1:30, Gardens of the World; 1:30-2, 20th Century Portraits; 2-3, Legal Forum; 3-4, Children's Classics; 4-5, Brain Teasers; 5-6, Who's News?; 6-6:30, Local Programming; 6:30-7, Winning at Cards; 7-7:30, Wildlife Habitat; 7:30-8, Castle Tour; 8-10, Town Meeting; 10-11, Local Programming; 11-12, Fiction Workshop

Wednesday: 6-7, Wake Up with Nature; 7-8, Starting Your Business; 8-9, Basic Physics; 9-10, Jazzercise; 10-11, Landscape Gardening; 11-12, Classic Game Shows; 12-1, Alphabet Lunch; 1-1:30, Woodworker's Bench; 1:30-2, Fixin' Things; 2-3, Legal Forum; 3-4, Reading Circle; 4-5, Brain Teasers; 5-6, Who's News?; 6-6:30, Local Programming; 6:30-7, Pottery Studio; 7-8, Bytes and Bits; 8-9, Investor's World; 9-10, Political Landscape; 10-11, Local Programming; 11-12, Drama Workshop

Thursday: 6-6:30, Early Birds; 6:30-7, Rural Tapestry; 7-9, Investor's World; 9-10, Jazzercise; 10-10:30, Thelma's Kitchen; 10:30-11, Fixin' Things; 11-12, Classic Game Shows; 12-1, Alphabet Lunch; 1-1:30, Gardens of the World; 1:30-2, 19th Century Portraits; 2-3, Computer Nets; 3-4, Children's Classics; 4-5, Brain Teasers; 5-6, Who's News?; 6-6:30, Local Programming; 6:30-7, Winning at Cards; 7-7:30, National Parks; 7:30-8, Mountain Views; 8-10, Town Meeting; 10-11, Local Programming; 11-12, Talk World

Friday: 6-7, Wake Up with Nature; 7-8, Starting Your Business; 8-9, Basic Physics; 9-10, Jazzercise; 10-11, Woodworker's Bench; 11-12, Classic Game Shows; 12-1, Alphabet Lunch; 1-2, Geo-Travel with Bob Florida; 2-2:30, Mountain Views; 2:30-3:00, Great Historical Moments; 3-4, Children's Classics; 4-5, Brain Teasers; 5-6, Who's News?; 6-6:30, Local Programming; 6:30-7, All about Grapes; 7-8, Weekly Wrap-up; 8-9, Ancient Art; 9-10, Political Landscape; 10-11, Local Programming; 11-12, Fiction Workshop

Call 800-253-8251 for service or installation.

New Visions offers you the most originally produced shows of any cable station in the region.

Enjoy educational TV viewing for your whole family.

Extra-Level

Design

7 Data Displays

Introduction to Data Displays

Data displays show quantitative information by transforming textual elements—usually numbers—into images. Nonlinear displays, which we examined in Chapter 6, are primarily textual in nature, with lines, arrows, gray scales, and spatial configurations structuring the text units. In contrast, data displays are *extra-level* in nature. Although they often include textual elements (titles, labels, and legends), data displays rely on nontextual signs—lines, bars, circles, shading, dots, color, and so on—to display information. Text serves only a secondary role by clarifying the nontextual elements in the display.

Data displays are useful rhetorical tools for at least three reasons.

1. Some readers of professional documents prefer to see *visual representations* of numerical data rather than to read the numbers in text form. These readers find data displays more interesting and more attractive; without the data display, they simply might not pay attention to the data.
2. Some sets of data are too complex for readers to use them in text (i.e., tabular) format. For example, a table containing the daily high/low/close data for the major stock market indicators over the past year would likely be unusable. Translating from a text to a graphic form gives readers access to data that would otherwise be unwieldy because of its size or complexity.
3. Some readers prefer a top-down perspective of the data. Tables are good for looking up specific pieces of data, for processing information from the bottom-up (e.g., a bus schedule or a wind chill chart). Data displays—if designed well—give readers a top-down view of the trends and relationships among the data.

And herein lies the most important and consistent rhetorical value of data displays: They greatly enhance our ability to *compare* numbers. If we wish to compare last month's sales total with this month's, we don't need a data display, as the text on the left side of Figure 7.1 demonstrates. However, if we want to compare sales totals for the last *12* months, in order to see the *trends* as well as the raw data, then the graphic rendering in Figure 7.1 would be helpful, if not absolutely necessary, for few people can hold 12 bits of information in short-term memory.

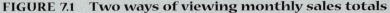

FIGURE 7.1   Two ways of viewing monthly sales totals

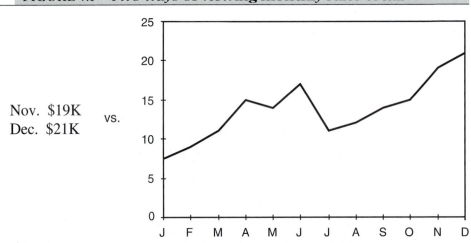

We could have designed this display in many different ways, each of which would have a different rhetorical effect. Instead of a line graph, we could have designed the sales data as a vertical or horizontal bar graph or as a pie chart—and then within each of these conventional genres we could have varied the graphic, spatial, and textual coding. For example, we could stretch our line graph vertically and reduce its width, accentuating the month-to-month differences among the data and thereby heightening readers' concerns about these differences. Or in the graphic mode, we could thicken the data line and add horizontal gridlines, enabling readers to gauge the data more precisely. Technology now provides a wide array of tools to design not only static displays but interactive ones as well. Obviously, you have an extremely flexible and rich visual vocabulary to work with!

The richness of this vocabulary may at first seem liberating because you have the freedom to design the data in so many different ways. And while the design process unfolds, you will, as Jacques Bertin shows in *Graphics and Graphic Information-Processing* (2–23), *discover* things about the data by shaping them visually. At the same time, however, this freedom may also be a bit perplexing because you have to control so many design elements—spatial, graphic, and textual. Just remember that the cognate strategies you use to shape your design are driven by the rhetorical situation. Using the rhetorical situation to guide your design process will help you manage this freedom, giving you the control you need to create an effective display for your readers.

Let's start our discussion of data displays by watching a professional communicator working with these variables. As the design process unfolds, notice especially how the rhetorical situation gradually steers the designer toward an acceptable solution.

Process Example—Data Displays

Ed Loeffler works for a large nonprofit organization that's planning to expand its membership. The current director of the organization, Laura McBride, has asked Ed to assemble some demographic data on membership over the past ten years and to prepare the data for presentation at a monthly Board of Directors meeting. Specifically, Laura's interested in knowing how the ages of members have shifted over these years. The trends the data reveal will help determine how the organization develops its new membership program.

After searching the databases, Ed has come up with the information in Figure 7.2 about the ages of members over the past decade, information that he's assembled into a table.

FIGURE 7.2   Ed's data in table format

Ages	2000	2001	2002	2003	2004	2005	2006	2007	2008	2009
Under 25	342	480	496	478	452	477	521	530	524	513
25–34	762	867	872	892	906	923	911	938	951	573
35–44	1197	1237	1342	1372	1360	1398	1453	1489	1521	1544
45–54	962	1003	1195	1411	1476	1545	1571	1653	1741	1785
55–64	653	802	836	880	997	1274	1359	1482	1637	1744
65 & up	497	590	642	762	902	1073	1288	1427	1571	1644

Scanning the table, Ed quickly realizes that in this form his readers can't see the trends in membership very easily or dramatically. To enable his readers to get the big picture more accurately and efficiently, he's going to have to display the numbers graphically. Getting the big picture will enable board members to make more informed decisions about how to design their membership program.

Analyzing the Rhetorical Situation

Before Ed begins to experiment with data displays, he assesses the rhetorical situation by thinking about the needs of his readers—what they'll want to know and how they'll actually use his data display.

- *Audience.* The readers will be board members—mostly successful businesspersons and professionals—who will inspect the data at their monthly meeting. Ed has attended many of these meetings and knows that board members are task-oriented: They like to get down to business and solve problems—the quicker the better. They depend on staff members like Ed to give them the relevant facts in a clear, concise form.

- *Purpose.* Board members will use the data display to decide how to pitch the membership drive. In talking to Laura, Ed knows that she wants to rethink the way the organization communicates with present and prospective members. Therefore Ed knows he'll want to highlight the trends in the data so Laura can garner support from the board to make some changes.

- *Context.* The data display will be part of the materials board members receive at the monthly meeting. They will examine the data display as they sit around the table in the conference room discussing the new membership drive. They may take the display home for further study, but they'll primarily use it at the meeting.

Invention

Ed begins by thinking about how he can graphically represent the numbers in the table. One possibility would be to create a series of pie charts, one for each year. Each chart would show the relative size of a given age group in a given year. So he begins translating the data into pie charts (Figure 7.3).

FIGURE 7.3   Ed's first draft—pie charts

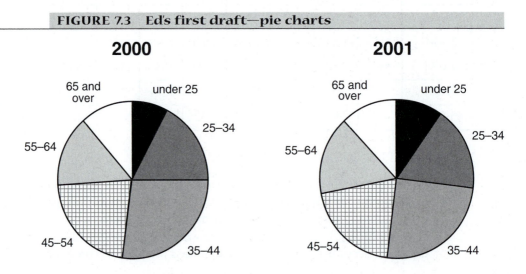

As he examines his first two charts, however, Ed realizes that this visual presentation, while it might initially attract the readers' attention, won't enable them to compare data very accurately from one year to the next. For example, how will board members be able to see the difference between the 35- to 44-year-old group in 2005 and in 2006? A series of ten such pie charts won't enable readers to make such comparisons. Besides, ten pie charts will clutter up the page, potentially frustrating Ed's readers as well as detracting from his ethos as the communication specialist. So Ed tries a multiple bar graph instead (Figure 7.4).

FIGURE 7.4   Ed's second draft—multiple bar chart

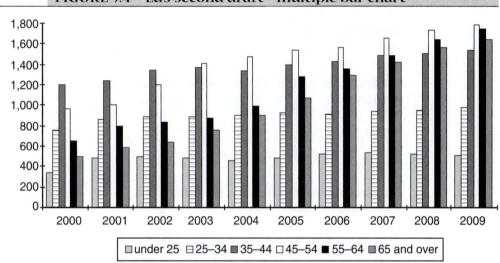

Switching from pie charts to a multiple bar graph enables Ed to show *all* of the data in a single display. Ed knows that his readers will appreciate the conciseness. Equally important, his readers also now have a consistent scale—the *y*-axis—by which to compare the data for a given category and year. So far so good. Ed prints his bar chart and tapes it to the shelf by his desk, satisfied that he's developed a workable solution.

Revision

Later that day, as Ed begins revising, he notices a serious perceptual problem in his graph: Readers will have to leap across a forest of bars to compare data in the same age group. For example, try to compare the 35–44 group in 2000 with the 35–44 group in 2005 or 2007. Ed imagines board members trying to make these perceptual leaps as they sit around the conference room table, and he can already see the puzzled looks on their faces.

To address these problems, Ed decides to change the orientation of the bars from vertical to horizontal, hoping that this arrangement will enable readers to compare the bars more easily (see Figure 7.5). By looking up and down the display rather than across, readers will be able to isolate bars within each age group, enabling them to see trends both within each group and from one group to another. Along with the horizontal bars, Ed adds light vertical gridlines so his readers can more precisely compare data. The gridlines provide benchmarks for comparing bars and also allow his readers to measure specific pieces of data more accurately, in case they need that kind of detail during their meeting.

FIGURE 7.5   Ed's first revision—multiple bar chart

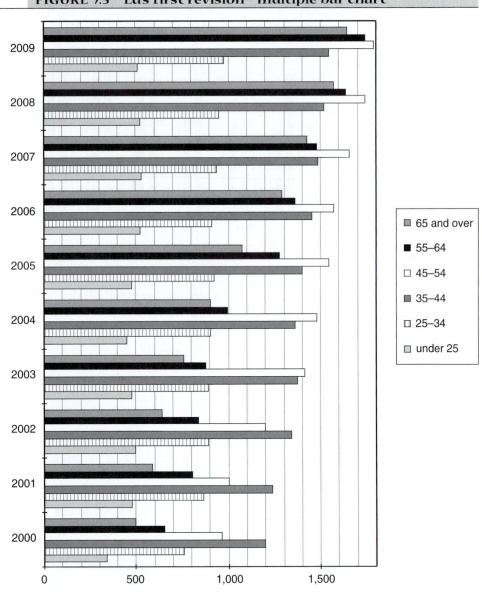

While Ed believes that his new graph is clearer than his previous displays, he thinks it still looks cluttered, preventing readers from making the comparisons Laura wants them to make. The big picture trends are still buried in a forest of bars, and readers will have to work too hard to uncover them. Besides, the graphic coding on the bars is busy and distracting, which not only reduces clarity and conciseness but looks unprofessional, damaging the display's credibility. So Ed decides to cut his losses and try a line graph instead, shown in Figure 7.6.

FIGURE 7.6   Ed's second revision—multiple line graph

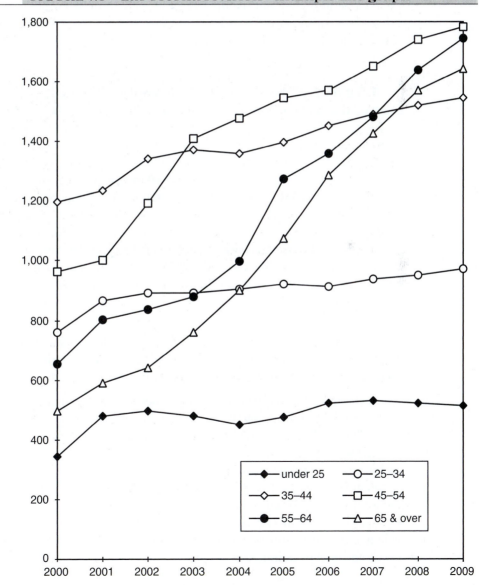

This arrangement of the data greatly improves the clarity of the display, as well as its conciseness. The clutter has evaporated, and readers can see the trends more clearly as they follow one age group—say the 45- to 54-year-olds—from year to year. Because it enhances clarity and conciseness, as well as ethos, Ed decides to stick with a line graph. Now he works on refining this display.

Visual Editing

Ed's getting close to a solution that he thinks Laura can take to the board meeting. The arrangement of the display gives readers quicker, more efficient access to the data because they can see the trends in each group from the top down. Now Ed sets out to improve the other five cognates in his next version (Figure 7.7), fine-tuning the line graph to increase emphasis, clarity, conciseness, tone, and ethos.

1. Ed thickens the lines so they have greater *emphasis*. He wants readers to focus on the trends and to compare the differences among the age groups. Strong figure–ground contrast helps readers to see these differences. However, Ed also doesn't want the lines to become so overbearing that they diminish the ethos of the display.

He accents the three steepest lines by making them darker than the other three lines. This enables Ed to highlight the growth in the middle and older age groups (45 plus), distinguishing this trend from the comparatively flat growth in the younger age groups (under 45). Designers have to be careful about emphasizing certain pieces of data and downplaying others because this can raise ethical questions. In this instance, however, Ed feels he's on safe ground: Laura wants him to emphasize such differences among the groups so that the board can more effectively plan the membership drive, and Ed's emphasis strategy will help Laura and the board achieve that purpose.

2. To enhance *clarity*, Ed adds light vertical and horizontal gridlines across the display so readers can compare values on the data lines. The gridlines will also help readers estimate specific values accurately, if they wish to do that.

3. To make the graph more *concise*, Ed deletes the legend and places labels next to the lines within the graph. By doing that, he can also delete the symbols on each line, reducing clutter and further emphasizing the trends. This more concise graph also enables readers to identify each line directly rather than having to shuttle back and forth between legend and line.

Removing the graphing symbols and the legend also enables Ed to adjust the *tone* of his display. To Ed, the existing symbols looked too technical for this context, as if they belonged in a physics or social science journal rather than at a meeting of volunteer board members. So by deleting the symbols and labeling each line, Ed lowers the level of technicality.

4. He adds a title at the top of the display. The title gives the graph an immediate identity on the page and a more finished, professional look, enhancing its *ethos*. The title also eliminates the need for a label on the *y*-axis: The title itself will tell readers that the *y*-axis represents the number of members.

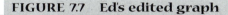

FIGURE 7.7   Ed's edited graph

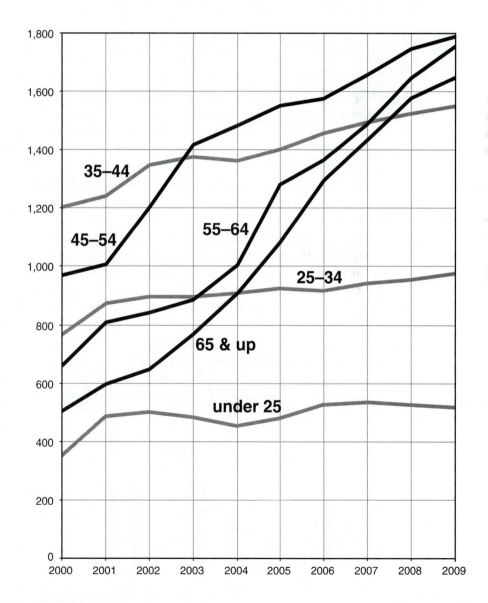

Growth in Membership by Age Groups

As Ed inspects his graph one more time, he thinks about some other adjustments he might make, such as adding color. Although he thinks his graph is very usable, he realizes that it isn't very inviting or exciting, especially to an audience of accomplished board members, who have high expectations and are easily distracted at meetings. So he decides to add some color to the lines, which enhances clarity by further differentiating the two data groups, and he shades the background with the light blue, which heightens the credibility of the display and reinforces its businesslike tone (Color Insert 1). Satisfied that his display is now a better fit for the rhetorical situation, Ed decides to delay any further editing until he gets some feedback from Laura.

Vocabulary of Data Displays

Ed's process makes it clear that designing data displays means selecting from an immense pool of visual language—pies, bars, lines, textures, plot frames, typefaces, and so on. Computer graphing programs can be remarkable tools for manipulating this vocabulary: They have huge lexicons of visual language you can use in your displays, though you might have to do some exploring to discover just how expansive that lexicon really is. Let's begin, then, by surveying the range of that vocabulary, dividing the lexicon of data displays into textual, spatial, and graphic elements.

Textual Elements

Because data displays rely primarily on sign systems outside the text—bars, lines, circles, dots, and so on—textual elements play a largely subordinate role. While spatial and graphic elements actually encode the data, text merely describes the data. Still, like wheels on an airplane, text often plays a critical role in making the display work.

Let's examine some of the textual variations in the bar chart in Figure 7.8. The data in this display may look familiar to you because it appeared in a table in Chapter 6. The textual elements on the chart include the labels on the *x*-axis (e.g., 2006) and the *y*-axis (e.g., 400) as well as the legend to the right.

FIGURE 7.8   Bar chart with textual elements

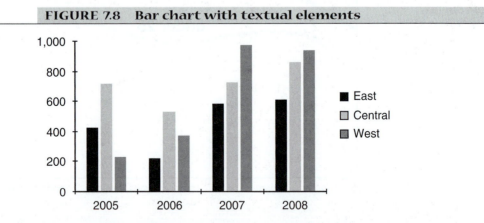

In Figure 7.9 we've added other textual elements to the same display: the *y*-axis title, labels every 100 units (rather than every 200), and the title at the top. These elements add descriptive information that users will find helpful, and they also add more visual bulk, competing for attention with the data bars. Other textual elements *could* be added—for example, data labels on each bar and a title for the *x*-axis. However, these items can quickly become superfluous—data need some breathing room to tell their "story" (Tufte 177).

FIGURE 7.9   Bar chart with textual elements added

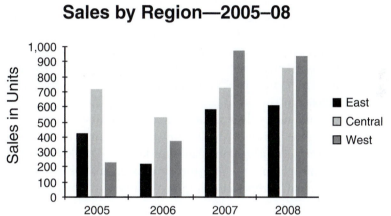

The degree of textual coding depends on other textual, spatial, and graphic elements and on the rhetorical situation. In our data display above, we could label each data point individually—there's enough space at the top of each bar—or we could add a horizontal grid. Doing *either* would enable a more precise reading of the data, assuming the rhetorical situation called for that much precision; doing *both* would probably be redundant.

Spatial Elements

Organizing a data display spatially can determine largely what it looks like and how effective it is. Although you have plenty of spatial decisions to make about the size, shape, and orientation of the display, conventions give you spatial templates to get started. Each conventional pattern has its benefits and drawbacks, depending on the amount of data, the variations among the data, and the rhetorical situation. Let's look briefly at some of these conventional forms.

Pie Charts.   The circular shape of pie charts lends itself to their purpose—to show the parts of the whole (Figure 7.10). Usually, pie charts situate the first slice at twelve o'clock and contain a maximum of six or seven slices. More than that and readers may have a hard time comparing slices.

FIGURE 7.10   Pie charts show pieces of the whole

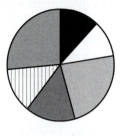

Bar Charts.   The *x*- and *y*-axes of bar charts create a grid for plotting data based on two variables, one of which is usually *time* (years, months). The *x–y* variables are usually interchangeable, which means that the bars can run either vertically (sometimes called a column chart) or horizontally. Bar charts come in many different forms, so let's look at two basic types: simple bar charts and complex bar charts.

Simple bar charts display data belonging to a single group; in the bar chart shown in Figure 7.11, let's say the bars represent sales in the East Region over the past three years. A *pictograph* is another kind of simple bar chart that, instead of extruding smooth bars to show the data, extends rows of icons that are topically related to the data—diplomas, dolphins, diamonds, whatever.

FIGURE 7.11   Simple bar charts show one data group

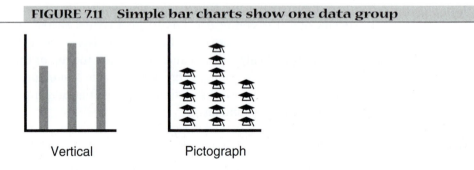

Vertical   Pictograph

Complex bar charts (Figure 7.12) display data from more than one group. In multiple bar charts, different sets of bars represent different groups of data. For example, in the multiple bar chart in Figure 7.12, the bars might represent sales in both the East and West Regions over each of the past three years. In divided bar charts, each bar is segmented into the parts of a whole (similar to a pie chart). In the divided bar chart in Figure 7.12, each bar representing the East Region might be divided into two subregions, the Northeast and Southeast.

FIGURE 7.12   Complex bar charts show more than one data group

Horizontal/Multiple

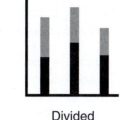
Divided

Line Graphs.   The *x–y* axes of the line graph work on the same principle as bar charts. Time is usually plotted on the *x*-axis. Line graphs differ from bar charts in their graphic coding of the data—lines connecting data points rather than bars that extend to them. And like bar charts, line graphs can be simple or complex: They can plot one group or, like Ed's line graph, they can plot several groups simultaneously, as shown in Figure 7.13.

FIGURE 7.13   Line graphs can plot groups simultaneously

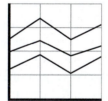

Scatter Plots.   Scatter plots show relationships between variables that are often unrelated to time (Figure 7.14).

FIGURE 7.14   Scatter plots show relationships between variables

Virtually any two variables can be plotted, for example, the relationship between:

■ The density of a tree species and the population of an animal species in a rain forest

■ Endorsement incomes of golf pros and major tournaments they won

■ Coffee consumption and GPAs of college students

The combinations of relationships are virtually unlimited, which makes scatter plots particularly provocative and useful, especially as discovery tools.

Data Maps. Because data maps reveal information about a given location—a country, a city, a building, a park—their arrangement depends on the space they represent and the relative location of the data in that space. In the map in Figure 7.15, the small circles represent, let's say, oil wells on parcels of land.

**FIGURE 7.15   Data maps follow spatial contours
of a given locale**

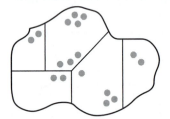

Gantt Charts. In bar charts and line graphs, time ordinarily serves as one of the variables, but those displays measure time in equal units (months, years). A Gantt chart, shown in Figure 7.16, displays time in varying quantities, according to the amount needed for a given task or project. Horizontal bars plotted on a grid represent varying segments of time—hours, days, weeks, months.

FIGURE 7.16   Gantt charts display time in varying quantities

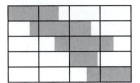

Graphical Matrix. Sometimes data—both quantitative and qualitative—can be displayed efficiently in a matrix through nontextual signs such as symbols and graphical codes. A matrix enables readers to see patterns across the whole data set as well as to access individual pieces of data. A graphical matrix, shown in Figure 7.17, is often used to display information about product performance (cars, TVs, mutual funds), accommodations at hotels and national parks, and the like.

FIGURE 7.17   Graphical tables show data in symbols and codes

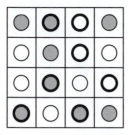

Because each of these conventional forms structures data differently, one convention will be more suitable than another for a given data set. Which conventional template is most appropriate for your data may not be readily apparent at the start, so like Ed you may need to try one, see how it works, then evaluate how well it fits the rhetorical situation. Fortunately, data design programs allow you to quickly transform data from one conventional template to another, so this initial process of trial and error should go fairly quickly. And on the Web, you'll notice that interactive displays often allow users themselves to choose a conventional form.

Once you've chosen a conventional form for structuring your data, you have several other spatial decisions ahead—mainly, the size and proportions of the display. If you select a bar chart, you need to decide the width of the *x*-axis and the height of the *y*-axis. Using the bar chart we began with in Figure 7.8, we can:

1. Shrink the *x*-axis, compressing the chart's horizontal space (Figure 7.18).

FIGURE 7.18   Chart with shorter x-axis

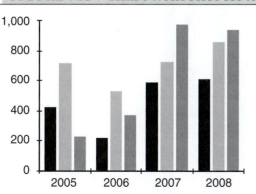

2. Stretch the *x*-axis, leveling out the differences in the data (Figure 7.19).

FIGURE 7.19   Chart with longer x-axis

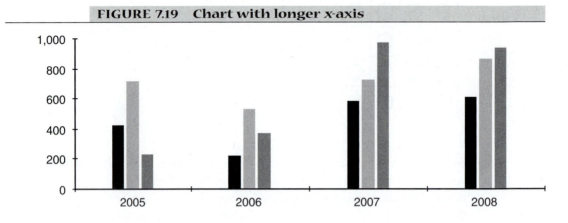

3. Stretch the *y*-axis, creating sharp peaks and valleys and emphasizing the fluctuations in the data (Figure 7.20).

FIGURE 7.20   Chart with longer y-axis

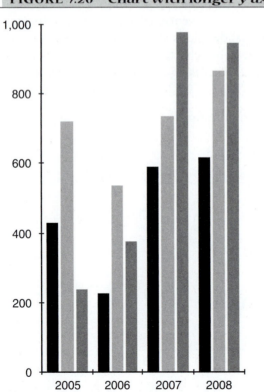

We can also switch the data on the axes, creating a horizontal bar graph (Figure 7.21). In all four charts we're working with the same data and the same graphic and textual coding. Space alone transforms these displays.

FIGURE 7.21   Horizontal bar chart

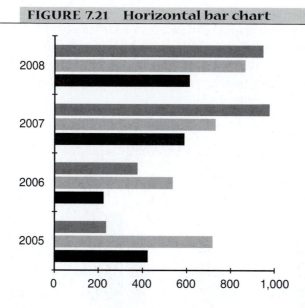

These spatial decisions have rhetorical consequences because they can lead readers to draw very different conclusions from the same data—a prospect that raises ethical questions. Stretching or shrinking the plot frame can jeopardize the accuracy and credibility of the information. For instance, note how the taller and narrower frame of the chart in Figure 7.20 makes the bars for 2007 and 2008 look much larger than in the shorter, more widely spaced version in Figure 7.19. When designing the spatial elements of data displays, especially in persuasive situations, you'll need to monitor carefully the potential impact of these variations on readers' interpretation of the data.

Graphic Elements

Graphic elements also play a powerful role in data displays, controlling the texture, weight, and color of lines, bars, plot frames, tick marks, and a variety of other forms. By making the data visible to readers, graphic coding brings the display to life, giving it form and substance. Perhaps even more than spatial elements, graphic elements can undergo an almost limitless variety of transformations, which can render your display a clear and usable communication or a cluttered mess.

We can divide our discussion into two kinds of graphic elements: those that actually represent the data—bars, lines, slices of pies, dots, and icons; and those that help define these elements—plot frames, tick marks, gridlines, legend boxes, and the like.

Graphic Elements That Represent Data. Most of the graphic coding in data displays does the important work of transforming numbers into abstract forms—bars, lines, slices of pies, dots, and icons. Although they may rely on text (labels, legends, titles) to define them, graphic elements do the heavy lifting because they alone represent the data.

Coding information graphically can take a wide variety of forms. If we return to our original bar graph (Figure 7.8), we can transform the display graphically by switching the coding on the bars and by thickening them (Figure 7.22). Or we can change the graphic coding to different textures, as well as thin out the bars, creating a more compact chart (Figure 7.23).

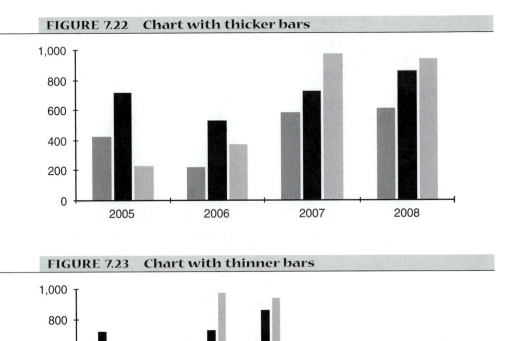

FIGURE 7.22   Chart with thicker bars

FIGURE 7.23   Chart with thinner bars

Similar variations are possible with line graphs, as we saw with Ed's final display where he thickened all of the data lines and also darkened those for age groups with dramatic increases in membership.

Graphic Elements That Help Define the Data.   Data displays rely on many other graphic elements to help readers interpret the data. These elements—gridlines, plot frames, tick marks, background shading, color, and the like—don't represent data; they simply help to define those graphic elements that do. In the display in Figure 7.24, we've added a horizontal gridline and a box outline, made the *x*- and *y*-axes thicker, and erased the tick marks.

FIGURE 7.24   Chart with horizontal gridlines

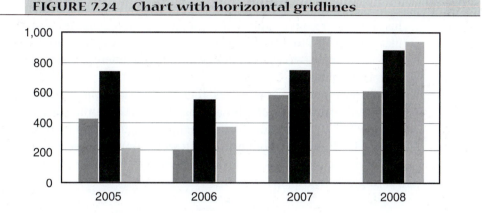

We could also add shading to the plot frame, providing figure–ground contrast for the reversed white lines in the graph. In addition, we could add color to both the bars and the plot frame. The results are shown in Color Insert 2.

And we could add pictorial elements to the plot frame that suggest the topic of the display (Figure 7.25).

FIGURE 7.25   Chart with pictorial elements

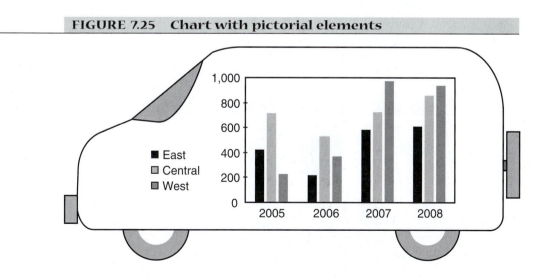

By adding conspicuous graphic elements that don't represent data, we're pushing the limits of conciseness. We also might be creating an ethical dilemma if these graphical elements distract the readers' attention from the data. On the other hand, we might raise an ethical flag if we trim all of the graphical elements, denying readers the tools they need to interpret the data. We'll discuss these ethical dilemmas further under clarity.

Synergy of the Coding Modes

Just as in other areas of information design, the coding modes provide a rich vocabulary with which to display information. We can use this vocabulary—textual, spatial, and graphic—to shape a display into many different forms, depending on the rhetorical situation.

To review the coding modes, then, we can take the pie chart in Figure 7.26 and transform it *textually* by adding the labels South, East, West, and North (Figure 7.27). We can transform it *spatially* (Figure 7.28) by rotating the slices in the pie to the right (though in doing so we flout the convention of starting at twelve o'clock), and we can transform the pie chart *graphically* (Figure 7.29) by varying the shading on all four slices.

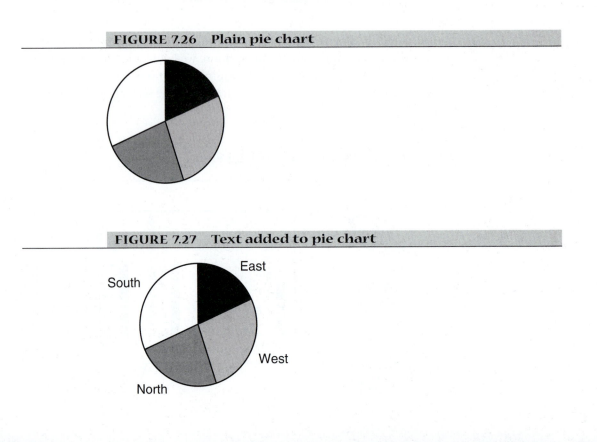

FIGURE 7.26   Plain pie chart

FIGURE 7.27   Text added to pie chart

FIGURE 7.28 Spatial alteration of pie chart (slice rotated)

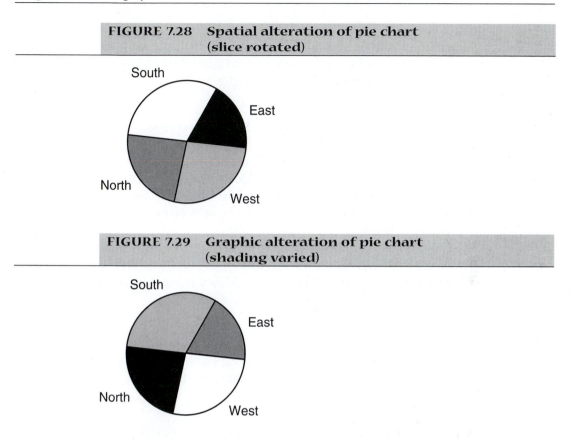

FIGURE 7.29 Graphic alteration of pie chart (shading varied)

In any given design problem the coding modes don't develop in isolation but together and in relation to each another. As your design process unfolds, then, you'll probably think in terms of all three rather than one at a time. So it may be more realistic to think about how we can simultaneously transform the pie chart in *all three modes,* as we've done in the two different forms in Figure 7.30.

FIGURE 7.30 Two versions of pie chart altered in all three modes

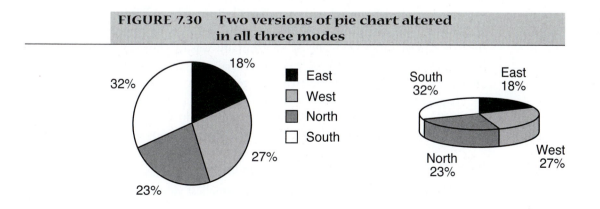

As you can see, the visual vocabulary of data displays is extremely rich and flexible, particularly if you consider the options available in data design software and interactive displays. Now let's look at how you can select from and control this expansive vocabulary as you apply the cognate strategies.

Applying the Cognate Strategies

Given the large vocabulary of visual elements you can choose from as you design quantitative information, how do you decide which elements to use or how to combine them? Should you use a large pie chart or a small line graph? Should you include gridlines or color, labels or legends, or a picture that signals the topic? Where do you begin?

Like other areas of document design, you need to begin by sizing up the rhetorical situation—who your readers are, what your purpose is, and how your readers will actually use the display. Once you've defined the rhetorical situation, you can use the six cognate strategies to develop the display.

Arrangement

Effectively arranging data begins with choosing a conventional genre—a pie chart, bar graph, line graph, scatter plot, map, or Gantt chart (Figure 7.31). These (and other) conventional genres serve as flexible templates within which you can shape data.

FIGURE 7.31   Conventional arrangements for data displays

Of course, early in the design process you may choose a conventional arrangement that doesn't work for the given readers, purpose, and context. As we saw in the process example, Ed started with pie charts but quickly realized that dividing the data into ten separate displays wouldn't suit his purpose. He then found that a bar chart, arranged either vertically or horizontally, was too busy and heavy-handed. So after experimenting with these conventional configurations, he finally decided on a line graph as the most effective arrangement for the rhetorical situation.

Arrangement, however, only *begins* with selecting an appropriate genre. You still have to decide how to order and situate the data within that framework. For example, how should you arrange the data in the simple bar graphs shown in Figure 7.32?

- Numerically, with 1 at the top and 3 on the bottom?
- According to size, from the largest to the smallest values?

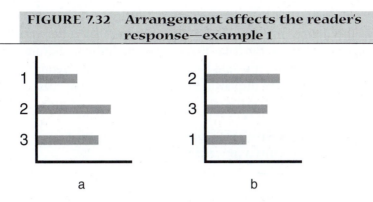

FIGURE 7.32   Arrangement affects the reader's response—example 1

a   b

What's the difference, in terms of the rhetorical situation? Let's say the three bars represent regional production in a company over the past year, with bar 1 representing the East Region, bar 2 the Midwest, and bar 3 the West. The vice president for production wants to use the data in an annual production report. How might the arrangements be interpreted differently by three regional production managers? Are the more direct, rank-order comparisons in version b likely to make the Midwest production manager gloat and the East manager run for cover? Does version *a* somewhat downplay the comparisons? Which display should the vice president use, *a* or *b*?

Of course, it depends on what kind of message the VP wants to send to the managers. For example, if the VP wants to heighten competition among the managers, version b might be a good choice. If the chart goes to the CEO, the VP might prefer version a because it shows a general growth pattern while downplaying regional differences that might reflect badly on the VP's administrative ability across a wide geographical area.

Likewise, how might a vertical rather than a horizontal orientation affect readers? As we saw in Ed Loeffler's design process, he preferred the horizontal to the vertical bars because he believed that for his data set (the size and the number of variables) the horizontal bars gave readers quicker access because they could scan more efficiently from top to bottom than across the display. However, the vertical arrangement of the bars (Figure 7.33) might look more formal and conventional to many readers and therefore be more appropriate in some situations than others.

FIGURE 7.33   Arrangement affects the reader's response—example 2

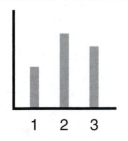

Arrangement decisions have rhetorical effects, and these decisions can take many other forms. You should also keep in mind that culture can play a role in arrangement strategies for data displays. For instance, in cultures where reading flows from left to right, it would be natural to show data trends in that same way. For Western readers, the display in Figure 7.34 shows an *increase* over time.

**FIGURE 7.34   Conventions for arranging data
                may vary across cultures**

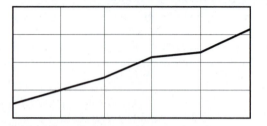

In a culture that reads right-to-left, however, even given the placement of the *y*-axis, some readers might interpret the data trend as *down* rather than up. All of this suggests a larger point that Lee Brasseur has clearly illuminated: that culture plays a major role in how we design data displays as well as how we interpret them.

Emphasis

Data displays give you enormous power to control which data—and which relationships among the data—to emphasize or deemphasize. You can level out a mountain of a line graph into gentle hills and valleys, or take skyscraper bars and reduce them to squat two-flats. That's a lot of power to transform data visually!

And with that power comes a responsibility to your readers. Emphasizing some patterns or data can make a huge difference in the way readers interpret the information—so much so that as a designer you need to be wary about using emphasis strategies that might deceive your readers. You have an ethical responsibility to help them make sound judgments and decisions.[1]

For example, the line graph in Figure 7.35 stretches the data across the plot frame, emphasizing each individual piece of data but at the same time deemphasizing the fluctuations among the three variables. Increasing the *y*-axis to 1,200 also helps to level out the data lines. Can you imagine a situation where such leveling might be seen as unethical? Perhaps the graph appears in a brochure where a life insurance company, represented by the circles, compares its costs to those of its competitors. Whose interests would be served by such a graph?

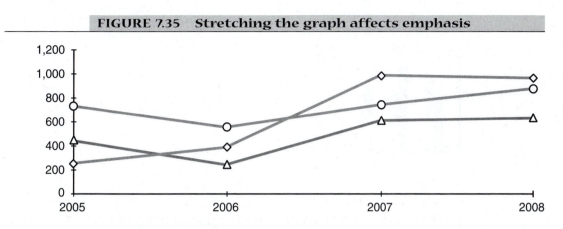

FIGURE 7.35   Stretching the graph affects emphasis

Compare that graph to the version in Figure 7.36, which reduces the *y*-axis to 1,000, stretches the plot frame vertically, emphasizing the fluctuations in costs, and uses a thick line to emphasize the company's performance. In this graph the company's costs are clearly trending upward while the competition's costs are leveling off, a fact that remains somewhat hidden in the first version.

FIGURE 7.36   Graphic coding for emphasis

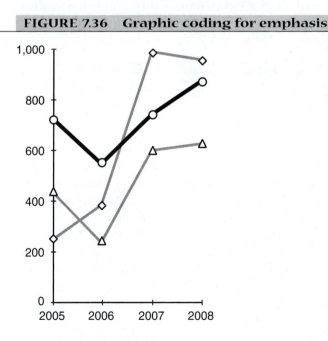

Or consider the bar graph in Figure 7.37. Using graphic coding can make one variable stand out and the other recede, again through the principle of figure–ground contrast. We can further enhance the emphasis strategy by labeling a single piece of data.

FIGURE 7.37   Textual coding for emphasis

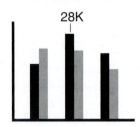

28K

Ultimately, what you choose to emphasize depends on the rhetorical situation—the readers, the display's purpose, and how readers use it. The importance of allowing the rhetorical situation to guide your emphasis strategies can be illustrated in the following fish story. Let's begin with the map in Figure 7.38, which plots the concentrations of walleyes in Lake Peter. Let's say that the data map will appear in promotional materials to be distributed at outdoor and boating shows to vacationers who might visit Lake Peter. Readers like to catch walleyes—it's their favorite fish—so it makes sense that the map emphasizes walleyes.

FIGURE 7.38   Lake Peter map—emphasis on walleyes

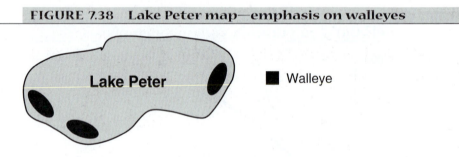

Lake Peter   ■ Walleye

Realistically, though, many readers probably won't catch any walleyes: They can catch them only one month of the year, and many readers will visit Lake Peter when walleyes are out of season. So readers need to know about the other fish too. What happens when we plot, for example, northern pike? Now that we have competing data codes, how should we distinguish one from the other? People like to catch northerns, but not nearly as much as walleyes. If the map were primarily informational—intended to help readers locate fish they could catch all summer—then maybe we should emphasize northerns over walleyes. However, the map is primarily promotional, rather than informational, so it's probably a good rhetorical choice to plot the northerns less emphatically than the walleyes (Figure 7.39). Most readers will like the idea that walleyes are swimming around in Lake Peter, even if they can't actually catch them.

And what about plotting the whereabouts of the lowly bluegill, the fish that readers will probably catch the most but which they'll find least attractive when

FIGURE 7.39   Lake Peter map—less emphasis on northerns

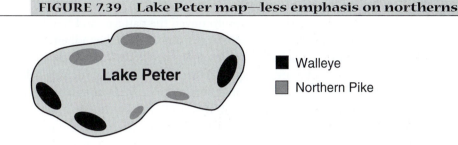

making their vacation plans? Because readers will largely dismiss bluegills as trivial, it will get even less emphasis, even though bluegills are by far the most common species in Lake Peter.

The more desirable the fish, then, the darker the data coding, the greater the figure–ground contrast, and the greater the emphasis, as you can see in Figure 7.40. Of course, the rhetorical logic here might not hold up in the heat of August when walleyes are out of season, northerns can't be found, and bluegills are the only fish biting. Then some early morning anglers may strain their eyes to find the bluegills on the data map. But using the map in a boat in the wee hours of the morning to find fish wasn't the purpose or the context the designer had in mind.

FIGURE 7.40   Lake Peter map—least emphasis on bluegills

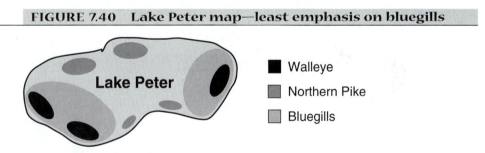

Emphasis can be further enhanced by using color to heighten the contrast between the fishing "hot spots" and the lake and between species (Color Insert 3). And if the colored map were posted on the Web, it could be converted to an interactive display, allowing readers to visualize any of the fish species, individually or in combination, as well as several others (bass, catfish, perch) that live in the lake. With an interactive display, readers can *self-select* what they want to emphasize!

Clarity

Clarity is the key to an effective data display. If the display doesn't show the data more clearly than a table, it won't earn its keep. The difficulty in achieving clarity may depend on the complexity of the data—a handful of data may not require much effort on your part to display it clearly, while a display with more complex data may need extensive revision to unveil the patterns and trends.

Clarity in data displays hinges largely on how well they adhere to perceptual principles, and this can help you troubleshoot problems your readers might encounter comparing data in a given display. As we outline these principles below, remember that the level of clarity will vary in different rhetorical situations and that the five other cognates will also influence your design decisions. For example, you might decide to forfeit some clarity to improve conciseness or to project a friendlier tone.

We'll organize our discussion of perceptual principles around four topics: benchmarks, area, gray scale/color, and perspective.

Benchmarks.   Bar graphs enable us to make accurate comparisons because they give us consistent benchmarks by which to measure the data (Cleveland and McGill 532–533; Cochran, Albrecht, and Green 27–29). In vertical bar charts, the x-axis supplies the benchmark; in horizontal bar charts, the y-axis creates the benchmark. Some bar charts, however, violate the benchmark principle. In the divided bar chart shown in Figure 7.41a, we can accurately compare the whole bar as well as the bottom segments, but comparing the middle or the top segments is not quite so easy.

Why? We need a consistent benchmark to make accurate comparisons, which for our divided bar graph might look something like the configurations in Figure 7.41b or 7.41c.

FIGURE 7.41   **Perceptual problems with bar charts**

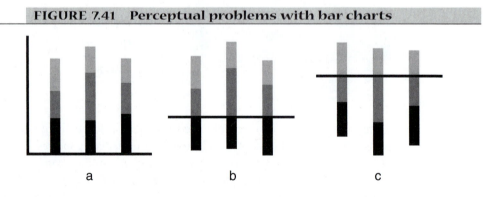

a   b   c

If you use divided bar charts, you shouldn't expect readers to make very accurate comparisons of some of the data in the bars. On the other hand, these charts have the benefit of being concise because they can display a lot of information in a relatively small space (here, four pieces of data per bar).

Making accurate comparisons can also be problematic in line graphs. Although line graphs are excellent tools for seeing the big trends, comparing data accurately from line to line can be difficult. For example, to compare the lines in the graph shown in

Figure 7.42a, we have to compare the variable space between the two lines (version b), which opens and closes irregularly across the plot frame. A grid (version c) can help by offering some benchmarks, though even here readers continue to pursue a moving target. Still, the line graph's ability to reveal the larger trends may easily compensate for this problem of comparing individual data points.

FIGURE 7.42   Perceptual problems with line graphs

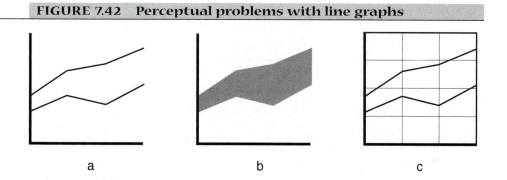

a   b   c

Areas.   Comparing areas that represent data can pose perceptual problems for readers (see Cleveland and McGill 532, 537; Cochran, Albrecht, and Green 27, 29–30; Macdonald-Ross 371–375), whether those areas take the shape of rectangles, squares, circles, or other shapes. Pie charts are particularly problematic because they require readers to compare slices with odd shapes (Cochran, Albrecht, and Green 27). While readers can get the general picture of how the data slices fit into the whole, they can't compare these slices very precisely. As a result, pie charts largely reveal generalities rather than specifics (Figure 7.43).

FIGURE 7.43   Using areas to represent data reduces clarity

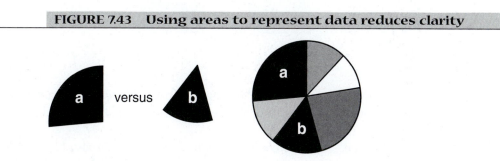

A related problem with area occurs when bars are transformed into pictures. The variations in the size of the picture bars suggest that their area—not just their height—corresponds with the size of the data. The chart in Figure 7.44, for example, suggests that the amount represented by bar 3 is about three times that of bar 4; actually, based on height alone (which was the designer's intent), amount 3 is not even twice as large as amount 4.

FIGURE 7.44   How much larger is bar 3 than bar 4?

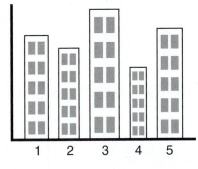

FIGURE 7.44   How much larger is bar 3 than bar 4?

Gray Scales/Color.   Gray scales can also be problematic if readers need to compare data (Cleveland and McGill 532, 536, 547–548; Macdonald-Ross 381). Let's say we want to use the gray scales in Figure 7.45 to represent varying amounts of annual rainfall. Would you have guessed that the amount represented by the gray scale on the left (15 percent) is half the amount represented by the one in the center (30 percent) and one-third the amount represented by the one on the right (45 percent)? You can partly compensate for this problem by labeling the gray scale values with the actual amounts or by using a legend, though even then readers may initially misunderstand.

FIGURE 7.45   Gray scales can be hard to compare

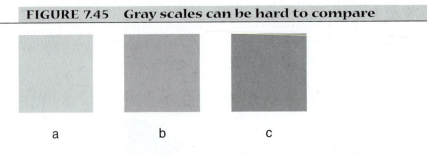

Similar problems occur with gradations of color. *Multiple* colors can be even more vexing because they can clash or compete with each other, further eroding clarity.

Perspective.   Making comparisons in 3-D charts can also be tricky business (Cleveland and McGill 532, 536; Cochran, Albrecht, and Green 29–30), largely because readers have to use perspective to judge size. In Figure 7.46, for example, how accurately can you compare the two bars next to the arrows? Is the bar on the left as tall as the bar on the right? Two-thirds as tall? Half as tall? It's a little like walking through a forest of redwoods and trying to judge the heights of the trees relative to one another. That may be an exhilarating walk, but it's not a very accurate way to compare.[2]

FIGURE 7.46   Perspective can also reduce clarity

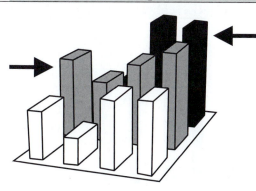

While the preceding perceptual principles should guide your revision, you needn't rule out a data display because it has perceptual flaws. Clarity is always relative to the task readers need to perform as well as to the other cognate strategies. Depending on the rhetorical situation, you may have to make some trade-offs with other strategies such as emphasis, conciseness, tone, and ethos.

Most of the clarity issues we've identified apply to screens as well as print. However, a few additional clarity issues surface when data displays appear online. Many online displays are interactive and give users a great deal of control over data visualization. For example, in interactive displays, users can select only the data that are the most meaningful to them to visualize, leaving other data buried in the database. Users can also often select which display genre (e.g., bar graph, line graph, scatter plot) provides optimal clarity. Still, interactivity doesn't guarantee clarity, and its success ultimately relies on the ingenuity and rhetorical sensibility of the designer (see Kostelnick) and on testing in the situations in which users interact with the displays (Mirel).

Conciseness

Like any other form of design, data displays can be lean and direct or they can be highly embellished and overwrought. Edward Tufte, in *The Visual Display of Quantitative Information,* proposes some methods for evaluating spatial and graphic conciseness. According to Tufte, conciseness can be measured spatially by what he calls "data density" (161–169) and graphically by what he calls "data-ink" (93, 105, 123–137). Let's look more closely at both of these concepts.

Spatial Conciseness. Tufte's "data density" formula measures how much data the display contains relative to its area (162). For example, Ed Loeffler's final display is about 4 inches wide and 5 inches high (20 square inches) and contains 60 pieces of data, or about three pieces of data per square inch. The data display in Figure 7.47, in contrast, measures about four and a half square inches and contains 12 pieces of data, so it's slightly less compact than Ed's final line graph.

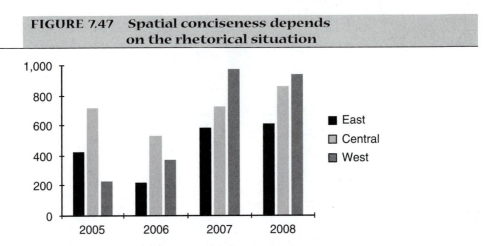

FIGURE 7.47 Spatial conciseness depends on the rhetorical situation

Some data displays contain only a few pieces of data, others show hundreds or even thousands. Is a dense display a better display? Maybe, maybe not. It depends on the rhetorical situation.

Graphic Conciseness. Tufte's "data–ink ratio" measures how much graphic coding a data display uses to show the data—bars, gridlines, tick marks, and so on. While Ed's line graph is only moderately concise in spatial terms, it's far more concise than his earlier bar chart. Bar charts use lots of graphic coding—a whole bar per piece of data, as you can see in the example above. Think of all the toner in the laser printer that these monsters consume! Divided bar charts are more concise graphically because they carry several pieces of data in the same bar. Scatter plots (Figure 7.48) are among the most efficient displays graphically, using only one dot per data entry. That's about as concise as you can get graphically.

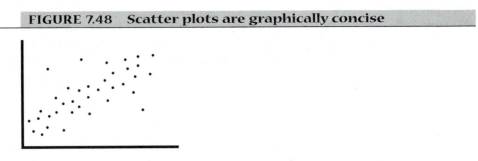

FIGURE 7.48 Scatter plots are graphically concise

Textual Conciseness. The conciseness of a data display can also be measured in terms of its textual cues—labels, legends, titles, and the like. Compare the example in Figure 7.48 with the one in Figure 7.49. Notice especially the extra labeling on the *y*-axis in Figure 7.49 that clutters the display.

FIGURE 7.49   Textual clutter

Sales by Region—2005–08

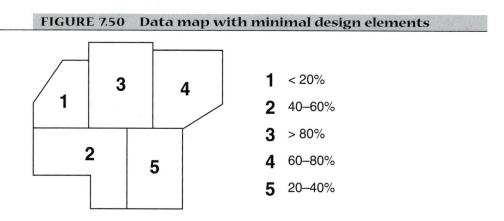

How much spatial, graphic, and textual conciseness is appropriate? That partly depends on the size of the data set and the purpose of the display. Data displays in some popular newspapers and magazines are not very concise, partly because they include pictorial elements—and color—to attract the reader's attention, like the one in Color Insert 4. Does the embellished seaside display lack conciseness? It depends on its purpose and audience. If its purpose is to grab the attention of casual readers who are uninterested in the data, it might do some important rhetorical work. It clearly has a different purpose and audience than data displays in a scientific article or a formal business report. In one rhetorical realm the display might be quite successful, while in another it might be a disaster.

While Tufte's methods are quite useful for gauging the compactness of your display, conciseness must be judged, not in a vacuum, but in relation to the rhetorical situation. Consider the data map in Figure 7.50. Let's say that the map represents housing ownership in the five districts of Westbrook, a fast-growing suburb.

FIGURE 7.50   Data map with minimal design elements

1   < 20%

2   40–60%

3   > 80%

4   60–80%

5   20–40%

And let's say that the map is designed for city council members who serve on a planning and zoning committee. Are council members well served by the map's visual conciseness? Probably not—the map looks pretty abstract, and its fuzziness erodes its clarity as well as its ethos.

We can add graphic coding—shading in each of the boxes to show the relative percent of home ownership in each district (Figure 7.51). Does the added visual bulk help readers? Because it gives readers quicker access to the data—they don't have to shuttle back and forth between map and legend to get the big picture—the additional graphic coding will probably enhance clarity.

FIGURE 7.51   Data map with more graphic coding

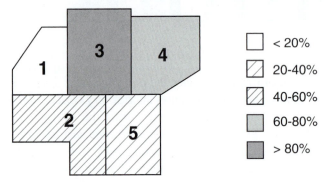

We can add still more graphic and textual coding—two main routes that cross Westbrook, orienting readers spatially along with the route labels, enlarged district numbers, and color in place of gray scale and hatching (Color Insert 5).

Which of the three versions serves its readers best? If city council members are nontechnical readers who need a quick and accessible view of the housing situation, the last data map—the least concise of the three—might well be the most appropriate.

Tone

Just like text designs, data displays reveal a certain tone of voice or attitude. One display might look formal, technical, and authoritarian, another friendly, accessible, and even humorous. Of course, selecting an appropriate tone depends on the rhetorical situation. For example, a formal, technical-looking display will probably seem more appropriate in a research article than in a brochure—unless the brochure contains highly technical information for specialized users.

Adapting tone visually for the rhetorical situation may require trial-and-error and revision. Ed Loeffler's first line graph looked fairly technical because of the symbols identifying each of the data lines. In his final display he deleted the symbols and the legend and inserted labels next to each line; he also thickened the lines and darkened some of them for emphasis. These changes transformed the tone of Ed's final display, making it look more conversational and approachable to his readers.

You can spot similar differences in tone in the two line graphs in Figure 7.52. Of the two, the one on the left looks more technical and precise because it uses graphic and textual coding to clarify the data. The one on the right looks more abstract because of its simpler design—the minimal textual coding along with the strong figure–ground contrast of the thick, reversed lines against the shading in the plot frame. In what kinds of documents would you expect to see these data displays? Maybe the one on the left would fit well in a monthly business report, where a precise, technical tone would suit readers; the one on the right might fit better in an annual report for shareholders.

FIGURE 7.52   Line graphs that differ in tone

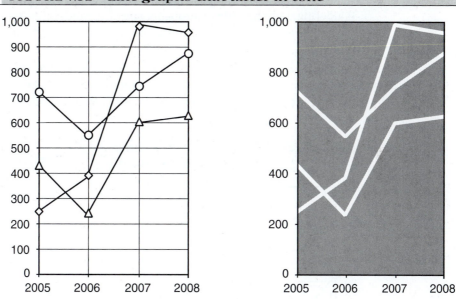

Like the other cognates, tone is always relative because it depends on the perceptual and rhetorical context. Although the tone of the display on the right in Figure 7.52 may seem informal, when compared to the color seaside graph in Color Insert 4, its tone may strike readers as a bit stodgy. Sometimes the tone of a display can be appropriately serious, stern, or even grim. Where the data represent human suffering or loss of life, Sam Dragga and Dan Voss argue that the display should not sanitize the data but rather be used to elicit an emotional response from readers.

Tone is not only relative across displays but also over time. As design conventions and trends change, readers' expectations change along with them. For example, full-color graphs and charts are conventional today in PowerPoint presentations and on the Web. In terms of visual tone, what would have been flamboyant a few years ago is today the norm.

Ethos

As you have probably gathered in our previous discussions about ethics, ethos in data displays isn't just a question of developing the reader's trust by looking professional, though that's always important. Rather, ethos begins with the question of honesty: Does the display tell readers an accurate story about the data, or does it distort the data? We've already looked at some of the visual tricks that data displays can play—stretched plot frames, misleading emphasis strategies, and perceptual problems with benchmarks, areas, gray scales, and perspective. What other kinds of design elements might raise flags for wary readers?

Tampering with the scales is probably one of the most common flags. The data display in Figure 7.53 cuts out 200 units from its starting point on the y-axis, skewing the data. Some break lines on the y-axis would at least fess up to this omission. Logarithmic scales can also skew the data for readers inexperienced with these types of graphs. The graph in Figure 7.54 transforms the data in Figure 7.53 into quite a different pattern, which may puzzle unsuspecting readers.

FIGURE 7.53   Tampering with scales can make readers suspicious

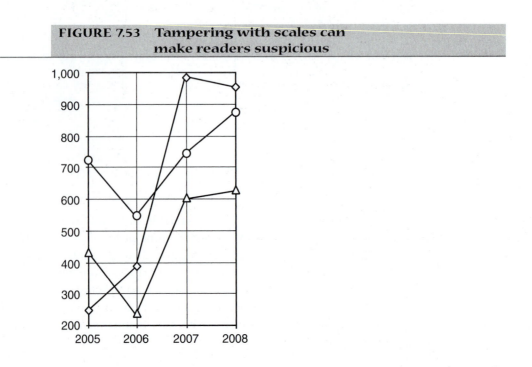

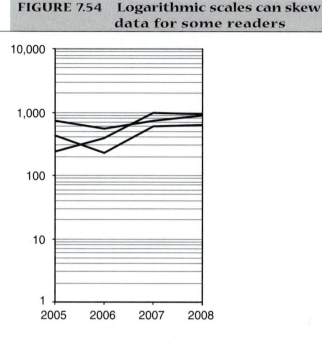

FIGURE 7.54   Logarithmic scales can skew data for some readers

Deception problems in data displays, then, can take many different forms. For example:

1. Readers might be deceived and *not realize it;* similarly, the designer may not realize the deception either, though this remains an ethical problem because the *designer is responsible for the displaying the data accurately.*
2. Readers might *detect* the distortion, and the designer's ethos plummets, even if the designer did not intend to deceive.
3. Readers might merely *suspect* deception, eroding credibility regardless of the designer's intentions.

The last condition could well apply to the forest of colored bars in the display shown in Color Insert 6, leading readers to question the designer's motives: What kind of tricks is the designer up to? Is he or she just caught up in the power of the computer and trying to show off? Or maybe the designer has a more worthy motive—to make reading more interesting. Whatever the motives, such a heavy-handed design may lead readers to question them, putting the designer's credibility at risk.

That's not to say that some aesthetic appeal won't build trust. The 3-D pie chart in Figure 7.55 isn't as flashy or complex as the forest of bars, so perhaps it will engender less suspicion. In spatial terms, the 3-D pie is actually more concise than a flat, 2-D version, though its perspective can obscure the data relationships. On

FIGURE 7.55   Aesthetic appeal can enhance ethos

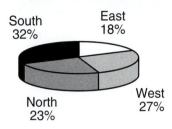

balance, perhaps its aesthetic appeal gives it more ethos than a flat version, especially in situations where precision isn't that crucial.

And then what about our playful seaside graph? Depending on the rhetorical situation, you can build ethos in many different ways, and we needn't equate ethos with seriousness and formality. In some places, the levity or novelty of a seaside graph can enhance the designer's believability. That place probably isn't in a research study or an annual report, but it may be in a newsletter or a magazine.

Interdependence of the Cognate Strategies

Like other forms of visual language, data displays require the designer to blend the cognates in response to a rhetorical situation. Let's look at how the cognates interact in a single display, shown in Figure 7.56. Here's the rhetorical situation: Dean Ng, an information specialist for the state drug enforcement task force, wants to design a display that shows the relation between money allotted to county sheriffs' K-9 units and the resulting "success" in drug enforcement as measured by the number of felony arrests on drug charges. No one has ever plotted these relations graphically, so Dean's readers, task force administrators, don't have any particular expectations. He designs the following scatter plot.

Overall, the graph quickly reveals the key relationship between the sheriff departments' K-9 units and the number of felony drug arrests in ten counties. Looking at the graph, you can immediately see that funds spent on K-9 units seem to have been a good investment. For instance, deputy sheriffs in Sanchez County, with 39 drugsniffing police dogs, made approximately 500 felony drug arrests from 2001 through 2009. On the other hand, Lafayette County, with only 17 K-9 units, tallied only 280 felony drug arrests during the same time period.

The graph also shows some mild anomalies, such as the fact that Calhoun County, which has 31 K-9 units, made approximately 330 felony drug arrests, while Grand County made 400 such arrests even though their sheriff's department maintained two fewer K-9 teams. The same kind of anomaly occurs at the high end of

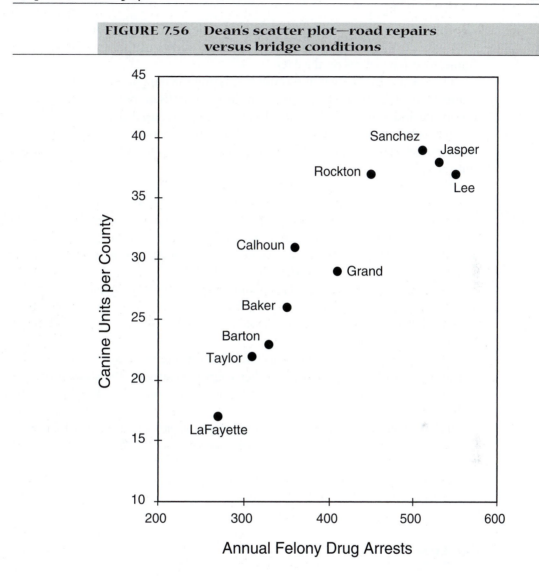

FIGURE 7.56   Dean's scatter plot—road repairs versus bridge conditions

Note: *y*-axis begins at 10; *x*-axis begins at 200.

the range, where Lee and Jasper counties show higher drug arrest statistics than Sanchez County but with slightly fewer K-9 units.

Perhaps the most notable *arrangement* strategy is the point Dean Ng chooses for the intersection of the graph's two axes. To prevent misreading and a possible ethos problem, he notes this at the bottom of the display. Had both axes started at zero, the graph would look significantly different, and the correlation between K-9 units and drug arrests would not be as visible to viewers. So the arrangement strategy directly affects *emphasis* as well.

Other less visible emphasis strategies include the large type on the two axis labels, the large size of the data points, and the line work that encloses the plot frame, focusing viewers on the data.

Dean achieves *clarity* in his graph by placing the data points and the county names near each other. This, along with the tick marks on both axes, helps readers locate individual data points. Dean could have used gridlines to enable greater accuracy in reading the data, but for now he knows his readers would be more interested in seeing the big picture rather than minute details. So he leaves out the gridlines.

Visual *conciseness* in Dean's display results from the relatively small number of graphic elements compared to the amount of data. Scatter plots offer less temptation to complicate the design with shading, cross-hatching, or other graphic bric-a-brac. Spatially, the plot frame could be reduced in area, but Dean will probably give the graph to his audience as a stand-alone document, so he isn't concerned much about space in this context.

The *tone* of the graph looks serious and official without being unduly technical. In large measure the tone results from the graph's open, uncluttered display area, the relatively large data points, and the sans serif labels on the axes and within the plot frame.

Ethos, of course, relates closely to tone, and this graph's credibility results primarily from a combination of the other cognate strategies: the straightforward arrangement, the clarity of the data points, the lack of visual noise, and the conventional typography.

The six cognates are interdependent in Dean's display—sometimes helping each other, sometimes balancing each another—so that overall the display responds appropriately to the rhetorical situation, in this case enabling state investigators (and perhaps the legislators who make funding decisions) to see relationships between two variables they hadn't previously compared.

Notes

1. The complex and perplexing ethical issues surrounding data displays have been addressed by theorists in a variety of ways. For example, Edward Tufte is concerned about reducing the "Lie Factor" that results from perceptual distortions of the data (56–73); Ben Barton and Marthalee Barton analyze how data maps limit readers' access to information that designers control visually; Donna Kienzler assesses the responsibility of designers to their readers; and Robert Lefferts discusses how to achieve "authentic credibility" (32) with graphics.

2. Based on her research with bar graphs on PowerPoint slides, Jo Mackiewicz recommends using 2-D rather than 3-D bars for better clarity.

References

Barton, Ben F., and Marthalee S. Barton. "Ideologies and the Map: Toward a Postmodern Visual Design Practice." *Professional Communication: The Social Perspective*, Ed. Nancy Roundy Blyler and Charlotte Thralls. Newbury Park, CA: Sage, 1993. 49–78.

Bertin, Jacques. *Graphics and Graphic Information-Processing.* Trans. William J. Berg and Paul Scott. New York: De Gruyter, 1981.

Brasseur, Lee E. *Visualizing Technical Information: A Cultural Critique.* Amityville, NY: Baywood, 2003.

Cleveland, William S., and Robert McGill. "Graphical Perception: Theory, Experimentation, and Application to the Development of Graphical Methods." *Journal of the American Statistical Association* 79.387 (1984): 531–554.

Cochran, Jeffrey K., Sheri A. Albrecht, and Yvonne A. Green. "Guidelines for Evaluating Graphical Designs: A Framework Based on Human Perception Skills." *Technical Communication* 36 (1989): 25–32.

Dragga, Sam, and Dan Voss. "Cruel Pies: The Inhumanity of Technical Illustrations." *Technical Communication* 48 (2001): 265–274.

Kienzler, Donna S. "Visual Ethics." *The Journal of Business Communication* 34 (1997): 171–187.

Kostelnick, Charles. "The Visual Rhetoric of Data Displays: The Conundrum of Clarity." *IEEE Transactions on Professional Communication* 51 (2008): 116–130.

Lefferts, Robert. *How to Prepare Charts and Graphs for Effective Reports.* New York: Barnes and Noble, 1981.

Macdonald-Ross, Michael. "How Numbers Are Shown: A Review of Research on the Presentation of Quantitative Data in Texts." *Audio-Visual Communication Review* 25 (1977): 359–409.

Mackiewicz, Jo. "Perceptions of Clarity and Attractiveness in PowerPoint Graph Slides." *Technical Communication*, 54 (2007): 145–156.

Mirel, Barbara. "Visualizations for Data Exploration and Analysis: A Critical Review of Usability Research." *Technical Communication* 45 (1998): 491–509.

Tufte, Edward. *The Visual Display of Quantitative Information.* Cheshire, MA: Graphics Press, 1983.

Exercises

1. Data displays often enable you to discover hidden relationships among data, which can lead to hypotheses about (if not direct insights into) an almost infinite variety of subjects. To that end, collect data for two variables and design a scatter plot that shows the relationships among your data. For example, you

might gather data from your classmates or friends about any of the following two variables:

- Cups of coffee consumed weekly and average hours of sleep per night
- CDs purchased in the past year and number of concerts attended
- Text messages made per week and text messages received per week
- Average hours spent watching TV and hours spent listening to the radio

You can probably think of dozens of other variables as the basis for collecting your data. After you've gathered your data from classmates or friends, display the data for each person on a scatter plot and observe the relationships that emerge. Then step back and make a hypothesis about human behavior.

2. Find an interactive data display on the Web. Topics might include finances or investments, travel, election results, population demographics, or sports. Analyze the interactive display, using the questions below as your guide:

   a. Which variables (time, display type, color, etc.) does the interactive display allow the user to control?

   b. How does this control enhance clarity for the user? What effect does user control have on arrangement, emphasis, and clarity?

   c. What are the limitations/drawbacks of the interactive display?

3. One of the four versions of the chart shown in Color Inserts 7 to 10 will appear in an annual report issued by the Golden Eagle Fund, an investment company primarily for senior citizens that seeks a competitive return without the year-to-year volatility of the stock market. The chart shows the mix of investments in the Golden Eagle Fund. Some readers of the annual report may only glance at the chart, but many will study it closely to assure themselves that the investment mix is a prudent one. Senior citizens are generally cautious investors, and they'll want to know that their money is safe and secure. Evaluate the four versions of the chart, using the questions below as your guide:

   a. Identify the differences in visual design—textual, spatial, and graphic—among the four charts.

   b. Discuss how these design differences affect one or more of the six cognate strategies.

   c. Choose the chart you would include in the year-end report. Explain your choice with respect to the audience: senior citizen investors.

4. You're writing an article about online dating services. Your research has shown that an important measure of "success" for such operations is the percentage of clients who report that they have "found a match" within a three-month period—someone with whom they have established an ongoing relationship. Because

these services are not free, the other significant measure of success is the cost of a three-month membership. In the table below are data showing reported match-success percentages and fees (rounded to the nearest $5) charged by the 22 dating services you've researched. For the sake of visual conciseness, the services are simply assigned letters, *A* through *V*.

Create a scatter plot that will allow the readers of your article to see which of these online dating services gives its members the greatest results for the cost.

Service	% Success	Cost
A	63	65
B	71	85
C	45	55
D	52	90
E	66	75
F	83	75
G	77	90
H	64	65
I	75	110
J	80	90
K	59	80
L	67	105
M	79	70
N	60	80
O	65	115
P	70	75
Q	61	105
R	74	75
S	76	125
T	57	65
U	51	90
V	58	85

Assignments

1. Triangle Sales & Warehouse Company is a distributor for several nationally known furniture manufacturers. Figure 7.57 contains data about Triangle's gross sales and net profit for their current fiscal year. Your job is to display these data in two different forms, one for each of the two following scenarios:

   a. The graphic will be included in an annual report to investors, who will want to see reasonably profitable patterns. Every investor report in the past has

---

FIGURE 7.57   Triangle Sales data table

Sales data for 2008–09 fiscal year, in thousands of dollars:

	Apr.	May	June	July	Aug.	Sept.	Oct.	Nov.	Dec.	Jan.	Feb.	Mar.
Gross	348	367	415	486	521	469	426	312	325	311	303	296
Net	91	107	113	129	123	118	97	71	60	53	49	42

contained information on sales trends, so readers expect to see some data on this. If investors get nervous about Triangle, they may withdraw their money and thereby jeopardize the financial health of the company.

b. The graphic will be included in a report from the new Triangle President, Ray Friedrich, to the Board of Directors. Ray wants to convince the board that Triangle needs to make dramatic changes in its operations to improve sales and profitability.

   As you develop your data displays and begin implementing the cognate strategies, think about the ethics of the two situations. What kinds of design choices will meet the different rhetorical goals without being unethical or unprofessional?

2. As an employee of the National Consortium of Local School Districts, you have been asked to crunch some data and come up with a convincing recommendation. The consortium was recently given a generous grant by the Noble Corporation, a significant part of which was earmarked for "Awards for Educational Excellence" (AEE), to be distributed to five outstanding school districts that are members of the consortium. Your job is to construct a recommendation report that offers a list of suggested winners of the AEEs, along with the rationale for choosing them. Here's the rhetorical situation:

   - *Audience.* Members of a special awards committee that will select the winners; the awards committee, which was created especially for the Noble grant, consists of five Consortium administrators along with five selected school superintendents from around the United States. Committee members are accustomed to dealing with lots of quantitative information.
   - *Purpose.* Your report should help the committee identify five winners of the awards and to persuade the committee that your choices are probably the right ones. With your report in hand, readers should quickly reach consensus on the five award winners.
   - *Context.* Committee members will receive your data displays at a convention in Boston, where they'll gather in the evening in a hotel conference room to

make their choices. Readers won't have much time to read text; they'll rely heavily on your data displays to reach a decision.

Twenty-six school districts were nominated for an AEE. You've been given the data in the attached table, which you'll use to make your recommendations for AEEs, with the top winner receiving a $500,000 prize, and four runners-up receiving $250,000 apiece. In creating your report, you will need to design graphics that help readers to identify—quickly and intelligently—the patterns and relationships that you want them to see in the data. In other words, you have to develop data displays that will sell your recommendations.

Identifying the Data Issues

As Edward Tufte has pointed out, every set of data has a "story" embedded in it (177). Your job is to uncover (through visual means) the hidden plot buried in the numbers (Figure 7.58), to find the important relationships among the data. In searching for the story you need to tell, use the following guidelines:

    a. Overall ITBS percentile scores and percentage of high school graduates going to college should be considered equal measures of excellence. That is, neither is more important than the other in measuring educational excellence.

    b. School districts defined as excellent should be those showing the most bang for the buck—that is, the best results in test scores and students going to college for the fewest dollars.

    c. You may sequence or combine the data in any way you wish in order to develop an overall ranking system. But be sure to explain and justify any computations you make so that your package of displays is clear, cohesive, and credible.

Displaying the Data

Though your report will include some text that will describe the data displays and explain your decisions, you'll focus your design efforts on the data displays themselves. As you design your displays, think about how you can implement all six of the cognate strategies—arrangement, emphasis, clarity, conciseness, tone, and ethos—to meet the rhetorical situation. Each visual element you include in your displays should do some rhetorical work—that is, each element should implement one or more of the cognate strategies. Specifically,

    ▪ Use *arrangement* and *emphasis* strategies to guide your readers toward your recommendation. Keep in mind that you're recommending a course of action to your readers. Arrange the data so that your readers can see the important patterns in the information; emphasize critical data that support your recommendations.

FIGURE 7.58   School districts data table

School dist.	Total annual $ per pupil	Overall ITBS percentile	% students to college
Ahr	2958	92.5	91.4
Breckenridge	2645	90.6	87.6
Cole	3254	89.2	90.2
Dean	2890	87.8	86.8
Escolas	2478	88.1	83.5
Frantz	3692	91.3	92.3
Gerber	3004	93.0	88.7
Holichek	3125	87.4	89.1
Igleski	2753	90.1	85.0
Jervis	3444	88.5	90.9
Kissack	3510	92.8	84.6
Licklider	2548	89.9	88.4
Martinez	3328	93.6	85.2
Nebeker	2616	91.0	89.5
Osuch	2840	93.2	92.9
Powell	3617	91.8	86.3
Quint	3186	88.4	91.0
Riche	3451	87.3	87.1
Soranson	2519	89.7	88.2
Thompson	2980	90.1	89.7
Underwood	3267	92.7	92.0
Vowell	2495	87.5	85.6
Weimer	3054	91.7	83.4
Xavier	2762	90.6	90.8
Yolanda	3569	93.2	86.9
Zowada	3316	88.9	90.0

- Use *clarity* and *conciseness* strategies to make your data accessible to your readers. In the flow of their meeting, readers won't have much time to process the information. Clarity will be critical. Lack of conciseness may frustrate readers. (This doesn't mean you can't use design to enhance tone and ethos; just make sure it does some rhetorical work!)
- Use *tone* and *ethos* strategies to make your data displays interesting, inviting, and professional looking. After a long day at the conference, where they've been inundated with other information, readers will be tired and unfocused. Your report should motivate your readers to explore the data.

A Note on the Color Insert

The insert on the next several pages contains color figures from Chapters 7, 8, and 9. In order to use the color figures, you'll need to flip back and forth from the text to the figures, a situation that we know isn't ideal in terms of supra-level design!

However, this was the only way we could include color figures, given the current economics and technology of print publishing. Given the importance of color, especially on the web, we believed that including color was extremely important in this edition, despite these limitations.

So please bear with us, knowing that in an ideal world, good supra-level design would locate the color figures much closer to the text.

Growth in Membership by Age Groups

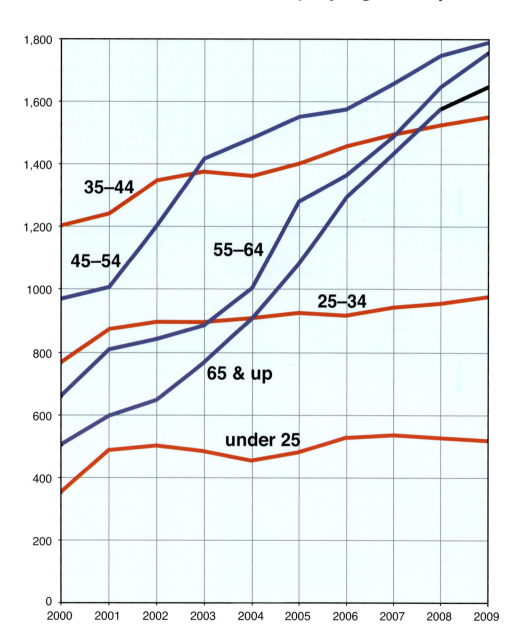

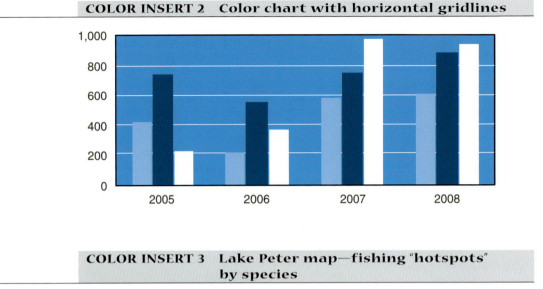

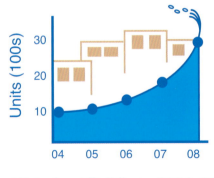

■ Walleye
■ Northern Pike
■ Bluegills

Waterfront Building—2004–08

COLOR INSERT 5   Data map with color coding

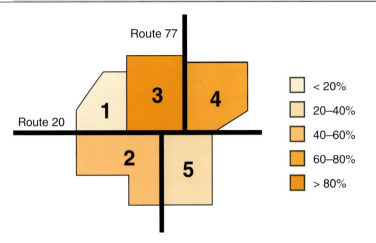

Route 77

Route 20

1 3 4

2 5

< 20%

20–40%

40–60%

60–80%

> 80%

COLOR INSERT 6   A heavy-handed design can perplex readers

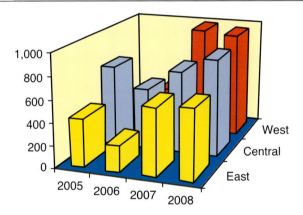

1,000

800

600

400

200

0

West

Central

East

2005 2006 2007 2008

COLOR INSERT 7   Golden Eagle bar chart

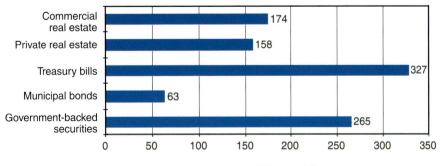

Commercial real estate	174
Private real estate	158
Treasury bills	327
Municipal bonds	63
Government-backed securities	265

0 50 100 150 200 250 300 350

Investments in Millions of Dollars

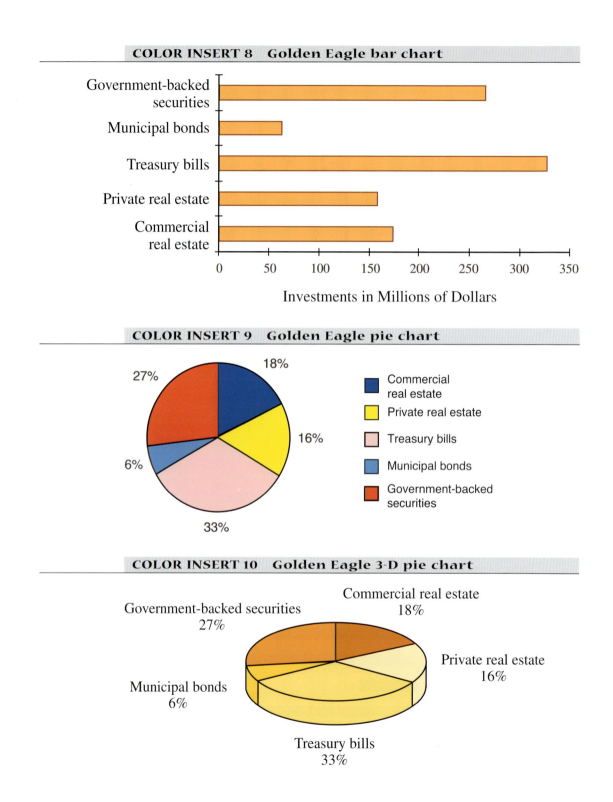

COLOR INSERT 8   Golden Eagle bar chart

Investments in Millions of Dollars

COLOR INSERT 9   Golden Eagle pie chart

- Commercial real estate
- Private real estate
- Treasury bills
- Municipal bonds
- Government-backed securities

18%
16%
33%
6%
27%

COLOR INSERT 10   Golden Eagle 3-D pie chart

Government-backed securities
27%

Commercial real estate
18%

Private real estate
16%

Municipal bonds
6%

Treasury bills
33%

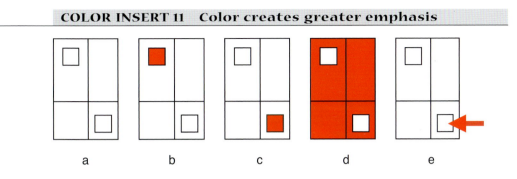

a   b   c   d   e

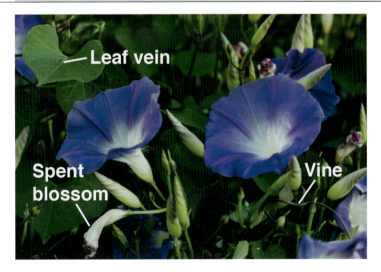

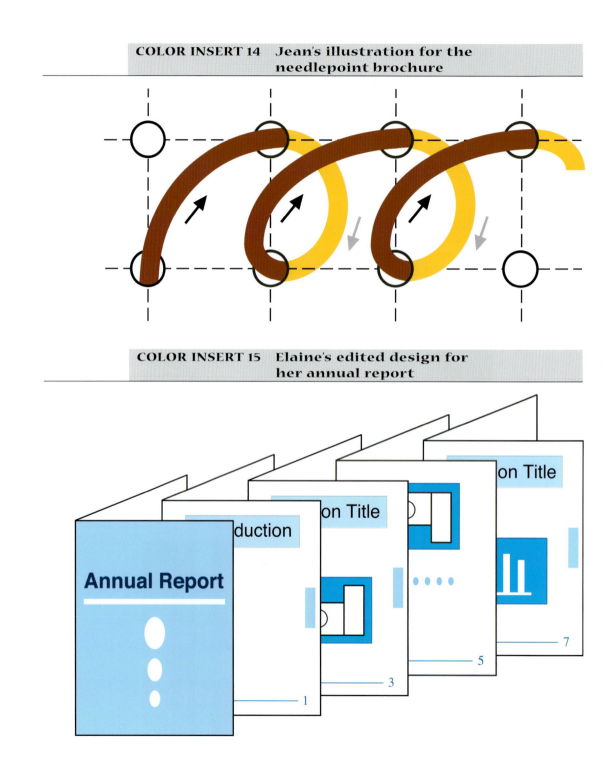

COLOR INSERT 14 Jean's illustration for the needlepoint brochure

COLOR INSERT 15 Elaine's edited design for her annual report

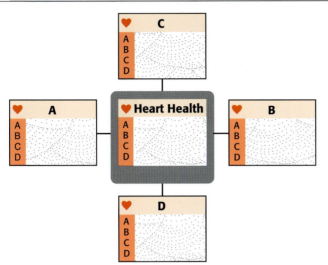

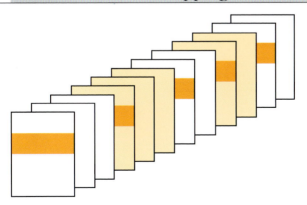

8

Pictures

Introduction to Pictures

Pictures can serve readers of professional communications in many different ways—they can instruct, persuade, motivate, announce a topic, or set the mood. Like text and data displays, pictures shape information for particular purposes and audiences. Some pictures are denser, richer, and more detailed than others, but all have the functional goal of responding to rhetorical situations.

As Rudolf Arnheim put it, "A picture is a statement about visual qualities, and such a statement can be complete at any level of abstractness" (137). Regardless of whether a picture looks realistic or abstract, whether it contains hundreds of pieces of information or just a few, a picture *statement* can fulfill some purpose with its readers. In our discipline, pictures that reveal very different "visual qualities"—a precise technical drawing, a sketch, a color photograph, a piece of clip art—can all perform effectively in their respective rhetorical situations. However, that also means that a picture well suited for one rhetorical situation may not perform so well in another.

As communications that respond to rhetorical situations, pictures function much like text. Although pictures obviously differ in their visual composition, they often perform much the same rhetorical work as text—speaking to readers about things they need to know, fulfilling their expectations, and often evoking emotional responses.

To understand how pictures do their work, we need to evaluate the rhetorical situation. Take the picture in Figure 8.1. What is it? Whatever you see in this picture—a ring, a contact lens, a pipe, the letter *O* standing on a tiny platform—will be shaped by your previous experiences. If we want readers to see what we

FIGURE 8.1   What is this?

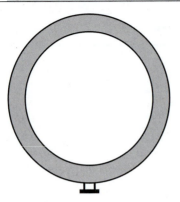

intended, however, they need more information because they're probably not used to seeing this object from this angle, unless they're looking down from a tall building or flying in a hot air balloon. The view in Figure 8.2 might help to clarify what we intended readers to see—an above-ground swimming pool.

FIGURE 8.2   Elevation of above-ground swimming pool

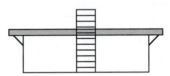

So what purpose does the picture serve and for whom? It might be useful to someone interested in buying the pool, and even more useful still if it had more descriptive information—for example, labels and a side view (Figure 8.3).

FIGURE 8.3   Elevation and top view of swimming pool

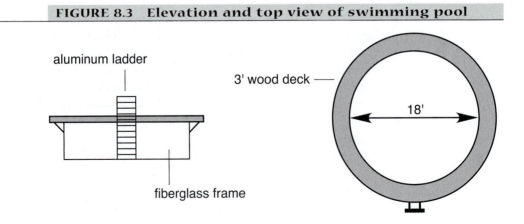

aluminum ladder

fiberglass frame

3' wood deck

18'

If these pictures were placed in a promotional brochure or a Web site, they might serve their purpose: to give readers an overview of the product that entices them to seek more information. As you might suspect, however, these pictures have a limited rhetorical range: They are too abstract to help lay readers assemble the pool or technical readers to manufacture it. For those readers and purposes, the pictures are hardly precise enough.

On the other hand, technical drawings of the pool that included the visual conventions of engineering would be appropriate for some readers, though for most lay readers those same pictures would lack clarity, and their tone and ethos would do more to intimidate than inform. As you'll discover in this chapter, pictures embody many conventions that readers learn, sometimes imperceptibly through their experiences in the world, sometimes through formal training.[1] If readers have acquired a working knowledge of the conventions used in the picture, they can probably extract the intended meaning. If not, they'll simply have to guess or give up, either of which may have serious consequences for the reader, especially if the picture has an instructional purpose.

When we create and evaluate pictures, we constantly need to consider audience, purpose, and context, just as we do with other forms of visual language. In this chapter that's exactly what we'll do, beginning with a case that shows the rhetorical situation driving the creative process.

Process Example—Pictures

In addition to her regular job as a technical writer, Susan Sievers does some freelancing for people she knows in the community. Recently, she was approached by Ben Parsons, a retired industrial arts teacher and naturalist who makes wood products in his spare time. Ben often travels to craft shows and other regional events to sell his creations. Now he wants to expand his business by creating inexpensive bird feeders that buyers can assemble themselves. He's particularly interested in selling his products to younger audiences—children involved in Cub Scouts, Brownies, youth camps, and the like—who might find building their own wood projects fun and educational.

To make his products useful to children, however, Ben needs some simple instructions to include with each kit of materials. So he wants Susan to design some illustrations that will make the job fun and educational for youngsters ages 8 to 10. Susan knows how to put the bird feeder together—Ben walked her through the process and then gave her the final product so she could design her illustrations. He also gave her an unfinished kit and one final piece of advice: "Keep your pictures simple; talk to them on their level. I want the kids to be able to do most of the work themselves."

Analyzing the Rhetorical Situation

Now Susan arranges the wood parts across her desk and imagines how to represent these items pictorially, given the following rhetorical situation.

- ■ **Audience.** Her audience will be children, ranging roughly in age from 8 to 10, who will put the bird feeder together themselves with some adult supervision. They'll be motivated to complete the project if they do it in a group setting and have a specific time limit. All of them can read, though the younger ones may not be very experienced, and some readers may not use English as their first language. Relying too heavily on words may be risky.

- ■ **Purpose.** Readers will use the illustrations to assemble the wood bird feeder. The instructions should be simple and clearly sequenced so readers can follow the steps. The instructions should also convey a sense of fun and accomplishment.

- ■ **Context.** Readers will look at the illustrations as they work through the project, referring to them to see how the pieces fit together. Since readers will be shuttling back and forth from task to page, the illustrations should enable them to find their place easily.

Invention

Susan puts the assembled bird feeder on the table by her computer and spreads out the parts of the unassembled feeder on the floor nearby. She begins by drawing a front and a side view (Figure 8.4), assuming that these views will make clear, concise, and accurate pictures for her readers.

FIGURE 8.4   Susan's draft of front and side views of the bird feeder

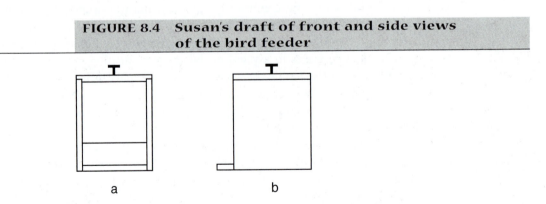

The front view and side views are efficient and complete, providing virtually all of the information her readers will need in a simple, compact form. This is a start—getting the key information in picture form. Susan doesn't consider herself an artist, but she's satisfied that the illustrations capture the size and shape of the object before her. The software on her computer has given her confidence to create and manipulate pictures, both the ones she draws herself and ones she scans from photographs and integrates into documents. She also has a large clip art file that she uses frequently for newsletters and promotional materials.

Revision

After Susan takes a break and returns to her computer with a mug of steaming coffee, she sits back in her chair and stares at her screen. She begins to worry that her pictures, which looked great a few minutes ago, now look too technical, that her young readers may not be able to understand them from these viewing angles. So she takes a sip from her mug and begins to revise.

When Susan imagines her readers completing this task, she sees them in motion, doing things—talking to each other, one moment giggling, the next moment with their heads down, intent on their work. Imagining that context, she realizes that her illustrations look too static, too focused on the finished product, rather than on the task itself. She realizes that to be useful the pictures need to walk readers through the procedure.

So she organizes the unassembled parts of the bird feeder—top, sides, and bottom—on the floor and sets about drawing them in an exploded view (Figure 8.5).

FIGURE 8.5   Susan's first revision—an exploded view

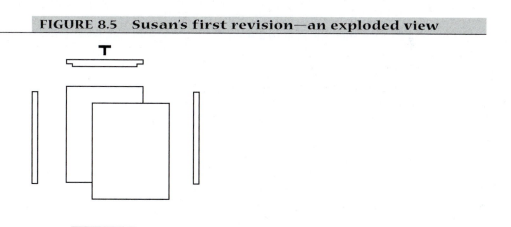

This is much better, she thinks, because now her readers can see the individual parts in relation to one another. However, when she remembers the age of her readers, she worries that they may not get it. They might scratch their heads and wonder why all these parts are floating in space. And they won't have a clue where to start. Then she recalls that she and Ben had discussed numbering the pieces. So she adds numbers to each piece along with arrows to show how they fit together spatially (Figure 8.6).

FIGURE 8.6   Susan's second revision—an exploded view
                    with pieces numbered

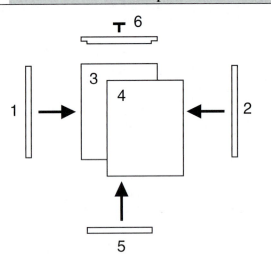

The illustration is better because now readers can distinguish one part from another and can see how the parts fit together. Susan puts her picture down for a few days, then shows it to a friend's nine-year-old son, Nick. Pointing to the pieces in the picture, Nick asks lots of questions: He wonders why some pieces are long and narrow and the others square; he wonders where the birds get the food; he wonders what the arrows are pointing at. Clearly, Nick's confused. Susan realizes that children Nick's age don't understand these kinds of pictures, so she decides to convert her flat two-dimensional drawings to a sequence of perspective drawings that show one step at a time (Figure 8.7).

These pictures are less concise—they take more space and repeat lots of information from one frame to the next. However, they are friendlier for young readers, Susan thinks. Her readers will be able to see each step and the changes that occur from one to the next. They can easily compare their bird feeders to the one in the picture, one step at a time, at their own pace.

Visual Editing

Susan now has lots of editing to do to increase the illustrations' effectiveness for her audience, purpose, and context. Like text, pictures demand attention to details. She needs to add a few more things, to tidy up the linework, and to make the flow of steps more cohesive. Her edited version is shown in Figure 8.8.

**FIGURE 8.7   Susan's third revision—a sequence
of perspective drawings**

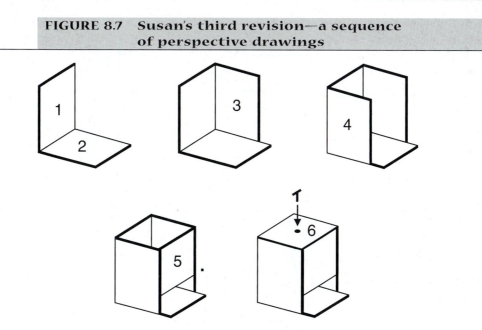

1. To increase *clarity,* she adds nails to the drawings to show readers where to fasten the pieces of wood. The perspective won't allow her to show all of the nails, but she hopes that readers will get the idea. Besides, Ben will predrill holes for the nails, so placing them should be easy once her young readers catch on.

2. Susan arranges the pictures on a landscape page and adds large numbers to identify each step. The landscape arrangement enables her to line up the steps in a continuous row, simplifying reader access. In addition, the numbers of the steps and the numbers on the wood pieces now correspond to each other. This *arrangement* strategy will help her readers follow the procedure more easily.

3. She adds a sixth drawing to show the finished product filled with bird seed, and she places the cover in the air above the container so readers can see the feed inside. She assumes that her readers will understand this convention and not think that the cover is literally flying in midair. Using this convention enables her to present this information *concisely.*

4. Susan gives the finished feeder a visual context by placing it in an outdoor setting with pine trees and birds. This lightens the *tone* a bit and, by showing the finished product in use, it motivates readers to complete the project and enjoy its benefits (or enjoy watching the birds benefit!). That should also enhance *ethos* because her readers will believe that the finished product merits the effort they'll expend to construct it. They can imagine themselves watching out the window as birds flock to the feeder they created with their own hands.

FIGURE 8.8 Susan's edited bird feeder instructions

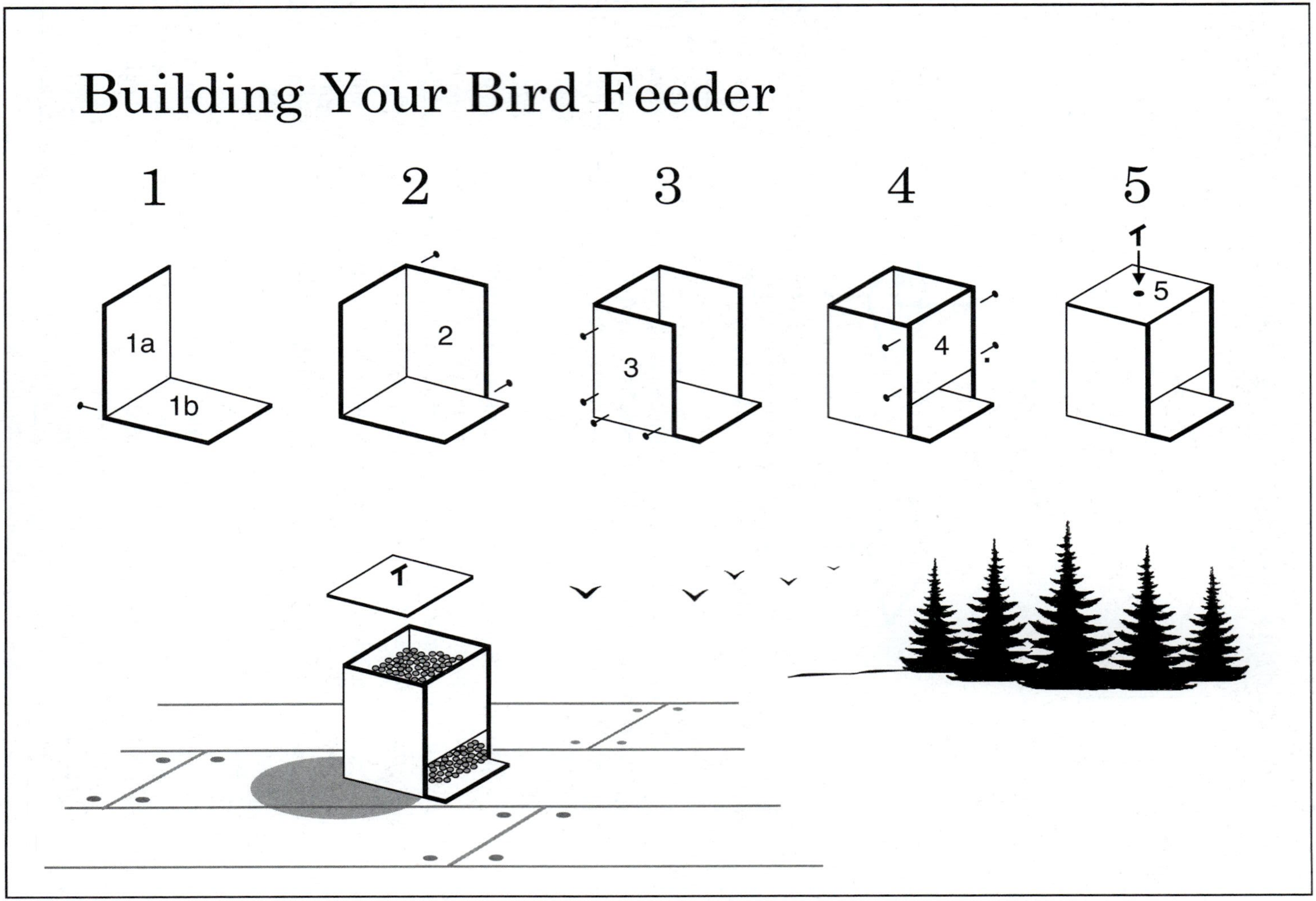

Building Your Bird Feeder

5. She includes a title so readers can quickly identify the document's purpose. For the font, she chooses New Century Schoolbook because it's traditionally used in children's materials and the tone looks nonthreatening.

Before she does any more editing, Susan wants to test her pictures again with her friend's son Nick. Testing pictures with the intended audience can provide lots of useful feedback during the design process (Floreak, Schriver). After that, she'll run it by Ben and see what he thinks. Susan will talk with Ben about future plans for the instructions, should the bird feeders become highly popular. Ben might want her to create an animated version of the instructions on a CD.

Vocabulary of Pictures

As Susan's design process unfolds, the rhetorical situation guides her decisions about the visual language she uses to construct her pictures. Just as if she were writing to her young readers, designing for them defines and limits her vocabulary—simple perspective drawings lined up on a single page. As the rhetorical situation changes, so will the range of Susan's vocabulary—the lines, textures, viewing angles, sizes, and conventions she uses in her pictures, from drawings and clip art to photos and animations.

Let's widen the lens and explore the wealth of visual elements—textual, spatial, and graphic—you can select and combine as you design pictures from one situation to the next. The visual lexicon of pictures is so expansive that we can't cover everything here. We'll use a broad brush so we can at least map the territory.

Textual Elements

In pictures, as in data displays, textual elements play a helping role—defining, clarifying, and modifying information contained in the images. They can be conspicuous (titles) or subtle (labels, call outs), and they can play a crucial role, a minor role, or no role at all in defining the picture. In the example in Figure 8.9, textual coding could play a crucial role in helping us understand the picture.

FIGURE 8.9   A picture without textual coding

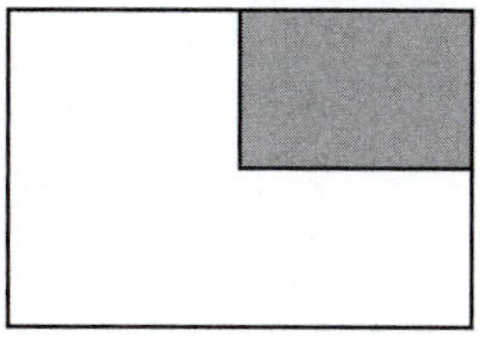

As in this case, pictures are often ambiguous without textual definition, leaving open the possibility for a variety of interpretations. However, adding textual elements quickly narrows the possibilities (Figure 8.10).

FIGURE 8.10   Textual elements help us interpret pictures

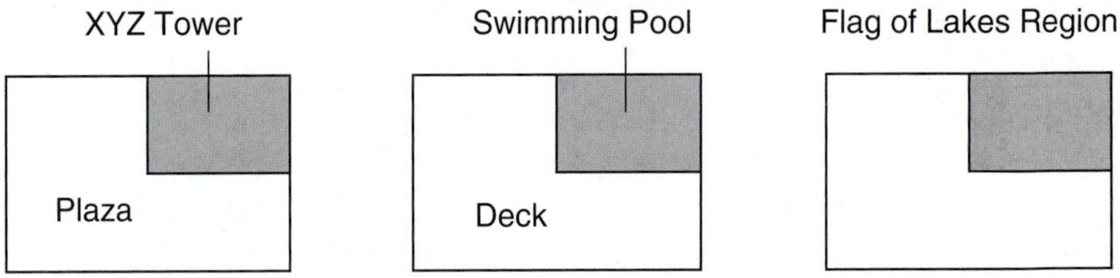

XYZ Tower   Swimming Pool   Flag of Lakes Region

Plaza   Deck

Textual elements can also add critical details—for example, precise measurements, such as the distance between the centerpoints of the two pulleys shown in Figure 8.11. And, on occasion, textual elements can claim the perceptual center of attention (Figure 8.12).

FIGURE 8.11   Textual elements add critical details

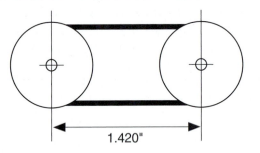

1.420"

FIGURE 8.12   Textual elements can even claim the center of attention

Landscape
Architecture
Building

Intensive English and
Orientation Program

Textual coding might also have greater visual presence in international communications—for example, illustrations for instructional materials—where the text might appear in several languages. On the other hand, some pictures intended for international audiences are designed to avoid textual coding altogether, thereby avoiding the issue of verbal translation.

Spatial Elements

Functional pictures organize information in space so readers can access, understand, and often use it. Just as Susan found with her bird feeder instructions, as an information designer you have lots of spatial decisions to make when you create pictures. Some of these decisions involve selecting the scope of the picture, its focus, and its viewing angle. Many of these decisions will be informed by spatial conventions.

Scope.   Just as you select material for anything you write, as you create a picture you need to consider how broad an area to illustrate, selecting what's important to your readers. You should ask questions like: Should I show part of the object, all of it, or all of it in a larger context? How wide should I open the lens? All of these are spatial decisions.

In the pictures shown in Figure 8.13, the lens progressively opens from left to right—first widening our view, then lengthening it.

**FIGURE 8.13   Spatial elements—widening
                   and lengthening the lens**

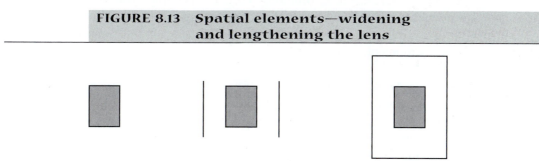

Susan made these kinds of spatial decisions as she created her bird feeder instructions. In her series of perspective drawings, she showed only a few parts of the bird feeder in step 1 and progressively added parts in the subsequent steps, until in her last picture at the bottom of the page she shows the feeder in a backyard setting.

Widening the scope progressively adds more information, which at some point may distract rather than help readers. In that case, the designer has to tighten the scope so that key pieces of information maintain their emphasis. Photographers do this by *cropping* a picture—cutting out the irrelevant information so readers can concentrate on the important part.

Focus.   Another spatial decision has to do with how *closely* we focus readers on the information in the picture. You can distance the reader from the information

(Figure 8.14a), or you can zoom in (Figure 8.14b), or you can get a close-up of a single element (Figure 8.14c).

FIGURE 8.14   Spatial elements—changing the focus

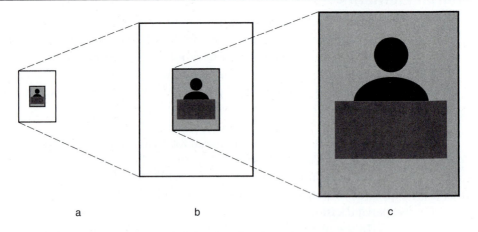

a   b   c

Of course, with each zoom in, we can reveal more precise information, but we also risk losing some of the surrounding context, which may create a problem for less experienced readers. One way to preserve the larger context while zooming in on the details is to create a blowup drawing of a key part, a spatial convention we'll discuss in a moment.

Viewing Angle.   When we represent an object on a flat surface like a piece of paper or a screen, we have to select a viewing angle—the top side or the bottom, the front side or the back, the left or right side, or two or three sides in perspective. Each viewing angle reveals different information about the object, as you can see in the viewing angles shown in Figure 8.15.

**FIGURE 8.15   Spatial elements—changing
                the viewing angle**

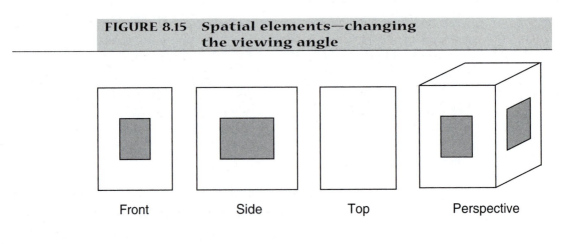

Front   Side   Top   Perspective

If you use perspective, you give readers access to a greater variety of information in a single picture, though that information might be less precise than if your readers viewed it from one side only. This was exactly the situation Susan found herself in as she went from one-sided views of the bird feeder to perspective views.

Spatial Conventions. Spatial conventions can increase the clarity and efficiency of pictures—as long as the readers are part of the discourse community that understands the conventions. Some useful spatial conventions include the following:

1. *Cross Section.* Cross sections show imaginary slices through things so we can see inside them—anything from a blood vessel to a building to a mountain. By cutting through things and revealing their internal parts, cross sections give us access to information that's usually concealed from our view. Some of the information we might be able to observe and then photograph or draw directly (the tree trunk in Figure 8.16a). Oftentimes, however, cross sections reveal information that we couldn't possibly see (the river in Figure 8.16b) or that we *could* see but probably never *will* (the foundation wall in Figure 8.16c).

FIGURE 8.16   Spatial conventions—cross-section drawings

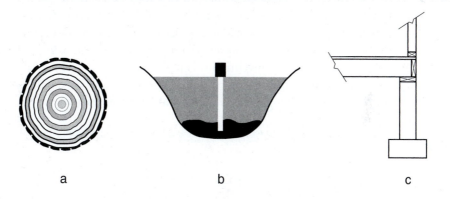

a   b   c

Like other kinds of pictures, cross sections reveal selective information. For example, the cross section in Figure 8.16a shows the growth rings of a young tree and some of their shading variations. The drawing in Figure 8.16b shows the river channel, the silt deposits on the bottom, and the probe that extracts samples. No fish, no boats, no sand bars—just the selective information that the designer chooses to reveal. The illustration in Figure 8.16c cuts through the concrete wall and footing as well as through the plywood floor and wood framing members. Notice another convention in this drawing: the "break lines" that signal that the framing lumber extends to the left and above the drawing.

2. *Blowup.* When crucial details of an object are too small for readers to see adequately, a blowup enables you to zoom in on those details while still showing the object in context. The picture in Figure 8.17a shows a blowup of a control panel, with the circle and line connecting the blowup to the whole drawing and locating it in the bigger picture. The picture in Figure 8.17b shows a cross section of a bookcase with a detail illustrating the construction of the top and a few shelves. A dotted line and an arrow signal the relationship between the whole object and the detail.

FIGURE 8.17   Spatial conventions—blowups

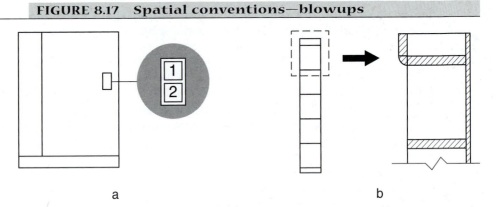

a   b

3. *Motion.* In many situations (for example, instructions) you may need to show how objects move through space. A couple of conventions can help you here: (1) showing how something looks before and after the motion, and (2) showing the motion step-by-step, or a combination of the two. The drawing in Figure 8.18 uses the before-and-after convention to show the movement of a lever from the off to the on position, with the arrow clarifying the direction. The picture shows the action from two different angles, a repetition that enhances clarity.

FIGURE 8.18   Spatial conventions—simple motion

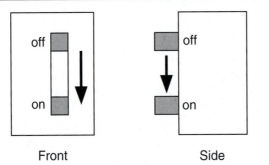

Front   Side

The drawing in Figure 8.19 shows another technique for illustrating motion, a step-by-step narrative of a baseball's path from the pitcher's hand to the catcher's glove. This picture uses graphic coding to illustrate the different flights of a fastball (the dark ball) and a curveball (the white ball). Of course, the picture doesn't tell the whole story: Curveballs usually move sideways as well as drop.

FIGURE 8.19   Spatial conventions—complex motion

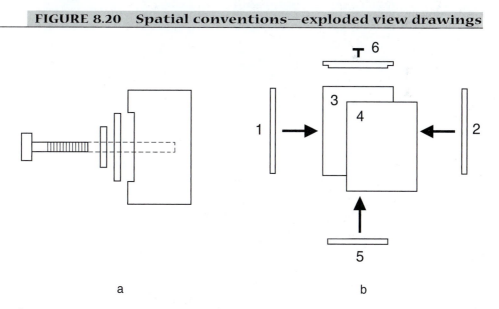

4. *Exploded View.* An exploded view enables readers to see how the parts of an object fit together. Separating the parts and letting them float in space can describe how they're connected or can show the readers how to assemble them. The exploded drawing in Figure 8.20a is purely descriptive. Notice how the dotted line (a graphic convention) shows the placement of the bolt through the washers and inside the object. Exploded drawings can be excellent instructional tools, but they can intimidate some readers. In the earlier versions of her bird feeder instructions, Susan created an exploded drawing (Figure 8.20b), but she later rejected this convention because it seemed too technical and complex for young readers. Like other kinds of visual language conventions, picture conventions are useful only to the extent that readers understand them.

FIGURE 8.20   Spatial conventions—exploded view drawings

a   b

Graphic Elements

Graphic coding gives pictures substance; it's the stuff that makes them visible—the lines, the textures, the shading, the broad strokes and the minute details. Depending on the medium you use to create a picture—a pencil, a computer, a camera, or a combination of these three—the graphic coding available to you may vary considerably. For example, on a computer the basic graphic unit will be lines measured in points (½ of an inch) and pixels, the tiny dots on the screen that make up any image.

Regardless of which medium you use, you can tell much about a picture's graphic coding by considering three qualities: level of detail or abstraction, shades and shadows, and graphic conventions.

Level of Detail/Abstraction.   Graphic coding reveals visual information. Intensive graphic coding makes a picture concrete and *realistic* because it reveals large quantities of information. Light graphic coding diminishes the amount of information, making a picture more abstract. Compare the pictures of a filing cabinet in Figure 8.21.

FIGURE 8.21   Graphic elements—level of abstraction

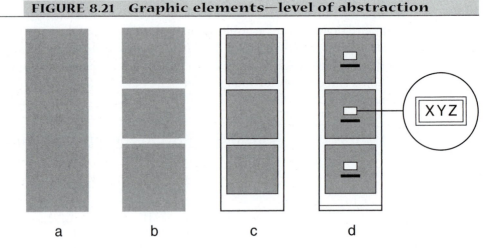

The shape on the left contains very little data about our filing cabinet—only a skeletal outline, a general concept, a generic volume that fills a space. Each version to the right adds information, with Figure 8.21d revealing the most precise and detailed description of the filing cabinet. Even this picture, however, has a fairly high level of abstraction, considering the other surface variations on this object— color, fasteners, textual elements, the reflection of light on metal, and so on.

The level of abstraction is relative, varying from one picture to another. As we've seen above, those variations are easy to see when the pictures record information about the same subject. You can see the same range from a high level of abstraction to low in the drawings of a walnut leaf in Figure 8.22: The first drawing contains far less information than the second, the second far less than the last.

These variations in graphic coding might lead us to conclude that concrete pictures are always more useful than abstract ones, but this is hardly the case. Too many details may be far less effective than just a few that are well suited to the picture's

FIGURE 8.22   Graphic elements—level of detail

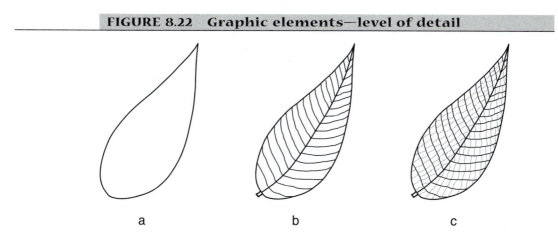

a   b   c

purpose. For example, the more abstract pictures of the filing cabinet or the leaf may be perfectly adequate for some situations—for example, a schematic drawing of an office layout or a field guide for identifying leaves by their shapes. On the other hand, the more concrete filing cabinet would be appropriate for readers interested in buying one, though it would still be far too abstract for engineers who had to evaluate its design.[2]

Of course, readers don't have to scrutinize every detail in order for the picture to serve its purpose. You might include some details for some readers, other details for other readers, depending on their needs. Or you might use a photograph or a piece of clip art to set the tone or attract the reader's interest in the subject, though in both cases the holistic effect of the picture, rather than the details, may produce the result you want.

Shades and Shadows.   Shades and shadows show the effect of light on an object and its surroundings and, like detailing, add useful information, making an object more concrete. In Figure 8.23a, the image displays no shade or shadow but rather stands sparsely on a flat plane. Without shade or shadow, readers could interpret the object as a flat piece of cardboard or a rectangular box. The image in Figure 8.23b adds shading which reveals the object as a cylinder with a lid. The image in Figure 8.23c adds shadows under the lid and behind the cylinder, revealing yet more information about the object. The shadow under the lid gives us some clues about its overhang, and the shadow behind the cylinder reaffirms its roundness as well as tells us something about the surface it rests on.

Does the additional information provided by shades and shadows always help the reader? Certainly not. A simple line or stick drawing, like the cylinder in Figure 8.23a, may work in some situations—for example, where the reader sees a plan view of the same object and needs information only about its size and proportion.

FIGURE 8.23   Graphic elements—shades and shadows

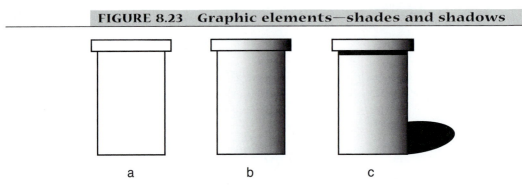

a   b   c

Conventional Coding.   Pictures contain many conventional features, some of which we've already seen in the spatial mode. Designers use graphic conventions to reveal certain types of information, several of which are listed below.

1. *Boundaries.* Graphic coding shows boundaries above and below the surface of the picture as well as in other directions. A variety of graphic codes conveys this information. For example, cross hatching or diagonal lines typically indicate a cross section, signaling to readers that an object (or part of it) continues in front of the picture. The cross-section drawing in Figure 8.24a shows the inside of a metal bar. Dotted lines show objects that extend in the opposite direction, behind the surface of the picture, as shown in Figure 8.24b, which represents the top view of a table with its supporting stand beneath. Break lines indicate that an object continues beyond the boundaries of the picture, as in Figure 8.24c, which represents a plastic pipe that extends to the right beyond the picture.

FIGURE 8.24   Graphic conventions—boundaries

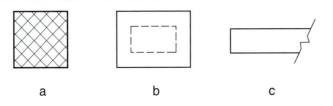

a   b   c

Lines can also reveal the relative importance or closeness of an edge or boundary. In Figure 8.25a (the front view of a boombox) and Figure 8.25b (the perspective of a piece of wood molding) the dark lines show important surface edges in the foreground, the light lines less important edges, often in the background.[3]

2. *Materials.* Many pictures use conventional codes to specify the materials that objects are made of. These pictures often display materials in cross section, as in the five examples shown in Figure 8.26.

FIGURE 8.25 Graphic conventions—relative importance or closeness

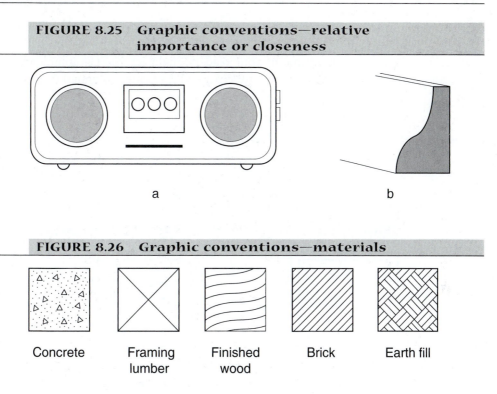

a   b

FIGURE 8.26 Graphic conventions—materials

Concrete   Framing   Finished   Brick   Earth fill
                lumber   wood

Graphic conventions exist for many other materials—metal, stone, glass, and so on—and some of these conventions may vary among different countries or regions around the world.

3. *Specialized Signs.* Many other conventional sign systems have been developed for specific purposes, both for the public and for specialized users within disciplines. Highway maps designed for a large public audience, for example, use conventional codes to designate interstates, state and county highways, and unimproved roads as well as many other features such as parks, campgrounds, and wildlife refuges. These sign systems usually include legends to ensure clarity.

Graphic conventions within disciplines typically have a narrower audience of users. Like technical jargon, graphic jargon has a specific meaning to members of the visual discourse community. For example, architects and structural engineers use blueprints to show how the components of a building fit together, geologists use technical drawings and computer modeling to represent topographical features, and radiologists use X-rays to diagnose bone fractures and diseases. Users of these graphic coding conventions have to learn the visual jargon to interpret these images. In some instances, professional organizations update these conventional codes to reflect current knowledge in the discipline.

Although you probably won't use many of these specialized conventions, they play a significant role in communicating technical information within disciplines. Remember that some of your readers might interpret graphic coding differently than you, so you'll need to anticipate if they belong to one of these specialized discourse communities.

Synergy of the Coding Modes

To review the coding modes, then, we can take the drawing of the computer in Figure 8.27a and add some *textual* coding to it—with the word *Start* on the screen and the label 7000Q on the computer itself (Figure 8.27b).

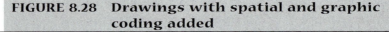

FIGURE 8.27   Drawing with textual coding added

In the *spatial* mode, we can change the viewing angle of the computer drawing, as in the perspective shown in Figure 8.28a. In the *graphic* mode we can shade the sides and the screen and add details to the keyboard, as in Figure 8.28b. And, in Figure 8.28c, we can transform the picture in all three modes: *textually,* by changing the message on the screen and adding the number below it; *spatially,* by focusing and zooming in on the monitor; and *graphically,* by adding some shading to the left and bottom parts of the screen.

**FIGURE 8.28   Drawings with spatial and graphic
                          coding added**

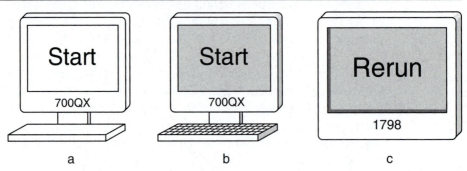

Like other forms of visual language, pictures are sensitive to changes in any of the coding modes. Changes in one coding mode will likely have a perceptual impact on other elements in the picture. Typically, you'll work in the spatial and graphic modes simultaneously, blending in textual elements as you need them.

Applying the Cognate Strategies

Like data displays, pictures are useful to the degree that you tailor their visual language to your audience, purpose, and context. A picture of a lion, a lily, or a lakeside resort that works brilliantly in one rhetorical situation may utterly miss the mark in another. Like other forms of visual language, adaptation is the key to effective picture design. Each of the six cognate strategies offers you an opportunity to adapt your picture to your rhetorical situation.

Arrangement

How you arrange information in a picture affects how much of it readers actually process and use. You might question whether you actually have any control over arrangement because pictures simply record reality, what's there. But like any communication, designing a picture entails *selecting* information: Arrangement is part of the selection process because it controls which information readers will actually see.

A variety of arrangement strategies—selecting an angle of view, positioning objects in space, zooming in and out—can control the flow of information. These strategies can create many different visual statements about the same subject, especially in instructional materials. Let's say in the example shown in Figure 8.29 we're arranging the parts of a tent pole to teach readers how to assemble them.

FIGURE 8.29   Which assembly arrangement works best?

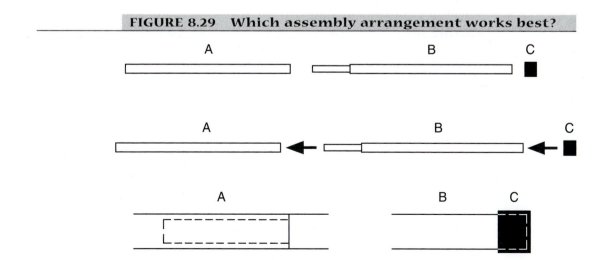

- In the first version, we've arranged the two pole segments (A and B) and the cap (C) along the line on which they need to be positioned so they'll fit together; the arrangement of the parts implies their method of assembly.

- In the middle version, we've inserted arrows that state the method of assembly more explicitly: "Place part B inside part A; and place part C over part B."

- In the bottom version we've included enlarged sections of the three parts and arranged them in their assembled position. This arrangement says, "In these two critical sections of the whole pole, this is what the pole segments and cap should look like after you've assembled them."

Which method works best? It depends somewhat on the readers, what they know, and what they expect. The top version is fairly passive—no motion, either stated or implied, which may puzzle some readers if the pictures are supposed to teach them what to do. Readers would have to make some inferences if they're going to get the tent up before dark. In the bottom version the designer assumes that readers know some conventions: the dashed lines to show the position of one pole segment inside the other, and the spatial gaps between the parts to show break points in the drawing.

Will readers get it? Some will immediately, some may after studying it a moment, and others may give up. The middle version might strike a compromise between the first and the last versions: Its conventions—arrows showing motion—are nontechnical and strongly suggest action. Although the middle version is more abstract than the bottom version, readers will readily understand how the parts fit together. Testing the pictures with the targeted readers would verify (or nullify) that assumption.

Another arrangement strategy for selecting and organizing information is the viewing angle we choose. In her bird feeder illustrations, Susan chooses to draw the feeder from the front left, as shown in Figure 8.30.

FIGURE 8.30   Viewing angle is an arrangement strategy

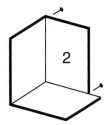

This angle gives her readers a clear view of each task, though it also conceals some information—for example, the nails behind part 2. But because that information is redundant—readers can see where two of the nails go and by analogy locate the other nails on the back surface, which have predrilled holes anyway—Susan feels confident that this viewing angle will work. She can weigh these benefits and drawbacks only in relation to the rhetorical situation: what her readers need to know and how they'll use the pictures.

Susan also decides *where* to place information in her pictures. For example, in the picture at the bottom of her page, she places the bird feeder in the foreground and the birds and trees to the right. Arranging the scene that way seems appropriate because the most immediate information (the bird feeder) appears on the left and the less important information (the birds and trees) trails off to the right.

Arranging the text in Susan's pictures is fairly simple, as she numbers each part as it appears in the sequence. Susan also grapples with a related arrangement issue—how to achieve cohesion among the steps. In her final version, she inserts large numbers above each step and places the steps in a horizontal line to ensure that her readers follow the sequence from left to right.

Emphasis

Pictures can map mountains of information in tiny spaces, sometimes so much information that readers can get bogged down in the details and lose sight of what's important. So designers have to be careful not to include distracting pieces of information that compete with those that readers need. For this reason, simple line drawings can often perform more effectively than photographs because they focus readers on the essentials and exclude extraneous information.

Even in a simple line drawing, however, the designer may need to focus readers on selected details, especially if the drawing has an instructional purpose. In the pictures shown in Figure 8.31, that focus may direct readers to push a button, observe a result, or locate certain parts. The first picture (a) singles out nothing for attention. Our eyes wander across the drawing without knowing where to stop. However, in the next picture (b) the figure–ground contrast of the gray box grabs our attention. The following picture (c) redirects our attention to a different gray box, while the strong figure–ground contrast in the next version (d) highlights both boxes. In the last picture (e), a dark arrow tells us unequivocally where to focus our eyes.

FIGURE 8.31   Graphic elements can create emphasis

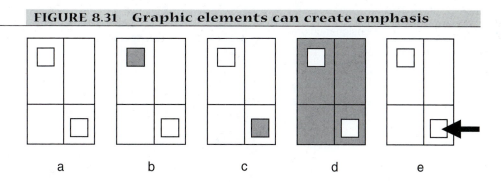

a   b   c   d   e

Even greater emphasis can be achieved with color. In Color Insert 11, spot color selectively highlights the same key elements of the picture. If this picture were used for an instructional purpose, what advantages would spot color have over gray scale? All of these *graphic* devices can be used individually or in combination with each other. We can also use *spatial* elements for emphasis—for example, by enlarging part of the picture, as we saw earlier with the tent poles. In Figure 8.32 a combination of spatial and graphic elements creates emphasis: The box is enlarged and it's accented with gray scale and an arrow.[4]

**FIGURE 8.32   Achieving emphasis by enlarging part
                                    of the picture**

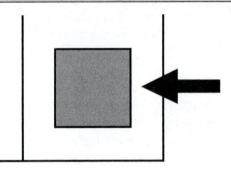

This drawing will certainly focus the reader's attention on the box. However, these highly explicit emphasis strategies may not compensate for the loss of spatial context afforded by showing the whole object. Some research indicates that providing such a larger context in instructions can help reader performance (Barnard and Marcel 54–56; Szlichcinski). In the above example, increased emphasis may slightly degrade clarity even though it enhances conciseness.

Finally, we can use *textual* elements to highlight certain features in the picture and use lines and arrows to point to these features, as in the new version of our filing cabinet (Figure 8.33).

FIGURE 8.33   Picture with textual emphasis

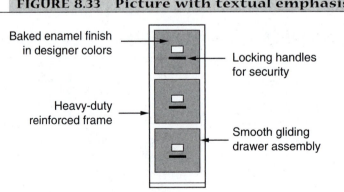

Call outs and labels—and even the figure title itself—are extremely useful emphasis strategies on both drawings and photos. In color photos, which typically contain a wealth of detail, textual elements and graphic pointing devices may be absolutely essential to guiding the reader's eye to relevant information. Compare the two photos in Color Inserts 12 and 13. The call outs in the two versions highlight different details, emphasizing some while implicitly deemphasizing others. Despite all of the busyness with the details and the color, what's called out for attention in one photo recedes into the background in the other.

Computer screens can afford some additional emphasis strategies: Animation or video can capture the reader's attention by setting parts of the picture in motion. In a Web site, these kinds of emphasis strategies can forcefully guide readers to key information, though they depend on the technical capabilities of the user's computer.

Clarity

To function effectively in most situations, pictures have to display information that readers can understand and use. However, because pictures often contain so much information, achieving clarity isn't always easy—or predictable. A higher degree of realism in a picture won't guarantee a high degree of clarity, nor will a lesser degree of realism necessarily result in poor clarity. Research in instructional materials bears this out (Dwyer).[5]

Readers will see many different things in pictures, things you can't always anticipate or control. Your readers' past experiences—viewing pictures and viewing the world—will shape their interpretations of your picture, as will their motivation, their information needs, and their viewing context. Given all the possible variables, the most you can do is to *manage* the clarity of your pictures. The best way to manage clarity is to seek input from your readers, as Susan does when she observes her friend's son Nick using her pictures. Aside from direct feedback from your readers, you can anticipate their responses by keeping four issues in mind: picture conventions, spatial orientation, picture size, and the level of abstraction. Let's look at each of these in turn.

Conventions. As we've seen in the section on visual vocabulary, pictures adhere to many different spatial and graphic conventions. Many of these conventions find their homes in visual discourse communities—some professional, others social or cultural. Readers who are familiar with conventions will expect and understand them, just as they expect and understand verbal language conventions.

Consider Figure 8.34, which shows a metal strap supporting a wood joist that in turn supports the floor above. Someone who understands construction details—an architect, engineer, or contractor—could easily identify the rectangle with crisscrossed lines as a wood joist, and the horizontal form with the diagonal lines as a plywood floor. However, the conventions of showing construction elements in cross

**FIGURE 8.34   Using picture conventions
                can help or hurt clarity**

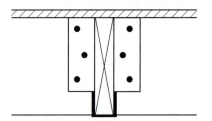

section, and showing them from this angle (beneath the floor), might not be as clear to someone outside the discourse community—for example, a homeowner not experienced in reading drawings of construction details. Understanding the conventions certainly helps clarity. Not knowing them might puzzle readers—at least until they learn the code (see Kostelnick and Hassett 83–96).

Users of picture conventions can also be defined by national boundaries or by cultural groups. Methods of representing the world may differ because of national standards or picture-making traditions, or things may simply look different across cultures or national boundaries. A picture of a bus in England or Canada may look like the drawing in Figure 8.35. But for readers from New York, Chicago, or Kansas City, this picture of a double-decker bus would look odd and exotic because it violates their expectations of what buses are supposed to look like.

**FIGURE 8.35   Picture conventions are often
                culturally specific**

In addition to visual forms, color conventions might vary across cultures. Yellow, for example, often has a negative connotation in the Western world (cowardice) but is associated with nobility in Japan (Horton, "Overcoming" 166).

Spatial Orientation.   The spatial orientation of a picture can affect how easily readers access the relevant information. In the cross section of the joist connection in Figure 8.34, readers see the construction elements directly head on, a viewing angle that allows them to compare the size, shape, and location of these elements. Rendering things in this mode is very precise, and if readers need that precision, this viewing angle will yield a high degree of clarity.

How you choose to orient your picture spatially, then, depends on your audience and your purpose. Recall that initially, Susan decided to draw front and side views of the bird feeder rather than a top (or plan) view because her readers will most often see the feeder from these angles. A top view (shown in Figure 8.36a) wouldn't reveal much useful information. Later she abandoned the flat, one-side only pictures and opted instead for perspective drawings (shown in Figure 8.36b) because they display information in a larger context, in relation to the whole object.

**FIGURE 8.36   Spatial orientation can help
or hinder readers**

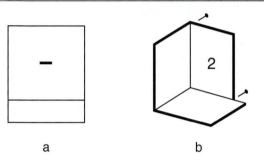

a   b

Perspective can weaken a picture's clarity if readers have to make accurate judgments about size, shape, or location. Fortunately, Susan's readers don't need that degree of accuracy, nor do readers in many instructional situations—for example, readers learning how to start and shut off a piece of equipment.

Size.   Closely related to spatial orientation is the issue of size. How big should the picture be for readers to use it in a given context? If they're using the picture at a desk, where they can study it carefully, the picture can probably be fairly compact and detailed without losing its clarity; if they're using it in other contexts—an industrial plant, a maintenance shop, or a greenhouse—the picture may need some enlarging to make it usable.

Susan's pictures contain relatively few details, and their repetition in a series enhances their clarity. However, if Susan's pictures were as small as those in Figure 8.37, they would be far less useful to her readers, despite the repetition.

FIGURE 8.37   Size influences clarity

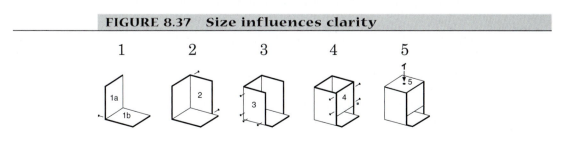

Even Susan's young readers would have to strain their eyes to extract the information they needed while they were constructing their bird feeders—that is, on a table or on a floor, with tools and snacks in their hands and other kids buzzing all around them.

Just like typefaces, picture size always depends on who's using the picture, why, and in what context. Few pictures in this chapter, for instance, would be large enough for an instructional poster displayed on the wall of a warehouse or industrial plant. On the other hand, many of the pictures here are larger than those that often appear on boxes containing instructions for products.

Like using small typefaces, using small pictures can cause ethical dilemmas if readers need to rely on the clarity of the pictures to avoid injuries or health problems. Here Web sites may have an advantage because if users find that a picture is too small, they can often click on it and view a larger version.

Level of Abstraction. Clarity also depends on the abstractness or concreteness of a picture. Like the other factors, the level of abstraction (or concreteness) should match the picture's purpose. In some situations, a high-resolution color photograph might overwhelm your readers, whereas a simple black-and-white drawing might provide a more direct medium.

For example, if you use a picture to evoke a subject, theme, or concept, the level of abstraction can be very high. For many readers, the picture in Figure 8.38 would suggest a house.

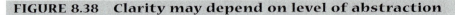

FIGURE 8.38 Clarity may depend on level of abstraction

However, this picture lacks realism: Most houses don't have windows this shape or size, they don't have roofs that slope this sharply, and they aren't this narrow. A photograph of a house would far more faithfully capture reality. Still, for many readers, the picture clearly conveys the *concept* of a house. Of course, if we use this image for another purpose, its clarity may be woefully inadequate—for example, if readers were thinking about buying a house like this, building it, or even renting it for a week by a lake. This picture has too high a level of abstraction for any of these purposes, and anything less than a photograph would probably lack sufficient clarity.

Clarity, then, has less to do with photographic realism than with selecting information that readers need for a given purpose. That may call for a highly detailed picture—a color photograph with crisp details right down to the roof tiles—or a hand-drawn picture with no more resolution than a cartoon.

Conciseness

Because pictures typically contain more information than readers absolutely need to make sense out of them, measuring conciseness can be difficult. Picture conciseness often depends on how its visual language affects the other cognates. Take the drawing of the table in Figure 8.39a. Although this picture is fairly concise, some editing could make it more concise. If we removed the lines (b), we'd still retain enough information to see its basic shape. In fact, we could edit it down quite a bit more, all the way to the ghostlike form in d, and still have the information we need to recognize its shape.

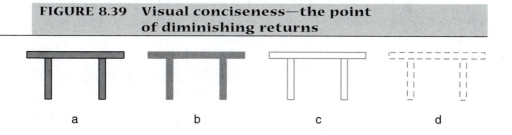

FIGURE 8.39   Visual conciseness—the point of diminishing returns

a   b   c   d

But like its verbal counterpart, visual conciseness eventually reaches a point of diminishing returns. Few of us would prefer to use pictures with dashed lines because to do so would sacrifice too much clarity. Achieving such a level of conciseness simply for the sake of economy might also strike our readers as a bit eccentric, undercutting our ethos. When conciseness efforts erode other cognate strategies, you need to put the brakes on!

In many situations extra information can help readers see things in context, enabling them to interpret the pictorial information more easily or completely. For example, we could illustrate the bolting for a deck joist to a column with fairly little surrounding context (Figure 8.40a) or with more context (8.40b). Can we justify the extra visual bulk in version b? Probably not, if the readers are architects, structural engineers, or professional carpenters. For these readers, the additional information—the 2" × 6" decking, the joist hanger, and the extended view of the column—is useless because their experience already supplies a larger visual context into which they can place this detail. However, if the readers are do-it-yourselfers with little experience, the added information may help them understand this detail, orienting them spatially so they can see the bolting in a larger framework. For these readers, the picture on the right has an appropriate level of conciseness while the one on the left is *too* concise.

FIGURE 8.40   Surrounding context may affect clarity

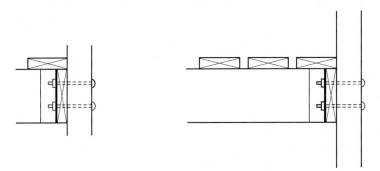

Conciseness in practical pictures, then, depends on the rhetorical situation, on whether the additional information does some work for the readers. In our table picture, we could add some details—the diagonal supports, the break in the center where the table opens up, the casters that meet the floor, shading to show the roundness of the legs (Figure 8.41).

FIGURE 8.41   Conciseness depends on the rhetorical situation

Are these details mere embellishments that erode conciseness, or do they help readers? Maybe, maybe not. For example, if the picture appears in assembly instructions, these details supply vital new information, and we can easily justify them. All of the other versions of the table that we saw previously are far too concise because they lack the information readers need in this situation.

When using pictures online, you can let your readers decide the level of conciseness. You can initially show readers small versions of the pictures—thumbnails—then give them the option to view larger versions or zoom in to see details.

Tone

Pictures speak to us in many different voices—formal, authoritative, conversational, matter-of-fact, technical, breezy, glib, even humorous. Perhaps more than any other form of visual language, pictures can elicit emotional responses from the reader (Ashwin). Pictures can make readers feel confident or intimidated, inspired or bored, amused or perplexed.

Compare the drawings of the bowl in Figure 8.42. How do they differ in tone? Often a picture that appears to be mechanically drawn (a) projects a technical and formal tone. Figure 8.42a looks as if the designer took some time to create it, to get the details and proportions exactly right. A drawing that looks hand drawn (b) seems more informal, personal, and relaxed, as if the designer quickly roughed it out with a pencil or a marker and didn't worry about getting it exactly right.

FIGURE 8.42   Drawings express different tones

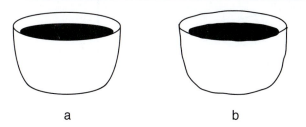

a   b

So which tone should you choose for your picture? Like the other cognate strategies, tone depends on the rhetorical situation. Figure 8.42a might work best in promotional or catalog materials selling kitchenware or ceramics because it's more precise and looks more professional, boosting the reader's confidence in the product. Figure 8.42b might be better for an instructional document such as a cookbook where readers need reassurance that they can perform the task. If drawing b could verbalize its tone, it might say something like, "Relax and enjoy yourself. If you make a mistake, don't worry about it. We don't expect you to become a gourmet chef."

Susan grapples with tone throughout her design process, concerned that her pictures will appear too formal and intimidating to her young readers. She partly addresses this problem by using perspective, selecting a familiar typeface to number the steps, and adding the deck and backyard scene. She especially hopes the backyard scene will motivate her readers by enabling them to envision the completed project. Overall, her illustrations maintain a simple, home-made look (Figure 8.43) that Ben prefers, rather than looking as if they came from an engineering office or a blueprint room.

Of course, there's sometimes a fine line between a casual, user-friendly tone and one that's patronizing and off-putting. Figure 8.44a looks more formal than Figure 8.44b, which seems more approachable because it appears to be hand drawn.
However, depending on the situation, the casual freehand drawing might erode reader confidence. If it appears in instructions for networking computers and is intended for technicians, readers will think they're being talked down to; worse yet, they might think the voice looks too nontechnical and tentative to warrant their attention at all. On the other hand, if the picture appears in a section of the company manual on e-mail privacy, its high level of abstraction and nonthreatening tone may be quite appropriate, especially for new employees.

Clip art and photo libraries offer lots of opportunities to use ready-made pictures to express tone. In fact, that's often the main purpose of these images—to get readers

FIGURE 8.43   Susan's drawings express a friendly, informal tone

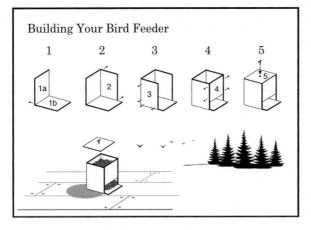

FIGURE 8.44   Appropriate tone depends on the rhetorical situation

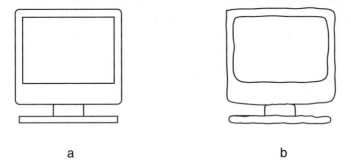

in a certain mood or frame of mind, especially in newsletters and Web sites. A few well-chosen pieces of clip art can turn a bland, stodgy communication into one that's inviting, upbeat, and even humorous or self-effacing.

All of this is not to say that pictures must be playful or emotionally charged to express a tone of voice. Far from it. Our cross-section drawing of the floor joist (Figure 8.40) has almost all emotion wrung out of it, but it still expresses a definite tone of voice: fairly technical and decidedly matter-of-fact, no nonsense, and plain spoken. For architects, contractors, and determined do-it-yourselfers, that's exactly the tone they'd expect.

Ethos

Pictures project ethos by building trust and confidence in the readers. To do that, pictures must convince their users that the picture-makers understood, and sincerely tried to satisfy, their needs and expectations. Because of the many variables possible in this process, ethos-building may occur with very different visual language from one situation to the next.[6]

Like other forms of visual language, the professionalism of a picture—how well-made it looks—can directly affect its ethos. A good-quality color photograph in a report, brochure, or Web site will probably engender ethos simply because, well, it's a color photograph. Like a fine piece of furniture or well-tailored clothing, it looks well made, and the appearance of quality may give it some instant credibility. On the other hand, lack of quality may cause ethos to falter just as quickly: Wavy lines, distortions, poor color or gray scales, and sloppy detailing might not reduce a drawing's clarity, but they may very well undercut its ethos.

Professionalism—how well a picture appears to have been produced—doesn't, however, automatically translate into trust. Let's say that one of the drawings in Figure 8.45 is intended for a dozen engineers and technicians working in an R & D department. For this audience, the freehand drawing (a) would seem incapable of engendering much trust. Compared to drawing b, it looks tentative, imprecise, and unprofessional. However, that doesn't mean this drawing would lack ethos for this audience in all situations. On the contrary, its creator might attach it to a memo asking readers for their feedback about a design decision. Unlike the straight-edged drawing, the freehand version may suggest to readers that their input is genuinely welcome, that the final design is not a done deal. In this situation, the unpolished freehand drawing may gain their trust if it convinces readers that the picture-maker sincerely values their input.

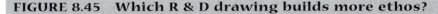

FIGURE 8.45   Which R & D drawing builds more ethos?

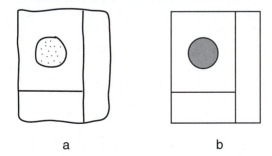

a   b

Ethos, however, involves more than how polished and professional, or tentative and negotiable, a drawing looks. Ethos also depends on how easily readers can *relate* to the picture, whether it speaks their language. Consider Susan's final instructions with the scene of the pine trees in the backyard. To children who live in rural areas, in the suburbs, or in northern climates, this scene might look familiar and natural, but to children living in densely populated cities or in milder climates, it might look distant and unfamiliar, causing them to question its authenticity.

Or look again at our picture of the house (Figure 8.46a). You might readily associate this picture with your concept of a house, even though you don't live in a house that looks like it. In fact, given its simplistic design, the chances are *very* slim that you do.

**FIGURE 8.46   Ethos relies on how readers relate
                 to the picture**

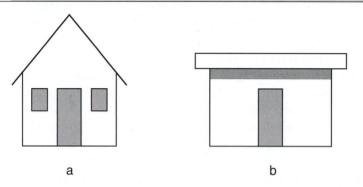

a   b

However, other readers, especially those in an international audience, might find such a house strange and exotic, or least mildly unsettling, because its language doesn't speak to them; it isn't part of their experience in the world—the houses they walk or drive by, live in, or visit. Such readers might relate better to the house in Figure 8.46b. If so, using this picture instead to evoke the concept of a house would probably restore the designer's credibility.[7]

In much the same way, human figures in pictures can affect ethos depending on whether or not readers identify with them. Skin shading, facial features, clothing—all of these can immediately tell readers if the designer considers them part of the audience. Some of these identity markers can be quite subtle—for example, hands that reveal clues about gender or dress styles that signal a certain time period or cultural setting.

Interdependence of the Cognate Strategies

Like other forms of visual language, when you design pictures you need to consider all the cognate strategies, not just one or two, as well as their effects on each other. Below we'll see how the strategies work together in a drawing intended for a specific audience, purpose, and context.

Jean is designing instructional brochures for a chain of fabric stores. The purpose of the brochures is to instruct users on how to create and embellish clothes, drapes, and decorative items. Her readers, primarily younger and middle-aged women, will use the brochures to complete these projects on their own, usually in their homes. Some readers may need motivation and assurance, so Jean wants to create simple, straightforward drawings that look professional but not particularly technical.

Jean is currently working on the needlepoint brochure. She's created the picture in Color Insert 14 that shows her readers how to do the first part of a running cross stitch.

In creating her picture, Jean blends a variety of the cognate strategies. Above all else, her picture must be clear and emphatic, highlighting key information that readers need in order to succeed at this task. So Jean decides to focus her picture on only a few tiny squares in the fabric grid. In doing so, she enlarges the fabric at least a hundred times its real size (an *arrangement* strategy) so her readers can see the movement of the thread through the holes in the corners of the squares. That strategy matches the context in which her readers will use the picture—as they perform the task.

Color enhances *clarity* by adding realism to the drawing. Still, the drawing is fairly abstract: the thread is too smooth and it's too thin in proportion to the squares it crosses. However, this level of abstraction enhances *clarity* because it focuses readers on the movement of the thread through the holes in the fabric rather than on the thread itself. In this way Jean's *emphasis* on motion enhances clarity.

Jean employs another arrangement strategy by repeating the cycle of the thread looping through the fabric so that users can get the hang of it. By clarifying the task, this repetition compensates for the loss in *conciseness*. Jean's arrangement strategy also relies on a pictorial convention—the ghosting effect created by the lighter-colored thread behind the fabric. Jean assumes that her readers will readily understand this convention of seeing through objects, and using the convention will not only add clarity but probably build *ethos* as well because her readers will sense that she's communicating with intelligent and competent learners and not trying to dumb down the instructions for hapless homebodies.

The *tone* of the drawing is objective, low-key, and businesslike, signaling to readers that the task requires some skill and concentration. At the same time, the simple lines and the lack of detail prevent the drawing from becoming unduly technical, off-putting, or pretentious. The use of color, moreover, enhances tone by making the image appear upbeat and inviting. One of the key purposes of the brochure, after all, is to promote fabric sales, not scare readers away. At the same time, the drawing's simplicity lends itself to an honest, straightforward ethos that subdues the persuasive purpose of the message.

Overall, then, as Jean develops her picture she integrates the various cognate strategies in response to the rhetorical situation. She can use these strategies again in other pictures in the same brochure as well as other brochures in the series.

Notes

1. Nelson Goodman makes the provocative argument that pictures are almost entirely conventional in nature. In Goodman's theory, readers understand pictures by learning the relevant conventional codes.
2. Arnheim provides extensive discussion about pictures and symbols and how they relate to the level of abstraction (137–139). Lilita Rodman specifically shows how level of abstraction applies to pictures in technical communication.
3. Research by Clive James Richards, Nicolas D'Amour Bussard, and Robert Newman indicates that a second line weight often benefits clarity in computer-generated technical illustrations.
4. Although we argue that arrows may be well suited as arrangement and emphasis strategies, the impact of arrows on clarity is less certain, as Robert Krull and Michael Sharp demonstrate in their study of arrows in procedural illustrations.
5. Studies by Francis Dwyer show that highly detailed pictures do not necessarily increase reader performance with certain kinds of educational materials (96–99, 133–135).
6. Drawing on classical rhetoric, Hanno H. J. Ehses shows how ethos-building can occur in promotional materials, specifically posters for Shakespeare's play *Macbeth*.
7. William Horton ("Universal") provides several useful guidelines for adapting pictures to international audiences. As James Mangan shows, culture deeply affects the picture conventions we use to illustrate the world we inhabit.

References

Arnheim, Rudolf. *Visual Thinking*. Berkeley: University of California Press, 1969.

Ashwin, Clive. "Drawing, Design, and Semiotics." *Design Issues* 1.2 (1984): 42–52.

Barnard, Phil, and Tony Marcel. "Representation and Understanding in the Use of Symbols and Pictographs." *Information Design: The Design and Evaluation of Signs and Printed Material*. Ed. Ronald Easterby and Harm Zwaga. New York: Wiley, 1984. 37–75.

Dwyer, Francis M. *Strategies for Improving Visual Learning*. State College, PA: Learning Services, 1978.

Ehses, Hanno H. J. "Representing Macbeth: A Case Study in Visual Rhetoric." *Design Issues* 1.1 (1984): 53–63.

Floreak, Michael J. "Designing for the Real World: Using Research to Turn a 'Target Audience' into Real People." *Technical Communication* 36 (1989): 373–381.

Goodman, Nelson. *Languages of Art: An Approach to a Theory of Symbols*. 2nd ed. Indianapolis: Hackett, 1976.

Horton, William. "The Almost Universal Language: Graphics for International Documents." *Technical Communication* 40 (1993): 682–693.

———. "Overcoming Chromophobia: A Guide to the Confident and Appropriate Use of Color." *IEEE Transactions on Professional Communication* 34.3 (1991): 160–173.

Kostelnick, Charles, and Michael Hassett. *Shaping Information: The Rhetoric of Visual Conventions.* Carbondale, IL: Southern Illinois University Press, 2003.

Krull, Robert, and Michael Sharp. "Visual Verbs: Using Arrows to Depict the Direction of Actions in Procedural Illustrations." *Information Design Journal* 14 (2006): 189–198.

Mangan, James. "Cultural Conventions of Pictorial Representation: Iconic Literacy and Education." *Educational Communication and Technology—A Journal of Theory, Research, and Development* 26 (1978): 245–267.

Richards, Clive James, Nicolas D'Amour Bussard, and Robert Newman. "Weighing-up Line Weights: The Value of Differing Line Thicknesses in Technical Illustrations." *Information Design Journal* 15 (2007): 171–181.

Rodman, Lilita. "Levels of Abstraction in the Graphic Mode." *Teaching Technical Writing: Graphics.* Ed. Dixie Elise Hickman. Anthology No. 5, Association of Teachers of Technical Writing, 1985: 1–9.

Szlichcinski, Carl. "Factors Affecting the Comprehension of Pictographic Instructions." *Information Design: The Design and Evaluation of Signs and Printed Material.* Ed. Ronald Easterby and Harm Zwaga. New York: Wiley, 1984. 449–466.

Exercises

1. Select a drawing from an instructional document for assembling or using a product. Do not select a photograph or clip art. Use the questions below to guide your analysis of the drawing.

   a. What purposes does the drawing serve?

   b. Does the drawing use any conventions? If so, will readers likely understand them?

   c. How well does the drawing implement the six cognate strategies?
      - Arrangement and emphasis
      - Clarity and conciseness
      - Tone and ethos

2. Visit a local park or recreation area and take several digital photographs. Select three of the photos for a brochure or Web site that promotes the park or recreation area to the public, especially younger people. Explain your

choice of photos for this rhetorical situation: how they fulfill the promotional purpose of the communication for this audience and how they implement several of the cognate strategies.

3. The picture in Figure 8.47 will be included in instructions that accompany a set of miniblinds. The purpose of this picture is to familiarize readers with the basic parts of the miniblinds before installing them. Identify at least five areas on the picture that need editing for either clarity or ethos (or both).

FIGURE 8.47   Picture for miniblinds instructions

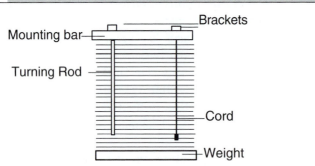

4. Find a set of instructions that contains pictures only or that contains pictures with text printed in several languages. Products like laser printers, photocopy machines, cameras, and computers often include picture instructions. Analyze the instructions in terms of the following two issues.

   ■ *Conventions.* What spatial or graphic conventions do the pictures use? Spatial conventions might include cross sections, motion, blowups, or exploded views. Graphic conventions might include arrows, dotted lines, or spot color. How well will international readers understand these conventions?

   ■ *Cross-Cultural Appeal.* Will the pictures relate better to readers in some cultures than in others? Why? Do you see any cultural conventions in the pictures (i.e., visual elements that reveal the influence of a certain culture)? How might these affect the ethos of the instructions?

5. On the next page are four exercises for creating wordless instructions. Use whatever graphic coding you think appropriate to maximize the clarity of your displays. Assume you're designing for an international audience. The images provide templates for recording your solutions. Use additional images if you need them. (Note: These exercises were inspired by the research of Carl Szlichcinski.)

a. Using the images in Figure 8.48, instruct the reader to turn the dial clockwise 180 degrees. Then tell the reader to turn the dial another 180 degrees clockwise to the original position.

FIGURE 8.48   Exercise 6a

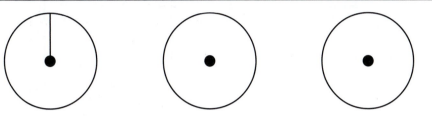

b. Using the images in Figure 8.49, instruct the reader to slide the shaded square to the right end of the box. Then tell the reader to slide the square to the left to its original position.

FIGURE 8.49   Exercise 6b

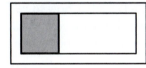

c. Using the images in Figure 8.50, tell the user to push the button so it's in the on mode. When the button is in the on position, it will light up. Then tell the user to push the button so it's in its original off position (the light will shut off).

FIGURE 8.50   Exercise 6c

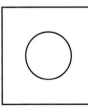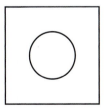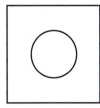

d. The water tank in Figure 8.51 holds 100 gallons of water, and the portable vat next to it is empty. Tell the user to turn the handle on the tank 45 degrees clockwise to release the water into the vat so that the vat fills two-thirds of the way. When the vat's two-thirds full, tell the user to turn the handle back to its original position to shut off the water.

FIGURE 8.51   Exercise 6d

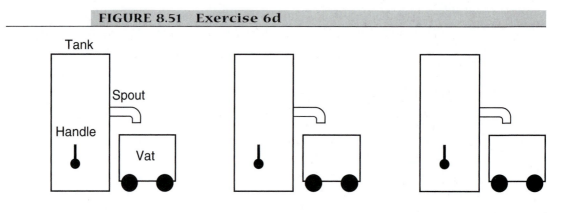

Assignments

1. Have someone demonstrate a simple craft technique—for example, a paper folding technique—that everyone in the class can quickly learn. Repeat the procedure a few times to make sure everyone knows it. Develop a set of instructions using both words and pictures that tell readers how to perform the task. Assume your readers are senior citizens who'll use the instructions to learn the procedure in their homes. Limit your instructions to both sides of a standard-size sheet of paper.

   What particular arrangement and emphasis strategies will you have to keep in mind to accommodate the special visual needs of your readers? Given the space limitations, what trade-offs might you have to make between clarity and conciseness? What can you do to give your document a light-hearted, conversational tone while building sufficient ethos so as not to patronize your readers?

2. For this assignment you'll design illustrations that teach readers how to use a piece of equipment. As you develop your pictures, you'll need to analyze your audience and purpose as well as the context in which your readers will use your communication.

Some Background Information

A biotechnology company has recently developed a new apparatus, the Wonderlight, that precisely emits high doses of ultraviolet rays on plants used in experiments. Agricultural researchers and scientists are excited about using the new Wonderlight apparatus because it replicates in a very short time the natural effects of sunlight on plants, thereby reducing the time experiments take.

You've been hired by the biotechnology company to design a communication that will enable users—technicians across North America, Europe, and South America who are involved in plant experiments—to operate this equipment. Because some of your readers may not read English, you'll have to rely exclusively on visual language to communicate the instructions (though you may use numbers if you wish).

The purpose of your pictorial instructions is to enable a first-time user to operate the equipment safely without any help. Users will probably use the apparatus inside a lab. Your instructions will be affixed to the equipment (i.e., glued or laminated onto the exterior surface), so they will be in close proximity to the task. To accommodate this supra-level constraint, limit your pictorial instructions to one side of two standard pages or one side of a legal-size page.

Some Criteria to Consider as You Design Your Pictures

As you develop your pictorial instructions, keep in mind some of these issues and guidelines relative to the rhetorical situation:

a. Consider the *arrangement* of information in each picture—the viewing angle (front, top, perspective), blowups to show details, and the placement of arrows and other graphic cues. Consider also the arrangement of your pictures in relation to each other—how changes in viewing angle might affect comprehension and how readers will know which task to do first, second, and so on. Obviously, you'll need to create cohesion among your pictures.

b. Use *emphasis* strategies to focus readers on essential information. Keep in mind the context in which your users will process your instructions (i.e., while they're using the Wonderlight apparatus in a lab). If you don't use emphasis strategies to keep readers focused on the task at hand, they might ignore the instructions, mishandle the equipment, and possibly injure themselves or the plant specimens.

c. Include information that's relevant to the task. You can supply details that enhance *clarity*, but be sure these details don't obscure key information, creating a *conciseness* problem. Consider also pictorial conventions your readers may or may not be familiar with, given the various cultural backgrounds of the readers.

d. Make the *tone* of your instructions businesslike and task-oriented but also nonthreatening. If the instructions look too formal, lab technicians may regard them as unusable.

e. Edit your instructions carefully so they project a professional *ethos*. The ethos developed in your instructions should also complement the kinds of work that users do—meticulously studying the natural world.

Design Information

Figure 8.52 shows the front, top, and side views of the apparatus, which measures approximately 4' high by 2' wide. Figure 8.52 also includes a sketch of the Wonderlight plastic container that holds the plant specimens. These containers are specially designed by Wonderlight for use in experiments. The directions for preparing plants for the specimen box are contained in other documents, so you don't have to worry about that aspect of the operation.

FIGURE 8.52   Pictures for Wonderlight assignment

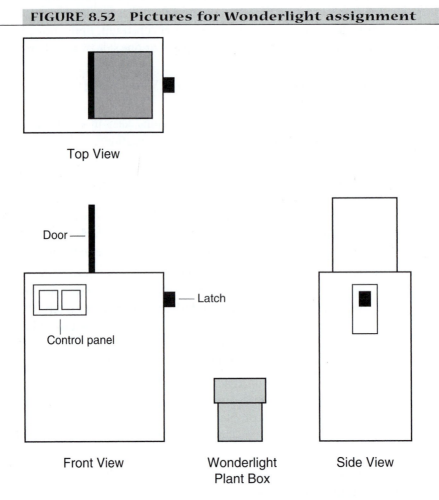

Top View

Door —

Latch

Control panel

Front View   Wonderlight   Side View
                     Plant Box

Your set of pictures should enable the user to complete the following tasks:

a. Turn on the apparatus with the button on the left of the control panel.

b. Place the plastic Wonderlight box containing the plant specimens inside the chamber of the apparatus.

c. Lower the door all the way so it rests horizontally on the apparatus.

d. Push the latch down so that the door is securely shut. Warning: failure to push the latch down might allow the door to pop open, allowing intense light rays to be emitted from the chamber within the apparatus.

e. Activate the light rays in the chamber by pushing the button on the right side of the control panel.

f. After 15 minutes, turn off the apparatus by pushing the button on the left side of the control panel. (Note that all Wonderlight treatments of plant specimens are done in 15-minute increments. The plants must be removed after 15 minutes or they might be damaged. The researchers will determine the optimum intervals between cycles and how many cycles are appropriate for a given experiment.)

g. Push up the latch and raise the door.

h. Remove the Wonderlight specimen container.

Note: These verbal instructions should not appear in your communication. Users should be able to extract this meaning from the pictures alone. You need not create a separate picture for each of the steps above; you might be able to combine steps in a single picture, or you might need more than one picture to explain a single step.

Document

Design

chapter **9**

**Supra-Level Elements:
Designing for Usability**

9 Supra-Level Elements: Designing for Usability

Introduction to Supra-Level Elements

In the previous two parts of this book we explored many different forms of visual language, ranging from text design to data displays to pictures and symbols. Now we'll look at design elements that coordinate, overarch, and unify all of these other levels to create whole documents. In this chapter we'll explore what we call *supra-level design*—the largest-scale visual language of documents, print or electronic.

Every communication, long or short, has supra-level design: a digital software manual, a rental agreement, a research proposal, or a Web site. Because supra-level design involves the largest and typically the most conspicuous design elements—major headings, tabs and dividers, the size, shape, and color of the page or screen, to name a few—supra-level design plays a unique and critical role in determining the document's *usability*.[1]

Let's look briefly at an example you're familiar with, a document you might be carrying around in your wallet or billfold—a business card. You may find it ironic that we've chosen such a tiny document to illustrate large-scale design, but the very compactness of a business card lets us see it in its entirety, as a whole communication. And that's what the supra-level entails, designing the whole communication as a functional object that readers use.

Business cards are conventionally printed on cardstock and measure about 2" × 3½", as shown in Figure 9.1. The size of these vital little documents makes them highly usable, mainly because they're portable and easy to store. If Kip Karakashi gives his card to people at a wedding he's DJ-ing, they can easily store

FIGURE 9.1 Kip Karakashi's business card

it in a wallet or purse. Imagine how awkward those transactions would be if business cards were, say, 5" × 8", or if they were printed on photocopy paper—they'd get bent, crumpled, and lost before his customers got around to looking him up. Adopting the conventional paper size and stock for a business card is a supra-level design choice driven largely by usability.

In addition to its size, shape, and landscape orientation—all supra-level choices—Kip's card has a large, dark green *S* zigzagging across the front, emphasizing the *S* in "sound" (the nature of Kip's business) as well as directing the reader's eye to key elements on the card. Graphically, the card has a light green shading, which gives it an identity and further enhances its ethos. Even a small document like this business card includes supra-level design in all three modes—textual, spatial, and graphic.

Consider a slightly larger and more complex communication that promotes a product or a service. Supra-level possibilities for size and shape abound, as you can see in Figure 9.2:

■ Standard portrait page (a)

■ Folded brochure, tent style (b)

■ Folded brochure, book style (c)

■ Tri-fold brochure with an N-fold (d) or a flap-fold (e)

■ Polygon shape (f)

■ Poster (g) or

■ Digital version for Web site (h)

Each of these shapes could significantly affect the usability of the communication, depending on how it's distributed to readers (personally delivered, mailed,

FIGURE 9.2   Variations in page folds and shapes

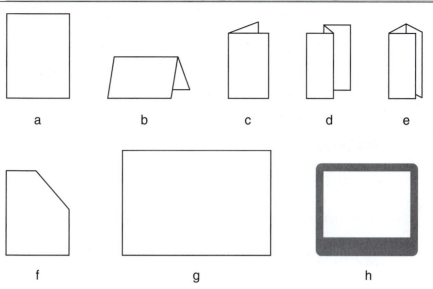

displayed in a rack, accessed on a computer screen), the context in which readers use it (at home, at work, on an airplane), or the time readers have to examine it. Multiply this list by other visual elements such as page texture, pictures or symbols behind the text, or the overall color scheme, and you get some idea of the tremendous variety and impact of supra-level design.

Both business cards and promotional documents are relatively simple communications. Imagine all of the supra-level choices in a more complex communication like a manual or a handbook. Some manuals and handbooks are too large or heavy to hold in your hand—or even two hands. Readers *use* these communications rather than *read* them. Users typically want specific information or need to complete specific tasks—and they want that information *now*. Readers get access to that information through a variety of supra-level elements—headers, tabs, field size and texture, color patterns, or field borders—to name only a few.

And if we open the lens even wider, supra-level design can encompass more than one communication—in fact, a whole set or series. For example, annual reports for an organization may have a consistent cover page, section headings, and page color and texture over several years (see Figure 9.3). Readers benefit from that continuity because they can easily place the document into a familiar set that they're comfortable using, thanks to its supra-level cohesion.

Catalogs, schedules, brochures, professional publications, and many other kinds of documents achieve this same supra-level cohesion—over months, years, and even decades (Kostelnick 28–30).

FIGURE 9.3   Supra-level cohesion in annual reports

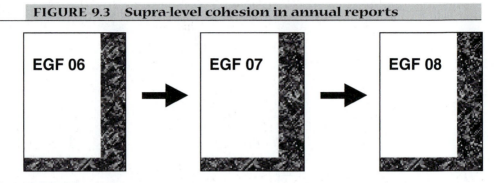

A Web site (see Figure 9.4) enables a more immediate kind of supra-level access by creating a digital network of fields that can instantaneously link one to another.

FIGURE 9.4   Supra-level access in a Web site

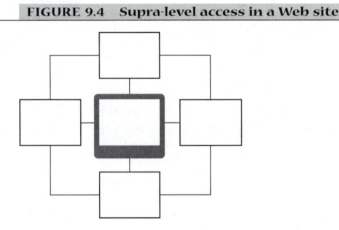

That immediate supra-level access within a single Web site is like riffling through a paper document or unfolding the panels of a brochure. What makes the Internet truly unique is that one Web site can simultaneously create supra-level cohesion across many other sites. The Web is truly a supra-level marvel, linking unlimited fields of information across space and time.

Because this chapter will examine visual rhetoric in its most holistic sense—that is, across the whole communication—on the following pages you'll see a range of supra-level design solutions. As with the other three levels of visual language, those solutions depend on the rhetorical situation, on how well they match the audience, purpose, and context. This may seem like a familiar tune by now, but satisfying the rhetorical situation is particularly critical here because supra-level design makes the first impression, orienting readers as it transports them from the outside world into the communication.[2]

Process Example—Supra-Level Elements

Elaine Seiler is an editor for a water conservation agency that's supported by private donations as well as by the state government. Each year the agency develops an annual report that goes to its donors and board members, numerous state and county officials, and interested members of the public, including city planners, engineers, and farmers. For many years the report has been created in a one-column format, printed on single-sided pages, stapled together, and inserted into an envelope and sent to readers. Elaine rarely gets any feedback from readers on the mailing list, and increasingly she's had the feeling that nobody reads the annual report, perhaps because it looks so stodgy and uninviting.

Elaine's boss, Leo Schaffer, the director of the agency, suspects the same. In a recent meeting with Elaine, he told her that he wants to upgrade the publication. "I don't want our report to languish in file cabinets," said Leo to Elaine. "I want our readers to *explore* it. I want them to *use* it. I'm afraid our current format won't cut it anymore. We need something more interesting and accessible."

Elaine is relieved that Leo has finally recognized the problem, but since the agency has a tight budget, she worries about cost. "Design a more attractive and usable document," said Leo, "and we'll worry about the cost later. If our readers actually use our report, it'll be worth every extra penny."

Analyzing the Rhetorical Situation

Elaine is delighted that she has the green light to redesign the report. Before she begins, she quickly assesses the rhetorical situation.

- *Audience.* Her audience will be quite broad and complex, including government officials, engineers and planners, business owners, environmentalists, farmers, and people involved in boating and fishing, both commercially and recreationally. Obviously, Elaine's readers span a wide range of educational levels and interests, public and private.

- *Purpose.* The report will have to be both informative and persuasive. Readers will need easy access to data and findings about water quality across the state. The report will also have to create a positive image for the agency, which needs to receive continued (and perhaps increased) monetary support from its many constituencies.

- *Context.* Readers will get the report in the mail and decide whether or not, and how much, they want to read. They will rarely read it cover to cover but instead will sample it section by section. Occasionally, readers will receive (and use) copies of the report at small-group meetings where Leo presents information about water quality.

Invention

Elaine has several pages of the report on her desk; she's reorganized them, placing headings in the margins to give readers quicker access to the information. Now she begins to imagine how these pages will cohere as a group.

She starts by thinking about spatial arrangement. Previously, pages were printed on one side only, stacked one atop the other, and capped with a plain white cover sheet. She has 14 pages of text, which, if she followed the previous design, would look like version a in Figure 9.5. To give the report a more professional look and better spatial cohesion, she decides to use facing pages on 11" × 17" sheets. This supra-level design will look like configuration b in Figure 9.5. Elaine figures she'll need eight 11" × 17" sheets, one for the cover page and back, and seven for the text, all of which she'll have folded and stapled.

Elaine likes the idea of the wraparound cover page because she thinks it will give the document a more finished and professional look, bolstering its physical presence and, consequently, its ethos. At last, readers will *notice* the agency's annual report!

However, when Elaine does a mock-up of this supra-level design, folding sheets of paper so she can visualize what it will look like, she quickly realizes that she can't have facing pages in the report without printing on both sides of the page. If she uses facing pages, then, she'll need only a total of four front and back pages. Including the cover page, the report will look like version c in Figure 9.5. Even with the extra paper for the wraparound cover page, Elaine's design will reduce the total amount of paper the report consumes, which allows Elaine to address an ethical issue that's important to the agency *and* her readers—conserving natural resources.

In reducing the number of sheets for the report, Elaine also realizes that she now has two blank pages. "What will I do with those blank pages?" she asks as she stares at her mock-up and worries about cost—and credibility. Two blank pages won't do much to help conservation. But after doing some thumbnail sketches, she realizes that the extra pages are actually a bonus because they give her the flexibility to reorganize the report by using titles, graphic elements, and space to enhance its usability.

Revision

Now that Elaine has made some decisions about the arrangement of her document, she thinks about how she can use additional design elements to make her report more usable to her readers. She starts by emphasizing boundaries between each major section of the report: She introduces each section with a bold title and a box at the head of the page; she ends each section with a row of Zapf Dingbats, leaving the rest of the page blank and placing the next section title on the following page. At the foot of each page she adds lines and mirror-image pagination, giving the pages cohesion across the whole document. She also places an internal tab on the edge of

**FIGURE 9.5   Elaine's supra-level invention
for her annual report**

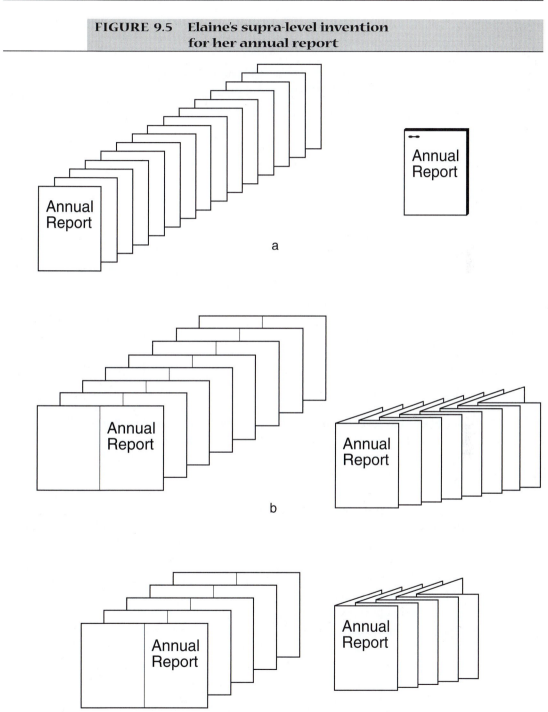

each section opener page; later she'll add key words to the tabs to give readers quick access. Her supra-level revision appears in Figure 9.6.

**FIGURE 9.6   Elaine's first revision—marking
                          section boundaries**

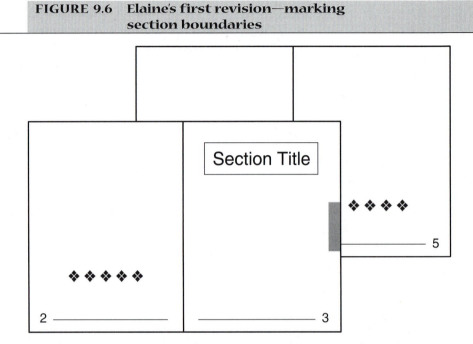

Elaine has several other issues to resolve—for example, where to place pictures and data displays. Now that she has facing pages, she has more flexibility in placing them close to the discussion in the text; therefore she begins to arrange them so they have maximum exposure (Figure 9.7).

She also selects a paper stock for the cover—a heavy tan paper to reinforce the purpose of the agency, conserving natural resources. In designing the cover, she includes the agency's logo (a drop of water) to add ethos; she centers the title to give the report a formal tone and uses a bold sans serif typeface to give it emphasis (Figure 9.8).

Elaine now goes back to her original text and begins to work it into her design. Having the two extra pages gives her some flexibility to create a more open and accessible document. Readers won't recognize the visual language of the report, having seen it in its old form for so many years, but she's hopeful the new design, when repeated in subsequent years, will create cohesion in the future. When the staff develops text for next year's report, she can anticipate how it will fit into the new design.

Elaine does another mock-up, using a recycled paper stock for both the cover and the text, hoping to bolster the report's ethos. Over coffee, she runs her design by Leo Schaffer, who likes its increased usability and professional look. Leo can't wait to distribute the report at meetings where he represents the agency. "How soon can we print them?" he asks, eyes bulging. Confident that she's on track, Elaine sets out to get a cost estimate for printing.

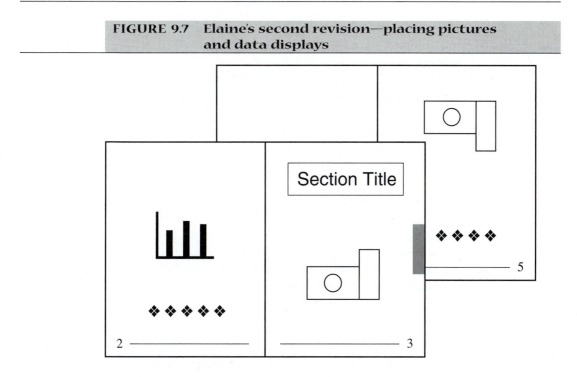

FIGURE 9.7 Elaine's second revision—placing pictures and data displays

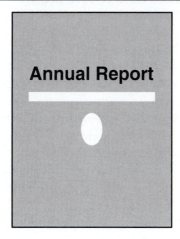

FIGURE 9.8 Elaine's design for the cover

Visual Editing

Discovering that her new design won't cost much more than last year's stodgy-looking report, Elaine reviews her mock-up and makes several supra-level editing decisions, including adding blue spot color throughout (see Color Insert 15).

1. Elaine discovers that she may have problems getting the internal tabs to print to the edge of the page. Consequently, she pulls them in a bit, an *arrangement* strategy, and colors them blue to bolster *ethos.*

2. The boxes surrounding each section heading look too plain and bold, diminishing ethos. Instead she uses a blue fill to enhance both ethos and *emphasis.*

3. She inserts dark blue mattes behind each picture, adding cohesion and ethos to the entire document.

4. Dissatisfied with the graphic element signaling the end of each section, Elaine simplifies this arrangement strategy by using a series of small blue drops, which also lightens the tone.

5. She thinks the cover looks too plain and underdesigned, a *conciseness* problem, so she edits the graphic elements—thinning the line under the report title and repeating the water droplets so they extend to the bottom of the page.

6. Elaine switches to a light blue paper stock for the cover because it will reinforce the theme of the report—clear, clean water—and give it a more serious and professional look, in both ways heightening ethos.

Now that she has the supra-level decisions firmed up, Elaine can go back through the internal parts of the report and do her final editing, both visual and verbal. Having a supra-level design in place will actually save her time because she can adapt the other elements to this larger visual framework.

Vocabulary of Supra-Level Elements

As we've seen with Elaine's annual report, designing on the supra-level means evaluating the whole communication—from the top down—and developing visual strategies that will immediately draw readers into it and provide access to its internal workings. Because supra-level elements are the reader's first point of contact, designing effectively at this level affects how, how much, and even *if* readers will use the communication.

Like other levels of design, the supra-level has its own rich vocabulary that includes a wide array of textual, spatial, and graphic elements. This lexicon is broad and deep, including everything from page headers to folder pockets to plastic dividers. Some supra-level elements you may not even consider within the purview of document design—things such as page size and texture—but these definitely have rhetorical impact and therefore deserve your attention. And like other levels of visual language, supra-level elements often conform to conventional practices, which shape and regulate this expansive vocabulary.

Textual Elements

Standing above and outside the text, supra-level elements often have the job of directing traffic—by initiating new sections of text and by providing cohesion among text fields. Supra-textual elements can also be expressive, setting the theme or creating a certain tone. Let's look briefly at the supra-textual vocabulary and some of its conventional uses.

Supra-Textual Vocabulary. Documents frequently use textual elements to initiate new sections and to create cohesion across text fields. A variety of textual elements accomplishes these two tasks. Let's look at each of these, using Figure 9.9 as a reference.

FIGURE 9.9   Pages with supra-textual elements

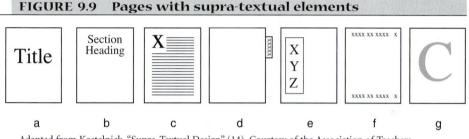

| a | b | c | d | e | f | g |

Adapted from Kostelnick, "Supra-Textual Design" (14). Courtesy of the Association of Teachers of Technical Writing.

Titles on cover pages (a) initiate a document; they are the nameplate, the neon sign above the front door. Section headings (b) signal major boundaries within documents, specifically where to enter a new section. Initial letters (c) tell readers where to start on a given page as well as create giant textual bullets within sections. Tabs (d) provide access points in longer communications, particularly instructional materials and procedure manuals; similarly, navigational bars (e) give users access to screens in a Web site.

Headers and footers (f) tie together pages or screens within a section, creating a stable benchmark from one field to the next. Background text (g) and watermarks can also link pages together by repeating the same text (the letter *C*) on several pages or by sequencing letters, numbers, or words across those pages. Of course, many of the other text elements (a–e) can also create cohesion; for instance, section headings and initial letters create visual parallelism among major units of the document.

Textual Conventions. Supra-textual elements often conform to accepted conventions, which themselves may derive from tradition—"it's always been done that way." Page headers and footers might be examples of this type of convention. Or the convention might be part of a genre (tabs for procedure manuals, navigational bars for Web pages). Or it might develop within an organization. For example, a corporation might have a standard title page for all internal research reports (Figure 9.10); because all title pages look alike textually, readers can easily see cohesion among the reports as a series, and they can easily store and refer to them because of it. For official documents the same corporation may use paper with the company name or insignia engraved on it (Figure 9.11).

FIGURE 9.10   Supra-textual convention—standard title page

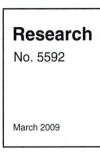

**FIGURE 9.11   Supra-textual convention—paper
with company insignia**

Depending on their origin and authority, supra-textual conventions may be very rigid (a title page format for an academic thesis), or they may be highly flexible and individualized (initial letters in a brochure). In the examples listed below, the supra-textual conventions are closely allied to genres, with some of the conventions being more flexible than others:

- Formal reports and PowerPoint presentations have title pages, often section title pages, and page headers or footers; Web sites also have home pages that introduce or provide links.
- Training materials often use tab headings to increase access; catalogs use internal tabs; Web sites use various kinds of navigational buttons for links.
- Newsletters and other journalistic documents use initial letters (or drop caps, a variation) to start articles.

- Official documents often have faint text, watermark text, or embossed text embedded in the pages.
- Professional journals have their title and their volume and issue numbers printed on the spine.

Spatial Elements

Spatial decisions on the supra-level have a major impact on the size, scope, and structure of a communication. Among other things, spatial decisions also determine how a paper document is physically contained—within a jacket, folder, pouch, binder, box, or laminated cover. In short, supra-spatial design determines the physical presence of the document, both visual and tactile.

Supra-spatial design also influences visual language at the other levels, as we saw in Elaine's design process. Some advanced supra-spatial planning will not only increase the quality of your communication but save you time. For example, you could design the perfect report on all the other levels, but some of that work will be wasted if you end up with two blank pages at the end because of poor supra-spatial planning. Let's look at the supra-spatial vocabulary you have to work with and some visual conventions that can help you shape it.

Supra-Spatial Vocabulary.   Documents, both paper and electronic, exist on surfaces of varying sizes and shapes; these surfaces supply the basic framework—the walls, floors, and ceilings—onto which the designer arranges textual and graphic elements. Let's examine the vocabulary of these surfaces, first with paper documents, then electronic.

Paper documents come in many sizes, which can be oriented to create a variety of working surfaces, as shown in Figure 9.12.

FIGURE 9.12   Supra-spatial elements—page size, shape, orientation

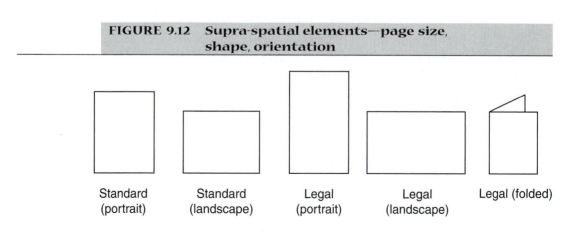

Standard (portrait)   Standard (landscape)   Legal (portrait)   Legal (landscape)   Legal (folded)

These surfaces can be folded, trimmed, or attached, creating many different combinations. Paper documents can also open up (like maps), starting small, then folding out into progressively larger fields. These supra-spatial variations are the basics, and many variations, refinements, and novelties are possible.

As shown in Figure 9.13, sometimes documents have odd shapes to attract attention (a), or they have holes (b) so they can hang on a door knob. Cover pages sometimes have cut-out boxes (c) so readers can see text on an inside page. Documents often use pouches or pockets (d) to hold other documents, and sometimes they have inserts that are physically attached to them (e). Finally, documents sometimes have perforated tear-off cards (f) that readers record information on and return to the sender.

FIGURE 9.13   Other supra-spatial variations

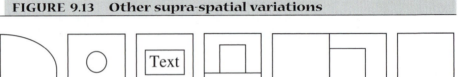
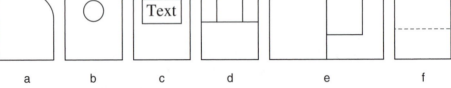

Adapted from Kostelnick, "Supra-Textual Design" (15). Courtesy of the Association of Teachers of Technical Writing.

Spatial elements also include the thickness of the surfaces—from photocopy paper to card stock—as well as any containers that hold or envelop them, such as a plastic lamination, a jacket, or a box. In these instances, supra-spatial design engages the reader's tactile as well as visual perception.

In an electronic medium the user's computer screen partly controls supra-spatial design because it acts as a window through which the user views surfaces. As shown in Figure 9.14, an electronic communication can be designed for a single screen the size of the monitor (a), or the document can extend vertically beyond the screen (b), requiring readers to scroll down, reshaping the field with each movement. Likewise, a screen can extend horizontally (c), as many databases and tables do, or both horizontally and vertically (d) to virtually any size. In each case, however, the user's computer monitor defines the field as the user navigates through supra-level space. On screens, supra-level space can also take the form of stacking or tiling of fields (e), or it can entail the use of links (f), as in a Web site.

And beyond a single Web site, links can extend supra-level space across dozens, hundred, or thousands of related sites (Figure 9.15). In this way, users can navigate spatially across screens, moving from one link to another, which may originate anywhere around the globe. So in creating supra-spatial depth, Web links can transport the user across many cultural boundaries as well.

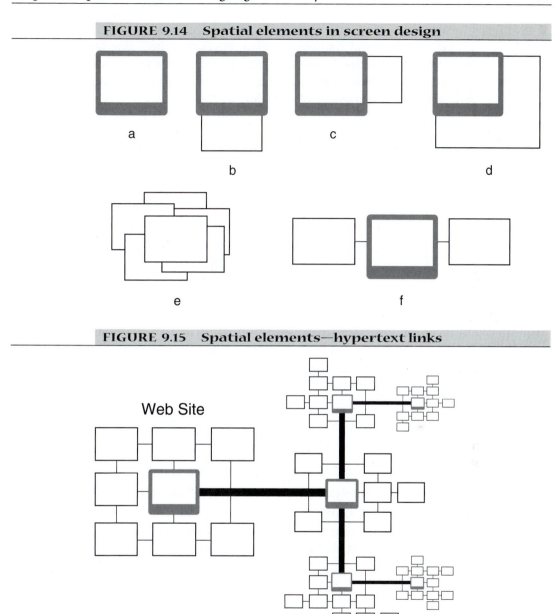

FIGURE 9.14   Spatial elements in screen design

FIGURE 9.15   Spatial elements—hypertext links

Spatial Conventions.   Like textual elements, spatial elements at the supra-level also conform to conventions, some of which are more rigid than others. For example, the use of 8½" × 14" paper is a fairly rigid convention within the U.S. legal community. Likewise, the size of business cards, including Kip Karakashi's, conforms to a widely accepted standard, though here you often see variations on the convention—for example, some business cards are twice as large, then folded in half.

Sometimes supra-spatial conventions are tied to, or at least perpetuated by, storage, retrieval, and transport systems. Envelopes, three-ring binders, and file folders (along with the drawers and cabinets that store them), conform to a standard page size (in North America at least), proliferating that page size in most business and professional settings (Figure 9.16).

FIGURE 9.16   Supra-spatial conventions—storage and retrieval systems

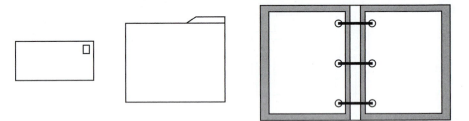

Along similar lines, Web pages generally conform to the width of standard screens, enabling users to see *across* the whole field, if not the full length. Sometimes, however, Web designers flout this convention, extending their screens horizontally into cyber-space, to the dismay of users trapped in their narrow screens.

These are only a few of the many supra-spatial conventions, some rigid, some flexible. Of the additional ones listed below, you can decide for yourself how rigid or flexible they are:

- Business memos and letters use a portrait orientation.
- Posters advertising graduate programs usually have tear-off cards that prospective students can fill out and return.
- Lengthy procedure manuals usually have page dividers that are thicker (e.g., card stock or rigid plastic) than the text pages.
- Highway maps fold into a common size that fits into a car's glove box.
- Envelopes and postcards conform to standards set by the postal system.

Graphic Elements

Supra-level design also includes a variety of graphic elements that can create boundaries between text sections, give the document cohesion, and express a theme or mood. In some kinds of communications, such as promotional brochures or Web pages, supra-graphic elements can be quite active and visible; in others (routine memos) they might not play any role at all. Let's look at the vocabulary of graphic elements, then at some conventions.

Supra-Graphic Vocabulary. Graphic elements give the communication shape and structure; often they're the glue that holds it together, that gives it an identity. As shown in Figure 9.17, these elements might include lines or shading in page headers and footers (a) or in the margins of fields, perhaps bleeding to the edge of the page (b). They include borders (c), icons repeated across sections of the document (d), or shading or color that ties textual elements together across the document (e).

FIGURE 9.17   Pages with supra-graphic elements

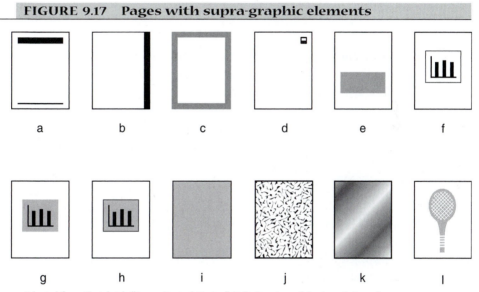

Adapted from Kostelnick, "Supra-Textual Design" (16). Courtesy of the Association of Teachers of Technical Writing.

Graphic elements can also create cohesion among extra-level elements. They can frame data displays (or pictures) with lines (f), shading (g), or a combination of the two (h). Graphic elements also include the background color of the page or screen (i), its texture (j), or its glossiness (k), as well as images placed on the field behind the text (l).

This rich vocabulary can serve a variety of purposes: signaling boundaries between sections of the document, creating cohesion, and setting the tone. Sometimes a single graphic element can do all three at the same time.

Graphic Conventions. Although supra-graphic conventions tend to be less rigid than those in the other two coding modes, they are easy to spot. They have visual, and sometimes tactile, impact. For example, certificates and awards often have ornate borders (Figure 9.18) that fortify the text within, giving it ethos. Annual reports often use glossy or semi-glossy paper to give them a finished look,

FIGURE 9.18   **Graphic convention—fancy borders on certificates**

again enhancing ethos (Figure 9.19). And instructional materials often signal warnings with bold icons that are repeated many times to create cohesion among these critical messages (Figure 9.20).

FIGURE 9.19   **Graphic convention—semiglossy paper for report cover**

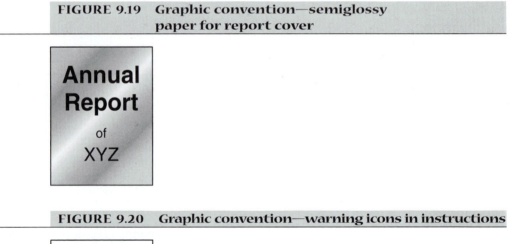

FIGURE 9.20   **Graphic convention—warning icons in instructions**

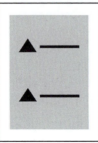

Most of the other supra-graphic conventions listed below are also flexible; depending on the situation, you can use them or flout them.

- Newsletters have bars or lines in the headers or footers (or both).
- Promotional materials often have glossy paper stock.

- Certificates and awards often are printed on parchment paper.
- Logos or background colors are repeated throughout screens in a Web site or slides in a PowerPoint presentation.
- Internal memos within organizations are sometimes color-coded—green, blue, yellow—relative to their function.

Synergy of the Coding Modes

To review the coding modes at the supra-level, let's say we're designing a manual for software that enables users to perform data entry procedures. The text and screen illustrations for the manual will consist of about 100 pages divided into 10 sections. What design choices can we make on the supra-level?

We'll begin in the *spatial* mode by selecting a square page that's typically used for computer manuals. And we'll make some other spatial decisions as well—to use facing pages, to start each section on a new page, and to attach the pages with a wire binding (Figure 9.21). In the *textual* mode, we'll place large headings at the start of each new section, and we'll include footers and numbers at the bottom of each page (Figure 9.22). And in the *graphic* mode, we'll shade the area behind the section headings, and we'll add lines above the text in the footers (Figure 9.23).

FIGURE 9.21   Manual with conventional page size and shape

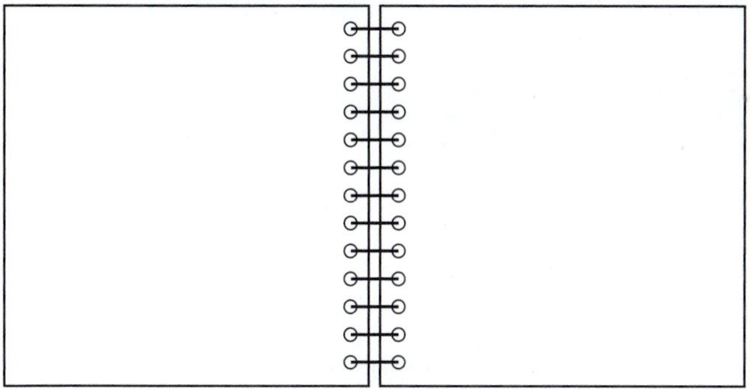

FIGURE 9.22   Manual with textual elements added

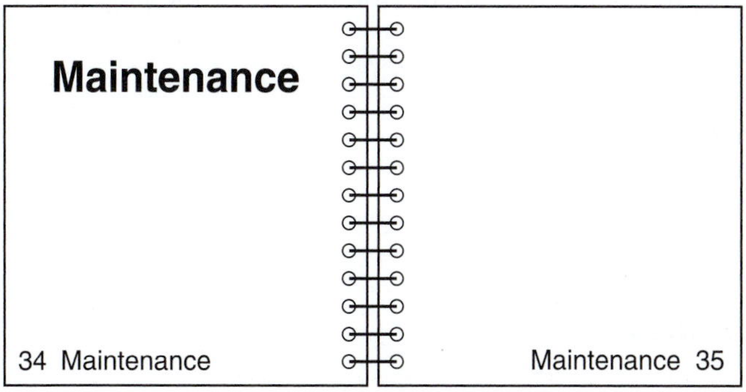

Maintenance

34 Maintenance

Maintenance 35

FIGURE 9.23   Manual with graphic elements added

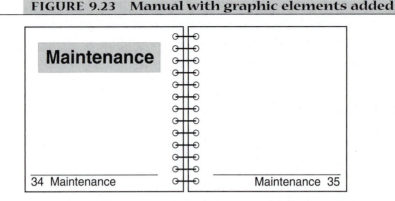

And we can revise all three modes together: *spatially*, by adding card stock dividers between major sections and starting each new section with a right facing page; *textually*, by adding a tab to each divider for easier access; and *graphically*, by accenting the divider with color or a gray scale (Figure 9.24).

FIGURE 9.24   Manual with elements added in all three modes

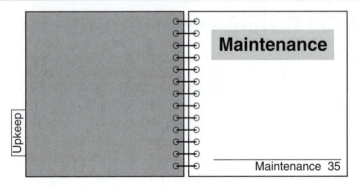

The same kind of synergy among the coding modes occurs in a screen environment. Let's say we're doing supra-level design for a Web site for a nonprofit organization that educates the public about heart disease. In the *textual* mode, we might begin with a prominent title for the home page (Figure 9.25). In the

FIGURE 9.25   Home page for a Web site on heart disease

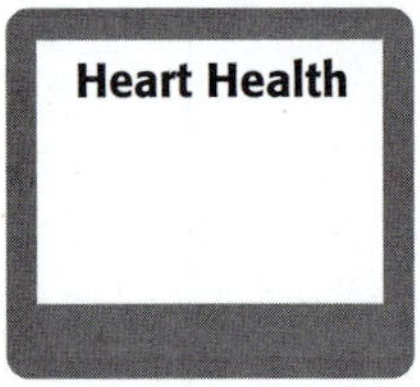

Heart Health

spatial mode, we might link the home page to screens that contain information on related topics (Figure 9.26). And in the *graphic* mode, we could add background texture to each page that defines them as a group, giving them cohesion across the Web site (Figure 9.27).

FIGURE 9.26   Web site with spatial elements added

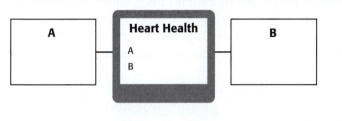

FIGURE 9.27   Web site with graphic elements added

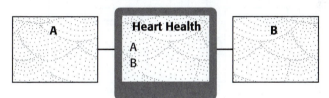

And then we might revise all three modes together: *textually,* by adding a navigational bar; *spatially,* by linking additional screens within the Web site; and *graphically,* by inserting a logo to strengthen cohesion among screens within the site and to differentiate them from those outside the site (Color Insert 16).

Applying the Cognate Strategies

Readers encounter supra-level elements first: They greet readers at the door and usher them into the communication, point out where the rooms are, which ones to enter first, and even what frame of mind to assume when taking the tour. Because of this, supra-level design profoundly affects how easily readers can use a communication. Of course, as the rhetorical situation changes—from a business card for a DJ service to online help for employees sitting at workstations—so does supra-level design.

Like other forms of visual language, then, supra-level design is a process of rhetorical adaptation, of striving for the best fit with your readers, your purpose, and the context in which they'll use your communication. You can make this process effective and efficient by implementing each of the six cognate strategies.

Arrangement

Supra-level design should route readers to points of interest. If the communication gives readers clear directions, they will travel quickly and efficiently to those points of interest; if not, readers will wander aimlessly, become frustrated, and maybe even give up.

Supra-level arrangement strategies can occur in all three modes, creating visual patterns that (1) give readers a quick map by identifying the key units and subunits, and (2) create cohesion among the units and subunits by bonding them visually. Both of these arrangement strategies apply to paper as well as electronic communications.

Take Figure 9.28, a report that uses several *textual* elements to identify the major parts and create internal cohesion among those parts.

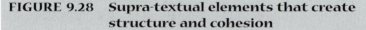

FIGURE 9.28   Supra-textual elements that create structure and cohesion

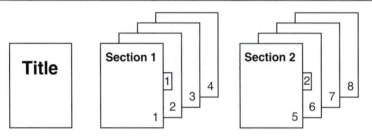

Graphic elements can perform these same arrangement strategies. Coding certain pages or screens with color or a gray scale (Figure 9.29a) signals the structure of the document as well as ties those pages together. For example, in a catalog the white pages might describe a variety of products, and the blue shaded pages might give information about prices and ordering. Dividers (b) can also show boundaries between major sections, and icons (c) can create cohesion within sections through visual grouping.

FIGURE 9.29   Supra-graphic elements that create structure and cohesion

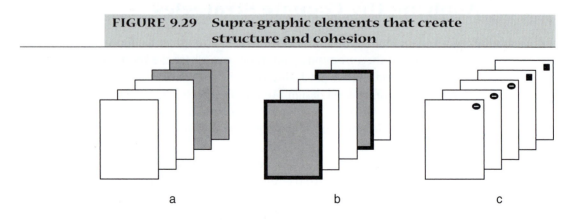

By revealing global structure, these supra-level elements give readers a top-down view of the document that immediately orients them.

In the *spatial* mode, repeated patterns of arrangement can take many different forms to make the communication more usable. Section divisions can be signaled in a variety of ways: by dividers made of card stock or solid plastic (Figure 9.30), or by the arrangement of text and pictures on pages that start a new section (Figure 9.31), a strategy that also applies to Web sites.

FIGURE 9.30   Section dividers made of different materials

FIGURE 9.31   Consistent arrangement of text and pictures to signal new sections

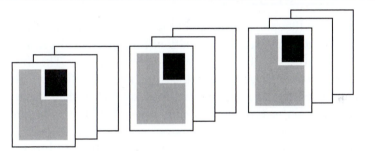

Creative spatial arrangements can greatly enhance usability. A page might open up into a larger page so readers can see the whole text, chart, or illustration on a single surface (Figure 9.32). Similarly, a Web site might allow readers to zoom out from a field that largely exceeds the size of the screen.

FIGURE 9.32   Pages that open up for usability

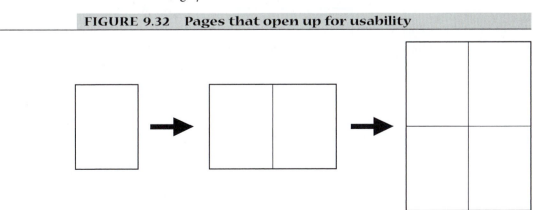

Creative spatial design also enhances the usability of the procedure booklet shown in Figure 9.33, where section headers occupy the margins of lapped pages that progressively increase in size with each subsequent section.

FIGURE 9.33   Cascading pages for usability

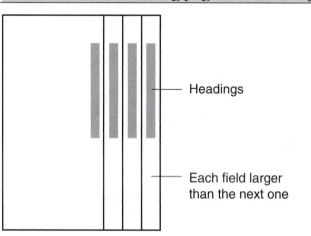

— Headings

— Each field larger than the next one

Sometimes the spatial structure of the communication conforms to supra-level conventions, meeting readers' expectations for a given genre. A six-panel brochure, shown in Figure 9.34, creates a ready-made framework: The three inside panels often cohere as a single group, and the front, back, and flap can be coordinated as well. Sometimes the flap complements an inside panel when the brochure is partly opened. If readers receive the brochure in the mail, the back panel may provide space for the receiver's address or serve as a return card. All of these arrangement strategies (see Figure 9.34) follow the spatial conventions of brochures and directly affect the brochure's usability.

FIGURE 9.34   Supra-spatial convention for brochures

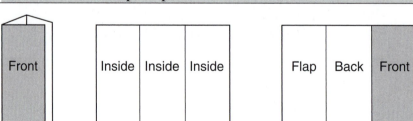

Arrangement conventions pervade many other types of documents, both paper and screen, fulfilling reader expectations about how the document is structured. In Web sites, for example, users expect to see a navigational bar on the left or right margin or at the top or bottom of the screen.

Emphasis

Emphasis strategies at the supra-level point readers to selected places in the communication, which can be a tough job because the communication itself may compete with other visual stimuli in the context in which it's used. A telephone book, typically used in a busy visual environment, includes an effective emphasis strategy to direct you to the business listings: You immediately notice the yellow pages without even opening the book. Let's look at supra-level emphasis strategies in all three modes—textual, spatial, and graphic.

In the *textual* mode, title pages, chapter and section titles (Figure 9.35), numbers, and tab labels (Figure 9.36) all signal major breaks in the document. They assert emphasis through contrast with text elements that are visually subordinate.

FIGURE 9.35   Textual elements that create emphasis

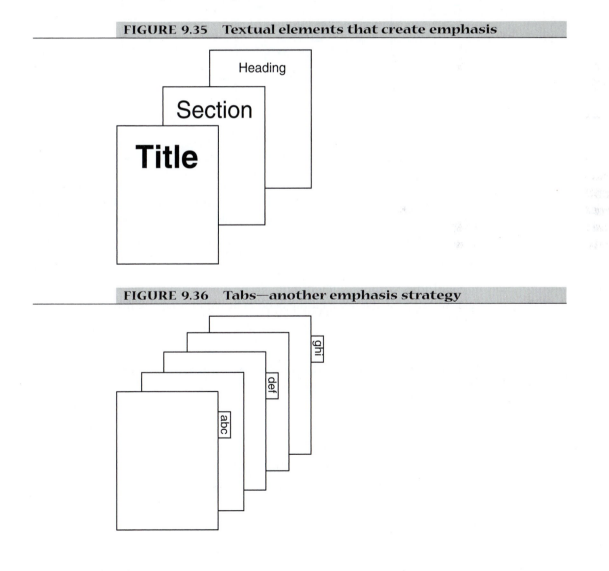

FIGURE 9.36   Tabs—another emphasis strategy

As we saw earlier in this chapter, such supra-level design choices aid usability by providing access points in both paper documents and online.

In the *graphic* mode, changing the color or texture of a page—or a series of pages that serve the same function—can get the reader's attention (Figure 9.37a). Using graphic cues around chapter or major section headers (b) can have the same effect, as can attaching icons to alert readers to important information such as signaling the next slide in a PowerPoint presentation (c).

FIGURE 9.37   Graphic cues that provide emphasis

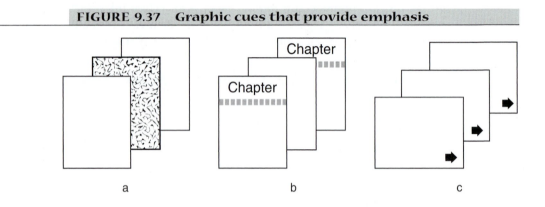

a   b   c

In digital communications such as Web sites, graphic coding for supra-level emphasis can be particularly dramatic, including color, pop-ups, and animations. These supra-graphic cues draw readers to links that can transport them from screen to screen.

Spatially, the most significant and frequently employed emphasis strategies include the size and shape of both pages and whole documents. For example, if important financial information were placed on a foldout (Figure 9.38), readers might not even be able to open the document without having that financial data unfurl in their hands.

FIGURE 9.38   Foldout supplements—another emphasis strategy

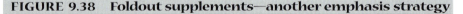

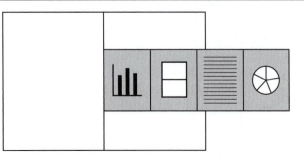

Foldouts, inserts, cutouts, pockets, flaps, thick dividers, odd shaped or oversized pages—all of these tug at the reader for attention, through both sight and touch.

For designers of digital documents, supra-level emphasis through size and shape variation plays a less important role because the design must always be filtered through a computer screen. You can stretch the screen horizontally all you want, but a user with a laptop might not even realize that the information exists out there—hardly an effective emphasis strategy!

Clarity

Supra-level elements can greatly enhance a communication's clarity by signaling its purpose, making its structure transparent, so as to give users access to its information, and making that information durable. To the extent that supra-level design accomplishes any or all of these things, it enhances clarity.

Type of Document and Purpose.   Supra-level language usually gives you clues about the type of communication you're looking at as well as its purpose. If you encountered a mix of documents strewn across a table, you could probably make some pretty good guesses about most of them by glancing at their supra-level features.

For example, most readers would immediately identify the document in Figure 9.39a as a brochure and infer that it has a persuasive purpose. Similarly, many readers would identify document (b) as a manual and infer that it has an instructional purpose.

FIGURE 9.39   Supra-level design clarifies genre and purpose

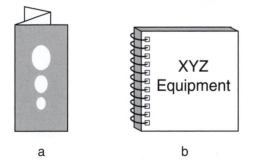

a   b

By providing these external clues, supra-level design orients readers to a communication's basic type and purpose. As readers, we rely on these supra-level signals to sort through all the communications we encounter; without them, we'd squander lots of time figuring things out.

Supra-level design, however, can also *camouflage* purpose. For example, despite the questionable ethics, sales letters are sometimes disguised as newsletters to draw readers into the text, though readers may eventually resist the strategy, just as they might when they realize that a TV infomercial is really an advertisement rather than a news report (see Kostelnick and Hassett 210–216). Can you think of any situations when supra-level design has misdirected you?

Structure/Access. As we've seen previously, supra-level elements enable readers to get a quick, top-down understanding of the communication's structure—the seams and boundaries, the major units and the subunits. By mapping out the structure, supra-level design elements like colored bands and pages clarify how the parts fit together and provide access points to the information (Color Insert 17).

In complex documents—manuals, annual reports, training materials—supra-level design can get readers where they want to go—fast. Textual and graphic features like tabs, title pages, icons, and color can help readers access information quickly and effortlessly (Figure 9.40).

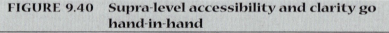

FIGURE 9.40   **Supra-level accessibility and clarity go hand-in-hand**

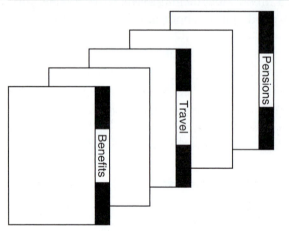

Durability. Clarity can also be enhanced by the supra-level treatments that preserve and protect information. Instructions used in a car repair shop where oil, heat, and dirt can damage them have to be laminated or encased in a protective covering to preserve their clarity. Similarly, maps used on boats, menus in restaurants, or recipes in kitchens might require the same kind of supra-level treatment to ensure both their clarity and usability.

Supra-level design can also *reduce* clarity, especially on the other levels. For example, choosing a dark color for print pages, PowerPoint slides, or Web site or screens dramatically affects the figure–ground contrast of the text. Color, whether used in print or on screen, can also create clarity problems if the document extends across cultural groups. The meanings readers associate with colors such as yellow, red, and green vary in different parts of the world, so designers need to use them cautiously (Horton 687). As the Web continues to expand its reach around the globe as a primary medium for professional communication across cultures, the use of color has become an even more important issue.

Conciseness

Because supra-level design is so conspicuous, its excesses are usually easy to spot. Designers have to be careful not to overindulge, creating so many variations that they cancel out each other, misdirecting readers and inflating production costs. For example, in a document with relatively short sections—say only a couple of pages for each section—using drop caps, linework, shading, tabs, *and* icons to signal the breaks would be redundant and wasteful. A Web site with multiple colors and icons, along with animations and videos, can overload the users' perceptual intake.

Like other levels of visual language, a communication's supra-level conciseness depends on whether the design elements help it achieve its purpose. Does the business card with the tent fold (Figure 9.41a), which doubles its size over a standard card, lack conciseness? Perhaps—if the added bulk fails to make the card more persuasive and useful. What about Figure 9.41b, the leather-bound report with the reading ribbon in the center? If it's a quarterly report to a manager, the supra-level design has clearly lapsed into supra-hype. On the other hand, if the leather binding envelops a formal legal agreement merging two multinational corporations, then it can probably justify itself, mostly in terms of ethos. Or what about the report encased in a plastic binder (c)? If the cover prevents the open document from laying flat on the reader's desk, the supra-level design will work at cross purposes with the document's usability—a serious conciseness problem.

FIGURE 9.41   Conciseness depends on a document's purpose

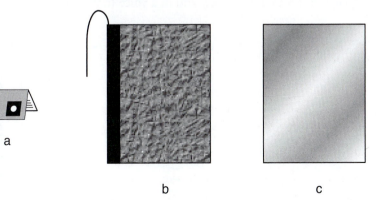

a

b   c

Like other forms of visual language, then, you can use functionality to measure supra-level conciseness. For example, a well-known grammar and usage handbook,

Diana Hacker's *A Writer's Reference,* features a spiral binding so facing pages can easily be laid flat, tab-pages to separate sections, colored tab markers at page tops to indicate subsections, and linework to clarify subsection divisions. At first glance this might seem like overkill, but given the highly complex subject matter and the extreme need for accessibility of information, the design displays supra-level conciseness. The same array of design choices in a totally different reference tool—say *Chemical Abstracts*—would be quite inappropriate and therefore not at all concise.

In a Web site, supra-level conciseness may have the functional goal of enabling users to scroll through a document without waiting continually for the screen to refresh. To increase the usability of the site, the designer might have to omit nonessential videos, animations, or interactive displays. Of course, the importance of Web conciseness depends on how often users visit the site: If they visit once or very infrequently, they might tolerate waiting for multimedia elements to load, but if they frequently access the site, they may resent the delay.

Tone

Supra-level elements immediately give documents a voice: serious, playful, trivial, calm, frenetic, objective, sincere, and so on. How readers gauge this voice may be critical to the document's success.

What tone variations does supra-level design reveal in the documents shown in Figure 9.42? Document a has a cut-out hole in it and a rounded corner, and its pages are bound with saddle-stitched staples. Does it look approachable, playful, humorous, and even a little self-effacing? (Do serious documents *ever* have holes like that punched in them?) Document b, much longer and thicker, has a sturdy wire binding and square pages. Does it look more functional, businesslike, and plain-spoken? How does document c sound, our multinational merger agreement with leather binding? Serious, high-brow, and maybe even elitist? Supra-level language speaks to us—quickly and in a voice that resonates.

FIGURE 9.42   What tone do these supra-level designs convey?

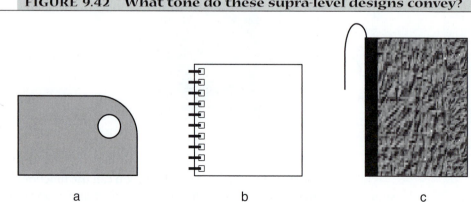

a   b   c

That visual voice can also be heard in web sites in the graphic composition of the screen—its texture, background images, multimedia-elements, and color.[3] The voice may range from light and breezy, to dark and mysterious, to low-key and matter-of-fact.

Like the other cognate strategies, tone is always defined by the rhetorical situation. If a supra-level design is repeated in different situations, the appropriateness of its tone may vary. If an internal memo report on excess travel expenditures used a heavy bond paper and color printing, it would look pretentious or silly and might even raise ethical questions about its author's character. But if the same design choices were used for a prospectus to an important client, it would probably look elegant, professional, and sincere.

Ethos

Supra-level design can strongly influence whether readers believe that a document speaks honestly or that its authors are competent enough to be trusted. Designers intuitively understand this principle; so do readers. As a result, designers often try to garner the reader's trust (both in the document and in themselves) by evoking a degree of supra-level formality. Some of these supra-level strategies are illustrated in Figure 9.43. Borders (a), textured or glossy paper (b, c), or embossed images (d)—each of these can indeed enhance credibility in the right situation.

FIGURE 9.43   Supra-level design has a powerful impact on ethos

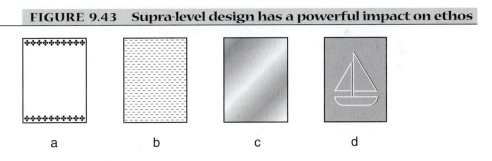

a   b   c   d

For example, someone who wins an award expects the certificate to look formal: A fancy border, a script font, and perhaps parchment paper can create a level of formality that's appropriate for the occasion. Similarly, a company's fact sheet that goes to potential customers is likely to be color printed on high-quality paper, with the company's logo in prominent places. In both situations, supra-level formality builds ethos by meeting reader expectations.

On the other hand, formality doesn't necessarily bolster credibility. Sales letters sometimes include fancy money certificates, like the one in Figure 9.44, that readers have only a slim chance of cashing in. All the supra-level ethos-building in the world—elaborate borders, script headline fonts, parchment paper—won't persuade many readers that they're really winners. In fact, such

FIGURE 9.44   Formality doesn't necessarily help credibility

Jane Marie Doe

Is Awarded

A Billion Dollars

supra-level maneuvers may engender only irritation or cynicism. Likewise, a charity that sends out a brochure soliciting funds may lose credibility if it uses glossy paper or embossing. A plain paper stock would probably give readers greater confidence that their money was supporting a worthy charity rather than a fund-raising promotion.

Web sites build ethos in many of the same ways that paper documents do, though they also have some unique areas of visual language. Animations and interactive displays, for example, can make a Web site more exciting, and perhaps more credible, if for no other reason than to certify the technical competence of the designer. (However, using complex graphic elements can backfire if they slow the user's progress through the site.) In addition, supra-level links to other sites with high credibility can also bolster the reader's trust. For example, a site for a chain of travel agencies might enhance its credibility by including links from its site to those of several cities, states, or national parks.

Visual conventions also figure importantly in building supra-level ethos. When documents violate supra-level conventions, ethos can quickly evaporate. For example, in legal proceedings documents are expected to be 8½" × 14"; communications appearing on another paper size would look unprofessional. Similarly, in most situations a newsletter would look cheap or zany if printed on actual newsprint. Violating supra-level conventions can severely undercut ethos.

Interdependence of the Cognate Strategies

As the supra-level design of a document takes shape, the cognate strategies develop a symbiotic relationship: They work together, reflect each other, and frequently balance one another. To demonstrate this interdependence, we'll examine both a promotional communication used by an independent real estate agent and a portion of the Web site of the National Park Service.

Real Estate Packet

Jim McGough has been a real estate agent for over 20 years. At times he has worked as a totally self-employed agent, while at other times he has been affiliated with regional realty companies. Jim uses a variety of professional communications, ranging from his business card to legal forms to informational materials for first-time home buyers. Because his business is highly relationship-driven, Jim has committed himself as much to developing trust and friendships as to selling houses. Jim understands a potential client may or may not buy or sell a house now, but if that person feels comfortable with him professionally and personally, the more likely he'll be to gain a client in the future.

Figure 9.45 is a drawing of Jim's information package developed by Sherry McGough, a senior lecturer in professional communication. The pocketed folder contains Jim's business card (fitted into the slots in the left-hand pocket) and a cascading stack of seven different documents.

FIGURE 9.45   Real estate packet

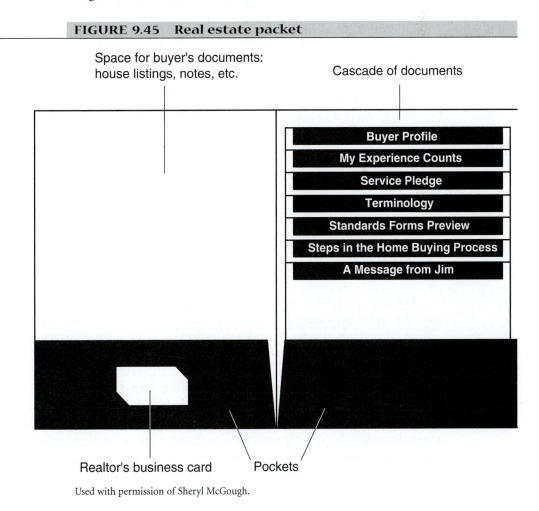

Space for buyer's documents: house listings, notes, etc.

Cascade of documents

Buyer Profile
My Experience Counts
Service Pledge
Terminology
Standards Forms Preview
Steps in the Home Buying Process
A Message from Jim

Realtor's business card   Pockets

Used with permission of Sheryl McGough.

The audience for these materials will range from young married couples searching for a starter home, to commercial investors looking for rental properties, to recently transferred executives who must sell their houses quickly, to families wanting more space, a more attractive neighborhood, or more luxurious amenities. The multiple purposes of the document package are reflected in the contents themselves:

- *A Message from Jim* is intended to introduce Jim and establish the theme of trust as well as the personal tone of the whole package. It's the shortest and smallest piece.

- *Steps in the Home-Buying Process* is an informational piece that presents its five major steps in a tabular format. The primary goal is to demystify the process.

- *Standard Forms Preview* is another informational piece that also has a persuasive goal: to build trust and confidence in Jim as an up-front real estate agent.

- *Terminology* is the lengthiest piece in the package (four pages) and continues the informational mode. It has a reader-friendly stance because the technical language of real estate transactions can cause anxiety for clients.

- *Service Pledge* is the most overtly persuasive element in the folder. Here Jim wants to assure potential clients that he is committed to honesty and service. This is where relationship-building really begins.

- *My Experience Counts* is another persuasive piece, intended to display Jim's extensive experience by implying that someone with this background must be doing something right.

- *Buyer Profile* is the one interactive element in the package, a form that clients fill out to give Jim a general profile of themselves. Because it helps Jim build relationships as well as gauge the potential client's needs and preferences, the document has both an informational and a persuasive purpose. It's the only standard size page in the package.

The context of Jim's communication package also varies, but usually he distributes the folder personally to people who have indicated an interest in buying or selling, or perhaps just looking at, real estate. He does not mail or hand out the package to people who have not requested it—this isn't a shotgun type of marketing communication. Now that we've outlined the rhetorical situation, let's examine how this document's supra-level design enacts the cognate strategies.

The *arrangement* of the communication displays several interesting supra-level elements. For example, the pocketed folder serves as the container, a design choice that enhances usability by leaving the documents loose so that readers can quickly pull out the communication they need rather than having to turn pages. Of course, this arrangement choice has its risks—a client might drop the folder and scatter the documents all over the floor or the car seat. However, Sherry was willing to take this risk because she believed that the folder itself, made of heavy paper stock, would provide a businesslike *tone* and lots of *ethos.*

The most unique and eye-catching arrangement strategy is the cascading stack of pages that gives each one a distinctive size and shape. The vertical size differences aid both *clarity* and *emphasis* because this alignment allows immediate access to all of the titles at once in a way that virtually any kind of binding or stapling wouldn't allow. Readers can see all of the section headings at a glance rather than having to turn pages. Supra-level emphasis strategies also include the white-on-red (white-on-black here) title bars for each document, which enhance the usability of the entire packet and also build *ethos* because they reflect Jim's confidence in himself and his real estate experience.

Conciseness strategies at the supra-level include the placement of the cascading documents on only one side of the folder. This supra-level conciseness—Sherry could have cascaded the documents on both sides of the folder—enhances the packet's usability because it frees up the pocket on the left to hold the client's miscellaneous notes.

Sherry could have used any one of a number of supra-level designs for the package, some of which would have been more conventional. But her willingness to take supra-level risks, particularly with respect to arrangement and tone, enabled her to add interest while still emphasizing the right things and building ethos with Jim's clients. And driving the whole design is the concern for usability—Sherry understood that home buyers or sellers rarely read documents from top to bottom, first to last. The pocketed folder, the prominently placed business card, and the cascading stack of documents with their highly visible titles combine to create a usable package that sends the message of personal commitment, efficiency, and sound business practices.

National Park Service Web Site

The National Park Service (NPS) is one of the best-known entities of the U.S. government. The online directory of national parks and historical sites contains over 400 entries. The NPS Web site has as its audience the entire American public as well as tens of thousands of visitors from other countries throughout the world. To appreciate the supra-level design of this site, you can access it at www.nps.gov.

To illustrate how well the NPS has achieved its supra-level design, we've selected its home page and two others: a secondary page showing the NPS map of Wyoming after we selected that state on the interactive home page display, and the main page for Grand Teton National Park, which of course is in Wyoming. These three screens contain considerable design work, so remember that our discussion here treats only the *supra*-level elements. Please feel free to flip back and forth among Figures 9.46, 9.47, 9.48, and Color Insert 18 as we discuss these features.

FIGURE 9.46   U.S. National Park Service home page, February 2009

Courtesy of the U.S. National Park Service.

Home Page.   See Figure 9.46 or Color Insert 18. The first thing to note about the NPS home page is that it's dynamic, not static. Except for the interactive map (see below), the items visible one day are not necessarily the same items visible the next day. This feature is true for many Web sites now—the basic layout stays the same but the separate features rotate among a series of set pieces or are updated weekly, daily, or even hourly. We took the screen shots you see here on February 19, 2009.

In terms of *arrangement*, note the black bar at the top of the page. It serves as a supra-level unifier and so you'll see this same bar at the top of every subsequent screen in the Web site. The three forest-green bars visible on the home page are also supra-level markers because they function much like divider tabs that you might find on a lengthy paper document. Other important arrangement choices include the two different kinds of links seen down the left side of the home page as well as the two series of thumbnails/links that run down the right side, most of which lead to video clips. (These will disappear on subsequent pages, while the simpler text-format links on the left side will remain.)

The black bar provides *emphasis* through contrast. Against the black, the seasonal scene (remember, it was winter as we captured the screens we are using here) stands out very strongly. The green bars provide emphasis as well, for the small thumbnails and the accompanying text in their respective sections.

Supra-level *clarity* is achieved through design choices such as the white type within the black bar, the green bars, and the winter scene photo itself, in addition to how the size and light color enhance the visibility of the interactive map.

The strategy of *conciseness* at the supra-level is represented by the "main event" of the home page—the interactive visual that allows the user to find national parks state by state. Think of how much text would be required to list all 50 states and the five territories, especially if they were grouped by geographical region. Instead, the map of the United States allows users to select the state or territory in which they might be interested, and—at least in the case of the 48 contiguous states—it *shows* the locations instead of having to list them.

The home page's supra-level *tone* is friendly, professional, and rather high-tech. The pictures scattered about the screen encourage exploration, and shades of greens and browns visually connote nature and the environment. The pop-up (which does not appear in our screen captures but is visible on the Web site live when you put your mouse over the individual state) confirms that the NPS design is in touch with the times. The fact that the center display is interactive also demonstrates that the NPS makes effective use of modern technology, which builds the Web page's *ethos*.

Wyoming state page.   See Figure 9.47. Major *arrangement* choices remain intact, including the black bar at the top, a photo just below (but purposely blurred), and a green bar as major header. Now the interactive map focuses on Wyoming, but

FIGURE 9.47   NPS Web page showing national parks in Wyoming, February 2009

Courtesy of the U.S. National Park Service.

surrounding states are also visible. The left-side links remain the same but the thumbnail/links on the right side are now gone (which is also a *conciseness* strategy, of course). In the interest of space we can show only 3 of the 11 "abstracts" that are visually keyed by a picture and contain a short (about 50-word) summary/description of each of Wyoming's national parks or trails.

An important example of supra-level *emphasis* is the medium-green area indicators of the larger parks in Wyoming, such as Yellowstone and Grand Teton, as is the slightly darker shading that allows Wyoming to stand out from its neighbors.

Both *clarity* and *ethos* at the supra-level are achieved through design redundancy: users can get to park-specific Web pages (see Figure 9.48) either by clicking on the park's actual location (or its label) on the interactive map of Wyoming *or* by scrolling down to the appropriate abstract and clicking on the name or one of the specific secondary pages for that park or trail area (such as Directions).

The supra-level *tone* of the Wyoming page remains friendly but also high-tech, and presence of the pop-up feature confirms this, as it did on the home page.

FIGURE 9.48   NPS Web page for Grand Teton National Park and John D. Rockefeller, Jr. (Memorial Parkway, February 2009)

Courtesy of the U.S. National Park Service.

Grand Teton National Park page.   See Figure 9.48. Once again some major *arrangement* choices remain unchanged, in particular the black bar and the left-side links. But at this level the forest-green bar has moved up by the left side of the picture, which now runs only partly across the width of the screen. These design choices also create *emphasis* through contrast, including the white typography against the black and the green.

A supra-level *clarity* strategy is the column of QUICKLINKS just to the right of the standard links and below the green bar. These links show the specific kinds of information available about the park—information that will likely be useful and desired by users who've come this far into the NPS Web site.

A *conciseness* factor is that the QUICKLINKS lead to new pages devoted to the items listed such as News Releases, and so do the primary "chunks" contained on the page, such as the section titled Planning a Visit During Winter? These supra-level choices provide a positive "redundancy"—and also contribute to *ethos*—because key information appears in multiple places and in multiple forms.

The visual *tone* of pages such as this one continues to be friendly and high-tech, and the increased specificity of the information available is sure to be exciting for users who by now may be seriously thinking of putting Grand Teton National Park on their itinerary.

In all, the National Park Service Web site includes a variety of textual, spatial, and graphic elements that work together on the supra-level to implement the six cognate strategies. Remember that, as always, the strategies are interdependent—they rely on and influence one another—in making a complex Web site an accessible network of screens for users interested in these wonderful natural resources.

Notes

1. In *Dynamics in Document Design*, Karen Schriver demonstrates procedures for evaluating the usability of whole documents—both visual and verbal elements—by getting feedback directly from readers.
2. Robert H. W. Waller outlines a scheme for analyzing what he calls "macro-level" features of text, comparing their rhetorical impact to "micro-level" cues such as punctuation. Waller's work provides an excellent foundation for examining supra-level aspects of functional document design, particularly book-length documents. His work certainly stimulated our thinking on the subject.
3. Web site color stirs the emotions of readers, as Anne Richards and Carol David clearly demonstrate. Color, therefore, can be particularly effective in creating supra-level visual tone.

References

Hacker, Diana. *A Writer's Reference*, 3rd ed. Boston: Bedford/St. Martin's, 1995.

Horton, William. "The Almost Universal Language: Graphics for International Documents." *Technical Communication* 40 (1993): 682–693.

Kostelnick, Charles. "Supra-Textual Design: The Visual Rhetoric of Whole Documents." *Technical Communication Quarterly* 5 (1996): 9–33.

Kostelnick, Charles, and Michael Hassett. *Shaping Information: The Rhetoric of Visual Conventions*. Carbondale, IL: Southern Illinois University Press, 2003.

Richards, Anne R., and Carol David. "Decorative Color as a Rhetorical Enhancement on the World Wide Web." *Technical Communication Quarterly* 14 (2005): 31–48.

Schriver, Karen A. *Dynamics in Document Design: Creating Text for Readers*. New York: John Wiley & Sons, 1997.

Waller, Robert H. W. "Graphic Aspects of Complex Texts: Typography as Macro-Punctuation." *Processing of Visible Language* 2. Ed. Paul A. Kolers, Merald E. Wrolstad, and Herman Bouma. New York: Plenum, 1980. 241–253.

Exercises

1. Collect brochures or other short marketing documents that exhibit at least four different supra-spatial designs—for example, size, thickness, fold patterns, or field orientation. Be prepared to discuss the rhetorical situation of each sample, and then write a brief explanation of how supra-spatial design choices implement one or more of the cognate strategies.

2. Discuss the appropriateness of the supra-level design elements for the documents described below. Focus your discussion on usability as well as tone and ethos.

    a. A fund-raising letter from an organization that sends food overseas to the poor; the letter is printed on a bond paper stock with a half-inch gold border.

    b. Training materials for a two-day seminar on how to start your own business; the materials come in a purple three-ring binder; all 100 pages are printed on a light green paper.

    c. Instructions for how to assemble components for a top-of-the-line stereo; the instructions open up into a double-sided 24" × 36" white page divided into 10 columns that include text and pictures.

    d. A 20-page proposal from a scientific research institute to a major governmental funding agency for a $750,000 grant; the proposal (including the cover page) is printed on both sides of 8½" × 11" plain paper and stapled in the upper-left-hand corner.

    e. A Web site for discount prices on hotel rooms; the home page has links to five categories of hotels, with each linked category extending 10–20 scrollable screens (the screens contain tables with locations, dates, amenities, and prices).

3. Create a five- to eight-slide PowerPoint presentation that provides an effective set of instructions for planting a small tree (say, in a homeowner's yard) or for

transplanting a household plant. Assume that the audience would be customers of a garden center and that the slide show will include a narrative voice-over and be burned onto a CD that customers are given along with the trees or plants they purchase. Borrow any necessary drawings or photographs from Web sites of your own choosing, and be sure to cite your source(s) somewhere in your presentation. Don't forget to include a list of materials and tools needed for the project.

Make sure that your slide show attends to the following supra-level design concerns:

- Lines or bars as unifying design elements
- Frames for graphics (e.g., boxes, background color, or gray scale)
- Picture or text placed in the background
- At least two different slide colors

4. Find a longer document—an annual report, a manual, an investment prospectus, a catalog, training materials—and evaluate how well the document's supra-level design establishes ethos with its audience. Below are some supra-level elements you might consider:

- Binding (stapled, perfect, spiral, three-ring)
- Paper stock and quality (plain, laid, glossy, card stock, recycled)
- Page headers/footers, including pagination
- Page color; spot color that unifies like elements
- Graphic elements that unify sections (or the whole document) or distinguish them from one another

How exactly do supra-level design elements affect the credibility of the document? Do the design choices conform to conventions? Meet (or exceed) readers' expectations? What suggestions for supra-level design do you have for improving the document's ethos?

5. Do a supra-level conceptual design of a small Web site (three to five pages) for a local nonprofit organization or for a small start-up company.

   a. Begin by defining the rhetorical situation for the Web site: its audience, its purpose, and the context in which users will visit it.

   b. With a pencil, pen, or marker, create thumbnail sketches for each Web site page that match the rhetorical situation. Include in your sketches conventional design elements like title/logotype, navigational bar(s), text and photo blocks, graphical elements, and so on. Be sure that the Web pages have supra-level design cohesion.

   c. Cut and paste your thumbnails on a single page (sometimes called a "storyboard"), and critique the whole set, using the rhetorical situation and the cognate strategies as your guide.

Assignments

1. The engineering consulting firm you work for is creating a feasibility report for a *very important* client. The report contains a detailed analysis of three possible sites for a hotel, sports, and entertainment complex adjacent to a major international airport. If the client likes your work, they might award your company a large contract to engineer the complex.

The information and data have been gathered and analyzed, and the feasibility report, both the prose and graphics, has been drafted. Because this project could generate a lot of future business, the manager in charge has asked you for some design suggestions.

"I want this document to look classy and professional," she said. "It'll have to if we're going to get this client's attention. They're high-rollers who spend half their lives in stretch limos making deals."

"But I don't want all glitz," she adds. "The report has to be usable too. We'll distribute at least twenty of these to the client, and different readers may have different informational needs. So make it pretty yet functional."

Assume that the document now contains approximately 42 standard ($8\frac{1}{2}" \times 11"$) pages, which include two pages of front matter (title page and table of contents) and five sections of eight pages each. The document also includes about 20 illustrations scattered evenly throughout the text. Assume also that you will be able to fit the text, illustrations, and data displays onto just about any page size and layout you choose. In other words, the text and images can be edited to accommodate your supra-level design.

Invent two significantly different supra-level designs for the report. You can do a small-scale mock-up of your designs, or you can draw thumbnail sketches (similar to the process example early in this chapter). Make sure that each design includes:

- Page size and orientation; page thickness, colors, or textures
- Physical containment devices such as binding and a cover page
- Framing devices for the pictures (maps, plans, drawings of buildings)
- Design elements (textual, spatial, and/or graphic) that signal the beginning or ending of major sections
- Cohesive devices—line work, shading, color, other graphic elements

Be prepared to defend on rhetorical grounds the design you prefer.

2. Find a real-world communication problem with a well-defined audience and purpose. You might, for example, locate a business that needs an updated employee manual, a government agency that needs a series of informational brochures, or a company that needs help with a research and development proposal. Below are some other scenarios:

- Set of instructions for a how-to task or for using software
- Newsletter for a local organization

- Informational materials—fact sheets, schedules, a directory
- Web site for a new small business
- Annual report for a campus or nonprofit organization

The more realistic your project, the better you'll be able to pinpoint the rhetorical situation—who your readers are, what you want your document to accomplish, and the context in which your readers will actually use it. Defining your audience, purpose, and context is critical because your primary goal in this assignment will be—as always—to adapt visual language to the rhetorical situation. Choose a real-world project so that you're making design decisions in response to a well-defined rhetorical situation.

Because you'll be working primarily with the *visual* language of the document, your project may entail designing (i.e., redesigning) a communication that already exists. However, because designing and writing are interactive processes, you should expect to make the *verbal* changes necessary to complement your design.

Although this assignment might appear to be very large and open-ended, your search for a design project should emphasize quality over quantity. It's more important to experience the design process at all levels—starting with the supra-level and working down to local decisions—than to work on "something big." As you shape or revise your document visually, use whatever software is appropriate for the project. And unless your instructor directs otherwise, feel free to use expedient techniques (photocopying, cutting and pasting) that will enhance your document and/or save you time.

Adapting Your Design to the Rhetorical Situation

As you begin to brainstorm ideas for your design, analyze the rhetorical situation—audience, purpose, context—asking yourself how visual language might respond to these variables. When you discard design ideas, discard them because they flounder rhetorically; when you discover ideas worth keeping, keep them because they do rhetorical work for you. To decide which ideas to keep and which to discard, ask yourself questions like these:

- How do you want the visual language of your document to affect your readers? Will visual language attract their interest, help them process information more easily, persuade them to do something, guide them through a set of instructions? Exactly what kind of rhetorical work do you want the visual language to do?
- How can you implement the six cognate strategies—arrangement and emphasis, clarity and conciseness, tone and ethos—to meet these objectives?
- What visual conventions are readers familiar with? What do they expect visually? How can you meet these expectations with your design?
- How can visual elements make the document more usable to your readers? How can supra-level design help here?

As you invent, revise, and edit your design, continue to adapt its visual language—typefaces, page layout, pictures, icons, whatever—to the rhetorical situation.

Materials for Your Design Project

Below are some guidelines for submitting your design project and for preparing your oral presentation.

a. Hand in an original copy of your project that's as close to the final printed version as possible, including the choice of paper stock. If you want to save your original copy for a professional portfolio, please hand in a second copy (or a photocopy of the original) for written comments. If you are designing an online communication, print each screen and e-mail your instructor the URL.

b. Write a brief (2-3 page) analysis of your audience, purpose, and context in which you explain how you've adapted visual language to the rhetorical situation. Below are two things you should consider including in your analysis.

- Briefly describe the rhetorical situation—audience, purpose, context. Who were your readers and what did you assume about their attitude toward and knowledge about the subject? What were you trying to accomplish in your document? How will readers actually use your document?
- Analyze the visual strategies you used to meet the rhetorical situation. How did you use arrangement and emphasis strategies to respond to the rhetorical situation? Clarity and conciseness strategies? Tone and ethos strategies? How did visual conventions figure in your use of these (or other) strategies? What role did gestalt principles or empirical research play?

Your analysis will guide your instructor's evaluation of your final project, so be as explicit and detailed as you can about how your design responds to its rhetorical situation.

c. Prepare a brief oral presentation (about 7 to 10 minutes) in which you narrate your design process, explaining the rhetorical strategies you used in shaping the visual language of your document. Explain the purposes and content of your communication, and identify the intended readers and the context in which these readers will use your document. To explain the rhetorical evolution of your project, you might show some earlier drafts, or you might design a flowchart outlining the stages of your project.

*G*lossary

Below is a brief summary of several terms we've used in this book. For easy reference, we've divided them into two groups: rhetorical terms and visual vocabulary. **Note:** Terms that appear as separate items in the list are in italics.

Rhetorical Terms

Arrangement. The spatial organization of visual elements in a line, *field, data display, picture, symbol,* or across an entire communication. Arrangement strategies perform a variety of functions: They create structure, give readers access to information, and give visual elements balance and proportion. Obviously, because arrangement strategies pervade document design, they strongly influence the other cognate strategies.

Clarity. The degree to which visual language enables readers to understand the message. Clarity is an issue in virtually any form of visual language—typography, *fields, data displays, pictures,* and *symbols.* On a perceptual level, reducing noise from visual language can ensure a measure of clarity. Empirical research can also serve as a guide. On a semantic level, however, clarity may hinge on the reader's prior knowledge of the subject, familiarity with visual *conventions,* or cultural background.

Cognate strategies. Strategies for shaping visual language that parallel strategies applied in verbal rhetoric (e.g., *arrangement* is a verbal communication strategy as well as a visual communication strategy). In this book we focus on six cognate strategies, which we divide into pairs: *arrangement* and *emphasis, clarity* and *conciseness,* and *tone* and *ethos.* The designer or writer implements each of these strategies, visual or verbal, in response to the *rhetorical situation.*

Cohesion. An aspect of arrangement; the bonding together of visual elements, often through the *gestalt* principle of grouping. The visual elements can be text, *data displays, pictures, symbols,* or *supra-level* markers.

Conciseness. The appropriate amount of visual language for a given rhetorical situation; the opposite of conciseness is overdesigning. You can test for visual conciseness by asking whether a visual element does enough rhetorical work to justify itself. Given this definition, then, a communication with dozens of visual elements may be visually concise while one with only a few may be overwrought.

Conventions. Accepted visual design practices, especially within a given *visual discourse community.* Readers learn conventions in a variety of ways: world experience, membership in a discipline, training, or trial-and-error. By using conventions, designers can tap into readers' prior knowledge about visual language as well as meet their expectations. Conventions develop from many sources, including disciplines, *genres,* and cultural traditions.

Editing. Fine-tuning design elements so they better match the rhetorical situation. Editing also ensures that elements with like functions have consistent design across the entire communication. Like verbal editing, visual editing usually occurs late in the design process.

Emphasis. The strategy of calling the reader's attention to selected visual elements—for example, using a larger, bolder typeface for certain text; darkening a line on a graph; highlighting a detail on a picture with an arrow. Emphasis strategies often rely on *figure–ground contrast* for their impact.

Empirical research. Data about readers' responses to visual language that's collected through testing, observation, or other means. Empirical research can take two forms: universal and contextual. Universal research involves the use of controlled experiments (e.g., Tinker's studies of typography). Contextual research is document-specific, with the designer gathering feedback from potential readers through observations, surveys, interviews, or focus groups. Both kinds of empirical research can help designers make informed decisions.

Ethos. The degree of credibility that visual language achieves in a given rhetorical situation. Ethos often depends on how professional a design looks—the designer's attention to consistency, quality, and details—though this isn't always true because a professional-looking design may fail to build ethos with its readers if they find it irrelevant or insincere. Visual language can also project the ethos (or character) of the designer's organization—for example, progressive, traditional, casual, customer-oriented, and so on.

Figure–ground contrast. Perceived distinction between an image and the visual field around it. All marks on a physical surface—a typeface, a line, an icon—display some level of figure–ground contrast. The designer can use figure–ground contrast to solve a rhetorical problem by creating the needed emphasis or by enhancing clarity.

Genre. A type of communication—résumé, annual report, newsletter, manual—that embodies distinct visual features that readers typically associate with that type of communication. For example, newsletters have nameplates, Web sites have navigational bars, legal documents have longer pages than business documents, annual reports have glossy pages, training manuals use three-ring binders, awards use script typefaces, and so forth.

Gestalt. An approach to human perception that posits a variety of theoretical principles describing how the eye and brain respond to stimuli in a visual field. In this book we focus on two gestalt principles—*figure–ground contrast* and *grouping.* While gestalt principles in themselves are nonrhetorical in nature, designers can use them to respond to the *rhetorical situation.*

Grouping. A *gestalt* principle of perception that describes how readers structure visual information that appears in a *visual field*. In this book we conflate several gestalt principles into this category, three of which include likeness of form, spatial nearness, and division. Grouping is a powerful design tool because it enables the designer to structure a communication visually by creating *parallelism* among some visual elements and hierarchical relations among others.

Integrated communication. Blending of visual and verbal elements to satisfy the rhetorical situation. In most effective communications, visual and verbal elements cooperate to implement the cognate strategies. However, sometimes visual and verbal elements enact strategies differently (e.g., the visual *tone* is upbeat but the verbal language is neutral), which may or may not result in an effective communication.

Interdependence of the cognate strategies. Influence of cognate strategies on one another. For example, the rigid *arrangement* of text will also affect *tone* and *ethos;* using a freehand drawing for an illustration will probably affect tone as well as *emphasis, clarity,* and *conciseness.* Sometimes interdependence results in negative trade-offs: A script typeface may make the tone of a letter more personal, but it may also erode its clarity; the designer has to decide if, on balance, the trade-off helps to adapt the message to the *rhetorical situation.*

Invention. Generation of design elements in response to a *rhetorical situation;* the design equivalent of writing a rough draft. Invention can occur anytime in the design process but is usually the most intense at the beginning. Visual invention involves creativity (e.g., brainstorming new ideas) as well as imitation (e.g., identifying relevant *conventions*).

Legibility. The visual equivalent of readability—the ease with which readers can process text on the word and sentence level. Typographical design choices directly affect legibility, whether on paper or on a screen. Although *empirical research* has yielded useful findings, legibility defies a purely scientific analysis because it depends on the composition of the *audience* as well as on the perceptual and informational *context* in which that audience encounters the text.

Parallelism. Similarity between visual elements that creates *cohesion* among them. Parallelism can include a wide range of elements—typefaces and sizes; placement of text in a field; line work and bullets; size and style of drawings or data displays; frames around drawings, *data displays,* or text; and so on.

Perception. How readers process visual language through the interaction of eye, brain, and image. While perception itself is nonrhetorical, it can be tapped for rhetorical ends.

Process. Design activities, including *invention, revision,* and *editing.* Like the writing process, an effective design process depends on how well the designer understands the *rhetorical situation* and adapts visual language to that situation.

Revision. Like writers, designers resee their work, continually shaping it to fit the *rhetorical situation.* As in writing, revising visual language is often crucial to creating an effective communication.

Rhetorical situation. Exigencies of a communication problem that drive the design process. The designer's task is to make visual language responsive to the rhetorical situation: the audience, the purpose, and the context of the communication.

- *Audience.* The intended readers or users of the message. Who the audience is, their familiarity with the subject, the conventions they know, their needs and expectations—these and other characteristics directly affect their responses to visual language. Anticipating these responses is one of the keys to effective design.

- *Purpose.* The aim or goal of the communication that's fulfilled by both the visual and the verbal elements. In general, purpose can be persuasive or informational or both, though each communication has more specific purposes—for example, to enable readers to find answers to questions about how to use their computer, to motivate them to attend a workshop, and so forth. The visual and verbal elements of a communication may or may not fulfill exactly similar purposes.

- *Context.* The circumstances under which the reader will actually interact with the visual language: the reader's physical surroundings (sitting at a desk, standing outside) and the tasks the readers perform (assembling a piece of furniture while using instructions). Context also includes previous communications between the sender and receiver, including the visual language contained in those communications.

Tone. The voice of visual language that reveals the designer's attitude toward the audience and the subject. Visual tone, like verbal tone, can express a range of voices: casual or serious, informal or formal, threatening or nonthreatening, empathetic or authoritative, and so on. Design strategies involving tone often interact with other *cognate strategies.*

Usability. The degree to which design elements give users ready access to the information they need in the way they'll actually use it. For example, a usable business report allows both executives and technical specialists to find what they need without getting bogged down in the others' material; a usable convention program enables readers to identify panel sessions and speakers while standing in a hotel concourse. Usability differs from readability, the measurement of how efficiently readers process text. Although all four design levels contribute to usability, *supra-level design* often plays the critical role.

Visual discourse community. A group of readers who share certain knowledge and expectations about visual language. Visual discourse communities can be small—employees of an organization (a software company) or members of a discipline (electrical engineers)—or they can be quite large—inhabitants of a country or an entire cultural group. An individual can, of course, claim membership in many different visual discourse communities.

Visual Vocabulary

Coding modes. The raw materials of visual language, consisting of three types: textual, spatial, and graphic. During the design process, a *synergy* develops among the coding modes.

- *Textual coding.* Words, letters, or numbers on a *field, picture, data display,* or *symbol.*

- *Spatial coding.* Distribution of textual and graphic elements on a *field, picture, data display,* or *symbol,* including such elements as *leading,* margins, viewing angle or depth in pictures, *x–y* axes of data displays, and page size and shape.

- *Graphic coding.* Any nontextual marks on a *field, picture, data display,* or *symbol,* including elements such as bullets, lines, borders, bars, textures, shading, and color.

Data displays. *Extra-level* sign systems that use primarily *graphic* and *spatial* coding to show quantitative data. Bar charts, line graphs, pie charts, scatter plots, Gantt charts, and maps are some of the key *genres.* Below are some of the conventional features of data displays.

- *Gridlines.* Horizontal and vertical lines within the plot frame of bar charts, line graphs, or scatter plots that guide the reader's eye to data points.
- *Legend.* Interpretive tool that enables the reader to decode a data display.
- *Plot frame.* Rectangular area defined by the *x*-axis and *y*-axis. All data are located within the plot frame.
- *Tick marks.* Short lines on the *x*-axis or the *y*-axis that locate intervals in the data quantities.

Extra-level design. The domain of visual design where information is communicated primarily through spatial and graphic elements, with text serving a secondary role as tags, labels, and titles. Extra-level design includes *data displays, pictures, icons, logos,* and *symbols.*

Field. A distinguishable area of visual interest or attention that readers can process as a unit. Field design occurs at the *inter-level.* A field can consist of a page (or a two-page spread), a brochure panel (or contiguous panels of an open brochure), a computer screen, or a business card. Most visual fields are complex and contain subfields—for example, a boxed or shaded insert on a page of text. Below are some visual elements typically used in field design.

- *Bleed.* Extension of a graphic element to the edge of the page; after the page is printed, it's trimmed so the element "bleeds" off the edge—that is, there's no margin.
- *Column.* A text unit running vertically down a field. Most fields contain one, two, or three columns. More columns are feasible in landscape orientation or in very large fields.
- *Hairline.* A fine vertical or horizontal line used in field design, often to separate text columns or other chunks of text or graphics.
- *Hanging indent.* A protruding text or graphic element, usually in the left margin. Numbers and bullets in lists, for example, look more emphatic if they hang rather than have subsequent lines of text running flush left.
- *Initial letter.* A large letter that initiates a unit of text. Initial letters sometimes take the form of drop caps. Occasionally, they are embellished with pictorial elements related to the subject.
- *Justified/unjustified text.* Justified text is vertically straight on both left and right margins; unjustified text is ragged on either the right or left margin.
- *Leading.* Vertical space between horizontal lines of text, measured in *points.*
- *Page orientation.* The general spatial arrangement of any rectangular page. Portrait pages are tall and narrow, landscape pages short and wide.
- *Pull quote.* A short piece of text repeated in a much larger type size, isolated spatially on the page, and often set off graphically for emphasis. Pull quotes act as teasers, drawing readers into the text.

Icon. Concise *extra-level* element whose design signals its meaning. Icons can signal warnings or topics in text, or they can function alone. For example, an icon in a train schedule may indicate that dining service is available.

Inter-level design. The domain of visual design that governs the display of text and graphic cues on a *field*. Inter-level design occurs in all three coding modes: textual (headings, numbers, letters); spatial (lists, justified text, matrices); and graphic (bullets, hairlines, boxed text). Inter-level design includes both *fields* and *nonlinear components*.

Intra-level design. The domain of visual design that governs local typographical cues: textual (type style and size, bold, italic, upper case); spatial (loose or condensed text, super- and subscript); and graphic (punctuation marks, underlining). In this book, *linear components* and intra-level design mean the same thing.

Linear components. Visual language that controls continuous text running on a single line. Design issues relating to linear components include type style and size, upper- versus lowercase, italics, bold, underlining, kerning, and so forth.

- *Downstyle/upstyle.* Downstyle is lowercase, upstyle uppercase. Small caps is a variation of upstyle. Up-and-down style means that the first letter of each "important" word is capped, but the rest (articles, prepositions) are in lowercase (Like This, a Good Example).

- *Kerning.* Fine-tuning of the horizontal spacing between letters.

- *Monoline.* A typeface that has strokes of consistent and equal width.

- *Pica.* Typographical unit of measurement; six picas make one inch.

- *Point.* Typographical unit of measurement; 72 points make one inch.

- *Serif/sans serif.* The "feet" at the bottom of a typeface. Sans serif typefaces have no such feet. Serifs come in a variety of shapes and styles: square, round, thick, thin.

- *X-height.* The height of the middle part of a typeface; the height of a lowercase *x* in a given font compared to letters with ascenders (such as *h*) or descenders (such as *p*). X-heights can vary dramatically from one font to another, even if the fonts have the same point size (measured from the top of the ascenders to the bottom of the descenders).

Logo. Abstract image that represents an organization, program, or project. To be effective, logos must have strong *clarity* and *ethos*.

Nonlinear components. A form of *inter-level design* that includes tables, matrices, organizational charts, flowcharts, decision trees, and concept diagrams. In nonlinear components the syntax of text relies heavily on spatial and graphic cues. For example, in a table the relation between two text fragments is defined by the intersection of a column and a row.

Picture. *Extra-level* form of communication that reveals information about its subject's visible traits. As communicative acts, pictures respond to *rhetorical situations*. Pictures can be realistic or abstract, visually dense or terse, highly informative or highly expressive. Whether they appear in print or on screen, pictures can perform a variety of functions—describe, narrate, persuade, motivate, and so on. Below are some conventional features of pictures.

- *Blowup.* Detail on a drawing that shows an enlarged view of part of a picture. Blowups are often framed by circles or boxes.

- *Cross section.* A drawing that shows an imaginary slice through an object—anything from a machine to a mollusk to a mountain.

- *Elevation.* A drawing of a side view of an object without any perspective.

- ■ *Exploded view.* A drawing that shows the parts of an object pulled away from each other, usually along a centerline.
- ■ *Level of abstraction.* Amount of detailed information in a picture or a *symbol*. A highly abstract picture contains structural information but little detail.

Symbols. Images that represent concepts. Unlike pictures, symbols are more abstract; they suggest rather than represent.

Supra-level design. The domain of visual design that governs large-scale elements across the whole document—the cover, the binding, dividers, page headers and footers, and frames around pictures. Supra-level features have significant impact on the *usability* of a document. Because readers encounter supra-level elements first, they play a crucial rhetorical role in giving readers access to information and in creating a first impression.

Synergy among coding modes. Decisions in one *coding mode* (textual, spatial, or graphic) usually affect those in another coding mode and vice versa. A design evolves not in isolated parts but as a whole, integrating textual, spatial, and graphic elements as it unfolds.

Credits

Table 3.1, Visual Language Matrix, Adapted from Kostelnick, "Systematic" (33), "Visual Rhetoric" (79). Used courtesy of the Association of Teachers of Technical Writing.

Figure 3.22 © Visco Manufacturing. Used with permission.

Figure 3.24 Used with permission of Iowa State University Office of Institutional Research.

Figure 5.37 Note: Seminar description is from "Introduction to Nondestructive Evaluation (NDE)," courtesy of the Center for Nondestructive Evaluation, Iowa State University.

Figure 5.38 Note: Text is from the Federal Aviation Administration Center for Aviation Systems Reliability, Iowa State University.

Figures 9.10, 9.14, and 9.19 adapted from Kostelnick, "Supra-Textual Design" (14), (15), (16). Courtesy of the Association of Teachers of Technical Writing.

Figure 9.45 was used courtesy of Sheryl McGough.

Figure 9.46, 9.47, 9.48, and Color Insert 8 courtesy of the National Park Service.

Adobe Illustrator, Adobe Photoshop, Adobe Type Basics, Birch, Lithos, and Tekton are registered trademarks of Adobe Systems Incorporated.

Canvas is a registered trademark of ACD Systems International, Inc. (and formerly of Deneba software).

Helvetica, New Century Schoolbook, Palatino, Peignot, Univers, and Times are trademarks, which may be registered in certain jurisdictions, of Linotype-Hell AG and/or its subsidiaries.

Index